D1282712

Regionalism and the South

The FRED W. MORRISON

Series in Southern Studies

Regionalism and the South

Selected Papers of Rupert Vance

Edited with an Introduction

by John Shelton Reed and

Daniel Joseph Singal

The University of North Carolina Press

Chapel Hill

© 1982 The University of North Carolina Press

Manufactured in the United States of America

Library of Congress Cataloging in Publication Data

Vance, Rupert Bayless, 1899–
  Regionalism and the South.

  Bibliography: p.
  Includes index
  1. Southern States—Social conditions—Addresses,
essays, lectures.   I. Reed, John Shelton.
II. Singal, Daniel Joseph, 1944–   III. Title.
HN79.A13V36   975   81-16235
ISBN 0-8078-1513-6   AACR2

Contents

Acknowledgments

The idea of this book took shape while Dr. Vance was still living, and the selections from his work included here reflect in large part his own assessment of what, among his copious writings, is still of importance—although neither editor could resist adding a few of his own favorites as well. Many other people have contributed, in one way or another, to putting this book together. In particular, Dr. Vance's wife, Rheba, read the introduction and gently corrected us on a number of points. Several of Vance's former colleagues were also helpful.

The University Research Council of the University of North Carolina, Chapel Hill, came across with an outright grant to support the publication of this book, and the Department of Sociology at the university subsidized its preparation in a variety of less conspicuous ways. We appreciate both sorts of support, and also that of the University of North Carolina Press and its director, Matthew Hodgson, which has so far been moral, but may turn out to be financial as well. Without Mr. Hodgson's encouragement and personal interest in the project, it would probably have been abandoned some years ago.

We also appreciate the assistance of two able young people, both associated with the Department of Sociology at Chapel Hill: Lynn Whitener, a graduate of that department, who prepared the bibliography and standardized the citations; and Bruce Geyer, a clerical employee, whose services went far beyond the secretarial, and well into the editorial.

We acknowledge elsewhere the cooperation of those who hold the copyrights on this material, but we wish, finally, to thank them collectively and less perfunctorily for their generous contribution to what is, inevitably, something of a memorial volume.

Introduction

Rupert Vance was born in Plummerville, Arkansas, in the closing months of the nineteenth century. He died in Chapel Hill, North Carolina, three-quarters of the way through the twentieth. For him, the South was always "home," and in his lifetime he saw the region transformed.

Vance's birthplace was a region still recovering from the Civil War. Its white citizens were suffering the consequences of defeat, occupation, and exploitation, and were engaged in inflicting some of the same experiences on southern blacks. In 1900, close to 90 percent of Vance's fellow Southerners lived in the countryside, and the region's cities—with a couple of exceptions—did not amount to much. The vast majority of Southerners were farmers and farm workers; nearly all were supported, directly or indirectly, by agriculture. They were supported, as Louis XIV once put it, the way a hanged man is supported by the rope. Southern personal income, per capita, was roughly at the level of Trinidad's today—and was considerably less than half of that in the rest of the United States. Southerners, both black and white, were leaving the region in increasing numbers for employment, or the chance of it, elsewhere. When Vance was born, southern state legislatures were busy transforming discriminatory custom into the formidable structure of Jim Crow law, designed to fix the Negro "in his place" for eternity. Informal efforts to the same end were commonplace: blacks were being lynched at an average rate of two a week.

When Vance died, his adopted hometown had a black mayor, who was soon to take a cabinet position in the state government of North Carolina. Within a year, the Democratic party would nominate for president a former governor of Georgia, a "born-again" peanut farmer–businessman, backed by Southerners of both races and a good many non-Southerners as well. From the political left came warnings of a sinister entity called "the Sunbelt": this region, which combined the South and Southwest, was alleged to be draining population, wealth, and influence from the old Northeast and achieving a baleful dominance in national affairs from a base of "agri-business" and extractive industry. Certainly the flow of population had reversed—more blacks and whites were moving to the South than were leaving it—and if per capita income in the South was still lower than that in the rest of the country, the gap had narrowed substantially, and in absolute terms the great majority of Southerners led comfortable lives. Like the rest of the United States, the region had become an urban society. By 1975, less than a third of its people were rural, and fewer than one in a dozen actually worked in agriculture. For better or for worse, Atlanta had become the model of the "New South"— a hackneyed phrase popularized by an Atlantan over a century before.

Rupert Vance came to Chapel Hill in 1926 to join the Department of Sociology and the Institute for Research in Social Science at the University of North Carolina, both of which had been founded a few years earlier by Howard W. Odum. For the next half century, the South, its problems, and the changes taking place there occupied much of his attention. In a half-dozen books and scores of articles, in his classroom teaching and his work with graduate students, in lectures to varied audiences throughout the South and beyond, Vance applied his intellect and the tools of his discipline to the problems of his native region and, with Odum and his other colleagues, developed the intellectual apparatus of "regional sociology."

Although Vance is probably best known as a student of the South, he easily ranked among the leading sociologists of his generation not only in the South but in the nation (and, for that matter, in the world). In 1944, he was elected president of the American Sociological Society (now Association). The depth, quality, and encyclopedic range of his work set a standard for southern sociologists which has never been equaled.

The breadth of his interests was especially striking. He began by writing the definitive study of the South's cotton tenancy system, moved on to a magisterial portrait of the region from the standpoint of human geography, then to studies of its complex population problems, and finally to examinations of the process that had transformed it from an agricultural to an urban and industrial society. Along the way, he found time to compose remarkably insightful essays on the South's politics, culture, and history, as well as more general contributions to sociological and demographic theory. Unlike the work of many scholars, Vance's has never seemed dated: his masterpiece, *Human Geography of the South*, can be read with almost as much profit today as when it first appeared in 1932. His accomplishments also included over forty years of teaching and directing graduate studies at the University of North Carolina, in Chapel Hill, where he was made Kenan Professor of Sociology in 1946, and service as a consultant to innumerable government commissions and agencies and to the United Nations (on international migration).

Vance's achievement is all the more noteworthy because he worked throughout his career with a severe physical handicap. Born in 1899 in a small central Arkansas town, he contracted polio at the age of three and soon lost the use of both legs. Unable to obtain treatment or even proper diagnosis in his hometown—"It was hell to live in the backwoods then," he would later recall—he and his mother spent two years at the McLean Orthopedic Hospital in St. Louis, where he learned to walk with the aid of crutches. Although the affliction kept him from entering school until age ten, he was able to enter in the fourth grade and promptly rose to the top of the class. Thereafter his paralysis had no significant effects on either his education or his career. Colleagues would later marvel at how Vance kept up a full round of professional activities, including a busy schedule of travel to meetings and conferences. Nor did his handicap exclude him from the normal boyhood pastimes: a 1950 profile in the *Raleigh News and Observer* reported that he often served as umpire for youngsters' baseball games. "He stood on crutches behind the pitcher," it noted, "and he never reversed a decision."

Like his mentor Odum, Vance grew up in a rural community typical of the South in that day. His grandfather was a Confederate veteran; his father a New South-style cotton planter who managed his work force of sharecroppers from behind the counter of his general store. Several times, the elder Vance tried to escape the narrow confines of the cotton system by raising peaches, cantaloupes, or livestock, but each time the vicissitudes of the national market brought financial disaster. His efforts to prosper growing cotton also met repeated failure owing to the sharp fluctuations in the price of that staple. During the agricultural depression of the early 1920s, he finally went bankrupt and lost all his land. To his son this spectacle of hard work and initiative culminating in failure came to epitomize the overall plight of the South. Why, he asked himself, were capable Southerners like his father forever frustrated in their desire to improve themselves? Was something grievously wrong with the South's culture, or economy, or social system, or perhaps with the genetic makeup of its people?

His education had given him a broad background to draw upon in his search for an answer. Taught to read at age four by his mother, he soon developed an appetite for books that his family found hard to satisfy, even though they purchased Dickens, Irving, and Scott by the set. The results of this early exposure were later reflected in his own writing, which was always clear (and not just "for a sociologist") and often elegant. He attended college at Henderson Brown, a small Methodist school in Arkadelphia, where he edited the college paper and yearbook, was president of the Young Men's Christian Association, and served as class valedictorian. Although he majored in English, his first love, he also encountered a gifted teacher named B. S. Foster who introduced him to social science. Intrigued by the new field, he accepted a scholarship to Vanderbilt to study for a master's degree in economics. His studies there with Augustus Dyer, a stodgy and resolute exponent of classical laissez-faire, left him with little taste for economics unleavened by sociological analysis. He found the double-distilled southern progressivism of Edward Mims (later to write *The Advancing South*) more attractive, though, and he was exposed to such fellow students as Ralph McGill (about whom he was later to tell some hilarious stories) and some young literati who were later to number among the Nashville "Agrarians."

After Vanderbilt, still unsure of his choice of profession and unwilling to enter law school (as his father advised), Vance entered a period of apparent drift, but one in which his social views were in actuality maturing rapidly. He took a job for two years as principal of a small Oklahoma high school, then taught English for three years at South Georgia College in McRae.

Vance later attributed much importance to his time in McRae. His social views were developing, he recognized, in a liberal direction, and while they had been fairly unremarkable in the Southwest and at Vanderbilt, they were enough out of place in South Georgia that his colleagues sometimes accused him of being a disguised Yankee. (This experience almost certainly had something to do with his life-long interest in sub-regional differences, an interest he turned to good account in his *Human Geography of the South*.)

All the while, he was avidly reading many books and periodicals, especially H. L. Mencken's iconoclastic *American Mercury*. (Until he met Mencken, Vance said, he had always assumed that the man ate little children for breakfast.) It was during this period that he also discovered Howard Odum's *Journal of Social Forces*, with its hard-hitting editorials cataloging the South's ills and proposing programs of action to meet them. This kind of *engagée* academic sociology appealed to Vance because it provided a way both to implement his commitment to reform and to satisfy his intellectual curiosity. And, after considering Columbia University and Chicago, he chose Chapel Hill as the place to do his graduate work, primarily because of the chance to work with Odum.

A young and energetic southern-born sociologist, Odum had come to Chapel Hill in 1920 to found an academic empire. He came as first director of the university's School of Public Welfare and as chairman of its new sociology department (the only one in the South). Two years later he began the *Journal of Social Forces*, with himself as editor, and in 1924, with support from the Laura Spelman Rockefeller Memorial, launched the Institute for Research in Social Science. His two basic goals were closely related: he wished to promote the scientific study of southern society so that people in the region could begin tackling their immense problems in constructive ways, and he hoped to provide an opportunity for talented Southerners to train in the new social science disciplines unhampered by financial cares or constraints on their freedom of inquiry. To those ends the institute offered fellowships to promising graduate students willing to investigate aspects of southern life. The stipends were high and the length of tenure was open, and there was no obligation to teach. Vance was one of the first to take advantage of these attractive terms, and so began an extraordinary association that was to last until Odum's death nearly thirty years later.

Odum was in his early forties when Vance came to Chapel Hill at age twenty-seven, and from the start relations between the two men were warm and mutually admiring. Keenly aware of Odum's sensitivities, Vance always maintained the humble role of student, of the loyal disciple both grateful to and slightly in awe of his master. And there was much to be grateful for. Odum provided Vance not only with institutional support and personal encouragement but, just as importantly, with the drive to theorize and generalize which would ultimately raise Vance's work well above simple description. In addition, Odum reinforced Vance's sense of mission about the South—an unapologetic assumption that something must be done about the problems they were studying. Vance always acknowledged his intellectual debt to Odum: one of his last published articles was, in effect, an act of homage to his mentor, an attempt to rescue one of Odum's concepts from what Vance thought was undeserved neglect. For his part, Vance contributed as much as anyone to realizing Odum's vision of Chapel Hill as a center of regional scholarship and what is nowadays called "policy research." In both volume and quality, his publications helped put North Carolina on the national academic map.

Yet Vance proved to be different in many ways, both temperamentally and intellectually, from his master. Odum's training had been in the organicist brand of sociology which was dominant before World War I. As a result, he tended to view the ideal society as a seamless web in which all groups and social institutions functioned harmoniously with one another. Odum regarded any sign of conflict as aberrational and potentially dangerous; political conflict as the worst. Thus, his ideology of "regionalism" included a blueprint for southern society in which consensus was so strong that the projects of academic social planners and the desires of the common folk would be instantly, automatically reconciled. More solidly grounded in the newer developments in social science, Vance had no such illusions. For him, conflict was at least a given, if not a positive good, as evidenced by a memorandum he wrote to Odum after reading the manuscript of Odum's *American Regionalism*:

> I believe I must be wanting a more hard-boiled view of social conflict. Conflict we will always have with us. How does Regionalism take [sectional conflict] out of the realm of hard knocks and place it in the realm of discussion and reasonable "due process" of policy-making? And what about class conflict? . . . Maybe it comes down to this, that we can't take a point of view without taking sides. Still I have the feeling that we need to be sure of the alternatives, if necessary to argue one side and then the other, show the interest involved.

Vance's graduate school paper on "Stuart-Harmon" (a thinly disguised picture of McRae, Georgia) contains a forthright treatment of class, racial, and generational conflict, and his dissertation, while it makes a scapegoat of no one, nevertheless recognizes that tenant and landlord necessarily have some divergent interests.

Vance's fascination with southern politics, a subject not for those squeamish about conflict and one that Odum largely ignored in his own work, led him to undertake a series of articles on populist-style southern politicians, beginning with a sketch of Jeff Davis of Arkansas, "A Karl Marx for Hill Billies," published in *Social Forces* in 1930. This article, perhaps more than any other, shows Mencken's influence. Vance was not the only reform-minded young Southerner to read the *American Mercury*: as Fred C. Hobson, Jr., has pointed out, Mencken was something of a hero to many. Having flayed the South in his famous essay "Sahara of the Bozart," Mencken was encouraging those Southerners who were trying to remedy the situation that he had (exaggeratedly) diagnosed, and he published works by many of them in his magazine. His relations with

Odum and his students were warm and supportive, and Vance admitted in later years that his piece on Jeff Davis was written with the *American Mercury* in mind. Still, it appeared in Odum's journal, not Mencken's.

Vance also differed from Odum in the style and approach of his writings. What someone once said of Kant could be said as well of Odum: he was both like and unlike Jehovah—he spoke through a cloud, but without the illumination of the thunderbolt. Vance's work, on the other hand, was always lucid and well organized, proceeding through clear-cut logical analysis to an identifiable conclusion. In some ways, Vance served as an interpreter for Odum, clarifying and substantiating the latter's ideas on regionalism, making them comprehensible to readers who could not pin Odum down in person for an explanation. On at least one occasion, Vance even tried valiantly to repair Odum's prose, after plowing through the draft of a 1938 book:

> My first impression [wrote the former English teacher] was that the materials were undigested and the manuscript was rather hastily done. [For example,] I look for a resolution, a point of view or a summary at the end of many chapters, and I find sometimes an abrupt conclusion and sometimes a quotation. . . . I would like to see [in] the manuscript the emergence of what might be called a point of view. Some of the most original and challenging of your ideas are stated as assumptions rather than emerging from the discussions as conclusions. Again, I see certain slants that are taken without being explicitly defined or argued.

This memorandum (which goes on) tells us something of the nature of the relationship between the two men. So may the fact that Odum apparently left the manuscript unedited.

These contrasts between the two were apparent in Vance's *Human Factors in Cotton Culture*, a revised version of his doctoral dissertation, published in 1929. Whereas Odum's writing on the South tended to be upbeat and optimistic, Vance's portrait of how Southerners were trapped by what he called "the cotton culture complex" was strongly pessimistic. Ever mindful of his father's experience, he stressed the ruinous unpredictability of the system, emphasizing how the cycles of the cotton market or the vagaries of the weather could destroy men's livelihoods virtually overnight and lead them to irrational behavior. He employed statistics and graphic literary detail to depict the lives of ordinary tenant farmers, again drawing on his personal recollections, and presented anything but a pretty picture. The resulting book was, as one reviewer aptly put it, "a rare combination of sound economics and human interest."

The book eschewed easy solutions. Far from holding out hope for reform, Vance concluded that the dependence on King Cotton led to a "vicious circle" almost impossible to break, a system whose participants "form an economic harmony that often benefits all except the producer, a complex whole that is so closely interconnected that no one can suggest any place at which it may be attacked except the grower; and the grower is to change the system himself, cold comfort for advice." The book introduced a needed note of sober realism to subsequent discussions of the South's problems in the 1930s.

Still, in *Human Factors*, Vance did not really answer his basic causal question of what had gone wrong in the South; that answer came in his *Human Geography of the South*, which appeared in 1932. This massive work, with a bibliography long enough to boggle the mind of even the most compulsive scholar, surely belongs among the classics of American social science. Borrowing techniques from the French school of human geographers and from the new science of ecology, Vance tried to see if some natural factor—some inescapable attribute of the physical environment—could account for the ills of southern life. Methodically, he reviewed the region's physical features as they had interacted with its social development, only to conclude that all, from topography and soil content to water supplies, had been sufficient for prosperity. An especially provocative chapter on the southern climate showed that, if anything, the region's weather should have given it a clear advantage over the North in industrial production. Chapters on the supposed biological inferiority of the southern people demonstrated that what many observers had described as "laziness" could more accurately be attributed to inadequate diets and parasitic diseases like hookworm and malaria. The South's plight was not the fault of nature, then, but was in fact man-made. Natural forces may have played a role, but in the end, Vance insisted, "history, not geography, made the solid South."

More precisely, according to Vance, history had left southern society arrested in the frontier stage. Adapting his thesis from the work of the historian Ulrich B. Phillips—whose influence on Vance was second only to that of Odum—he maintained that the social and economic patterns of the South had been shaped essentially by the plantation, a frontier institution which produced cotton by almost literally mining the soil. During the nineteenth century, the rest of the country shed its colonial status as an exporter of raw materials to become an industrial society. Because of its dependence on the plantation system and, later, the devastation of the Civil War, the South failed to keep pace. The region never built up a capital supply of its own and remained backward in technology and industrial skills. The result, Vance argued, was a "colonial economy," frantically exploiting its natural resources to pay for manufactured goods produced elsewhere. The North (he quickly added) was not to blame; rather, the tragic course of southern history had condemned the region to its poverty and dependence. To escape this fate, Vance believed, Southerners would have to strive consciously for urbanization and industrialization, and for a more diversified agricultural system that was less dependent on staple crops. More cautiously than Odum, he endorsed regional planning as the quickest and most efficient route to a mature economy, but he characteristically pointed out that any such program would have to take into account the entrenched folkways of a people still under the sway of the plantation mentality.

The publication of *Human Geography of the South* cemented Vance's reputation as a leading figure in sociology. Invitations began pouring in for him to serve as consultant on various projects, both scholarly and governmental, and Vance was usually quick to take them up. He actively lobbied for passage of the Bankhead-Jones Farm Tenant Bill and, after its enactment in 1938, frequently acted as advisor to the Farm Security Administration, which was created by the new law. In addition, he was among the founders of the Southern Sociological Society in 1935 and became its third president in 1938. His most important contribution to the organization, he liked to recall afterward, was seeing to it that the society met from the start only in hotels where its black members could attend all functions, including formal dinners. Finding such facilities in the South of the 1930s was not always easy, but Vance and others persisted in this policy, with the result that some other professional associations then getting under way in the region followed suit.

At the same time, Vance was becoming increasingly interested in the fledgling field of social demography. In 1938 he published a *Research Memorandum on Population Redistribution within the United States*, for the Social Science Research Council, attempting to set forth an agenda for research in an area whose importance was just beginning to be recognized by sociologists generally.

In fact, by the mid-1930s, Vance had begun to view population as an alternative explanation of the South's dilemma. The solid, scientific feel of demographic theory strongly appealed to him; it was hard to argue against numbers. More important, as Vance was to demonstrate in *All These People: The Nation's Human Resources in the South* (his next major study, published in 1945), there could be no question that the South since the Civil War had been dramatically overproducing people. Again the fault seemed to lie with the system of staple crop agriculture, which encouraged families to have as many children as possible in order to have hands available for field labor. But, as Vance showed, whatever the short-run advantages for individual families, this system led to long-run disadvantages for the region and nation, since the huge reservoir of underemployed workers which resulted kept wages in the South at a bare subsistence level. Here, Vance thought, was the root cause of southern poverty. His solution once more was an industrialized and urbanized society, arrived at through planning, precisely because urban life and higher living standards would of themselves help to lower the birth rate and thus to solve the South's population problem. He had only limited faith, however, that such planning would actually come about. More realistically, as early as his 1936 article "The Old Cotton Belt," Vance foresaw the process in which the South would export its surplus population to the urban slums of the North, with tragic consequences for the country as a whole.

Vance continued his interest in demography, becoming president of the Population Association of America in 1952, but in the latter part of his career he focused his attention primarily on the subject of urbanization itself. In a 1955 article he claimed, accurately as it turned out, that a major "breakthrough" had taken place in the South around the middle of the preceding decade: the cities rather than the countryside had finally come to dominate the society. For Vance, the main significance of this development was its meaning for the South's relationship to the rest of the nation. As he observed in *The Urban South*, a symposium he edited at this time with a Chapel Hill colleague, Nicholas Demerath, the South in one critical area after another was finally catching up with the other regions. The indices of southern deficiency which he and Odum had charted for years were at last disappearing. Put another way, the circumstances that had prevented members of his father's generation from succeeding, despite their best efforts, appeared to be past.

Although this view was correct as far as it went, it clearly failed to take into account the other major change that was occurring in southern life during these years: namely, the civil rights movement, which in 1954 and

1955 saw both the Supreme Court decision in *Brown v. Board of Education* and the Montgomery bus boycott. Vance may well have hesitated to "trespass" in an area he regarded as the domain of his friend and colleague Guy Johnson, but in any case, despite his own liberal racial views, the changing structure of southern race relations simply did not receive the attention in his published work that, in retrospect, it clearly deserves in any account of the South's modernization.

Another difficulty the contemporary reader may find in Vance's work is the concept of regionalism itself. To a greater extent than is usually recognized, Vance was as much the father of regional sociology as was Odum. Indeed, Vance's explorations in human geography, his charting of subregions and resources, led directly to Odum's *pointilliste* portrait of the South in *Southern Regions*, an imposing study published in 1936. Vance was always far more conversant with modern social theory than was his mentor, and the gap between that theory and regionalism troubled him. To the charge that regionalists were engaged in "mere description" of particular locales rather than in the attempt to build a general science of society, Vance replied that description was a necessary preliminary operation: "The truth in the statement I do not find too disturbing provided one can go from description to generalization by good empirical methods. There are certainly sufficient regions and sufficient societies to offer basis for valid generalization." To the accusation that regionalists in attempting to understand a region by dabbling in history, geography, and economics were doing everything *but* sociology, Vance replied ruefully: "I have sometimes said that it must be fun to be a dilettante, but dilettantes are not supposed to work very hard." He added: "Regionalism focuses many disciplines on the one area under study, and anyone who follows this line takes a calculated risk that leads to trespassing on other people's preserves."

Nevertheless, he acknowledged (in a 1948 letter) that "all of these things [his extrasociological interests] have enabled me to examine one region from different facets, but they have not brought me much closer to the core and essence of sociology." This lack of connection still troubled him over a decade later. In 1960, he was writing that "regional sociology has been much better at taking in other people's washing, relating its contributions to those of geography, economics, political science, and so forth than it has been in relating regionalism to its own domain, that of general sociology."

This uneasiness may have been aggravated by the postwar development of the South. Since its origins lay in a concern with the economic and social problems of the region, regionalism faced a dilemma when those problems appeared to be on the way to solution. Vance was delighted with the South's modernization, but realized its consequences for his own style of research. As he put it in 1960: "The New Deal has been dealt. . . . As the affluent society crosses the Mason-Dixon line, the regionalist of the 1930's turns up as just another 'liberal without a cause.' "

Whatever the reason, it is ironic that by the early 1950s, when Vance produced for a symposium on regionalism what is probably the clearest statement available of what the "regional sociologists" were up to, his own work had largely left regionalism behind. As something of a valedictory gesture, although it may not have been intended as such, he and Charles Grigg presented a paper to the American Sociological Association in 1956 which proposed a synthesis of the declining subdiscipline of regional sociology (purged of its particularistic emphasis on the South) and the ascendant one of human ecology. Unlike corporate mergers, intellectual ones are not a matter of public record, but if this one took place, it resembled many corporate mergers in that the smaller party effectively vanished. Still, the student of intellectual life who is looking for regionalism's impact on its parent discipline of sociology must seek it in the work of present-day human ecologists. If regionalism produced a third generation, it is effectively disguised.

In the years after 1960, however, Vance's attention did return occasionally to the South. The later papers in this collection deal with aspects of the region's social structure and "quality of life" which are more subtle than those linked directly to per capita income: education, family life, high culture. In addition, Vance became concerned with Appalachia, largely bypassed by the urbanization and industrialization that transformed the rest of the South. Appalachia's problems were much like those of the South as a whole thirty years earlier and seemed susceptible to study and treatment in the old "regionalist" framework.

But if the relation of Vance's interests to one another and to those of his discipline of sociology occasionally troubled him, it need not concern his readers. When he "trespassed" on other disciplines, he did it well, and the natives recognized that. Although he never studied human geography, population, human ecology, and social structure in the classroom, his authority in these areas was recognized. Although affiliated with a sociology department, he was always being mistaken—flatteringly, he said—for something else: "O. E. Baker nominated me to the Association of

American Geographers. . . . Carter Goodrich thought I was an economist when he asked me to work with the Study of Population Redistribution. There was a time when work in tenancy led some to classify me
with the rural sociologists. The editors of the *History of the South* per-
suaded me to attempt the last volume for their series [an attempt later
abandoned]."

These confusions and problems of classification are testimony to the
range of Vance's interests and the caliber of his mind. In his works on the
South, we see a vigorous and well-informed intellect addressing some of
the most pressing problems of his day. In the works on regionalism,
Vance pondered the questions of how to bring together many disciplines
without becoming undisciplined altogether, of how to study a region "as
a whole" without simply studying *everything*—questions still vital to
interdisciplinary enterprises.

As the appended bibliography reveals, the articles and essays collected
here are only a sample of Vance's scholarly work. We have concentrated
on works dealing with the South and with regional sociology, and have
attempted to provide a representative selection, spanning the last fifty
years of Vance's life, the middle fifty years of this century. Some excellent
articles later included as chapters in his books have been left out, as have
examples of his purely theoretical work and demographic articles not
dealing with the South. (Among other conspicuous omissions are his
presidential addresses to the American Sociological Association and the
Population Association of America.) While by no means unimportant,
those facets of Vance's work seemed to us to be of less interest to readers
other than professional sociologists.

Above all, we sought selections that would indicate how broad his
interests were and how he brought those interests to bear on the trouble-
some problems of the American South. He was very much a man of his
time. As the citation accompanying his honorary degree from the University of North Carolina accurately observed, he "contributed not only to
the understanding of the human problems of this century, particularly
those of his native South, but to the solution of many of them." In doing
so, however, he also exemplified some virtues of an earlier time. Like
others of his colleagues at Chapel Hill, Robert Coles has observed, he
carried on "an older tradition of social science, and a Southern one. [The
titles of his books] suggest, in their directness and simplicity, what disciplines like sociology and psychology have lost in recent years"—*Human
Factors in Cotton Culture, The Human Geography of the South, All*

These People: The Nation's Human Resources in the South—"books meant to alert the reader, keep his attention, and (in the Southern tradition) describe. Narrative power is what those books have." When Gunnar Myrdal made a related point, in *An American Dilemma*, he undoubtedly had Vance and his colleagues in mind: "Social science in the South has never, as in the North, lost the tradition of reasoning in terms of means and ends; the few leading scientists have not become 'purely scientific' to the [same] extent as in the North. The significance for human happiness of the problems under study is always a present thought in the South, and statesmanship enters more naturally into the writings of its distinguished social scientists."

But if Vance addressed the problems of his day in a style recognized even then as an "older" one, he was also, in an important sense, ahead of his time. Whatever the final verdict on "regionalism," Vance's excursions into geography, history, economics, and political science evidence his vision of a unified social science, his conviction that a complicated modern society like the American South cannot rightfully be vivisected for the convenience of academic departments. It is a measure of his foresight that this fact is only now becoming obvious to the rest of us.

John Shelton Reed
Daniel Joseph Singal

Regionalism and the South

1. Stuart-Harmon

Social Distance in Twin Towns (1928)

Originally a paper for Professor Steiner's graduate seminar in community studies at North Carolina, this was Vance's first professional publication. Ironically, it was not published under his name. As he told the story in later years, Steiner was unable to find a publisher for a collection of his graduate students' papers, but found one readily enough for a manuscript with his name as author and the acknowledgment "Among those who have collaborated with me in the preparation of these community studies are the following. . . ." Nevertheless, Vance always included this chapter in his bibliography. "Stuart," Georgia, is, in fact, McRae, where Vance had taught English at South Georgia College before coming to Chapel Hill. The opening paragraphs are probably Professor Steiner's.

INTRODUCTORY NOTE

American towns in general have been located in a haphazard way with little reference to their relation to other towns in the same region or to the particular nature or needs of the territory immediately surrounding them. In some sections of the country this has resulted in an oversupply of towns, many of which cannot look forward to any satisfactory growth, or development. There can easily be found hundreds of such towns whose future has become even more precarious with the development of more rapid means of transportation. During the pioneer days of settlement there may have been some justification for their existence, but with the coming of railways, improved highways, and automobiles, they play a declining role in the territory they were designed to serve.

Especially unfortunate in its location is the town which either through accident or design finds itself immediately adjacent to a rival town which is separately incorporated. In such a situation business interests suffer for the available trade must be divided between two rival business sections.

From Jesse F. Steiner, *American Community in Action: Case Studies of American Communities* (New York: Henry Holt and Company, 1928), pp. 226–45.

Moreover, when the people in each town differ in race or nationality or social or economic status, as is frequently the case, divergent attitudes develop which foster misunderstanding and make cooperation impracticable. While it is true that if the two towns were incorporated as a single municipality, the same class divisions would remain, yet a unified town government would at least insure cooperation in public utilities and schools as well as prevent the growth of rival business districts on the main street of each town.

Stuart-Harmon, the twin towns described in this chapter, are representative of similarly situated small communities where one town is compelled to play a subordinate role to the other. Stuart, longer established and possessing prestige as the county seat, far outclasses Harmon, the railroad junction, with its inferior buildings and less cultured people. This difference in social status prevents normal association between the people of each town and creates unfriendly feelings which drives the people still further apart. Separated by no discernible boundary, either natural or artificial, each town has its own government, post office, railroad station, water system, retail stores, and churches. Through this duplication of institutions each town is impoverished and the people receive an inadequate return for the money spent in their support.

Without doubt this inefficiency in social organization must largely be traced to faults in the community structure. A great deal of time and effort are sometimes wasted in trying to overcome by improved methods of organization evils that are inherent in the structure of the community itself. This case study of Stuart-Harmon indicates quite clearly the necessity of more expert attention to the location and planning of towns as a fundamental first step in making community organization effective.

It should not be thought, however, that all the shortcomings of these two towns arose from their disunity and double organization. The dark picture that is painted showing the lack of wholesome recreation, the breakdown of traditional methods of social control, and the monotonous, aimless life of the young people, is true of many small towns more fortunately located. Nevertheless, the deficiencies characteristic of Stuart-Harmon were enhanced by their peculiar situation and present a problem which has thus far defied all attempts at solution.

GENERAL SETTING

Located in the "flat lands," the coastal plains of the South Atlantic, Stuart-Harmon is the center of the small but productive agricultural region in southern Georgia. The major commercial crops are cotton, corn and turpentine and its derivatives from the pine woods. Sweet potatoes, watermelons, cantaloupes, peaches, dewberries, peppers, and strawberries are grown, and only await the development of a cooperative marketing system to become profitable. Sugar cane is also an important crop and the cane grinding and making of syrup is a popular folk festival eagerly looked forward to by the country people. A few progressive farmers have found poultry raising on model chicken farms to be very profitable. The Stuart Board of Trade and the local Farm Bureau are attempting to introduce tobacco raising, and some slight beginnings have been made.

The majority of agricultural operations, here as throughout Georgia, are carried on under the tenant system. The terms "good farmer" and "good nigger" mean docile, hard working tenant. As a matter of fact, many of the tenants are shiftless, complain of having hard luck, fail to pay out, and almost every winter move to another farm in the vain hope of gaining a better living.

RISE OF STUART-HARMON

Of this region Stuart-Harmon is the cultural and economic capital. Stuart is an old settlement, of Scotch Presbyterian origin with a population of about 2,000. In 1874 it was incorporated and named for the pioneer Stuart family whose descendants still dominate the town. Colonel Alex Stuart, formerly a State Senator, now holds the position of mayor. Another scion of this old family is the leading physician; still another is president of the Citizens Bank. Economically the majority of the people of Stuart are well situated. In general their living is gained as retired farmers, farm owners, turpentine men, professional men, county officials and merchants and employees of the thirty mercantile establishments. It is in Stuart, older, larger, and more assured of its social position, that the landlords live to whom the tenants must repair for directions and supplies.

The town has its fair share of graduates of the State University, Georgia Institute of Technology, and the various denominational colleges. If one happens to go into Watson's department store he may be waited on by a young man wearing a Phi Beta Kappa key. Cultured, courteous, conservative, and proud of their old traditions, the "best people" of Stuart may be regarded as typical of "The Old South." Because of their intolerance of new ideas, new ways, and new people, they have not until recent years encouraged the coming in of outsiders. Many of the old residents have refused to sell desirable building lots, a fact which has hampered the growth of the town.

This conservative attitude of the people together with their exaggerated feeling of importance was largely responsible for the establishment of the town of Harmon. When the Great Eastern Railway desired to extend its main line through Stuart some of the property owners in the town declined to sell the right of way at a reasonable price. Confident that the railway would eventually be built through Stuart, its leading citizens did not take seriously the conflict over the purchase of the right of way. From the point of view of the more conservative, the coming of a new railroad was not a matter to get excited over, since the town was already on the main line of the Southern Railroad. When finally the Great Eastern officials broke off negotiations with the profiteering landowners and announced that a right of way had been secured a mile west of Stuart, the town people began to realize the mistake they had made. At the junction of the two railroads there was established a rival town named Harmon which because of its superior transportation facilities grew rapidly until it had a population of about 1,200, and became a shipping center of local importance.

SOCIAL AND ECONOMIC CONTRASTS

Since Harmon is primarily a railroad town, most of its citizens earn their living as railroad employees. Sitting over a midnight cup of coffee in Harmon's all night restaurant, one may see engineers, firemen and brakemen bolt a last bite before they pull out for Atlanta or Savannah. Among the few local industries in the town where employment may be secured are the town's ice plant, the turpentine still, and the two sawmills. No professional men and very few people of means and retired farmers live in Harmon. When a successful farmer wishes to move to town, he prefers to reside in Stuart where his children can have better surroundings.

While the people of Stuart realize that they are to blame for the establishment of Harmon they have never become quite reconciled to its existence. They look upon the town as an unwelcome rival and give expression of their resentment by building up social barriers between the two towns. From their point of view the people in Harmon simply "do not belong." Economic contacts are many, but intimacies are few. Harmon has had an inferior status thrust upon it which is resented but not denied. No one would suggest that this amounts to complete segregation, yet the social relationships and opportunities of Harmon people are very much restricted.

If Harmon is industrial, Stuart likes to think of itself as the business center. But Stuart's thirty stores are more than the surrounding region can really support. Prices are high, stocks lack variety, and many merchants eke out a hand-to-mouth existence. "Fire sales," "removal sales," "bankrupt sales," "going out of business sales," are too common to attract attention. The only time when business flourishes is on Saturdays during the autumn months when the tenants haul their cotton to town and pay their bills. At such times the streets of Stuart are crowded with gaunt farmers, anxious women with weary children, and strolling groups of Negroes. To the casual observer it seems as if these people were laying in a year's supply of shoes and clothes, flour and side meat. It is too often true that anything they need later will have to be advanced by their landlord or "bought on time."

Harmon, on the other hand, has no crowds of Saturday customers to make up for the monotony and poor business of the week. With the exception of the drug store, the all night restaurant, and the two garages, the establishments in Harmon look musty and forlorn. They exist to serve only the people of Harmon, and many of their expected customers go to Stuart. On Saturdays in Harmon, the shopkeepers standing in the doors of the four stores, give one the impression that they too would like to move to Stuart. Their struggle to make a living has especially been discouraging since the failure of Harmon's bank a year ago. This cast a pall of discouragement over the town from which it cannot easily recover. While Stuart has thus far escaped a similar catastrophe, business has recently been at a low ebb and the people are constantly talking of hard times.

DUPLICATION AND COMPETITION

The chief difficulty of course, is the folly of attempting to support rival business districts in the twin towns. Stuart-Harmon suffers a high per cent of business failures and pays higher prices for groceries and clothing because of its over supply of stores. Many people realize this fact, but civic pride if nothing else makes impracticable any merging of business interests.

In the field of public utilities there is a similar division of effort with its resulting inefficiency. Stuart and Harmon each has a volunteer fire company, and neither has been successful in putting out any fires that have gained headway. The separate water systems cannot maintain sufficient pressure for effective fire prevention. The rate of fire loss in Stuart-Harmon is high, and fire insurance premiums are almost prohibitive. The Harmon town government leases its electric current from the Stuart lighting plant, and the Harmon people pay a higher rate than is required of the citizens of Stuart. No less do the churches of the town suffer from this division. Each community supports a Methodist and a Baptist church, while Stuart has, in addition, an abandoned Episcopal church and a Presbyterian church which meets occasionally with a young pastor who comes from Savannah. The Stuart Methodists worship in an old barn. The two ministers in Harmon preach twice monthly to small and struggling congregations that rarely succeed in paying their ministers' salaries in full. Occasionally when some one dares to criticize the churches or the town governments for not being more cooperative he is regarded as indulging in mild sarcasm and no further attention is given to it.

The young people of the two towns know each other fairly well but mingle rarely. Occasionally one of the prettier or "better class" Harmon girls attends a Stuart party in spite of the social distinctions that are usually enforced. Formerly any Stuart boy who went to see a Harmon girl was likely to be attacked by a fusillade of rocks and compelled to scurry home. The reason for this was simple: With what good purpose did a Stuart boy visit a Harmon girl? It was as if West End should keep company with East Side. While the feeling of distrust is gradually declining, the association of the young people of both towns is still looked upon with great disfavor.

SCHOOLS: A COOPERATIVE ENTERPRISE
THAT DOES NOT UNITE

Education is apparently the one interest that tends to unite the twin towns, and to the school the young people owe what solidarity they have attained. That the Stuart-Harmon public school is a cooperative enterprise is an historical accident which cannot be explained without briefly reviewing the history of Slidell College. Almost thirty years ago, in a day when public high schools were little known in Georgia, a Methodist Academy was founded at Stuart for the Christian education of boys and girls. By means of gifts and tuition it struggled along as a local boarding school. At first its curriculum included the primary grades. It had a good high school department for that day, and many students came to it since it was the only academy in the country around. With the growth of public education the two towns organized the Stuart-Harmon public school district, rented a building from the Academy, and took over the first seven grades. The Academy retained the high school, added two years of college and adopted the official title: "Slidell College, a Methodist Junior College for Boys and Girls."

The administration of this college which serves the two towns as a high school, presents some difficult problems. As a private institution it is under the control of the college board of trustees appointed by the South Georgia Methodist Conference. This board selects the President, passes upon the teachers, and determines the policies of the institution. A large share of its appropriations, however, comes from both county and town boards of education and, theoretically, at least is subject to the control of these public school authorities. It is doubtful if the situation is legal, but no one has ever cared to carry the case into court, for the towns want neither to lose the college nor to be forced to issue bonds for the erection of a high school building. Those who do not belong to the Methodist Church dislike to see the high school dominated by the Methodists. The administration usually tries to avoid this criticism by employing at least two teachers who are active members of other denominations. But with all the concessions the Methodists are willing to make it still bears the earmarks of a denominational school, and as such is a constant source of dissatisfaction to many of the residents of Stuart-Harmon.

As might be expected, this effort to build up a cooperative school system of this nature did not prevent clashes between the children of each town. Formerly, Stuart-Harmon gangs had a mutual agreement to hang around the school grounds after four o'clock in order to fight. The boys no longer fight, but the girls from each town go around in little cliques. In the high school a group of hard-working students from Harmon seem conscious of inferiority and spend an excessive amount of time in study. The Stuart girls refer slightingly to the "Strawberry Blonds" who are said to peroxide their hair. Something, no doubt, is lacking in the taste in which some of them dress, and their manners likewise give little evidence of refinement. On the other hand, there are Harmon students who say that several of the Stuart girls think they are in society and are too good to speak to anybody. In the senior classes, however, this factional spirit seems much less noticeable. The parties, picnics and other social occasions which they attend create a feeling of comradeship. By the time commencement arrives, the class seems bound together by a haze of sentiment which temporarily at least drives into the background the social distinctions that separate the people of the two towns.

SOCIAL CLASSES WITHIN STUART

Social distance divides Harmon and Stuart, but it also operates in Stuart itself. Calloway Street is the select residential district. Here stand the beautiful homes of the Stuarts, the lawyers, the doctors, the retired farmers who own turpentine lands, and the leading merchants. It is the women of Calloway Street who run the civic and patriotic clubs just as their menfolk run the town. Membership in the Stuart Improvement Club, the Daughters of the American Revolution, and the United Daughters of the Confederacy is limited to the elite who guard jealously their rights as leaders in civic and social affairs.

In a less desirable section of Stuart is the middle class residential district locally known as "Shintown." The people who live here have modest incomes and reside in bungalows attractive enough in appearance but far outclassed by the stately mansions on Calloway Street. In their social life, the women of "Shintown" have nothing in common with those in the higher social circle. The Parent-Teachers Association, the Woman's Christian Temperance Union and the American Legion Auxiliary furnish an outlet for their social and civic interests. In the work of these more plebian organizations the women of Calloway Street maintain a friendly interest, but make it quite clear that they are too busy to attend any of their meetings.

Lowest in the social scale are the people who live in the rows of ill-kept houses located in the outskirts of the business section. Some of these are cheap boarding houses and several have a rather unsavory reputation about which wild stories circulate from time to time.

Across the railroad lies the segregated quarter known as "nigger town." White women from the best families drive over there occasionally to take their laundry or look for a cook, but they never seem to notice the tumble down shacks or become concerned about the squalor amid which the Negroes live. A Methodist and a Baptist church and the "Twin City Seminary" provide for their religious and educational needs. This Negro school boasts a domestic science department which is a great source of satisfaction to the white people of Stuart because it insures for them a supply of well-trained cooks. Everybody will tell you, "We have a good bunch of Negroes: they give us no trouble for they know their place and keep it."

THE YOUNG PEOPLE AND THE
BREAKDOWN OF SOCIAL CONTROL

It is in the social relations of the young people of Stuart-Harmon that the conflict of social attitudes and loosening of the bonds of social control are most clearly seen. There are many of the older people in the two towns who say that the young folk are going to the dogs. Anxious mothers have found cigarettes in the vanity bags of their high school daughters. Many young sons and daughters have assumed control of the family car without the parents realizing how it happened. Some of the town's best men are drinking rather heavily on the sly. The change in social attitudes is well brought out in a comment by one of the "nicest girls" in Stuart: "Six years ago, if a boy had offered me a drink of whiskey I would have been insulted; now I merely laugh and say, 'No thank you, I don't drink!'" Boys and girls go out driving until one or two in the morning and cut off the remonstrances of their parents with the reply: "Well, everybody else does." Many students drop out in the first year of high school to go to work and are afterwards seen loafing in the streets. In the high school senior class which numbered twenty last year there were only two boys and one of them failed. Some of the older families in Stuart have decided to send their boys off to a military academy. Occasionally an adolescent boy runs away from home to the surprise and chagrin of his parents, and is captured and brought back to face the ridicule of his fellows. Once in a while a vaguely vile story goes the rounds about a Harmon girl, and later it is reported that she has been seen clerking in a ten cent store in Atlanta, Savannah or Macon.

The agencies of social control have found the mediation between the old and the new a thankless task. Some of the patrons have said that the school board should pass a rule against the school children going downtown at night, and that the teachers should enforce it. Several years ago the Ku Klux Klan, then rather popular, secured a passage of a curfew ordinance which was enforced for two months. Four revivals are held each year in the two towns, and the changes are rung on the refrain: "The young people are going to hell." Dancing, petting and car riding come in for their share of attention. It is proved to the satisfaction of the pulpit if not the choir, that one who plays bridge is in the same category with a "crap shootin' buck nigger." Some have begun to wonder if the revivals really do much good. Nevertheless the evangelists come back each year and they always carry off a liberal collection even though the salary of the local ministers may remain unpaid.

DULLNESS VERSUS VICIOUSNESS IN RECREATION

In this conflict of social attitudes between the new and the old the complaint is frequently heard that the young people do not work as did those of a former generation. Certain it is that they have a great deal of leisure for which the community has provided nothing in the way of organized recreation. There are no Boy Scout or Camp Fire Girl organizations nor boys' and girls' clubs of any kind in Stuart-Harmon. Organized play exists only in the public school calisthenics and football and baseball at the college. The young people do little reading outside their class room work, for the twin towns have no public library, and the shelves of the college library (which are not open to the public) have been filled with dusty tomes on divinity, the gifts of benevolently disposed ministers. The few plays and other programs given during the year for the purpose of raising money for the Woman's Christian Temperance Union and the American Legion are held at the college auditorium. Usually these plays are put on by traveling directors who furnish the costumes, and get a percentage of the receipts. As a matter of custom, the same boys and girls from Calloway Street are cast in all these plays. During the performance the town "bad boys" sit out in the dark in cars, smoking and talking in boisterous tones. Around Christmas they are likely to amuse themselves by exploding firecrackers under the windows. Since there are no music, drama, or literary clubs, these plays constitute the young people's chief means of developing their esthetic and cultural interests.

Two centers of conflict of social attitudes are found in the dance and the cheap carnival. With the aid of the community the American Legion has built a club house in which dances are sometimes held by the younger married people and their friends. Often a dance is followed by a sermon against dancing by one of the local pastors after which the young people may suspend the pastime for several weeks as a matter of prudence. Several times the more strait-laced Legion members have been outraged to find some of the high school pupils holding an impromptu afternoon dance in the club house without permission. In the spring and summer no carnival for miles around fails to come to Stuart-Harmon. Side shows and amusement devices draw good crowds, but the perennial gambling booths appeal most to the town boys and the callow youths from the farm. The carnivals are usually sponsored by the American Legion which gets a percentage of the receipts after the city license fee has been paid.

LOAFING AND SOCIAL DISORGANIZATION

No discussion of the recreation of the young folk of Stuart-Harmon would be complete without a mention of loafing. From early afternoon until closing time at eleven or twelve at night, small groups of young people can be seen idling away their time in and about the garages, restaurants, and drug stores, for loafing is a popular means of recreation with well-established hangouts. Gangs of boys, gossiping and playing pranks on each other, have the garages and all-night restaurants practically to themselves. In the four drug stores the phonographs blare forth their jazz from afternoon until closing time. Young boys gather around the counter, matching for drinks and joking with the soda fountain clerk, while the giggling girls sit around the tables in intimate conversation. When a boy bends over the group and speaks in a low tone after a hasty glance around, one may be sure that he is telling a sex joke left by the last commercial traveler. More or less subtle wordplay upon the theme of sex is indulged in by all groups from the Shriners to the fourth grade boys. It is true that in the shops the barbers now cast a glance around the room before asking "Have you heard this one?" and the "Police Gazettes" have disappeared from view, but girls awaiting their turn for a hair cut seem hardly at ease. One observes that they sit rather primly, get their necks shaved as quickly as possible and hurry out.

It is in this failure to provide wholesome social activities that the social disorganization of Stuart-Harmon is most apparent. People deplore the fact that their children spend so much time on the streets, but no one has advanced the idea of a community playground or attempted to organize girls' and boys' clubs of a wholesome kind. The ministers continue to talk about a religious revival and the older settlers bemoan the good old times, but nobody seems to know just what to do about it. In the meantime the parents hope that John will finally settle down and May will quit gadding about town. The school seems powerless to deal with the problem for its classes are already crowded and the overburdened teachers can give no special attention to those who fail in their studies. Occasionally a young clerk, recently married, tells a high school teacher how he missed his chance at education because of his unwillingness to attend school. The teacher nods sympathetically and puts the matter out of his mind. It has been a generation since a man from Stuart-Harmon has gained success in Atlanta, Macon, or Savannah. The boys usually marry and settle down at the home of their parents or their wife's parents until they can afford to build. Some of the girls who graduate from high school teach in the country, but they look forward to marriage rather than to teaching as a profession.

LACK OF SOCIAL SERVICE AGENCIES

Stuart-Harmon like most small towns makes no adequate attempts to deal with dependents and delinquents. There is no professional social work. When a family reaches the starvation level, some friend carries a subscription list around to all the merchants, who put down small sums because "everybody else is helping." Tender-hearted housewives continue to feed tramps at the back door provided they do not become too numerous. An occasional vagrant or suspicious character is put in the town lock-up, but usually, if molested at all, such persons are given a few hours to get out of town.

RECENT EFFORT AT BOOSTING

During the past year and a half, Stuart, like many other American towns, has become dominated by the booster spirit, and led by the Board of Trade, has sought to gain prosperity by increasing its population. Situated on the Southern Railway and on a state highway leading from Atlanta to Jacksonville, the people of Stuart have watched for a number of years the automobile tourists and the Pullmans of the Royal Palm passing through the town. But none of the tourists ever settled, and then the roads were so poor that the cars began to use another route. Faced by this situation, the Board of Trade entered upon an extensive program designed to improve conditions. The private ferry on the Coropeake River, which during high water was always out of commission, was replaced by a bridge that was opened by the governor last May with appropriate ceremonies. A good roads campaign was inaugurated which resulted in Stuart voting a bond issue that made possible eight blocks of paved streets, a white way, and side-walks in a hitherto unpaved residential district. Finally after a long struggle against the efforts of the embattled farmers, a county bond issue of $325,000 was voted to match state and Federal funds for paving the two highways the length of the county. The banks and the Board of Trade have called in experts from the State College of Agriculture to explain the advantages of diversified farming. Poultry raising is being encouraged, and a carload of registered Jersey bulls from Virginia were auctioned off to the farmers.

Nor has the Board of Trade neglected to advertise in the effort to attract new residents to the town. Editorials have appeared deprecating the prejudice against Yankees and "foreigners." It is pointed out that lynchings (from which McKee County is singularly free) create a prejudice against a community. The section has been written up in an attractive manner in the "Atlanta Journal" by a special correspondent who put most of his emphasis on the history and the future of the community. An eighteen page McKee County Photogravure Section in a 1926 issue of "Georgia, A Magazine Devoted to the Development of a Greater Georgia" was paid for by the Stuart Board of Trade. In its folders, the section is "sloganized" as the "Paradise of Real Agriculturists" and Stuart as the "City, Wholesome and Substantial." The publicity pamphlet concludes with the statement: "The people are satisfied and happy and work in perfect harmony to make their county and towns better places in which to live. We have no divisions among our people and both white and black work for their own advancement along the same lines." On the strength of these and similar statements the McKee-Sterling Land Company has been organized for the purpose of selling developed farms to newcomers.

In the meantime tourists have come back from Florida, and have stopped in McKee County only for gas. Every day, it is said, the Board of Trade gets inquiries from up North and mails back its folders. The new-comers have not yet arrived, but the people still look hopefully toward the future. At any rate they do have the sidewalks, the pavements, and the white way, which were needed so long. But the conflict of social attitudes and the results of cultural isolation still remain.

STUART AS IT IS TODAY

This effort on the part of the Board of Trade to boost Stuart did not result in better relations between the two towns. Harmon gave no help in getting out the publicity and is mentioned only once in the Photogravure Section. Stuart, still conscious of its superiority, continues to ignore its neighboring rival as it has in the past. The old traditions and attitudes of the people persist in spite of the effort to make Stuart a more progressive town. The boys still drop out of school to loaf on the streets. The presi-dent of the Woman's Christian Temperance Union repeats her lectures to the boys and girls on "purity" and "cigarettes" whenever the school principal will give her a chapel period. The biology teacher is warned not to mention sex or evolution in class, and the statement: "My grandfather was not an ape" is good for a laugh at "those fool scientists" in any church in town. Some of the boys and girls like Zane Grey and Harold Bell Wright, but many of them care little or nothing about reading. The two Methodist churches voted overwhelmingly against unification, al-though the leading lawyer in town favored it. The town is still talking about the college girl who, on her way to the State University to begin her second year's work, met her old sweetheart on the train, eloped with him to South Carolina, and brought him back to live with her folks. Chip Norman, minister's son and a college graduate struggling along in a blind-alley bookkeeper's job, tried to kill himself recently. All his friends knew that he was drinking secretly, and the best girls would no longer associate with him. Three boys in the town ran away from home and sent their frantic parents word that they were going to South America. A good one about the drummer and the old maid is going the rounds of the drug stores. A tenant farmer told the crowd at the garage that if he had his way "All these niggers and damn foreigners would be deported." A lawyer drew a good laugh in the barber shop by saying, "I don't object to niggers going to heaven. I suspect my shoes will still need shining up there." In a recent Sunday sermon the minister informed his congregation that the South contained the "only pure Anglo-Saxon blood in America." Downtown, slim, giggling mulatto girls who hardly need the face powder they use, gaze, rather conscious of their beauty, into shop windows. The Dixie Carnival and Tent Show has just left town, and a new revival is to start soon at the Methodist Church. The white way and the paved streets have done little to relieve the drabness and monotony of life and the town seems to be settling back into its old lethargy with dwindling hopes of future improvement.

THE OUTLOOK IN HARMON

Over in Harmon the two hotels, erected with high hopes at the junction of the two railway lines, are having a hard time remaining solvent. "Business is dead in Harmon" is a common saying, and the owners of the stores would gladly sell out if they could find a purchaser. As the town gets older its appearance is getting more unkempt and its chances of improvement become increasingly meager. To the outside observer the people of Harmon appear uncouth and lacking in appreciation of the finer things in life. Under the circumstances little else could be expected for the struggle for existence has been hard and the inferior status forced upon them by Stuart has been disheartening. In Harmon, pretty young girls grow up, go to school and marry, and within a few years childbearing and household drudgery have wiped off the bloom; they are wrinkled, slovenly, and commonplace. The only girls who can look forward to a different lot are those who have gone to other communities to teach and have found there a permanent home. But it is hard to get out. Mac Bowman, son of expressman Bowman of the Great Eastern Railway, won highest honors in the senior class of Slidell and planned to go to Duke University. But his father got him a job as baggageman, and the boy gave up his hope of a college education. In Harmon families need money, and children are expected to go to work as soon as they can get paying jobs.

Stuart-Harmon seem fated to continue to struggle along side by side, yet separated, one placed above, the other placed below. Competition rather than cooperation characterizes their relations with each other. Each little move of progress in one town is an occasion for jealousy in the other. The two long streets between Stuart and Harmon are filled in the evening with cars of joyriders from Stuart. But no one would think of taking a joyride around the Harmon shacks across the railroad. The attitudes of the people, their economic status and habits of life form a gulf between the two which cannot be easily crossed. If through some miracle of industrial expansion Stuart-Harmon should greatly increase their population they might outgrow their isolation and merge their double organization into a united municipality. But as it now is, isolation shuts out the people of Harmon, and social distance no less divides those of Stuart. Unable to live together, the twin towns are yet unable to live apart.

2. Cotton Culture and Social Life

and Institutions of the South (1929)

This article is a gloss, for an audience of professional sociologists, of Vance's dissertation (published the same year), Human Factors in Cotton Culture, *from which, in fact, it is largely drawn. His characteristic style, his ability to shift effortlessly from statistical data to the gritty reality behind them, and the range of his interests and erudition are already evident.*

The spatial and temporal distribution of the activities of man as conditioned by the environment is coming to be regarded as the especial study of human ecology.[1] Instead of a crude geographic determinism, the point of view taken by human ecology is that of an adjustment of previously existing cultures to such factors of natural environment as climate, soil, land forms, and societies of plants and animals.[2] In the American South it is possible to trace the adjustment of culture to the demands of the cotton plant.

R. Mukerjee writes:[3]

> Whenever man depends upon agriculture and has found a permanent abode, the growing of different staple crops such as rice, wheat, or Indian corn, and the rearing of different domestic animals, selected from among the native stock of a region, govern not merely man's interests and habits but also his social organization.

Nature's harmony of the soil, the rainfall, the frostless season, and the flaming sun has fitted well with a transplanted tropic plant, a transplanted tropic race, landless white farmers, and the slow but all surviving mule to make the American South a distinctive region, the Cotton Belt. In less than 3 per cent of the world's land area, Professor O. E. Baker[4] has estimated 60 per cent of the world's cotton supply is grown. In this area 42 per cent of the crop land was in cotton in 1919 and the value of the cotton crop was equal to the value of all other crops combined.[5] In

From *Publications of the American Sociological Society* 23 (1929), pp. 51–59. Reprinted by permission.

the terms of the student of anthropology we may regard this highly specialized agricultural region, the Cotton Belt, as a culture area[6] and speak of the cotton-culture complex. The plantation, cotton tenancy, seasonal routines, food habits, family labor, attitudes of speculation, shiftlessness, and mobility, for the purpose of this paper, may be considered as culture traits surrounding the cultivation of cotton. With respect to these traits the one-horse cotton farmers are more nearly standardized.

Historically cotton culture conditioned the development of the South through the plantation system. The production by means of routine methods, applied to unskilled labor of a staple from which the plantation could not escape has tended to set the mode by which human factors in southern agriculture shall be regulated. Robert E. Park[7] has well said:

> The history of slavery in America is an incident in the history of the plantation system. . . . Slavery has disappeared, to be sure, but the plantation system in one form or another remains, not merely in the South but in many parts of the world. The abolition movement when seen in its proper perspective is merely an episode in the history of a particular type of industrial organization.

"Its concentration of labor under skilled management," writes Ulrich B. Phillips,[8] "made the plantation system with its overseers, foreman, blacksmiths, carpenters, hostlers, cooks, nurses, plowhands, and hoe-hands, practically the factory system applied to agriculture." The change from the cotton plantation to cotton tenancy gave the agricultural worker mobility, legal freedom of contract, and wages or a share of the crop in return for his work. It brought the landless southern white man within the cotton system, created share tenancy and cotton cropping, a system whereby labor is secured "without wages and loans are made without security." The Census of 1900 showed that of all farmers to whom cotton offered the chief source of income, 67.7 were tenants.[9] By 1910, although Negro farmers cultivated 52 per cent of the total cotton acreage, the white farmers produced 67 per cent of the total crop.[10] In cotton-growing areas in ten southern states in 1920, 55 out of every 100 farmers were tenants, and out of every hundred cotton renters 21 were cash renters, 37 were croppers, and 42 were share tenants.[11]

The effect of the seasonal cycle of the cotton plant is shown in the social routine of the people. The periods of slack work come in mid-summer—July and August—and in midwinter—December and January.

After cotton is laid by in July and August summer terms of school are held in many places, and rural people attend protracted revival services. One cotton planter[12] writes of the practice. "It seems sensible to me. Cotton anyway must be grown by a series of spurts rather than by a steady daily grind." During the hot season "about the best thing for croppers to do is to quit work, visit around and attend the protracted meeting. Then if they haven't killed each other *ad interim* they are physically fit when the rush of cotton picking begins." Cotton picking mobilizes all the available cheap manual labor in the South. This un-mechanized process takes the cooks, maids, roustabouts, idlers and men-of-all-work out of the southern towns, mothers out of the homes, and children out of school. In many places the country schools close until the harvest is gathered. The amount of the farmer's time required to pick an acre of cotton would, it is estimated by the Department of Agriculture, produce three acres of corn in Iowa or four acres of wheat in Kansas.[13] H. C. Brearley[14] found in a study of 1,601 homicides in South Carolina from 1920–24 that:

> months of high homicide rates concur rather closely with the seasons of little farming activity, with one peak coming during the winter vacation and the other during the midsummer lay-by and camp meeting time. Two of the three months of least homicides, May and October, are also the months when farm labor is most busy.

Among the most obvious of the material culture traits associated with cotton are the food habits of its growers. The immense amount of man labor in planting, chopping, and picking cotton comes at times which interfere with the cultivation of other southern crops. Consequently, the family on the one-horse cotton farm has been "driven by compulsion to the most efficient of all the foodstuffs that can be made to suffice."[15] Corn is suited to the southern climate, and is an efficient producer of cereal carbohydrates. A dietary survey conducted during the war found that the maize kernel constituted 23 per cent of the total food intake of Tennessee and Georgia mountaineers, 32.5 per cent of that of southern Negroes, but only 1.6 per cent of the diet of 72 northern families in comfortable circumstances.[16] Hogs thrive on corn and, since they complete their growth in one season, may be regarded as comparatively efficient producers of strong meat. In fact, H. P. Armsby has estimated that about 24 per cent of the energy of grain is recovered for human consumption in pork as compared with about 18 per cent in milk and 3.5 per cent in beef and mutton.[17] The cheaper cuts of fat pork, salt cured, become the year round staple of diet. Surveys have shown that pork often amounts to 40 per cent of the value of all articles of food consumed by southern farmers.[18] Sorghum and sugar cane are eminently suited to the southern climate and produce, without demanding too much labor, a food of high sugar content.

Thus it comes about that the Negro cropper, the white tenant, and the small cotton farmer live upon a basic diet of salt fat pork, corn bread, and molasses. This forms the "three M diet," meat, meal, and molasses, noted by Dr. Joseph Goldberger[19] of the United States Health Service as pellagra producing when made up in conventional proportions. When cotton farmers purchase food, these are the articles of diet they purchase; first, because all three are cheap, and second, because food likes and dislikes come to be matters of habit imposed by culture. Exclusive reliance on this diet impairs health and economic efficiency, and thus may serve to cement the cotton farmer closer to his basic diet.

The southern rural attitudes toward the field labor of women and children to a great extent grow out of the seasonal demands of cotton. The unmechanized processes of chopping and picking call for a large amount of unskilled manual labor. The time element also enters. "The limiting factor is the amount of cotton the average farm family can pick before the cotton begins to deteriorate."[20] One small mule can easily till more cotton than the average farmer can chop and pick. It is true, then, that the most successful cotton farmer is the one who can command a large amount of human labor within his own household. "It has been said with some degree of truth," writes Alexander E. Cance,[21] "that successful farming rests on the unpaid labor of women and children." Of the 1,084,128 women listed in the 1920 Census of Occupations as engaged in agriculture, 80 per cent were found in the ten chief cotton states.[22] Practically 20 per cent of all females over ten years of age living on farms in these states were listed as field laborers. Out of every hundred women field laborers, 68 were Negroes and 32 white. In a report of family labor employed per farm[23] October 1, 1927, the South Atlantic states averaged 3.83 and the South Central 3.62 persons as compared with 1.79 for the Western states, 1.82 for North Atlantic and North Central states, and 2.51 for the United States as a whole. Large families are an economic asset. A young cotton tenant wrote:

A young married man single-handed can hardly rent land to farm on, as the landowner wants a man with a large family, children large enough to work so he can realize on their labor. . . . What must the young people among the renters do? They are practically denied the land to farm on until they rear enough children to gather a good-sized cotton crop; that is what the landowners want.[24]

Children thus may be said to cost the cotton farmer less and pay him more. Forced by the demands of the plant and his economic needs, the one-horse cotton farmer accepts the fieldwork of his womenfolks and children as a matter of course. This attitude on the part of rural families is carried into cotton-mill villages. It is everywhere met in attempts to enforce compulsory school attendance.

Closely connected with devotion to cotton, indeed a part of it, is the speculative attitude engendered by the fluctuations in the price of cotton. A prominent cotton factor in the Eastern Belt writes:

This attitude—a matter of degree, a degree beyond the legitimate risks of normal business—spreads itself in a thoroughgoing way and permeates the economic life of the South. Our most successful and so-called conservative business men grow up with it and are often not aware of its dangers until a crash comes. Meantime, in general, the cotton producer, lien merchant, and dealer has no other outlook, and has learned to live from year to year on the fortunes of risks over which he has absolutely no control, and upon the hazards of which he will stake his all. And when he happens to combine some other line of business with cotton, the risks he exposes himself to are in proportion.

Cotton impinges in yet another manner upon the culture patterns of the South. The cotton growers' flow of money income is subject to a seasonal cycle and to the cycle of cotton prices. This serves to give the cotton growers not only a shifting standard of living, but also serves to prevent them from acquiring habits of thrift. It has been shown that the average money income from cotton has ranged from $35 to $200 a bale and from $10 to $60 an acre. Without an income which can be counted upon, it is almost impossible for a family to plan and live according to a budget. The consumption of goods by the family thus tends to run in cycles corresponding to those of cotton prices rather than to be equalized over a period of years. The cótton farmer is too much given to alternate periods of splurging and deprivation.

The cotton farmer stands to make or lose his income all in one lump at one time. In the Cotton Belt luxuries are likely to be bought on the spur of the moment, during a good season in cotton, and paid for by deprivation in next year's living. Planters are apt to lament the phonographs, sewing-machines, organs, player pianos, automobiles that their tenants buy during seasons of prosperity as evidences of inherent traits of lack of judgment and extravagance of Negroes and poor white people. The culture trait, however, draws an origin from the cyclical nature of cotton itself. A period of deprivation during the growing period is relieved by a supply of ready cash income secured practically all at one time. The income of the cotton grower has its peaks of high prices, but these peaks are not expected, they are not planned for, and they do not always serve to level up the general standard of living.

Two other sets of attitudes peculiar to southern farmers have grown out of the conditions of tenancy and cotton culture. The first attitude may be described as the shiftless attitude of the renter toward the place on which he lives. The common complaint of landlords is of houses allowed to go to ruin, fences torn down, and land lacerated by erosion. Law gives the tenant no interest in his tenancy. A tenure of twenty years gives the renter no more right to remain than a tenure of twenty days. In this the American practice differs from the English. In addition the law gives the tenant no claim for improvements made. The tenant then does not look forward to a future but only to a present use of the farm. In self-defense his is the philosophy of get what he can while he can. To fix fences, clear land, stop gulleys from washing, to repair a shed, or shingle a roof is from his viewpoint a foolish waste of time and energy. From this attitude it may be only a step to the use of fences for firewood. Much of the shiftlessness of southern tenants, regarded in this light, is a self-defensive adjustment.

Mobility furnishes a closely related trait of tenants growing out of a lack of attachment to the farms which they have cultivated. A study by the Department of Agriculture in 1922 estimated there then was a shifting of occupants on 19 per cent of all farms in the United States, 27.7 per cent of tenants and 6 per cent of owners shifting. In eight cotton states, however, 30 to 40 per cent of all farms showed a change of occupants.[25] "White croppers reported much shorter average periods of occupancy than colored croppers," ranging from a third of a year to a year and a half.[26] In almost any region the form of share rent, a third of corn and a fourth of cotton, set by custom, can take no adequate account of variations which exist in the fertility of cotton-producing soils in a given area. Variations in character of landlords also exist. Having nothing to lose the tenant is easily led to move by a desire to secure better land, or to find a more agreeable landlord. Poor housing, inferior educational facilities, and health conditions may be regarded as additional factors inciting to mobility. There is always the chance that the tenant may find a better place for no greater expenditure. Let him move a number of times and mobility itself tends to become a habit; the renter has then acquired the reputation of being a shiftless, roving tenant.

When traits such as we have described are confronted in the behavior and attitudes of individuals, these traits are described in terms of personality and character defects. Thus the manager of a large Arkansas plantation owned by Frank O. Lowden writes of the cotton laborer:

> He has nothing, wants nothing, expects nothing, does not try to have anything, but does waste and destroy any and everything. He is wild for money, but when he gets it, it is not worth five cents on the dollar to buy his needs. That is for waste, his needs are bought on credit.

The inadequate adjustment of the inefficient one-horse cotton farmer group, however, does not operate against its survival in the succeeding generations. Exclusion from urban culture patterns has left the farmers of lower economic levels with less knowledge of contraceptive practices. For the same reasons his attitudes toward the restriction of families partake more of the old, the traditional, and the conservative. Moreover, children are less of an economic handicap in that he is not expected to do as much for them. They are more of an advantage because they furnish unskilled farm labor. After having aided in cultivating the family crop, many sons of farm owners as well as of renters enter maturity and the ranks of cotton croppers and tenants at the same time. The exhaustion of free land and the differential birth-rate in favor of the farmer, accounts in part for increasing tenancy rates. Cotton culture, it may be said, after rendering some of its producers inefficient, makes for their survival both in the economic and biological sense. They are the marginal farmers, for they exist on the outer margin of culture. "They constitute a more or less disturbing factor—a miserable support for themselves and a disturbing menace to the success of others that must always be counted in the estimate of production and consumption and in any proposed legislation."[27]

NOTES

1. R. D. McKenzie, in *The City* (Chicago, 1925), Robert E. Park, ed., pp. 63–64.

2. H. H. Barrows, "Geography as Human Ecology," *Annals of the Association of American Geographers* 13 (1923): 4.

3. R. Mukerjee, *Regional Sociology* (New York, 1926), p. vi.

4. O. E. Baker, "Agricultural Regions of North America," part 2, "The South," *Economic Geography* (January 1927), p. 65.

5. Ibid., pp. 77, 79.

6. Clark Wissler, "The Concept of the Culture Area as a Research Lead," *American Journal of Sociology* 32 (1926): 881–91.

7. *American Journal of Sociology* 33 (1927): 290–91.

8. "Decadence of the Plantation," *Annals of the Association of American Geographers* 25 (1930): 37.

9. U.S. Census Monograph 4, *Farm Tenancy in the United States* (1920), p. 33

10. U.S. Census Monograph, *Negro Population in the United States, 1790–1918*, pp. 594–96.

11. Rupert B. Vance, "Human Factors in Cotton Culture," MS, Institute for Research in Social Science, University of North Carolina (1928), p. 77.

12. Alfred G. Smith, "The Cropper System," *Country Gentleman*, September 4, 1930.

13. *Seedtime and Harvest*, U.S. Department of Agriculture, Circular 183 (1922), p. 39.

14. "Homicides in South Carolina, 1920–1924," MS, University of North Carolina (1928), p. 22. South Carolina's population was 82.5 per cent rural in 1919.

15. W. J. Spillman, in *Farm Income and Farm Life*, ed. Dwight Sanderson (Chicago, 1927), p. 194.

16. U.S. Food Administration, *Food and the War* (New York, 1918), cited in E.V. McCollum, *The Newer Knowledge of Nutrition* (New York, 1922), p. 128.

17. "Roast Pig," *Science* 46 (1917): 160.

18. H. W. Hawthorne et al., *Farm Organization and Farm Management in Sumter County, Georgia*, U.S. Department of Agriculture, Bulletin 1,034 (1922), p. 37.

19. U.S. Public Health Reports, *Pellagra in the Mississippi Flood Area*, Reprint 1,187 (1927), p. 16.

20. Spillman, *Farm Income and Farm Life*, p. 194.

21. Ibid., p. 77.

22. *Occupations*, U.S. Census, 1920, vol. 4, chap. 3.

23. On farms of crop reporters, *Crops and Markets* 5, no. 10 (October 1928): 362.

24. See *Report of Senate Industrial Relations Commission*, Senate Document 415, vol. 10 (1916), 9262.

25. *Department of Agriculture Yearbook* (1923), p. 590. Kentucky, a state of tobacco tenanacy, also showed a farm mobility of from 30 to 40 per cent.

26. Ibid., p. 593.

27. *Condition of Agriculture in the United States and Measures for Its Improvement*, National Industrial Conference Board (New York, 1927), pp. 8–9.

3. A Karl Marx for Hill Billies

Portrait of a Southern Leader (1930)

This sketch of "Jeff Davis the Little," an Arkansas populist, was the first of a series of studies of Southern politicians which Vance hoped someday to consolidate in a book, "Spellbinders of the Old South," a book that was unfortunately never completed. It is written in the American Mercury *style and displays Vance's journalistic flair to good advantage.*

In the noble discipline of political science there has lived and practiced in these United States no more astounding savant than the late Junior Senator from Arkansas, Jeff Davis the Little, Karl Marx to Hill Billies. He was no replica of the patriarch of the Confederacy and remains unadored of the U.D.C. Professional man of the people, thrice governor, twice elected to the Senate, it was at one time the dearest wish of good Arkansawyers to see their tribune of haybinders matched in joint debate with Theodore Roosevelt, then President of the United States.

Opposed by almost every newspaper in the state, he liked to quote their description of him as a "carrot-haired, red-faced, loud-mouthed, strong-limbed, ox-driving mountaineer lawyer that has come to Little Rock to get a reputation—a friend to the fellow that brews forty-rod bug juice back in the mountains." He loved to quote it because the ring of invective had a mouth-filling sound and because it won him votes.

Dead these seventeen years, Jeff Davis possesses a name that Arkansawyers, usually an outspoken race, mention before strangers with bated breath. In Arkansas one must first learn the politics of an acquaintance before deigning to criticize or to blame. For every man who loved not Jeff Davis the Little, hated him with a holy passion. A man of might in the days when politics was politics, he evoked a hierarchy of angels and demons in which there were no neuters. At every cross roads and hamlet in that most berhymed and bedeviled of commonwealths he wrestled mightily with powers and principalities, spirits of light and of darkness. For Jeff Davis divided in order to rule and stirred up strife that victory

From *Social Forces* 9 (December 1930): 180–90.

might light on his banner. Since his day Arkansas has elevated to the governorship a banker and a farmer, sundry lawyers, a professor of sociology from the state university with his Ph.D., and a travelling salesman; has sent to the Senate the redoubtable Joe T. and Thaddeus the Terrible. But the land of the Slow Train, where fact becomes folklore if it is allowed to simmer over night, has produced and will, God be thanked, produce no more consummate master of politics than Jeff the Little.

In a state that possessed no aristocracy against whom they might rebel Davis led a revolt of the dispossessed poor whites. Whoso would understand politics beneath the Smith and Wesson line must cease from the contemplation of Bishop Cannon to give his days and nights to the lives of Vardaman of Mississippi, Pitchfork Ben Tillman and Cole Blease of South Carolina, Tom Watson of Georgia, and Jeff Davis of Arkansas. Before the Civil War the governors of South Carolina were good Episcopalians and held with the speaker on the floor of the Virginia legislature that "It is conceivable that a man may go to heaven by another route than the Episcopal Church but I am sure a gentleman would choose no other." After the struggle her rulers came from frontier Methodist and Baptist stock. The toad under the harrow had stood it long enough. The wool hat boys were climbing into the saddle and when the carpetbaggers released their weakened grasp hell began to pop all over the South. It was farmer against planter, common man against enfeebled aristocrat, Populist against Democrat, rustics against city dudes. But if Arkansas had no aristocracy to overturn, its towns had grown up and were developing a professional class of lawyers, doctors, merchants, and absentee landlords rising mildly above the dead level of reconstruction poverty. The capital had already grown into the wonder and envy of the haybinder. As Davis was to tell them, the horny-handed sunburned sons of toil yearly pulled the bell ropes over old Jerry only to have the price of their fleecy product set by the gamblers of the New York Cotton Exchange. Things were not well. And if they were wrong, a conflict must be precipitated or an ogre must be improvised. No discussion of economic principles would win votes; but to dramatize a struggle, that was different. The material was at hand. The terror of the nineties, the trust, was beginning to be noised abroad. It was not difficult to inspire in the minds of simple rustics the fear of machines, rings, pools, railroads, mergers, and combinations. Jeff carried on a whirlwind campaign against industrialization, corporate business, and capital in a state which needed all three and had not the remotest chance of getting them. In no abstruse terms of economics he led the red neck and the patched britches brigade on a holy crusade against the malefactors of great wealth. Instead of seven against Thebes it was Arkansas against the trusts. Before he reached the Senate this Jeff the Giant Killer who had never heard of Karl Marx was to carry his truly grotesque version of the class struggle to the coves of all the mountains, forks of all the creeks, and banks of all the bayous in Arkansas.

In the South one must understand that politics like agrarian religion is likely to be the outgrowth of poverty experience. A clear conscience and the witness of the spirit to the soul's salvation, things denied the wealthy, compensate the rustic for his ungained competence. Likewise the poor but honest yeoman of the plough arises on election day, and with the untainted ballot thrust in his hands by Democracy, strikes down the minions of pelf, pride, and plutocracy. What if for two years he hearkens with knitted brows to the gathering murmur of graft and boodle in the state house. Election day again rolls around and again the freeman strikes for his altars and his fires. There but needs arise each time some man of the people, nurtured on rock clad hills, trained at plow handles, and polished off within the law office of some county seat. Elected prosecutor, he becomes the stormy petrel of politics and proceeds judiciously to fill the jails of his district with Negroes until their feet stick out the windows. By this time he is being duly persecuted by the corporation, the whiskey gang, the pardon mill, the state house ring, and the text book trust; his good name is about to be taken from him or dragged in the mire, and his children are soon to be left orphans. There remains but one recourse; he must offer himself to the people, sacrifice himself on the altar of patriotism, hug all the darts of venom to his bosom that he may be seen of men and rewarded. And if in measured periods he pays sufficient tribute to pure southern womanhood, to noble men in gray with empty sleeves, he may carry his share of the burden for the machine and be duly rewarded from the public treasury. In a state where business, art, science, and letters open few avenues to wealth and prestige, politics has become a business. Men of keen and crafty intelligence after reading law waited carefully for the least prod from behind to flop into the puddle of politics. Public office is a private trough, and if no great graft exists it is because no great wealth exists. Moreover, where there is found no alien strata in a megalopolitan complex, politicians remain closer to the people.

Nor in Arkansas politics have great slush funds proved necessary— even for purposes of corruption. Mightier than tons of publicity or high powered space in newspapers were leather lungs and the ability to travel day and night to attend the barbecues. Not a reading people, the Arkan-sawyers regarded over-much reliance on printed matter as a form of highbrow evasion. Better than a circus, they loved their political meetings and they wanted them hot. Not to meet an opponent in joint debate was cowardice of the highest order; to furnish forth to the audience a pre-pared effort was to invite both contempt and defeat. To omit the per-oration to southern womanhood, the defiance to Negro equality, the apostrophe to Confederate valor, the homage to the horny handed sons of toil showed bad training but might be forgiven. But, while baring this devoted bosom to the arrows of political enemies, to fail to threaten with death any opponent who dared offer one insult to "my withered mother and the sweet little wife whose home I have mortgaged for this cam-paign"—such failure marked a man as no man, and defeat must be his portion.

For Arkansas lingers in the fields of romance and in its politics ogres, demons, and phantoms may be encountered on every hand. The state has never learned to laugh at itself and knows not the use of irony as a social corrective. It still winces under the implication of Thomas W. Jackson's *vade mecum* of the smoking car, *The Slow Train Through Arkansas*. It has never forgiven a native son, Opie Read, who somehow just missed greatness with his gently ironic novels of Arkansas planters. When the Arkansas Advancement Association sought to have H. L. Mencken de-ported for the alien he is because of animadversions on the state, it was regretfully informed by Thaddeus the Terrible that the offender appeared to have been duly and legally born in Maryland Free State. No young Walter Hines Page has ever arisen in the state to scribble mummy letters, to picture the missionary society ladies as old hens around a puddle, and to raise the chant that the frying pan and the Confederate veteran must go.

Davis' life followed the pattern but like many a greater man luck made Jeff. At the age of sixteen he failed, to the great detriment of the state, of obtaining a scholarship to West Point because, among other things, he preferred to spell separate, "seperate." If it be true, as General Jackson once observed, "I would not give a damn for any soldier who cannot spell in more than one way," orthography was to prove even less of a necessity to an Arkansas politician. He failed to stay at the state univer-sity or Vanderbilt law school long enough to graduate. On his way to Vanderbilt, like any country boy, he took the wrong train out of Mem-phis and had to count ties back to the station. He was licensed to practice law at the age of nineteen, "his disabilities being removed." Prosecuting Attorney of the Fifth Judicial District at thirty, he ran for the office of Attorney General at thirty-six. Opposed by a Professor Goar, head of the Arkansas Law School, he fought a losing contest. Instruction had been given in favor of Goar in practically every county. Recognizing defeat before the Democratic convention Davis was planning to move to Oklahoma, the Mecca of disappointed Arkansawyers, when the luckless professor dropped dead addressing a meeting of voters. The state convention obligingly furnished the obscure candidate for an obscure office a majority of one vote and unwittingly started Jeff Davis the Lesser on his meteoric rise.

Again fortune favored. The bucolic legislature of 1899 enacted a futile populist statute, the Rector Anti-Trust Law. As weird as any statute ever concocted in Kansas it provided that any corporation transacting business in Arkansas "that shall become a member of any pool or trust, shall be fined $200 to $500 for each day it operates." The blow to commence was staggering, but against the protests of the budding business men of the state Davis seized an opportunity to create an issue that would go home to the boys in the forks of the creek. He construed the law to apply to all corporations and associations and proposed to enter suit against every foreign chartered body in the state. The legislature appropriated $5,000, and Jeff boasted: "I sued the Standard Oil Company, I sued the American Tobacco Company, the Continental Tobacco Company, the Cotton Oil Trust, I sued the express companies, I sued everything that looked like a trust. I sued them all." Because of their participation in rate associations, Attorney General Jeff extended the prosecution to all insurance companies operating in the State.

Every effort made by the now thoroughly frightened men of affairs to unscramble the scrambled eggs of business redounded to the credit of the tribune of the people. He sought strife, he provoked business men to ludicrous and unpolitic retaliations. On this issue he made the race for governor and carried the fight to "the one gallus boys that live up the forks of the creek and don't pay anything except their poll taxes." His ready power of invective and abuse drove several able men from the governor's race, and when the smoke rolled away over the carnage of trusts he had carried all but one of seventy-five counties.

His election literally wrecked the organized political systems of half a century, demoralized and revolutionized the administration of public affairs, and wrought ruin in the established partisan order. Entering upon an audacious warfare against the old traditions he appointed to office men who could have expected no promotion under the old regime. "My friends are always right to me" became his oft repeated motto. "No man can be appointed to office under my administration unless he is a white man, a Democrat, and a Jeff Davis man."

From then on Jeff was never to lose a struggle, so we may leave him on his uninterrupted march from victory unto victory while we ponder the bearing of his example on the processes of politics. Davis belonged to an old order, an order that southern liberals devoutly hope is passing. He would find no place in Professor Odum's *Southern Pioneers in Social Interpretation*. He was of no ante bellum aristocracy, neither did he play Henry W. Grady to a conquering industrialism. He belonged neither to the old nor the new South; his intellect was neither conservative nor critical; it was the apotheosis of the poor white and spent itself in vulgar ridicule and war on phantoms. All the tricks that democracy gives play to in its leaders were his, and it is easy to dismiss him as a demagogue.

But Jeff had his *raison d'être* in a magnetic quality of personality and the appeal to the human element. Many a harassed governor of these states has given an apparent welcome to the poor man that comes into his office, but Davis could relieve his embarrassment and make the poorest and humblest feel at home. Driving along the county roads to the hustings he has stopped many a plodding farmer with: "Captain, I would like to get a chew of hillside navy. My name is Governor Davis and I sure am glad to meet you." Politics dictated that his emotions rule his head, and Jeff's heart became his book of etiquette and his manners, the promptings of a rough and ready human nature. He ended by becoming the most miscible element in that fluid mixture called politics, and his democratic manner became an Arkansas sentiment, a belief, a creed, and a fetish. Today any Arkansas politician who could realize on the good will inherent in the trade name *Jeff Davis* would find his political fortune made.

He knew what it means to the common man to eat with the great ones of the earth. At the speakings with dinner on the ground the Governor walked around under stately oaks, ate pie at one place, custard at another, a slice of country ham, then a slice of chicken until he got around to more than a dozen places and announced at each that he had a good notion to telephone his wife to send his trunk out to Rosebud. Before he had finished two hundred farmers gathered around, admiringly watching the tribune of the people at his food. "I had rather eat turnip greens, hog jowls, and corn bread with you fellows out here around the wagon than go in the hotel and eat with the high-collared crowd." Returning on the train, he chuckled to his admiring associates: "I caught that entire crowd of farmers by staying out at that farm wagon, eating that good country grub, and bragging on Mr. Shirley's children."

Like Napoleon, Jeff knew that to decorate a private is to win the army. Singling out some man of the people Davis would learn his name in order to address him during his speech: "Just look at Uncle Jim Betts here, with his homespun clothes, with his home-knit socks. These are my kind of folks—fellows that chew hill-side navy, smoke a corn cob pipe, and sing in the choir." . . . "I don't know that I will ever marry again, but if I do I am coming out here in the country and marry one of these big fat country girls that can cook an oven of hot biscuits, throw them up the chimney and run around and catch them before I can get my boots on." He ended many of his campaign speeches with an invitation to visit him at the governor's mansion. "If you red necks and hill billies ever come to Little Rock be sure and come to see me—come to my house. Don't go the hotels or wagon yards, but come to my house. If I'm not at home tell my wife who you are, tell her you are my friend and you belong to the sunburned sons of toil. Tell her to give you some hog jowl and turnip greens and we will eat eggs until we have every old hen on the Arkansas River cackling. She may be busy making soap but that will be all right."

There was a gusto about Davis; he played the demagogue but he liked it. It was not a distasteful business to him; it was glorious fun. Nor did he despise the people with whom he played the game. If the common people heard him gladly, let it be said he offered himself for their amusement—and his profit—gladly.

None knew better how to meet the embarrassed and inarticulate hay-binders from the forks of the creek, to shake hands with their bedraggled wives and kiss their grubby children. His opinion that cotton should sell for fifteen cents sounded like an edict from the state. When he asked a farmer how his crops were growing, how many melons he had, how much hill-side navy he raised, the very pleiades twinkled. The Governor never spoke without a reference to his Confederate father, his wrinkled mother, his little wife, his twelve children, four dead, and his nine pointer dogs.

Jeff sensed the analogy with that transcendent demagogue and called his wool hat brigade in jean pants the Old Guard. His closing appeal still reverberates down the lanes of Arkansas politics: "If the Old Guard will rally around once more, if the boys in the hills will only touch hands with the boys in the valley, we will win one more victory for good government, and in the meantime whip these Yankees out on dry land and let them stink themselves to death."

He played an easy game. His appeal was to the back townships, the rustics and the bumpkins whom he sought to turn against the town dwellers. He ridiculed the harmless institutions of society until formal dress and bridge whist seemed crimes against nature. He described the mythical men of the cities as "the crowd that when they shake hands with you only give you the tips of their fingers . . . wear collars so high they can't see the sun, except at high noon, looking over their collars. . . . You can't tell from their tracks whether they are going or coming back." With many a homely and vulgar phrase he shook laughter from the bellies of haybinders and sent their old wool hats up among the trees until they looked like buzzards flying over. Withal in his many campaigns he averaged 61 per cent of the total vote of the state's 75 county seats and 71½ per cent of the vote of the 185 largest towns and cities. Like Chick Sale he proved that we have but recently moved in from the country.

Arkansas, to whose farmers money never talked except to say good bye, has been shown by the recent census to have the smallest amount of unemployment in the union. It is thus a state in which men work but not for gain. Jeff never expected nor did he long for a remedy for agrarian ills. His attack on the trusts was never in terms of economics. "Old Armour and Cudahy never raised a sow and pigs in their lives, yet the price of meat is so high I can hardly buy breakfast bacon in Little Rock enough to support my family. I just buy one little little slice, hang it up by a long string and let each one of my kids jump up, grease their mouths and go on to bed." To the simple farmer in the river bottoms he described a visit to the New York Cotton Exchange: "These men were sitting there tearing open telegrams and going yow, yow, yow. I could not understand what they said, but in less than five minutes a price had been posted and they had changed the price of cotton five dollars a bale all over the world. And had they ever grown a bale of cotton, my fellow citizens?"

"The Populist party advocated one of the grandest doctrines the world has ever known—that you can legislate prosperity into a country." But the Governor was happy and content to voice the unrest of a raw and raucous democracy. To have solved the ills of the body politic would have left Jeff without a mission and the hill billies without their safety valve.

In the rough and tumble hustings Negro baiting always proved a trump-card. President Roosevelt's visit furnished the Governor enough ammunition to win a dozen elections. Roosevelt was to speak on *Law Enforcement and Public Righteousness.* Gauging the audience, Jeff with characteristic audacity introduced him with a peroration to southern womanhood with its inevitable conclusion. "And, oh, Mr. President, when the husband or the brother, the father or the sweetheart of one of the angels of earth comes home in the evening and finds her in the throes of death, when he sees the cruel clutch mark on her snow white throat and watches the pulse beat grow fainter and fainter as the end draws near, there's not a law on the statute books of Arkansas to prevent him from avenging that crime at once and without apology to any tribunal on the face of the earth."

An affront to Roosevelt's companion, Clayton, Arkansas' Reconstruction governor, he later magnified and capitalized in his campaigns, "The papers say that I did not treat the President courteously. I stayed with him all day. I showed him all the courtesy any official could show to another, but when we came to the banquet table I found that Powell Clayton was to eat at the same table and I said: 'Mr. President, I can not eat with that old one-armed villain; his hell hounds murdered my aunt in Little River County during Reconstruction.' I delivered the President to the banquet hall where the luncheon was being served and I said to the guard, 'Cut the ropes, let me out. My God, let me away from Powell Clayton and his nigger gang.'"

Called to account for a serious tactical error in race relations, Governor Davis added to jurisprudence a new doctrine of presumption of innocence. "But they say that I pardoned a Negro for assaulting a white girl. Gentlemen, I am a southern man imbibing all the traditions and sentiment of the southern people, and you know I had good reasons for so doing. In our country when we have no doubt about a Negro's guilt we do not give him a trial; we mob him and that ends it; and I want to say to you, my fellow citizens of Carroll County, that the mere fact that this Negro got a trial is evidence that there was some doubt of his guilt."

Jeff's contributions to the science of penology are equally valuable and have been too long neglected by criminologists. On the eve of an election the legislature made an appropriation to cover a deficiency incurred by the state penal institutions. "Oh my fellow citizens, this penitentiary gang is mad today; they are mad as they can be. Why? Because I have dehorned that crowd in Little Rock. . . . One Saturday afternoon I felt a veto spell coming over me and I vetoed $150,000 of this foolish, reckless appropriation before I went to supper; when I came back I vetoed a lot more. . . . I said to them: 'Gentlemen, you can steal what the convicts, eight hundred in number, make but I swear by all the gods in the calendar that you shall not steal and use in riotous living the money of the taxpayers of the people of Arkansas. If you can not make these convicts self-sustaining, you will have to get another Governor and another legislature before you can steal the tax money of the people of this state to support them.' "

It is doubtful if the criminologists fully realize the immense value of the power of pardon in politics. If an umbrageous citizenry can be kept silent, every pardon means a new block of votes. Jeff gave fair warning in his first campaign: "I promise you here and now that I will run the pardon mill fair and impartial and none but my friends need come around me begging for pardons." Charged with releasing nine hundred prisoners, many richly deserving punishment, whose reprieves were secured through pardon attorneys, he evaded the issue and struck straight at the tear glands of his audience.

"Ladies, they call me the pardoning Governor of the State; I am glad to be called the pardoning Governor. I am glad that I have been able during my administration to lift so many shadows and sorrows from the hearts and homes of the people of my state. . . . My fellow citizens, never criticize a man because he is merciful. What is mercy? Mercy is God. God is Mercy. Without mercy we would have no God. The sunshine, the flowers, the fields, the trees, the brooks—everything in nature tells us in glad loving tones of God and his mercy. . . . I have a little boy at home eight years of age, God bless his little soul. If he should get into trouble in after years and get into the penitentiary I would kiss the very feet of the governor who would give him a pardon. I would wash his feet with my tears. If it were your son, I could not write the pardon quick enough. Judge Wood said the other day that any old woman could get a pardon at my office who came there crying. I want to say to you, my fellow citizens, that I thank God that my heart has not become so steeled, so cold and callous that the tears of the mother in Israel will not move me to pity. . . . God bless you old mothers in Israel and when you offer up your devotion tonight, if you can spare one moment, lisp a prayer for the pardoning governor of Arkansas. If you don't want your boys pardoned, don't come crying around my office because I can not stand it, and do not try to stand it."

In North Carolina every decent risque joke is attributed to Senator Zeb Vance; in Arkansas every rough and ready political trick goes back to Jeff the Little. Campaigning against one Brother Adams, an ardent prohibitionist, Davis had a bottle of whiskey slipped in the brother's old grip. "Old Sodapop, when did you come to town? I can take two green persimmons and squeeze on you and make you so drunk you wouldn't know your heels from a shot gun. Open up your old grip and let the crowd see that whiskey." The whiskey was found and the crowd, glorying in their idol's gift for practical jokes, yelled for Jeff.

Politics according to Jeff possessed the rough and tumble of the frontier, a Rabelaisian quality that accepted human nature and gloried in its crudities and vulgarisms. Campaigning against a bachelor, Jeff drove straight at old human nature. "Judge Bryant, you come up here on the platform; come up here where the ladies can see you. Ladies and gentlemen, I want to show you the color of one man's hair that never hugged a woman in his life." Cowardice held no place in the hustings. "Bob Rogers, you threatened to kill me. I am not afraid of you. I can take a corncob with a lightning bug on the end of it and run you into the river."

Of all southern politicians Jeff seemed least to fear the Methodist and Baptist political hierarchy. Excluded from fellowship in the Baptist church on serious charges, Jeff had more ammunition to sweep the state. "My fellow citizens, I was excluded from the Second Baptist Church of Little Rock. A lot of high combed roosters turned me out of the church for political purposes without a trial, without a hearing, thinking they could ruin me in that way; but when the little church at Russelville, where I was born and raised, heard of this indignity, this outrage, they sent for me to come home and join the church of which I had been a member for twenty years, and more than a hundred members were present when I was restored."

What if the charges were first preferred by a little country church at Monmouth Springs, manifestly lacking in high combed roosters; what if the charges were allowed to lay over until after the primary; what if a church committee delivered them to Governor Davis and took his written receipt; what if on the date of the trial he went on a fishing trip to Chicot County; what if only twelve persons were present at the historic restoration at the mother church; what if many of these were relatives; well, what of it? What the hell do you want for politics in Arkansas?

Jeff was doubly fortunate in the enemies he made. So astutely could he fan the flames of partisanship to unequal and unreasonable heat, that, all other expedients failing, he fell back on the cross of martyrdom. Asked why he supported Jeff, many an honest native has answered: "Because he was persecuted all his life." In many of his campaigns when denounced in unmeasured terms for misrepresentation Davis failed to retaliate, neglected to fight back, to cut, stab or shoot—either with bullets or epithets. He simply and pathetically said to his audience that his opponent had been put in the race to kill him, that he knew his life was forfeit before the race was over. "But," said he about to die saluting them, "all I ask is that when I am dead you bury me in the old graveyard and write on my headstone the words: 'He died a martyr to the common people.'" And Jeff, master of the vulgar comic, never cracked a smile.

Jeff understood as well as any demagogue that politics is a matter of jockeying for alliances. "My friends are always right to me," he said, but he was never averse to changing friends. His secret of success, as his colleague, Senator James P. Clarke, analyzed it, was that he never halfway fell out with anyone; he tolerated no concealed enemies or half-hearted friends. They were forced into the open. When a former ally took up service with the enemy Jeff ridiculed him into a state of complete helplessness. Like Wilson, Jeff's path was strewn with cast-off supporters, but, unlike Wilson, he was able literally to force reconciliations with any cast-off he needed. And then he so dealt with the erring one as to drive home the conviction that no resentment of past differences remained. He left no non-committal element in the state and he never courted sympathy. His enemies would never extend it, and his friends were bound by more virile and enduring forces.

Davis possessed no scholarship and expended no industry to acquire it. The curse of the southern politician, superficiality, bound him hard and fast. With an almost cynical clarity rarely met in eulogy, his colleague, Clarke, said in the Senate: "He was not a widely learned man nor did he desire to be. He was not willing to devote the time and self denial involved in acquiring familiarity with the views and methods of those who had gone before. He absorbed enough out of the general intelligence of the country to be fairly familiar with many of the leading questions of the day and could discuss them before an audience with a sufficient show of knowledge to impart all the lessons they seemed willing to absorb. He never concerned himself about mastering in full scope and detail great and absorbing questions since he felt that he could only make use of such aspects of it as his auditors were willing and desirous of understanding, and that he was therefore engaged in a wholly unprofitable service when he talked over their heads."

The gift of superficiality so valuable in Arkansas hustings was to prove rather too thin for even the greatest deliberative body in the world. His Senate career, full of fireworks though it was, furnished an anticlimax. He had told his Arkansas audiences: "If you will send me to Washington I will let that gang know I am in town. I will pull off a speech that will knock down the cobwebs before I am there two weeks." Ignoring the conventions that demand silence and hard work from a new Senator for at least a year, Jeff, eleven days after being seated, delivered a philippic against the trusts and the complacent and conservative Senate. He ended with a fervid peroration to Arkansas. In an interview widely published he naively told the newspaper boys he had swept the cobwebs off the ceiling of the Senate Chamber. Although the Arkansas papers had always opposed him, they had paid Jeff the honor of taking him seriously. But now he became the sport of the metropolitan dailies to whom he was another of the populist monstrosities occasionally spewed forth by the South and West. The echoes from the press goaded him to return again to the fray in the manner of the barbecue forums of Arkansas politics.

"But, Mr. President, insignificant as I am, let them sharpen their blade, for I will be here at the appointed hour and while here only God can stay my voice in behalf of organized, united labor and the yeomanry of America. . . . Let scavengers of plutocracy howl! Go! damnable imps of pelf and greed, I defy your torments! Tear to fragments my political career, if it comport with your execrable will; stifle and distort my every utterance; not satisfied if such be your brutal frenzy, lash my poor form into insensibility; then if it be your further pleasure, gnaw from my stiffening limbs every vestige of quivering flesh; howl in wretched bestiality through my own innocent blood as it drips from your fiendish visages; drag then if you want what remains into the filth and vermin of your foul den and burn it upon the altar of Baal, or scatter it before the friendly winds of heaven to your betters, the carrion crows of the field. All that they may do and more if there yet be open further depths of infamy to a polluted, besotten press."

Davis was a type of the lazy and superficial orators with which the South has blessed the Senate Halls since the War. Before the Senate, in a eulogy of his colleague, Senator Clarke, who owed his election to Davis, continued his critical analysis with cold logic: "I happen to know that he was not satisfied with his career in the Senate. . . . When he first appeared in the Senate he was smarting under the resentment of wholesale and unwarranted attacks that had been made upon him, and a sort of retaliation seemed to linger with him and control his actions and expressions. . . . In the last days of his life I found him more disposed to diligently investigate affairs of larger import than in former days, and I noticed an increasing absence of that intemperate form of expression which usually characterized his comment on official matters. . . . He said it was his purpose to take upon himself the task of mastering some of the problems of the day and he hoped to make himself useful in evolving and applying remedies of a substantial character. . . . I was much impressed with the belief that it was his fixed purpose to achieve a name here that would be creditable to him, and he knew affairs of this life well enough to know that he could only do this by the severest toil and the closest application to his duties. A large number of devoted friends reassured themselves with the conviction that he had a real capacity for statemanship and that after he had achieved a position where his own tenure was secure and his apprenticeship ended, he would manifest the qualities of industry and constructive ability that would show him to be a real man among men in managing the affairs of the nation. The question may now never be answered to the satisfaction and acceptance of all."

Like Bryan, Secretary of State, Jeff spent most of his senatorial term recouping his private estate, seriously drained in many a campaign. Moreover, after denouncing the corruption and red tape of the Senate, Jeff had his wife and all his children placed on the Senate payroll as clerical help and laborers. None of them left their homes in Little Rock.

Times are changed now. The antitrust law is a dead issue, forgotten long ago. Arkansas' great need now, and the eating clubs repeat it every Wednesday and the prayer meetings every Wednesday night, is fewer politicians and more business men. Arkansas is again hot foot on the trail of the corporations, but this time she hopes to entice them into the state. Greater than the Governor, the greatest man in the state today is a power magnate, H. C. Couch, who told Hoover what to do about the Mississippi flood when he came South. H. L. Remmell, a Republican, constructor of the Remmell Dam, comes next. The University has published a bulletin on the "Need for Industry in Arkansas." The research was done by Professor Dickey but the foreword is by the University's astute president, J. C. Futrall. Hugh Hart has gone to the New York office of his insurance company at fabulous thousands of dollars a year salary. The state is beginning to regret its exported resources of man power and wish it might keep them at home. Professor Brough went on the Chatauqua circuit from the governor's chair to extol the glories of Arkansas to whomsoever would listen. Oil, discovered at Smackover, made near millionaires of many a populist farmer. "Arkansas on Wheels" has toured the country often inviting investments and immigration. Only last year the governor headed a party of legislators and business men who visited the Carolinas examining the technique of attracting cotton mills to cheap labor.

There may yet arise a reincarnation of Jeff Davis to sweep the state. Business men and city dudes sometimes fear phantoms, and God knows the plight of the Arkansas peasantry is frightful enough to evoke phantoms. An old Confederate soldier, mellowed with bug juice and under the spell of barbecue oratory, once saw Jeff as Jefferson Davis, the patriarch, endowed with eternal life. "I fought for him in the sixties and I'm going to go on voting for him if he lives forever. He is the greatest and longest lived man that ever was." Even so, much meditation by one crowned with the bays of poesy by the populace has added this hope of another millennial dawn to the already overcrowded theology of Arkansas:

> If Jeff could only come back now for one small day
> And see the petty politicians' peevish play.
> In fancy I can see the old guard fall in line
> With guns unlimbered waiting for the first faint sign
> To forward march—God, what a change would mark the day.
> If Jeff could only come back now to lead the way.

4. The Profile of Southern Culture (1935)

No sooner had Vance completed his doctoral dissertation on the vicissitudes of the cotton system than he turned his attention to southern society as a whole, as seen primarily through the lens of the newly established field of human geography. When viewed in this fashion, the region broke down readily into six subregions, each distinctive in its geographic and economic features, yet all interrelated by common cultural patterns. It was a far more complex and accurate vision of the South than any previously offered, and it was soon to become the conceptual basis for Odum's regional sociology. Vance developed these ideas at length in his second book, Human Geography of the South, *but the essential scheme can also be found in this summary article prepared for a symposium on southern life and culture. Although it did not appear in print until 1935, the essay was in fact written in 1931.*

Any geographer, by the very nature of the species, must be equally impatient of two dogmas that have arisen concerning the South. The implication of that ritualistic phrase the "solid South" is matched only by its untenable counterpart, "No North, no South." In a common touching devotion to the Democratic party and in a certain attitude of condescension toward the Negro, the South was once supposed to be solid. But, unlike the Middle West, the South is not one region but many. History, not geography, made the solid South, and to the extent that the area forgets its history and allows the geography of the region and resource to assert itself will the South refashion its cultural landscape along many and varied lines. This, in part, it has already done and more it is doing.

Any portraiture of culture in the South or elsewhere is of necessity soon forced to soar into realms of the imponderables; our discussion sets itself an easier goal. Ours is the bread and butter survey: to take a quick glance at the regional cupboards, to estimate their degree of bareness and plenty, and to describe the consequent mode of life of Dixie's Mother Hubbards and old Ladies of the Shoe. We shall find that these regional

From *Culture in the South*, edited by William Terry Couch (Chapel Hill: University of North Carolina Press, 1935), pp. 24–39.

cupboards are arranged in a neat series, and that, moreover, their respective supplies are changing.

The new regionalism serves to show that the South's many areas are not flung together in disordered array, but follow each other in the unity of natural sequence. The most typical land form to be encountered on the globe's surface is the profile of physiography as it slopes upward from a region's seacoast to its mountain core: Patrick Geddes calls this profile the *valley section* and finds that it may be divided into some six or eight zones—each serving as habitat of a cultural type with characteristic mode of life and livelihood. Sloping down from the land core, these zones— mountain ledge, highland dip slope, piedmont plateau, central plains, coastal plains, and maritime plains—furnish the life stage of the miner and the backwoods peasant, the factory wage earner, the woodsman, the rich planter and the poor peasant, the truck gardener and the fisherman. However much they may hide behind urban disguises, these belong among the earth's perennial human types. As the French sociologist, Le Play, pointed out two generations ago, they have developed out of that inevitable net which enfolds us all—the nexus of place, work, and kind of folk.

The fourteen states called southern, stretching from Virginia and West Virginia to Texas, possess a physiognomy that corresponds to the profile of culture. Whether approached from the Atlantic, the Gulf, or the Mississippi Delta, the South slopes upward in the sequence of the valley section. Its area of 887,272 square miles supporting in 1930 a population of 35,473,496, falls into natural zones, some of which swing around the southern terminus of the Appalachians in crescent shape. Let us follow the regional profile down to the gulf and sea, glancing at regional cupboards as we go. We shall encounter the highland area, the piedmont plateau, the sand hills, the gulf, coastal, and alluvial plains comprising a cotton belt, the piney woods, and the coastal fringe.

I

Cutting across and athwart the South, the great spines of the Blue Ridge, Appalachians, and Cumberlands furnish the apex of the valley slope. The South, it will be recalled, came out of the frontier, and here the region stands nearest its frontier past. E. A. Ross notes what isolation and mountain topography have made: "The mountains come down like the letter 'V.' Down this crease brawls a petty river; leading into this from a smaller valley will be a creek; into the creek a branch, into the branch a fork. Each settlement is a shoestring along one of these water courses and constitutes a world within itself, for it is insulated from its neighbors by one or two thousand feet of steep wooded ridges."

The zone is really two. The mountain escarpment with its mining culture is best presented by coal and iron areas of West Virginia, Kentucky, and Tennessee; the dip slope with its frontier farming centers in Kentucky, North Carolina, and Tennessee. As S. H. Hobbs points out, the region best illustrates farming as practiced before the era of commercialized agriculture. This section is responsible for the fact that the South has a larger number of practically self-sufficing farms than any other important section in the United States. The cash income from the farm is as low as in any section, and the products sold from the farms represent a small proportion of its products. Of all southern areas, this ranks highest in proportion of white population, farm ownership, and number of meat and milk animals per farm. Its churches and schools are among the poorest, while its illiteracy rate is the highest for white people in the nation.

In their wilderness ways, their domestic economy, colonial *mores*, and Elizabethan English, the real mountain folk come near representing a projected frontier, the colonial South carried forward into the twentieth century. Family ties are strong, and the denizens of isolated communities are closely related. The highlands were settled by native whites who wanted to get away from the slave belts and their class distinctions. In ante-bellum politics they proved of an earlier day. Following the nationalism of Washington and Jefferson rather than the sectionalism of Calhoun and Davis, they shouldered arms in defense of the Union rather than of the cotton kingdom. To this day they possess two attitudes whose combination is incomprehensible to the southern common man of the cotton belt. They hate Negroes, yet vote the Republican ticket.

Offering a replica of its terrain, the Ozarks, settled mainly by its emigrants, have repeated the social economy of Appalachia. But these frontiers, preserved so long as museum pieces to remind us whence came the old South, are changing rapidly. Life in urban centers and fertile river valleys of the mountains has no doubt always equalled the levels of livelihood for their states, and now coal mining, railroads, highways, and industrialism are coming to change further this section of the map. The art of cheesemaking in the little mountain cheese houses has brought steady income to many a cove. The ribbon of North Carolina Route 10, winding magnificently from sea through mountains, wages incessant war against isolation. Prohibition has changed mountain moonshining, however much we may deplore it, into a capitalistic industry with many economic ramifications. Kingsport, Tennessee, once a mountain hamlet, has reached out for northern capital to capture eighteen nationally important manufacturing plants. Aluminum, rayon, paper pulp, lumbering, coal, gas and oil are making new mountains even though but a small fraction of the wealth goes to the native owners of the soil. Missionary effort and equalization of state funds have come to level educational opportunities. The South's retarded frontier is passing, but the picture is not all bright. There are areas which remain so isolated, so barren of resources once the timber is cut, that they should face frankly the need of a new policy. Good schools and churches, missionary efforts and community organization which cannot and will never be financed from within, should not be used to hold population on eroded ridges and isolated, worn out, sub-marginal areas. The South may have to consider seriously the removal of population from such areas with their reversion to state controlled forestry.

II

The Piedmont, one of the South's oldest regions, has become its newest. Here, in Geddes' phrase, the rustic type is assuming its urban disguise. Curving from Birmingham through north Georgia and the Carolinas to Danville is the piedmont crescent. Here lived a frontier yeomanry which largely came down the great valley from Pennsylvania. Separated by the fall line and the pine barrens from the early tidewater aristocracy, they carved out an area of small farms. Today this emerging zone of industrialism represents the South's most coherent effort to break with its rural past of frontier and plantation. Ranking among the nation's leaders in increasing urban and industrial ratios, sections of this map have seen Henry W. Grady's dreams come true.

The piedmont is in the main a manufacturing area of towns, not of great cities. Basic to its industry and accounting for its even distribution is the network of high tension power lines. Spreading with startling rapidity throughout the area, these lines have created a southern superpower zone and carried potential cotton mills to every hamlet. This is one of the country's few places where the little town is flourishing. There are no great cities, if one excepts Atlanta, but, unusual for the South, the North Carolina piedmont shows a majority of its population urban. The new industrialism still firmly links the South with its past in the processing of its cotton. Its labor, cast out by a niggard highland economy and a decadent cotton system, has been harboured in paternalistic mill villages. Its workers were once untrained as factory operatives, but capital came, training developed leadership, and natural resources anchored the South's industrial renaissance in the piedmont. As for the Negro in the piedmont, although barred from the textile industry, he is an urban dweller rather than a peasant farmer. The proletariat of the odd job, the Negro occupies densely settled slum areas in most piedmont cities. Durham is unique as the capital of the Negro business world, and has created more than one Negro fortune of respectable dimensions. In Winston-Salem, also in Durham, the Negro works in tobacco; in the Birmingham district he helps to man the heavy coal and iron industries.

Birmingham, for all its iron ore, coking coal, and dolomite, never made more than pig iron until taken in hand by United States Steel and George G. Crawford. North Carolina and Virginia, for all their stock of tobacco, never realized on them until the Dukes, the Reynoldses, and others created brands, mass production, slogans, billboard advertising, and fortunes. High Point has almost come to equal Grand Rapids as a synonym for furniture, though the forests are retreating from her borders. The country's leading textile area, possessing a monopoly of the main branches of tobacco manufacture, the new cotton kingdom harbours the South's largest supply of wage earners and, as we shall see, goes far to set the standard of living for the new economy.

III

The fall line with the narrow sand hills marks the transition in the South's profile. Beyond center two great zones, the piney woods and the cotton belt. Stretching in a huge crescent through gulf and coastal plains and flatwoods of seven states, the piney woods comprise a third zone, closely linked to the South's past. Once covered with millions of pine, short leaf, long leaf, slash, and loblolly, it furnishes a passing problematic belt in which can be traced the cycle of forest exploitation in the South. First the frontiersmen, facing the shadows of the forest, felled trees for the sake of free land and sacrificed timber as a useless by-product in the great bonfires of log-rollings. Early desired for their naval stores, slash and long-leaf pines were next turpentined to death in a crude and wholesale massacre of a great industry. Having retreated from North Carolina, which once really deserved the name Tar Heel state, to Florida, the naval stores industry appears to some observers on its last legs. In the third stage "turpentining ahead of the cut" became a recognized practice, and lumbering had to clean up quickly in order to get the pines before they decayed after turpentine butchery. Exploitation all along the line from high class to "woodpecker" mills is bringing the South to the verge of its resources of yellow pine. Abandoned mill towns, decadent communities with economic support removed, great mills and logging railways whose whistles have blown for the last time, show how pressing is the problem created by the passing of the piney woods. With only cut-over lands left as taxable support for roads, schools, and community services, the population is left stranded. One mill town in Louisiana was picked up bodily and moved to a new forest in Arizona. These thousands of cut-over acres are not needed in the South's farming system, and on lands lacking sodded pastures it seems quite useless to expect a return to the stock ranching conditions of the early western range.

The South continues to rank second to the Pacific coast area in production of lumber; and the transient camp, the woods' riders, and turpentine still remain the features of the deep South's naval stores industry. Without new policies they can not continue. Reforestation and the long-time view find lumber men interested in cutting, not in regrowing timber. On the other hand, native inhabitants, hostile to large timber interests and intent on preserving the free range for their scrub cattle, burn off the woods each year. This practice and the hardy porker make the life of the pine seedling hazardous indeed. The demand for pulpwood, the manufacture of kraft paper, and the movement of paper companies South are making serious inroads on young growth. Some few corporations have reforestation projects under way, but the movement waits state action on marginal and tax forfeit lands. Thus there is changing before our eyes another of the South's subregions.

IV

Much of the piney woods has already fallen before king cotton. Highlands, lowlands, and uplands, these areas may be considered as fringe belts nibbling at the hitherto undisturbed core of the geographic and historic South, her fourth zone, the great cotton belt. Coastal plains, gulf plains, deltas, black belts, and clay hills combine with the beaming sun, the Negro, the landless white, and the mule to supply the world's demand for a cheap fabric. On three per cent of the world's land area 60 per cent of the world's cotton supply is grown. If the highlands represent a relic of the frontier South, the cotton belt stands as a survival of the mid-century South, the cotton kingdom. The historic link which binds cotton culture to the past is the plantation. The plantation demanded four factors: fertile, plentiful land, either level or rolling; a labor supply, docile and of low social status; management involving social as well as economic supervision; and a staple crop. The plantation system came before slavery and outlasted it. Victorious in conflict with the frontier farming system, the plantation set its everlasting stamp on piedmont, black belts, and deltas. In the South it has produced five staple crops: rice, indigo, tobacco, sugar, and cotton, and cotton has outlasted and outdistanced them all. Staggered by the abolition of slavery, the plantation reorganized its labor element into a unique cropping and share tenancy system, admitted the dispossessed poor white farmers into its bounds, advanced upon the western lands of Texas and Oklahoma, and extended production to dizzy heights before unknown.

So deeply has the culture of cotton entered in the mode of life of the American South that the whole area is characterized by activities and attitudes which have grown up about the cultivation of the plant. First of all, the cotton plant lays down an annual cycle of activities concerned with the planting and cultivating, gathering and marketing of the crop which in turn has its effect upon social life and institutions. Thus the school, the church, and other community agencies find their season of intense activity during the two respites of cotton culture, for a few weeks in the late summer between the last chopping and the first picking and for two or three months in the winter between the last picking and the preparation of the ground for the next crop. The demands for hand labor perpetuate the field work of women and children, place a premium on a high birth rate and otherwise affect the standards of domestic life. The demands of the cotton plant are greatest at precisely the period required for the tending of other crops and thus impede diversification. Furthermore since cotton is food for neither man nor beast, and cannot be disposed of except through the local ginnery, it furnishes an excellent basis for the crop lien system of credit, which in turn further fixes the tradition of the one-crop system upon the cotton belt and limits the diet of the cotton farmer to the deadly monotony of meat, meal, and molasses.

The cotton farmer is peculiarly subject to the speculative risk of the market, since his is the one staple grown in America that can contribute nothing directly consumable by the farm family. Moreover, he is entirely dependent on a money economy, upon a crop whose gyrations in market prices make it deservedly called dynamite. Thus the risks of the cotton market combine with the risks of the weather and the weevil to make the climb to ownership all the more difficult and to encourage speculation, to perpetuate tenancy and its attendant evils: inadequate housing, inefficient methods of agriculture, isolation, dependence on credit, backward community institutions, illiteracy, mobility, shiftlessness, and lack of thrift. Chained by inability to finance experiments, diversification, and other types of farm enterprise such as dairying, southern agriculture seems bound today to landlords and supply merchants who hold the economic keys, but are unable or unwilling to unlock the chains.

All study of change in the cotton belt must take into account the fact that it is not one belt but four: southeastern, gulf, delta, and southwestern prairies. The southeastern belt is in the worst way. The upland staple is getting shorter each year, so that much of it has to be exported to cheaper foreign markets, while piedmont mills import delta staple. The region, cropped since colonial times, uses as much fertilizer as the rest of the United States together, and fertilizer costs are mounting. Moreover, rough topography forbids the extensive use of labor saving machinery and large-scale farming. Cigarette tobacco introduced as the economic salvation of light sandy soils in this area is proving an economic Frankenstein, devouring by its endless demands for hand tasks and fertilization the farmer's surplus of labor and investment with no sustained adequate returns on a gyrating market.

The gulf states with their warm rains have proved most vulnerable to the inroads of the boll weevil and have made unsuccessful attempts to create a permanent agriculture of the velvet beans and peanuts type. Cotton has resumed its sway, however, and in the Mississippi delta with its long staple reigns supreme as always. Delta farmers, organized in levee districts, long burdened to the point of bankruptcy by their hopeless efforts to keep back the Father of Waters, have gladly seen the federal government assume charge. In some sections Mississippi farmers have led a successful escape from the cotton system. Lacking the urban markets for fluid milk, they have attracted the capital and the plants and now sell processed milk—cheese, ice cream, condensed and evaporated milk—in addition to running giant glass tank cars of refrigerated liquid milk to New Orleans.

As for the southwestern belt, it can grow cotton at a profit while all other areas are losing money. The dry heat of the great plains area places a limit on the range of the boll weevil and relieves the area of the expense of weevil doctoring. The level topography makes possible the use of tractors, gang plows, mechanical choppers, and sledding takes the place of hand picking. Moreover, new and improved gins have been introduced which clean bolls and scraps out of sledded cotton with comparatively little damage to lint. The area is comparatively newly cropped, rains have not bleached out its fertility, and the gigantic fertilizer bills of the southeast are unknown. Thus it happens that while the southeast, gulf, and delta may be clamoring for acreage restriction to save the cotton farmer, the southwest is perfectly satisfied to expand acreage. It has consistently done so, and many are the old cattle ranches that have fallen before the advancing cotton croppers of the southwest. The one great drawback is the possibility of drought.

The greatest change possible to the South hinges on a new technology in cotton. There are two such developments within the range of possibility: the perfection, first, of a cotton picker successful under field conditions; second, the chemical processing of rayon out of the whole stalk. It is impossible to foresee all social effects, but either would knell the passing of ten acres, a Negro, and a mule. Cotton could be harvested mechanically, its culture would assume the aspects of the great wheat ranches, and production would be immensely cheapened and expanded. Tenant croppers and small farmers would be turned loose to drift as seasonal laborers, and we would face the emergence of a new cotton plantation transformed into a mechanical giant and monster. The great Scott plantation in the Yazoo-Mississippi delta points the way. Here 37,000 united acres, owned and managed by a corporation of English mill owners, ship some 15,000 bales yearly to England.

v

From the sandbar islands of North Carolina Sounds, the South's fishing fringe extends out past the Georgia-Carolina sea islands to the shrimp, sponge, oyster, and deep-sea fisheries of Florida and the Gulf. Bordering the fringe may be found a great trucking area reaching up from the Rio Grande Valley to Virginia's eastern shores. Centering in Florida, these various areas follow the season up the coast and vie with one another in express shipments of fruits and vegetables to metropolitan areas. Intensive cultivation demanding brains, capital, hand and knee farming, and much fertilization, has cut across the pattern of southern agriculture and changed sandy flats into priceless acres. But neither trucking nor fruit growing is a universal panacea for a decadent agriculture. Two per cent of America's arable land can supply all her vegetable needs, and an orchard once planted can survive the bankruptcy of many owners.

Combining trucking with citrus fruits, Florida has developed an orchard and winter garden culture comparable to that of the tropics. In her beautification program based on speculative exploitation of nature's gifts of air and sea, lakes, beach, and sunshine, she has led the South's largest increases in urban population, saddled south Florida's municipalities with well-nigh hopeless debts, and shown of what grace the tropic shore line of the South is capable in architecture and landscaping. Throughout she has merely repeated much southern history in waiting for outside capital to lead the development. When in tidewater Louisiana and Texas immigrant farmers from the midwest in 1885 first used the machinery of the wheat belt on the coastal prairies with their artesian wells and impervious clay hardpans, they created a new form of rice culture. All hope that the rice areas of Georgia and the Carolinas could recover from the abolition of slave labor came to a speedy end. Here one man with machinery can grow as much rice as seventy orientals.

Again the famed sugar bowl of Louisiana represents the strange adjustment of the sub-tropics plantation to the factory system. Hundreds of acres are bound by the network of a plantation railroad, supervised by a director of transportation, to a great compressing mill. Seasonal Negro laborers work at breakneck speed to harvest cane before the frost. The introduction of the P. J. O. variety of cane, blight resistant and of high sucrose content, bids fair to revive the hitherto waning sugar zone.

VI

A sixth region, possibly too young to chart accurately, may be found for our profile in the gulf and high plains of the southwest. The grassy stretches of Texas and Oklahoma were first occupied by that cultural type, the stock herder. The long horn and the cowboy were two Mexican heritages that developed into American types. When grass and the range were free, cattle roamed afar and only brands could be owned. Barbed wire closed the open range and final notice was served to that effect when the Texas legislature in special session made fence cutting a penitentiary offense. The second stage was reached when ranges large as counties fell before the advancing horde of tillers of the soil and were cut up into small farms. The Negro and the cropper followed, and Oklahoma and the Black Waxy of Texas have their cotton tenancy areas to equal those of the old plantation belts. The recent advance of cotton upon the semi-arid plains has been recounted.

There has been erected largely on the foundations of gas and oil an industrial superstructure for the southwest. The transient oil boom town, the derrick, the pipe line, the refinery, and the tanker constitute the main features of its cultural landscape. Although engaged in a crude and lavish exploitation of limited resources, the oil industry has accumulated much of the capital that in the hands of Texas and Oklahoma millionaires will carry on the future constructive development of the area. Its latest achievement has been to pipe gas from its Louisiana fields to Birmingham and Atlanta and from its Texas field to Chicago by means of relay pumping stations. Tulsa, Oklahoma City, Fort Worth, Dallas, and San Antonio have grown greatly. Texas is over 40 per cent urban, and Houston and Galveston are pushing New Orleans, the nation's second point of export.

VII

We have spoken of the South's profile of regions with their varying stages from frontier through plantation to industrialism, and of the changes that man is making on the map. Geography, however, offers one factor of superlative importance that has been regarded as not subject to change by man. Let us talk of the weather. Everything from southern high tempers to the section's rank in industry has been accredited to the South's climate. At least one industrious student, Ellsworth Huntington, has assigned the South a low rank in civilization and accounted for this status on the basis of subtropic climate. Although man's technology of apartment house architecture and steam heat has almost conquered cold regions for human habitation, it is noteworthy that man's ingenuity has not proceeded further than ice water, Palm Beach suits, the frigidaire and artificially cooled movie palaces in combatting enervating heat and humidity. Changes are possible, however, in adjustment to climate, and it is notable that many southern deficiencies and inadequacies find climate a secondary rather than primary factor. Such was yellow fever of unhappy memory, happily passed away. It used to be solemnly asserted by doctors that in the southern climate yellow fever waged war with malarial fever, the first ruled the cities, the second conquered the country. The South has been the home of diseases, whose low death rate has concealed their tremendous importance in lowered vitality and efficiency.

Much of the South's retardation popularly charged to the climate may indeed be rightly transferred to the credit of hookworm, malaria, and ill-chosen diet. Thriving in areas of sandy soils, heavy rainfall, warm winters, and barefeet, the hookworm larvae have largely created the stereotype of that lean, cadaverous, yellow-complexioned, shiftless southerner known as "poor white." It is noteworthy that after two decades of work on the problem, the International Health Commission's announcement of victory over hookworm closely parallels the upward economic and industrial surge of the South. The menace remains in a very weakened form only for the rural white population of school age living in sandy areas. Malaria, the pioneer's scourge and bar to settlement, has proved the South's handicap to energy and industry. A public health official writing of the South's mosquito-infested sandy flats, coastal swamps and river deltas, said: "The major health problem of this desolate region is simple enough. Drain all the swamps, sink holes and barrow pits, screen all the houses and put shoes on thousands and then train them all to cleanly habits of living. In brief, the whole thing is as simple and easy as it would be for a one-armed man to empty the Great Lakes with a spoon."

Public health officials and the Rockefeller Commission, it is true, have attained no such triumph of preventive medicine with malaria as with hookworm. Sparsely populated countrysides are still subject to the drain of chills and fever and many southerners unsuspectingly carry malaria microbes dormant in their blood streams. But any city or town that is willing to pay the price may clean up and police its environs to secure freedom from the *Anopheles* mosquito. The South, however, awaits a practical method of control attainable by the countryside.

Pellagra, although primarily confined to the warm South, probably owes nothing to climate as a contributing factor. Serious and until recently increasing in its ravages, it is of chief importance as indicating the dietary maladjustment of a whole section. The social heritage of a crude frontier diet and the exigencies of cotton cropping have brought the southern common man to a diet at variance with his climate. "Several years of experience in the southern field," writes a home demonstration agent, "convince me that pork fat, starch, and sweets constitute the basis of diet at all seasons. Even in growing seasons vegetables are rendered more or less useless by long cooking." E. V. McCollum has said: "Animal experimentation, human geography and history all point in an all but conclusive manner to diet as the principal cause of our health troubles in so far as these are not brought about by communicable diseases." In a land of profusion in plant life, it is tragic that deficiency in fresh fruits, green vegetables, lean meats, eggs, and milk should have produced an insidious and baffling disease and lowered the level of human adequacy. When the reign of hookworm, malaria, meat, meal, and molasses is completely broken, the South may expect a further release of the energies of its people sufficient to throw off cultural stagnation and the domination of the cotton system. The handicaps of the South are not inherent in the geographic and biological scheme of things. They partake of the nature of historical accidents and economic blunderings; they are amenable to science and social engineering; and they may be overcome.

VIII

Thus have passed in hasty review the panorama of the South's changing regions. A promised glance at the regional cupboards and we have done with this survey of material culture. At what levels of material well-being does the South exist? Clarence Heer, after surveying all the statistical evidence available, holds that incomes and wages in the South range around some two-thirds of the norms for the rest of the country. Just as competition between the South's many regions tends toward but never reaches a sectional plane of living, so does competition between sections fall short of a national plane. In a nation so characterized by mobility as ours, many workers, mainly Negroes, may migrate northward; some industries may move South, but sectional difference in income so far persists. To complicate the picture further there are the differences between occupations and economic classes within the nation and the section.

The twelve southerners who issued a clarion call for the South to return to the agrarian way of life are, of course, aware that the South has never deserted agriculture. In this year of grace it is only 32 per cent urban in a nation preponderantly cityfied. Agriculture sets the mode for southern standards of living, and the cotton belt sets the mode for southern agriculture. Agriculture represents the main source of livelihood for nearly half the South's population, and it is in agriculture that income differences with the rest of the country reach their greatest. Farming, as Mr. Heer shows, pays its southern farmers just about one-half of what it pays its followers elsewhere in this country. At the bottom is the cotton cropper, next the share tenant, above him the small owner, and highest in the scale the planter-landlord. All are likely to pay tribute to the supply merchant and furnisher who takes the dangerous risks of the gyrating cotton market, along with 25 per cent or more for credit. Moreover, many farms outside the cotton belt, capable of sustaining the backwoods mode of living of an earlier day, can never be made to yield the income sufficient for a modern standard of living.

The occupations in the South whose returns approach nearest to national standards are those which have erected highest the barriers of skill against raw recruits from the farm. Very nearly the country's average wage is paid in the railroad shops and the higher mechanical and building trades. Casual farm laborers, on the other hand, obtain about 48 per cent of the wage paid elsewhere. That the greatest wage differential appears in unskilled trades reflects among other things the presence of the Negro. The cotton mill which excludes the Negro lies especially open to invasion from the cotton farm. The mill village furnishes a house, and the mill technique offers no insuperable barrier of skill. If the jobs were open and it were moving time in the cotton belt, thousands would go tomorrow— so slender and so precarious are the returns from cotton farming. Wages in textiles grow progressively lower the farther we penetrate into the deep South from Virginia to Alabama. This is a measure of the influence of the threatening hordes on the farm. In cold figures Mr. Heer shows that returns from the 1927 census of manufactures assign average annual earnings of $825 to southern factory workers, $748 to laborers in lumber, $671 to cotton goods operatives, and $519 to farmers.

So far our discourse has been of the southern common man. But the South, we are told, has been the home of aristocracy. How fare the leaders in this economy? That leadership has shifted since the Civil War from agriculture to trade and industry. Moreover, our income differentials go back as far as the Civil War, possibly further. If Pitchfork Ben

Tillman of South Carolina be taken to typify the men who wrested political leadership from the old aristocracy like Wade Hampton, then the Dukes, Wash and Buck, represent the new economic leaders from the middle class. Both prestige and wealth have passed from the landed planters to the new industrial leaders. Moreover, much of the development in rayon, aluminum, gas and oil, coal and iron, even in trucking and orcharding has been carried on by outside capital and outside leaders. Thus the gains and losses are absorbed outside the area. Moreover, the South has the largest proportion of the nation's population employed, but with a smaller proportion in the learned professions. This is no doubt due in part to the fact that the census lists as employed a large number of southern farm women and children whose contribution to agriculture may be slight and sporadic. There are certain indices which, following Mr. Heer, point to the South's comparative rank in large incomes. The proportion of persons in the South with incomes large enough to require the filing of a Federal Income Tax Return in 1926 was one-third as great as in the nation—1.43 to 4.01 per cent. Comparative incomes in certain professional and clerical pursuits in the South show city school teachers with 67.6 per cent of average for teachers in the rest of the country, college professors with 87.7 per cent, clergymen with 73 per cent, and male clerks in manufacturing establishments with 91 per cent. Since the great fortunes are averaged in the figures of income per capita, they furnish another striking comparison. From 1919 to 1921 income per capita for ten southern states ranged from 55 to 42 per cent of the rest of the country. The conclusion is foregone. The South's upper economic classes are not as large and do not receive returns proportionate to those of the nation. Its material culture has not yet provided that economic surplus above bare necessity which in our civilization makes its characteristic appearance in large fortunes. Nor is the agrarian South yet prepared to support learned and professional classes at national standards. Insofar as the development of those imponderables, science, literature, philosophy, and the arts depend on wealth and leisure, the South must admit handicaps. In the main the depression of 1929–1934 has served to make more evident the fundamental weaknesses of southern economy—all along the line from the debacle of the cotton system to the virtual break-down of public education in more than one southern state.

Up to now the South's most striking achievement has been the futile one of fighting the Civil War to a standstill. If the upper class demonstrated its leadership by maneuvering the conflict, the southern foot soldier, by his tenacious conduct of that same conflict, should have forever laid to rest the bogey of poor white. With its obsequies completed by anti-malaria and hookworm campaigns comes a dawning respect for the Negro, engendered by his modicum of success in the arts and in northern industry. It is time, then, for the South to cease repining at climate, stock, and Reconstruction and to turn to a task greater than the Civil War—that of regional planning.

Here are tasks enough to occupy the next hundred years, but may one ask in no facetious spirit, what else has the South to do with its spare time? Mississippi flood control, with federal direction and support, bids fair to recover the country's most fertile and hazardous area—the delta. Next should come the task of redistributing the highland population now held on barren ridges and marginal areas. A program for reforestation of cut-over lands will conserve resources in the waning piney woods. The stabilization of rural-urban ratios and the development of live stock and dairying to the point reached in certain Blue Grass areas should follow. The orderly exploitation of the South's untouched resources, largely in the field of the chemical industries, vies with the social mastery of industrialism and the attainment of labor codes as enlightened as those of New York or Massachusetts. Towering above all is a challenge that must not be denied. The rationalization of cotton production with realignment of the cotton system and its human factors ranges all the possibilities from co-operative marketing, diversification and controlled production to a new technology of mechanical harvesters and production of rayon from the whole stalk. The domestic allotment program for cotton and tobacco promises a needed reduction in southern crop surpluses; the Industrial Recovery Act permits integration on a higher economic level for the disorganized southern industries of lumbering, coal mining, and cotton textiles; while the creation of the Tennessee Valley Authority promises the development of the great Muscle Shoals power system in connection with a balanced rural economy based on adequate land utilization and part-time rural industries. Until these tasks are accomplished we may continue to talk of the new South and of its strivings for culture and the imponderables. But the poorer regions on the South's profile must still give us pause before the question of Sirach of old:

> The wisdom of the scribes cometh by opportunity of leisure;
> And he that hath little business shall become wise.

How shall he become wise that holdeth the plow,
That glorieth in the shaft of the goad,
That driveth oxen, and is occupied with their labors,
And whose discourse is of the stock of bulls?
He will set his heart upon turning his furrows;
And his wakefulness is to give his heifers their fodder.

5. Is Agrarianism for Farmers? (1935)

The publication of a book by a Georgia Tech economist gave Vance the opportunity to express his views on "Agrarianism," a back-to-the-land program advocated by a number of conservative southern intellectuals, among them several men that he had known as a student at Vanderbilt. Vance was more sympathetic to at least some elements of the Agrarian platform than were most southern progressives. He was by no means a fellow traveler, however, perhaps because he had grown up on a farm, unlike most of them. Nevertheless, he attempted to make his criticism constructive, which was characteristic. Also characteristic is his emphasis on concrete, political steps to implement reform.

For many the agrarianism of *I'll Take My Stand* afforded more of controversy than of exposition, and for a while it appeared that the brilliant group centering at Nashville were to be known by what they opposed rather than by what they advocated. Agrarianism, we were told, was a movement against mediocrity in art and letters, against American nationalism, against communism, against southern liberalism, against the tariff, against farmers' keeping books, against Yankees, and against the Juggernaut, the last being the outcome of the Civil War. Now this, no doubt, is a fine list of things to be against except that it appeared to leave the agrarians only one thing to be for—notably the ante-bellum southern planter. "The South, it appears," a caustic friend wrote me in those early days, "is to have its Ghandi—not one but twelve. And the alternative they offer to industrialism is much more glamorous than the spinning wheel—nothing less than an antebellum colonial mansion." Howard W. Odum has phrased it more wisely: "If the Old South were what we know it was not; and if we could go back, as we know we cannot—would it not be a relief from the maladjustments of an industrial society?"

The maladjustments have accumulated, but overnight the call to defend the rural South against the onrush of factories and payrolls became

From *Southern Review* 1 (1935): 41–57. Reprinted by permission of the Louisiana State University Press, © 1935–36.

a work of supererogation. With the retreat from industry no longer a choice but a necessity, agrarianism now has the chance to tell us what it stands for, rather than what it is against. It is as though the leaders of a rear guard action were suddenly offered command of the country from which they had prepared to flee. Today the agrarians are hearing less about the futility of tilting at windmills and of trying to turn back the clock. They are, in fact, being asked for programs. It needs only that they abandon a somewhat gratuitous defense of Jefferson Davis for the agrarians to change from nineteenth century romanticism to twentieth century regional planning.

The time is past when the needs of a great region can be served by a historical legend, no matter how lovingly fashioned. Nostalgia must become program, and this program if it is to seek national acceptance, owes the duty of candor—a candor which shall conceal no bias of race or class. This, it seems to me, is the significance of Mr. Cauley's book;[1] it marks the transition from a literary movement to agricultural economics. Nor should this come as a surprise to those who have followed the pages of the *American Review*.

I

It is not the purpose of this paper to discuss agrarianism as a theory of art, or as the defense of a tradition. As a philosophy of American history it has a good lineage all the way from Jefferson, who spoke of those that labor in the earth as the chosen people of God in comparison with urban mobs, down to Ben Tillman, who spoke of the textile mill workers of his state quite simply and fervently as "the damn factory class." As a movement it is entirely possible that agrarianism has claimed too much. It has, rightly no doubt, looked askance at economic materialism; and yet in realms of art and the spirit it has somehow assumed that once a section accepted an agricultural mode of life, all things would be added unto it.

Agrarianism can, no doubt, strengthen its defenses by consolidating its position. An examination of what comprises a feasible program for agrarianism may offer some suggestion as to what territory may be claimed and what should be abandoned by the movement. To hold, for example, that the choice is between agrarianism and industrialism is to claim too much. No one doubts that both will continue, and the best that agrarianism can expect here is a decreasing rate of industrialism. If the benefits of technology can not be made available to mankind under capitalism as we know it, they will be conserved under some more collective system. There is now no turning back from industrialism; there is only the hope that the agrarian section of society can be saved from exploitation at the hand of the industrial sector.

Similarly Mr. Cauley, it seems to me, claims too much when after defining Agrarianism as "an economic system in which agriculture is the chief but not the sole means of making a living, and in which people generally own sufficient property to insure them a decent living and the basis for a satisfying degree of economic freedom" he holds that "as against both Capitalism and Socialism—twin products of highly-developed machine production—Agrarianism is a third possibility." One may accept his definition and yet find it impossible to believe that men will to any great extent give up machine production. Rather, if capitalism fails to give mankind the abundance of goods they need, they will give up the price system and keep the machines. In any case industrialism will continue in all but the most backward countries, and agriculture will exist as an adjustment either to capitalism or socialism. Nevertheless, there exists some justification for the impulsive distrust of the socialist state shown by the agrarians. Certainly both Marxist theory and Soviet practice seem to indicate that, failing the introduction of the factory on the farm, that is, the mechanization and collectivization of agriculture in mono-culture, the Socialists would subordinate the farm population to the urban proletariat.

Because of Capitalism's partial adherence to private property and individual autonomy, the agrarian masses may be expected to retain their traditional allegiance to the system, provided it can supply them with cheap and adequate manufacturers' goods. Mr. Cauley and the agrarians generally propose to get around this need by reducing human wants to a minimum level. For the rest they are content to refer to manufactured products somewhat emotionally as gadgets with the implication that men use them largely because they are suggestible to advertising. The one answer to this is that lacking the gadgets of water at the tap and electricity in the home, the farm wife becomes a water-pumping, diaper-washing gadget herself. Peasants the world over have through necessity taken a somewhat calloused attitude toward the drudgery and child-bearing activities of their women. For their next symposium, let us hope the agrarians will invite a hard-bitten farm wife to cast a cold and fishy eye on their proposals for diminishing the sum total of human wants.

If, to reverse the dialectic, agrarianism is not to be regarded as an ambitious theory of the "liquidation" of industrialism in a capitalistic crisis, precisely then what is left? The answer is that agrarianism remains a theory of agriculture, the advocacy of non-commercial or partly commercial as against commercial farming. The point should be made clear that agrarianism is not the theory that everybody should become farmers; it is rather the theory that farmers should farm for a living rather than for a profit in the price system. From the viewpoint of agrarianism for farmers we may well glance at the problems in the South (1) affecting future population trends, (2) capitalistic farming in relation to mechanization and the growing distinction between the Southeast and Southwest, (3) the problem of tenancy, and (4) the present crisis in the South.

II

First, we realize that the capacious maw of industrialism has until recently relieved agrarianism of the necessity of facing one of its most difficult problems—that of population increases. The depression on the one hand has effectively halted the southward movement of industry, on the other it has reversed the urban, industrial, and northward migration of the South's rural population. When we realize that the South, irrespective of the Negro, has the country's youngest population with the highest ratio of persons in the reproductive period of life, the country's highest birth rate, and the highest proportion of children to child-bearing women, this seems a Pyrrhic victory for Agrarianism. Moreover, some one and a quarter million souls have returned to the Cotton Belt, displaced by failing industrial production.

What this means is suggested by an estimate of the National Resources Board. With migration blocked and present population trends projected, by 1960 the rural population of eleven southeastern states will be increased over nine million with Texas and Oklahoma accounting for another two and three-quarters million increase. If migration continued at the 1920–30 rate, the increase would be only some two and one-fourth million for all the states mentioned. No one expects the urban migration to cease entirely but on the contrary no one expects it to resume at the rate set by Coolidge prosperity.

The South's farms have long furnished a reserve army of unskilled labor. This army, industrialism for a long time now will decline to receive, except in decreasing numbers. Its members are thus thrown back on the farm. Farms are already too small in the South and the ratio of tenancy is far too high. Yet it is true that if peasant proprietorship on optimum size farms could be established by fiat, present population trends would eventuate in the subdivision of holding and the recruiting of new armies of tenants from the too numerous sons of farm owners.

The demand, then, is for a population policy for agrarianism. Pressing on the capacity of westward migration, of the South's uncleared lands, and of urban industry to absorb their population increases, Southern farmers may well take a look at the French peasant. To this peasant his farm is a permanent thing to be tended with loving care and handed down undivided. As a result his family affairs are the despair of the French militarists. He hopes to rear to adulthood two children, preferably one son who will inherit the family domain and one daughter who will marry a neighbor's son who will also inherit. In such a stable order he hopes that no child of his will have to till another's land nor seek his fortune in that wicked Paris.

Here is the challenge to agrarianism. Non-commercial farming is more devoted to conserving the integrity of population on the land than to the increase of efficiency for the profit of the few to the displacement of the many. Nevertheless, to avoid the trend of subdividing farms and taking up poorer lands, the size of the farm family needs to fall more in accordance with the number that industry and agriculture will decently absorb. Otherwise agriculture will continue to thrust its population increases on the bargain counter of a heedless industrialism.

III

The orthodox view of agriculture as a commercial enterprise may be presented as follows:

The farmer is nothing more nor less than a business man in command of land and capital. As such, it is his function to specialize his crops and mechanize his methods so as to increase his production and cut his costs. He can best do this by engaging in mono-culture, the production of one staple cash crop. In the meantime he can add to his success by judiciously anticipating the rise in land values, thus reaping his share of the unearned increment. To secure these laudable aims the farmer should place a mortgage on his land since this discounts the future and places him in command of more capital to expand production and increase efficiency. True, he will encounter the vicissitudes of the price cycle; but lowered prices may be met by increased efficiency, and the way to increased efficiency is by way of increased production per unit of overhead, the overhead consisting of said mortgage and said machinery. This procedure, it is very likely, leads to increased size of farms, and increased amount of wage or cropper labor.

At this point the reader may refuse to be taken in and arise to inquire as to whether the author is presenting a travesty of the old doctrine of "buy more land and grow more cotton to buy more Negroes, to grow more cotton to buy more land . . ." and so on *ad infinitum*. It is of course the orthodox economist's picture of economic man farming for profit in the price system. The picture, however, must be finished. Soon agricultural surpluses mount, price levels fall, the machinery and the mortgage remain to be paid for on the old level, and increased production even with the aid of increased efficiency soon lands the farm and the farmer in the hands of his creditors. Mr. Cauley phrases this matter very neatly when he says: "As a producer of goods agriculture in this country may be accounted a success; but as a business it is a distinct failure, and to a very large extent, its success in production is responsible for its failure as a business."

If agriculture is in the way of being a good provider but a poor bargainer, then agriculture must provide more for itself and less for those with whom it must bargain. This is not the denial of the economy of abundance; it simply holds that abundance like charity begins at home. It has proved much easier in our fluctuating price system to produce a steady flow of goods than a steady flow of income with which to purchase those goods or their equivalent. The general or all-round farmer is the only one of our artisans who can produce anywhere near the number and variety of goods sufficient for his own consumption. When in the interests of efficiency he concentrated on one staple crop, he threw away this immunity and became a business man subject to all the risks of the market. Such farmers enjoy none of the benefits of capital reserves or semi-monopoly and reduction of output found in industry, and like ripe plums are ready to be shaken down by the winds of depression and price failure. But wherever one finds farmers who provide first for the family living, with a change of pace for whatever cash crops the market will absorb at decent prices, one finds survivors of price changes. To one who did not buy his farm on the last rise and has no intention of selling on the next, the changes in land values can not mean so much.

In its more sober tones the Land Planning Committee of the National Resources Board has endorsed such a national policy.

> Even if we were assured of opportunities of employing all the population that could be spared from agriculture, it seems probable that a middle course will be safer and perhaps socially more wholesome than an extreme form of commercial agriculture. The latter might imply, for instance, large capitalistic units dependent in part on hired labor and characterized by a high degree of economic instability. On the whole, it appears wiser to strive for the family farm characterized by a reasonable degree of self-sufficiency interrelated with forest, wildlife, and recreational resources of the countryside, and integrated as far as practicable with other forms of employment for family labor.

The advocates of agrarianism in all candor may set down their reactions toward increased mechanization as promised in the much discussed Rust Brothers cotton picker. One can see that cotton prices will fall, farms capitalized on the basis of previous returns will go on the block, and population will be thrust off the land; all with the end-result that fewer owners on larger holdings will for a time make bigger profits in commercial agriculture. The one admitted gain to society will be cheaper cotton goods—a gain for which society may have to pay in relief of the displaced and dispossessed farmers. This is the picture in the Southeast, much of whose topography is too rough for machine cultivation and harvesting.

But let us follow the changing picture in the Southwest. The great gains to be made in cotton production before the price finally reaches a level slightly above the cost of production, say six or four cents, will lead to a consolidation of farms in immense holdings. Capitalized on the basis of the first profits of mechanization, many farms thus purchased will not be able to sustain the early rate of return as cotton prices continue to fall before the spread of mechanization. The costs of expensive machinery and of land bought on a speculative rise will leave the new cotton zones vulnerable to the next price recession. Combines and great wheat farms, as we know, failed to save the Wheat Belt. In addition occasional droughts in the Southwest may be expected to accelerate the rhythm of failure and bankruptcy. Yet all the while, farmers raising the family living and using family labor will continue to grow some cotton for cash income, and many of them will continue to survive the weeding-out process of price fluctuations.

It is significant to note that these conflicting views of commercial agriculture marked a geographical division of the specialists attending the Southern Regional Conference on the Cotton Economy at New Orleans in March of this year. Almost uniformly the representatives of the new Southwest area, Oklahoma and Texas, advocated specialized cash farming, mechanization and increased efficiency. They regarded tenancy as either a form of employing labor or as a stage in the climb to ownership, but in neither case an alarming social problem except possibly for mobility. Further rises might be expected in land values, and absentee landlords might still be expected to discount those values and pay prices higher than the present worth of the land, thus keeping them out of reach of the tenant-cultivator. The only urgent remedy needed at the present was to restore the export market, to lift restrictions on production and allow the inevitable march toward mechanization, efficiency, and large scale production to wipe out the submarginal producer. The only objection voiced to this program was that such submarginal farmers would never know when they were wiped out.

Against this partial view may be set the more balanced view of optimum regional production advocated by Howard W. Odum and others. The forthcoming Southern Regional Study, for example, points out that to satisfy the minimum dietary requirements for milk in the Southeast would require some 245 billion gallons, that the deficit is over one-tenth of the nation's production and involves a 192 per cent increase in the region's present production. Moreover, all down the line the region has failed to incorporate livestock in its agriculture. To make up one-half the area's deficiency in cattle would require four times the pasture now listed. To cite the principle of comparative advantage against the Southeast providing these things for itself is to ignore the costs of transportation and distribution. Then there remains the previous threat that the Southwest will undermine the region's cotton, the medium of exchange with which it secures its subminimum requirements. And then we are brought up short with the realization that no man can make the transition from growing products for sale to growing products for use unless he owns the land he farms. At least not in the share tenancy of the cotton system.

IV

Accordingly all who propose the South as the native haunt of agrarianism must face the conditions of tenancy in the region. Of all the characteristics of commercial farming, tenancy, it seems, is the most extreme; and of all the tenant areas the South is the most distressing in amount and kind. The system exacts its toll in cash crops and furnishes its tenants their family living, such as it is, at extortionate credit. It is noteworthy that the theories of tenancy so far developed in America are barely more than defenses of capitalistic agriculture. As such they are subject to the same cool scrutiny that agrarianism gives to commercial agriculture in general.

A dread of tenancy, as R. T. Ely points out, was brought from Europe by every stream of agrarian immigrants coming from semi-feudal backgrounds. The ideal of the American farmer cultivating an economic unit sufficient to maintain his family in comfort with no overlord governed the policy toward squatters, the passage of the Homestead Act of 1862, and various state "Homestead Acts" exempting the homestead, up to a certain value, from seizure for debt. Nevertheless, speculation and land grabbing introduced the elements of landlordism and the rapid increase of tenancy became apparent upon the disappearance of arable free land.

The first tenure census of 1880, showing over 25 per cent tenancy, brought dismay to those who believed that America would pass beyond the land tenure conditions of the Old World. Only gradually came the realization that, lacking an effective bar on speculation, land grabbing, and resale of homesteads, giving away government land could effect a wide distribution of farm ownership only as long as the supply of free land lasted. By 1930 about 53 percent of the farmers operated leased land and 42 per cent rented all the land they tilled. No one, I suppose, now doubts that Federal long-time farm credits operated to aid the concentration of large holdings in commercial farming rather than to start tenants on the road to ownership. "Negatively, it may be said," writes B. H. Hibbard, "that the land policies of the government have failed to keep the land permanently in the hands of the tiller of the soil." An interesting example of this is cited by Secretary Wallace in our Federal reclamation areas. These developments were urged as a means of creating new farms to be operated by owners, but the same failure to guard against land speculation and the absentee landlord has resulted in the fact that some 40 per cent of the projects are now operated by tenants.

Until recently in this country no critical theory of tenancy has been developed which takes into consideration the fact that while the United States is drifting into tenancy, certain European countries with semi-feudal backgrounds, notably Denmark, Ireland, and France, have made the transitions to peasant proprietorship. The problem in America has been chiefly discussed either by Mid-Western economists to whom tenancy is an expression of capitalistic enterprise, or by Southern students with a definite racial bias, if not a predilection for the ante-bellum plantation. Of those acquainted with Mid-Western conditions, T. N. Carver may be taken as representing the orthodox point of view. Tenancy is related to the inefficiency of farmers. Thus owing to his greater efficiency, the able farmer achieves ownership while the inefficient is forced to become a tenant and farm under supervision. Possibly the most able attempt to rationalize the system is found in the agricultural ladder theory developed by W. J. Spillman. According to this theory the young and inexperienced farmer has to go through a series of progressive stages represented by the system of wage labor and tenancy in order to acquire the capital and experience necessary to farm ownership. Tenancy is thus a stage through which farmers climb rather than a status into which they fall. Spillman contends that the ladder strengthens the system of land-ownership. The ladder theory is sharply challenged by the fact that the percentage of tenants who are over 55 years old has been increasing for several decades. There are now about 375,000 who, as Secretary Wallace says, have struggled a lifetime toward ownership and in their old age possess no home of their own and no more security than when they started.

The whole trend of the Mid-Western school has been to minimize the extent and increase of tenancy in the United States and to point to the South as a special case. As late as 1912 an able authority could write, "With the exception of the Negroes in the South there is no tenant class of farmers in the United States." With white tenancy increasing at a more rapid rate than Negro tenancy, and especially in consideration of its spread to the Southwestern cotton areas where few or no Negroes are found, this statement is now doubtful. Of the one and four-fifths million tenants found by the 1930 census in sixteen Southern states, over 60 per cent were white. The period from 1920 to 1930 demonstrated the devastation that could be wrought by a fall in prices in an area of commercial farming. Because of migration there was a slight decrease in Negro tenants, but an increase of 69 per cent in the number of white croppers in the area.

It is also customary to hold that the Southern share tenant, and especially the cropper, is an agricultural laborer given a fictitious dignity by being called a tenant. Such procedure dismisses the problem from the category of tenancy and thus no doubt, serves to make the tenant situation seem immeasurably brighter. This is but an example of the practice, to which social scientists at times have proved addicted, of solving problems by shifting categories. It is best answered by pointing out that tenancy at its worst has tended to degrade its workers to lower levels and to deny their rights as tenants. Tenants with a fluctuating status are the best proof of the seriousness of the problem. In many cases the plain truth is that they are regarded as tenants when that status is to the profit of the landowner and relegated to laborers when that status proves more profitable.

Another view often advanced holds that Southern tenancy is the normal development of the abolition of slavery and the break-up of the ante-bellum plantation. The shifting of former slaves into the metayer or share-cropping system was simply the method whereby large landholders made use of agricultural laborers lacking property in land, implements, and workstock. Moreover at this point the banker, the credit merchant and the farm mortgage companies crept in to furnish the credit needed and to dictate the type of agriculture to be practiced. This explanation is perfectly valid, but it should not be accepted as throwing the problem in any favorable light. Slavery, it must be remembered, had come to be regarded by the enlightened opinion of mankind as an abnormal industrial relationship. The concentration of large landholdings in the plantation was undoubtedly bolstered by its existence, as it was by the speculative and land grabbing activities of the frontier. The persistence of the pattern after sixty years, is, therefore, no cause for congratulation even as it refers to the Negro farmer. To those who see tenancy as an ideal system, the problem must be regarded as even more disconcerting when it is realized that white tenants have entered the cotton system on even terms with the ex-slaves, have secured their family living in the same extortionate credit system, have exceeded them in number, have carried tenancy into the Southwestern areas where few Negroes are found. In the disastrous period 1920–1930 the evidence is unmistakable that when Negro tenants fled from the blighted cotton area to the refuge of northern industry, white tenants crept in to take their places. Racial inefficiency, and the shadows of slavery and the plantation here seem to explain too much or else nothing at all.

Behind the rallying defense of "Let the Negro problem alone" the South has let and has forced the nation to let tenancy alone, until now it sees fastened upon itself the incubus of a degraded white tenancy. Yearning for the symbol of the old plantation, fearing the Negro, and held in thrall by credit institutions that enforce the commercial agriculture from which they take their toll, the section has long stood in the shadow of laissez-faire as regards land tenure—so long in fact that it has almost rejected the hope of an independent free-holding yeomanry, living self-sufficient lives on family-sized farms, for the chimera of land concentration and the commercialized farming of the cotton system. In the Southeast the work of Carl C. Taylor, the late Eugene Cunningham Branson, and others, marks the turn toward a more realistic attitude toward tenancy.

v

There may be some viewing the spectacle of twelve cent cotton and government benefits all-around who have decided that the South need trouble itself no more about agricultural reform. But many discerning people in the South must feel: (1) That to reduce production reduces human labor; (2) that rental benefits go to landowners rather than to the masses of the rural population generally; (3) that instead, a larger number of the rural population goes on relief; (4) that these benefits are paid by consumers in higher prices of cotton textiles which are thus placed in a poorer competitive position; (5) that pegging the price of raw cotton holds the umbrella over competing cotton areas, granting them a certain minimum price with no necessity of corresponding reduction in output; (6) that American exporters paying the pegged price cannot meet world cotton prices; (7) that our cotton export trade may be vanishing before our very eyes. Volumes could be written on these texts, but they are slowly emerging from the realm of controversy into the realm of fact.

And yet why should one blame the Federal government? With the best intentions in the world, it has ventured to underwrite the cotton economy, only to discover what abysmal thing it is. With approximately one-eighth of the area's families on Federal relief, with two-fifths of the region's cotton lands rented by the government, and cotton prices pegged by government loans, does anyone think that the Federal agencies will soon be able to retire as guarantors of commercial agriculture in the

South? Let us ignore for the time being the controversies now raging around the displacement of tenants, the shifting of tenants to casual labor, the question as to how large a per cent of the total cotton income benefit payments have shifted from tenants to landlords. Nevertheless, the government has so deeply invaded the cotton system that it now can retreat with honor only by aiding in a reform of the system.

The way to this reform, now long overdue, is pointed out by the proposed Bankhead Bill to create a Tenant Farms Corporation. Some fifteen million acres of land, much of which is in the possession of Insurance Companies, Federal Land Banks and helpless owners, are estimated as available for settling tenants and share-croppers. The Corporation would start with $100,000,000 capital and the authority to issue a billion dollars worth of bonds. With efficiency and dispatch, it is hoped that within five years, 500,000 present farm families could be settled on their own lands. The farm would be about the size of the present tenant holding, graduated in accordance with the size of the family, and should cost from $2000 upward. With low interest and amortization charges the tenant might expect to gain possession of his farm with annual payments around $80 for some thirty years. The sum looms large in view of the fact that his cotton at present prices would bring only about $200 a year. Once settled on his farm he could be taught by county agents to grow a garden, keep pigs, pasture a cow and produce most of his own food. This would be clear gain, for in the commercial agriculture of the Cotton Belt the family living is purchased at extortionate rates of credit and paid for out of the cash returns from the cotton crop. Provided he gets good land, the tenant's annual payments will be much smaller than rent and credit charges exacted by landlord and time merchant. On the other hand, he will have to pay taxes and certain costs of production not usually charged against tenants. Here he has the advantage of cheap production credit, not available to tenants except where the landlord is willing to release his prior lien for the rent.

Difficulties remain which in all candor should be listed and faced by advocates of peasant proprietorship. First, the program, it will be recognized, is an attempt to escape some of the commitments of commercial agriculture. As such it is handicapped in the beginning by the fact that the purchasers are thrown back upon the money crop to meet annual payments. It will be recognized that the tenant must be allowed an equitable cotton or tobacco quota and that other crops and part-time employment should supplement his income. Even then, in order to carry through a desirable social policy, a realistic recognition of the relation between staple prices and the ability to keep up annual payments may be necessary. Second, the program must be guarded against the speculation and absentee ownership which have thwarted similar movements. If the farm owner cultivating his own farm is the goal, provision should be made that no purchaser can sell or mortgage his farm. If he wishes to relinquish his interest, the farm should revert to the corporation which can repay him a certain paid-up value and resell the farm to another tenant. Third, it should be realized that the very mould of his existence has made the tenant a creature of mobility and dependence. Every effort should be expended to encourage habits of stability while his need of dependence may be met by short-time farm credits and the supervision afforded by farm and home demonstration agents.

VI

The savor of sweet reasonableness that hovers about this proposal will not lead those who know the divided councils of the South to expect its easy acceptance. Certainly many Southerners who see no further than the interests of the credit institutions and large landholders which cluster about commercial farming may be expected to prate of "excursions into state socialism," "government extravagance," and "meddling with the South's peculiar institutions." Accepted before the country as representatives of, as well as experts on, the ill-understood cotton economy, no one doubts they have the power to block this measure.[2] If they choose they may fiddle the familiar string while the nation continues to pay rents to planters, processing taxes to the AAA, and relief to dispossessed tenants and laborers. And while the money rolls down the gutter to no permanent good, the cotton picker, sweeping across the level plains of the Southwest, may so wreck the commercial agriculture of the Southeast as to leave the landed interests demanding of their government the assistance they once denied.

The agrarians, one feels, are in process of unifying themselves around peasant proprietorship as a standard of economic minima for the region. Yet one runs across writers in a recent issue of the *American Review* who list attempts at land tenure reform as the Fourth Crusade against the South, following the Third Crusade against Scottsboro, and lay the conspiracy at the door of the tribe of sociologists who are now to assume a place in Beelzebub's hierarchy directly across from the Abolitionists. Mr. Cauley, I fear, will find himself consigned to this devil's group, for he expresses no flattering opinion of the place of tenancy in an agrarian order. Nor will he be alone. The Nashville agrarians are no mean warriors; they have, to my recollection, crossed steel with everything from Industrial Councils to the shades of Henry W. Grady and Walter Hines Page. Yet I venture it will be a new experience for some of the agrarians to find themselves accused of rushing pell-mell into the Fourth Crusade against the South. Manifestly there do exist class interests in the South, nor are all the foes to sweet reasonableness to be found among the Yankees.

No one believes that the success of the movement toward peasant proprietorship will equalize all the special disabilities of an agricultural section in an industrial nation. Manifestly it would not raise the new freeholders to unexampled levels of prosperity, restore export markets, nor equalize the tariff burden; but it should give the South a large group of sturdy independent peasant proprietors, black and white. Then will agrarianism cease to be a foible of literary men and become possible for farmers. And at last the agrarians, it seems to me, will be free to take up their rightful task—the formulation of the cultural and social values of an agricultural people.

NOTES

1. Troy J. Cauley, *Agrarianism: A Program for Farmers* (Chapel Hill: University of North Carolina Press, 1935). Both this volume and its relation to the Nashville group are deserving of review on their own account—a task not here attempted.

2. After this was written, the Bankhead Tenant Farm and Homes Bill passed the Senate in amended form by a vote of 45 to 32.

6. Planning the Southern Economy (1935)

By the mid-1930s Vance was caught up in Odum's enthusiasm for regional planning. Both saw planning as a means for dealing concretely with the South's dilemmas, and actually doing something about them. Moreover, with its strong emphasis on interregional cooperation, planning stood in sharp contrast to the traditional states' rights politics of the South. Yet Vance remained more skeptical than his mentor of the possibilities for successful planning. Aware that any efforts for social reconstruction must inevitably run the gauntlet of the political process, he envisioned no easy solutions. Perhaps that is why this article, like all his writing on planning, tends to focus on the specific problems facing the region rather than on the ways that planners might resolve them.

In our own day we have seen social planning by degrees invade the sanctuary once hallowed by the spirit of social resignation. Social resignation, whether it spring from belief in fate, in providence, in inevitable progress, or in *laissez-faire* economics, is, I take it, society's method of sitting still and letting something happen to it. But science and the technical arts in the hands of man have pioneered in making things happen rather than waiting for them to happen. No less encouraging has been the rise in our day of the new Southern regionalism to replace the old fire-eating sectionalism inherent in the doctrine of states' rights. Any glance at social trends in the South must take into account both the trend toward regionalism and that toward social planning.

I

Certainly, if either social or regional planning be regarded as a form of economic rehabilitation, then it can easily be shown that the South as much as any other region stands in need of such a program. Studies of

From *Southwest Review* 20 (Winter 1935): 111–23. © 1935 by the *Southwest Review*, published by Southern Methodist University Press.

trends show that in practically every per capita count of wealth, welfare, and economic competence the Southern states stand at the bottom of the nation's list. The South's deficiencies antedate the present crisis; concerning most of them it can be said that the depression has but served to reveal them in a more glaring light. In surveying the problem of social planning in the South, it will therefore be necessary first to characterize the basic regional economy, before going on to consider the present and probably future trends deriving from the agricultural crisis, the AAA, federal relief and rural rehabilitation, the breakdown of the tenancy system, and the inauguration of the submarginal land program in the rural South. We may save for the last a hasty glance at urban and industrial trends.

It is not enough to dismiss the economy of the South as agricultural. It is also colonial. The function of the region in a colonial economy, as every high-school student of American history learns, is to extract staple raw materials from its wealth of soils, forests, and minerals, export them to a mother country for fabrication, and then, if it can, buy them back. A colonial economy is a debtor economy. It begins as an investment on the part of a mother country, it accumulates but little capital of its own, it lacks the organization of credit, and as economic opportunities arise they must be financed from outside the area. The surplus returns are exported as profits, interests, and dividends to outside business men in command of capital. Thus the South has often sold out its undeveloped resources—pine forests, Kentucky coal, Birmingham iron, Arkansas bauxite, Texas petroleum—to outside interests at rockbottom prices, all for lack of credit to finance development. The rise of textile and tobacco manufacturing and the power industries in the Southeast represents the area's first transition from an economy exploited from the outside to one more indigenous.

It is a commonplace that the South's agricultural workers—croppers, share tenants, and small farmers, black and white—find themselves on the lowest rung of extractive economy alongside the peasants, the fishers, and the foresters of the world. This is the base line from which all other countries count their gains; Southern agricultural workers have a status comparable to that of the Chinese and Hindu peasant farmers. Moreover, these tenants and small farmers live in a credit system in which they must pay interest charges on consumers' goods of 25 per cent or more, buying what few manufactured goods they can in a high domestic market protected by the tariff. It is from these levels of living that workers in

Southern textile and tobacco factories, coal mines, lumber camps, etc., are drawn, to receive the low wages which the differentials sanctioned by NRA recognize.

In addition, the Southern region is hampered by a racial dualism which multiplies the need for all such social institutions as churches, schools, recreation centers, etc., while dividing their means of support. Competition between races adds its burden, falling heavily on the poorer white groups. The South continues to keep the Negro in his place, and the Negro continues to hold back the South. Furthermore, the Southern region, with its sparsely settled areas, possesses the largest proportion of young people and children to be educated, with the least taxable wealth for the support of education and the highest cost of assembling school children in consolidated schools. As long as industrial prosperity continued, migration, largely Negro, from the South into the North took the place of suspended European immigration. The South was thus in the position of rearing and educating, however imperfectly, the labor reserves of the rest of the nation. Now that the migration from the farm has stopped, the region's problem is the adjustment of a decreasing rate of population growth to an increasing utilization of regional resources. It may well be asked whether under these circumstances social planning can take the region from lower to higher levels of living.

II

Necessity has long been reputed the mother of invention, and it is no doubt true that out of prolonged and desperate social crises come first, the focus of public attention on neglected problems; next, social inventions and plans for their solution; and finally, the determination to carry these plans through. Of such parentage is the New Deal, and in the South no less than in the nation at large the depression has glaringly revealed the precarious foundations of our economy and posed the question of guidance and direction of social trends.

Now in any study of attempts to master the regional problems of the South, a distinction must be drawn between recovery programs and long-time regional planning. It is possible that a get-well-quick recovery program can be set up which will aim only at as speedy a return as possible to the *status quo ante*. The Negro preacher, you recall, defined the *status quo* to a bewildered parishioner as "the mess we're in." To many who think in regional terms the condition of Southern economy before the depression is far from representing a golden age to which we should wish to return. To their way of thinking, the present crisis and the recovery program will prove valuable only if they offer means and incentive to the reform, the rehabilitation, the rationalization of Southern economy.

What do we find that depression, relief, recovery, and national planning have done to and for the rural South, the great Cotton and Tobacco Belts? It is an old story that while the nation during war-time was adding forty million farm acres to replace the fifty million lost acres in Europe, the tobacco area slipped into high gear and the Cotton Belt expanded its domain westward at a dizzy pace. More than half of our cotton and more than one-fourth of our tobacco have been regularly sold abroad. The passing of war demands and the spread of the world depression found the South piling up cotton surpluses until it has stored more than enough to provide the world for a year if not a furrow were turned. Such conditions led inevitably to five-cent cotton—unfortunately, an old story for the South. With the AAA, the New Deal embarked upon the program of a gradual reduction of surpluses by the payment of subsidies to farm owners for restricting production.

Actual experience with the cotton-adjustment program has forced the federal government to recognize that the methods applied to wheat or corn and hog control in the Middle West encounter in the South a peculiar economy. It was inevitable that in the South the Agricultural Adjustment Program should become a landlord's code. In the rural South in 1934 a landowning minority were paid subsidies for reducing their cotton acreage 40 per cent and thus for throwing out of employment a proportionate number of the area's lowest-scale workers, croppers and tenants. Those who do not comply with the program find themselves confronted with the Bankhead bill which provides in substance that all farmers producing over their quota may be fined one-half the value of the overproduced cotton as soon as they offer it for sale.

Secretary Wallace himself has said that if we go all the way toward economic nationalism, "It may be necessary to have compulsory control of marketing, licensing of plowed land, and base and surplus quotas for every product for each month in the year." With such a program, he adds, "It may be necessary after a time to shift part of the Southern population." Already the truth in this prediction is becoming apparent. Southern croppers and tenants, to a number difficult to estimate except from relief rolls, have been severed from their connection with the land and forced into the status of casual laborers, retaining possibly permission to live for the present rent-free in their former tenant houses. Only direct relief and work relief, FERA and CWA, have aided in salvaging these new squatters, the dispossessed marginal men of the South. Landlords throughout the deep South have been able to release a portion of their accustomed tenants, see that they were furnished their share of Red Cross flour, and hire them when needed for fifty cents a day. Only the high levels of wages set by CWA went against the grain.

With the passing of CWA the federal government is beginning to attack the problem of relief on three fronts: (1) urban unemployment, (2) stranded populations whose one local industry has curled up and died, and (3) rural rehabilitation. In the last-mentioned program, rural relief funds are to be used to finance indigent farmers who give up growing a single cash crop and go in for diversified farming to supply their own needs but not to glut markets. In the South this program means that the federal and state relief agencies will supply the tenants with the production credit and supervision formerly furnished by landlords and supply merchants. A program of rural rehabilitation will place tenants in houses and on acres leased from landlords and land banks under the AAA, lend them cows and hogs secured from the adjustment program in dairy areas and corn and hog belts, allow part use of work stock and tools secured from landlords, and pay them wages for improving rural economic and social conditions. Thus relief is based upon the provision for the lowest-level groups of the means of self-sustenance supplemented by wages paid for making improvements. In addition to allotment payments, landlords are to receive as compensation the labor of the tenants in repairing their houses, terracing and draining their land, rebuilding fences, etc. Supplementary wages will be paid for the building of cooperative community projects, cooperative canning plants, market houses, community parks, and recreation centers, and the repair of local schools, etc. This program at the present is in a tentative stage; it has been announced but not put into effect.

The monetary manipulation plus the AAA have in a short time worked wonders with the gross farm incomes of the nation. The gross farm income of the United States, if one includes benefit and rental payments, in 1933 increased $1,240,000,000 over 1932, a gain of 24 per cent.* In this period the gross income from tobacco increased 62 per cent. The cotton

---

*Statistics made public by the Bureau of Agricultural Economics as this issue was in press show that the total cash income of farmers during 1934 exceeded the total for 1933 by $1,040,000,000. The increase was $645,000,000 from marketings of crops and livestock, and $395,000,000 from direct federal aid. The editors [of the *Southwest Review*].

growers saw the price of their staple rise from 4½ to 12 cents a pound and their gross income from cotton and cotton seed increased 56 per cent —to which the government has added $160,000,000 in rental and benefit payments. In this respect the improvement of the status of Southern farmers was exceeded only by that of the producers of grains, notably wheat, whose gross returns increased 86 per cent. Cattle and meat were not affected, and dairy products lost.

Nevertheless, twelve-cent cotton and the highest ratio of automobile sales in the nation for the rural South should not blind us to the fact that it faces two unsolved problems: the national problem of the restoration of agricultural exports, and the regional problem of what to do about tenancy. "Thus," says Secretary Wallace, speaking of the adjustment program, "we are sparring with the situation until the American people are ready to face the facts." Without the restoration of cotton to its place in the world markets it is useless to consider the resumption of business as usual in the Cotton Belt. But if the resumption of business as usual means the revival in full of the baneful tenancy system with its extortionate time-merchants, its overproduction of cash crops at the expense of food, feed, and cover crops, its absentee landlords, its wasteful method of cultivation, and its shifting, trudging, drudging croppers with the lowest levels of living in rural America, the revival of world trade means but an empty victory for the region.

Let us deal with the world problem first. If we are to continue to export agricultural products as of old, the United States, Secretary Wallace tells us, must accept annually in imports a billion dollars worth of foreign goods more than she did in 1929. Only thus can the balance of international payments be met.

In view of tariff history, of the pressure of Eastern against Southern and Western interests, and of the administration policy as developed up until Roosevelt's tariff message to Congress, it is futile to hope that the industrial interests will stand by and endow the agricultural groups to the extent of a billion dollars a year. Nor can reduction of the tariff reasonably be expected in the face of the horrible example Japan furnishes of what a nation can do to tariff barriers by deliberately depreciating its currency and debasing the living standards of its laborers. On the other hand, if we are to retire to a self-contained national economy, in which America consumes the total produce of her agricultural areas, we must erase from our map from forty to one hundred million acres of farm lands —forty million if we take out the most productive, one hundred million if we take out the least productive. More than half the South's cotton land and one-fourth of its tobacco acres must be retracted. Moreover, the land-utilization problem involved is a difficult one. From the point of view of making the best use of land resources, of securing cheaper and more efficient production, and of relocating farmers stranded in infertile areas, it would pay the nation to retire a hundred million acres of its poorest land from farming and devote most of it to grazing, forestry, and recreation. From the standpoint of the human factors involved, it will mean much less displacement and shifting of population groups to reduce a proportionate acreage of fertile farm land than to retire from cultivation whole areas of submarginal lands. In either case, the nation will be forced to retire farmers as well as acreage, and to prevent glutted markets these must be placed at subsistence farming in producing noncompeting crops. Secretary Wallace himself favors an intermediate course, the increase of our imports by some half a billion dollars and the retraction of our good land by some twenty-five million acres. Until the problem of foreign trade is settled, the South has no way of knowing where she stands.

As for the problem of tenancy, it seems to me there is no escaping the conclusion that the cotton system is overmanned, loaded down in normal times by the retainers who cling to it for a miserable sustenance. The unmechanized task of cotton-picking has been the neck of the bottle, and no doubt the plantation manager has always hoped for cotton-harvesting machinery, comparable to the wheat combine, that would enable him to dispense with many of his tenants. It can hardly be denied that the depression, the assumption of the burden of relief by the federal government, and the official enforcement of restricted production are showing Southern landlords means of relieving themselves of responsibilities of which they are glad to be rid. We may be witnessing in our own day a shift of many black and white farm workers from the status of tenants to that of casual laborers. Should the South, after a period of mass displacement, mobility, and swarming of tenant farm families to towns and cities to swell relief rolls, abandon tenancy for a system of casual labor, it will be casual labor with a difference. The casuals of the Wheat Belt winter in Chicago, where the problems afforded by their presence are confined to Hobohemia and the police courts; those of the Southwest, when their services are no longer in demand, retire to Old Mexico or the Little Mexicoes of the cities. The new casuals of the Cotton Belt must winter in their accustomed haunts, provided with but a meager pittance of a wage, the use of the worst tenant shacks, and what they can "pick up." From no standpoint of living standards, race relations, community conditions, or social welfare can the prospect be called inviting.

We have never devoted the serious study to this problem that England gave to Irish tenancy or Denmark to the condition of her farmers, nor have we attempted to emulate their solutions. Why? Partly because we have had the idea that this is purely a problem of the Negro. This notion is no longer tenable. There are more than 1,091,000 white tenants in the South, as compared with 698,000 colored tenants. And while one may not be surprised to note that more than half of the Negro tenants are croppers, it is startling to learn that more than one-third of the white tenants are in the same poverty-stricken class. Even more startling is the realization that from 1920 to 1930, a period of increasing difficulty in cotton production, Negro tenants in the South decreased by some 2,000, while white tenants increased by more than 200,000.

While the contention is true enough, it is hardly sufficient at this late date to point out that much of this situation has resulted from the concentration of the ownership of land in the hands of the few and their devotion of that land to the production of staple crops, to the exclusion of feed and food crops. Landownership itself has of late been a precarious game for the Southerner. Many landowners have been forced out by failure; and others would be content to retire on any equitable terms. Lands are never cheaper than during depressions—or more difficult for tenants to buy. Facing our vexing and unsolved problem of cotton and tobacco tenancy, I am inclined to wish that "forty acres and a mule" had come true. In the hands of a Franklin D. Roosevelt rather than of military administrators, carpetbaggers, and spoilsmen, less lavish with human lives and more lavish with public credit—with an RFC, an HOLC, and an AAA, with adequate payments to land-poor plantation owners for a portion of their holdings, with the inclusion of the landless whites in the scheme, we might have worked out a better system than the present one, in which more than 60 per cent of the farmers in eight Southern states are well-nigh landless wanderers on the face of the earth, croppers and tenants. In moments of weakness one may indulge in his private vision of every farmer living under his own vine and fig tree, tilling only the cotton or tobacco needed for cash incomes. Would "forty acres and a mule" have worked? I doubt it. But for one I should have been willing to see the new owner forbidden for a period of years to mortgage, sell, rent, or give away his farm. Die he might, but like the Roman sentry at Pompeii he would have died at his post. We might have thus created a peasantry in

the South, but at least the farmers would have been peasant proprietors
—and that is a stage we have not yet attained for more than half of our
farm families.

III

With all the region's wealth of good lands, a surprising number of farmers are living on farms that are infertile, rocky, eroded, isolated—in short,
on submarginal land. Even when measured by the backwoods standard
of living to which they have become accustomed, these farmers eke out
a poor existence. In our sandy flats, pine barrens, and poorer areas of
the Appalachian Highlands are to be found many of these families. On
the other hand, in fertile areas there may be found many farms which
have failed and have been abandoned, not because of soil deficiencies
but because of overproduction in cash crops or insect depredation. It is
the announced purpose of the submarginal land program to get these
stranded farm families from poor land to good unused land, to turn the
submarginal land they leave back to forests, parks, and grazing, where it
belongs. This is a plan to which the present Department of Agriculture is
committed, and no doubt it can be carried through by purchasing from
these stranded farmers their infertile farms, and applying the proceeds as
first payment on better lands now delinquent for taxes or held at a loss by
mortgage companies, etc.

In the present transition period, provision should be made to prevent
these farmers from upsetting the agricultural adjustment program by
wholesale production of staple crops. In their native mountains they are
accustomed to a live-at-home agriculture, and in more productive areas
they should be encouraged to follow this pattern of living with the gradual introduction of some staple farming to supply their needs for cash.
Such a plan fits in well with the rural rehabilitation program just discussed and with the operations of the new Division of Subsistence Farms
of the Department of the Interior.

IV

In this survey we should not neglect to consider Southern industry and
the effect of NRA and the recovery plans. Dr. Clarence Heer's classic

study showed that wages and income in the South before the depression were about two-thirds those in the rest of the nation. Differences were greatest in agriculture, but extended into teaching, the ministry, and all the learned professions. In the industrial world this low wage-scale offered the hope of enticing industry southward, and subsequently has become the basis of the South's differential for which Alabama coal operators and others clamor with mingled tears, patriotic exhalations, and threats of secession. Here again is felt the effect of the region's predominantly agricultural economy.

We all, I take it, admit the need of a better balance between town and country. The growth of well-distributed, medium-sized urban centers has furnished a much-needed market for the fruit, truck, poultry, and dairy products of both general and specialized farming, thus lessening to some degree the South's dependence on export crops. The growth of cities, however, goes hand in hand with the growth of industry, and this the depression has effectively halted. The South has in the main gained its new industries by underbidding and undercutting industries already established in the North and East. And here what the depression has temporarily halted, the NRA code in cotton textiles, as Dr. C. T. Murchison has pointed out, may permanently arrest. The textile industry has notably suffered from overproduction, and accordingly one of the major provisions inserted in the textile code forbids new installations of machinery without permission of the code authorities. This permission is to be granted only upon proof of justified demand in the market.

The effect of this regulation has been, as it were, to freeze the industry to the map as it is now distributed. In the past the Piedmont South, favored by certain lower costs of production, notably by cheap labor drawn from agriculture, drained the industry from New England by repeated installations which so flooded markets that Northern competitors had to fold up and move South or quit. This process cannot be repeated under the regulations restricting production and new installations. Mr. Donald Comer of Avondale Mills, Birmingham, is authority for the statement that out of 2,033 leaders taken from industry to serve on 210 code authorities, only 181 are from the thirteen Southern states. The textile code, I am given to understand, is the only one of major importance that contained a majority of Southerners. This is no doubt a fair enough index of the preponderance of industry in the North and East. Why then, one may ask, did the Southern operators agree to the regulations? Partly because regional competition and undercutting are processes to which they too have become liable. Arkansas, Louisiana, and Texas, counting on their reserves of cheap labor from tenant areas and submarginal farms, stand ready and willing to do for the Piedmont what the Piedmont once did for New England.

The adoption of the textile code, it will be readily admitted, served to prevent further disorganization in a highly disorganized industry. Nevertheless it should be realized that its faithful acceptance as a general principle may effectively halt the further southward migration of industry. Moreover, it may effectively thwart certain legitimate ambitions of the Southwest. Under such circumstances, "Industry Comes South" might well become a closed chapter in the history books, and that, I imagine, is no more a cheerful prospect to the student of social trends who seeks a balance between industry and agriculture, town and country, than, say, to Southern Chambers of Commerce. It is but reasonable to state, however, that with the resumption of more normal production and consumption these regulations may be relaxed—though not to the extent of the rugged individualism that existed in the far-off days, B. C.—Before Codes.

7. The Old Cotton Belt (1936)

This piece is typical of many others from the same period and illustrates Vance's mode of analysis well. Dealing with the same subregion that he studied in his dissertation, Vance examines the physical "givens," the institutional structure, and the historical and economic basis of the problem that concerns him, then evaluates the likely effects of government policy. Noteworthy is his description of how the southwestern cotton belt was rapidly supplanting the southeastern one and of the consequences in large-scale migration out of the region. It is probably fair to say that no other social scientist in the South at this time was as aware as Vance of the enormous exodus of people taking place as the sharecropping system broke down. His comments on what might happen if these people flooded northern cities proved all too prophetic.

The question of population redistribution finds the conjunction of emigration and regional poverty a demonstrated fact in the Southeast. The area's staple crop is cotton. From this fact there arises the one question with which we shall be deeply concerned: Why is cotton production not sufficiently profitable to afford Southerners a decent livelihood today?

In our attempts to answer, our first task will be to show the extent of pre-depression poverty in the Old Cotton Belt[1] as conditioned by the peculiar nature of the cotton economy and the land tenure system. Further, we shall find that the pressure of rapidly increasing population upon diminishing utilization of resources has been intensified by two recent crises: the advent of the boll weevil, and the loss of the world cotton markets. A study of the gains and losses in farms from 1910 to 1930, when the boll weevil invasion upset the area's precarious economy, will serve to throw light both on the migrations of the period and the emergence of competition from the Southwest. It also poses the question as to whether these areas suffered a permanent diminution of physical resources or a temporary breakdown in institutional and economic factors.

From Carter Goodrich et al., *Migration and Economic Opportunity* (Philadelphia: University of Pennsylvania Press, 1936), pp. 124–63.

The first crisis had to do with supply of American cotton; the second is tied to world demand. Now the mounting cotton surplus and the loss of world trade, together with competition from the Southwest, serve to cast doubt on the Old Belt's ability to continue to support population even at its previously low levels. While there can be but little question that, up to the present, the AAA has improved conditions as a whole, its crop reduction program in cotton appears better adapted in the long run to raise prices than to restore markets or to hold the maximum population on the land.[2] The extent to which this and various other governmental programs may alleviate the pressure toward migration is examined. The final task of the chapter is to present the alternatives facing the cotton economy, and to estimate the amount of migration called for under each hypothesis.

THE PATTERN OF RESOURCE UTILIZATION

The Land

It has been contended that anything can be grown in the southeastern states, a claim which receives support in the variety of plant life cultivated at one time or another from the Carolina low country to the Louisiana sugar bowl. The Coastal Plains are level, and much of the Piedmont is gently rolling country. Soils are, in the main, of fair to high fertility, and even where lacking in yield prove highly productive when fertilized. Other conditions favorable to agriculture—the basic occupation of the area—include a long growing season, plentiful rainfall with adequate seasonal distribution, fair transportation facilities, and low land values.

It has been usually pointed out, however, that with the excessive devotion to cotton the advantages for agriculture have not been adequately utilized. Part of the reason can no doubt be found in the history and institutions of the section, but the soil and climate contribute much of the answer. The Southeast finds itself in competition with regions better adapted than itself for the production of grain, forage, and livestock. But in cotton, the section has a plant peculiarly its own, for it can be grown on practically all well-drained soils, including the sandy soils to which fertilizer is applied.

The plant brings with it, however, physical disadvantages as well. Unlike the agriculture of grass lands and meadows, cotton culture is clean culture leaving the surface of the soil open to washing in summer and winter, with the result that over 50 per cent of all eroded areas mapped by the Soil Erosion Service are in the South. There are 200 counties in the South whose average land value falls below $15 an acre, a fact for which erosion is partly responsible. Nor is the damage, as Table 7.1 indicates, confined to the Piedmont and Brown Loams; it is also found in the Black Prairies and the Red Plains. Thirty-two and four-tenths per cent of all sampled areas in the South showed some form of erosion.

The Institutions

The heavy reliance on cotton as the one cash crop, and the economy its culture helped develop, have been expensive in more ways than one. Beside the cost in economic and human terms, the waste of erosion becomes a relatively minor item. The fluctuations in yield per acre and price per pound from year to year and the consequent risk and uncertainty, the intensive hand labor required and the consequent small acreage and farms, the shortage of local food crops and the consequent drain on the regional economy, the prevalence of tenancy with absentee ownership—all are in one way or another products of "cotton as king," and all contribute to the poverty of the region and the migration of the lower-level groups.

There are to be found in the world's agriculture, no doubt, good tenancy systems. It is felt by practically all students, however, that share-tenancy as developed in the Cotton Belt is ruinous of both land and men. In law and in actual practice both the share-tenants and croppers stand halfway between real tenants and laborers paid with a share of the crop. No method has been generally accepted in the Cotton Belt of applying share-renting to livestock or other products besides cotton and tobacco. Accordingly, there is little return of fertility to the land through the growing of cover crops and livestock. With no security of tenure and no permanent interest in the land, the tenant is content with a quick skimming of its resources before he moves to another farm. Indeed, to incorporate permanent improvement in land or buildings would, under the present system of law, be presenting a free gift to the landlord. Thus much of the tenant's spare time is wasted, and the landowner, unable or unwilling to afford improvements, often lets the land go unterraced and fences and tenant shacks unrepaired. The waste of human resources may be made clear by reference to the dietary problem of the tenant. The landowner, as indicated, gets his income from cash crops. Unless exceptional, he is not interested in the production of fruits, meats, milk, and vegetables to feed his tenants. Moreover the tenants, caught in the cotton routine and

TABLE 7.1

Estimated General Distribution of Erosion in the South, 1933
(in millions of acres)

Region	Total Area	Severely Impoverished or Soil Washed Off	Devastated	Total Erosion	Per Cent
Piedmont	46.0	12.0	4.5	16.5	35.8
Triassic Piedmont	5.0	1.2	.4	1.6	32.0
Appalachian Mountains	78.0	12.0	3.0	15.0	19.2
Miss., Ala., Ga., Sandy Lands	27.0	6.5	2.0	8.5	31.4
Southern Brown Loams	17.0	4.5	1.8	6.3	37.0
Tex., Ark., La., Sandy Lands	33.0	9.5	1.5	11.0	33.3
Tex., Ala., Miss., Black Belt	12.0	4.5	1.0	5.5	45.8
Red Plains of Texas and Okla.	36.0	15.0	3.0	18.0	50.0
Total for South	254.0	65.2	17.2	82.4	32.4
Total for United States		125.0	34.2	159.2	
Per cent South is of the total					51.8

Source: Adapted from H. H. Bennett, "Quantitative Study of Erosion Technique and Some Preliminary Results," *American Geographical Review* 33 (July 1933): 423–32.

steeped in the need of cash in an economy of debt, rarely acquire the means, the training, or possibly the inclination to produce their own food or feed crops.[3]

The failure of the tenant to grow his own food and forage for his stock would involve fewer dangers if he could afford to buy them. The returns from the one cash crop, however rarely prove sufficient to carry him, or even the small owner, over to the next season. Not infrequently the entire sum is absorbed by the obligation he has incurred to produce the crop and feed his family. The small farmers and tenants have always found it necessary to discount their crops with the credit merchant before they could be produced, and since the Civil War many of the large landholders as well have been forced on to a credit basis. Because of the large degree of risk and their poor bargaining position, the borrowers are often charged credit prices equivalent, on an annual basis, to 30 per cent interest. In times of good cotton prices the credit trade proves lucrative for time merchants and commissaries; in times of price failure sporadic exhortation to diversification and live-at-home farming is not sufficient to undo the tradition.

Of the 670,924 operators of farms in Georgia, South Carolina, and

TABLE 7.2

Average Value of Production per Farm, Including
Livestock, 1924–1928

	Average Cash Income	Gross Income
South Carolina	$765	$1,040
Georgia	815	1,139
Alabama	743	1,029
Mississippi	854	1,128
Louisiana	1,060	1,261
Arkansas	843	1,095
United States	$1,557	$1,836

Alabama, some 32 per cent are croppers who pay half of the money crop for rent of land, workstock, and equipment; 19.5 per cent are share-tenants who own and feed their workstock but pay one-fourth to one-third of their cash crops as rent; 14.1 per cent are cash tenants who theoretically pay six to eight per cent of the value of the land for its use. In addition there are approximately 210,000 white and Negro farm laborers, a group which constitutes 31.2 per cent of all operators of farms. These laborers are classified in the census as "male wage hands not employed on the home farm," and are hired mainly by the large owners by the month or as casual laborers. Employment is continuous for this group only during periods of cultivation and harvest.

Then there is a group, consisting of 4.8 per cent of the operators, who own part of the land they till, and 29 per cent who are full owners. Nor is this a completely significant figure, for about 40 per cent of the full owners report mortgages covering above 40 per cent of the value of their properties, on which indebtedness they pay interest and other charges of over 7 per cent in addition to taxes and normal production costs. On the other hand (if we are allowed to project trends from 1900 and 1910)[4] it can be estimated that 7 per cent of the operators own two to four tenant farms and 2.5 per cent own five or more farms. In the Special Census of Plantations in 1910, in 152 counties of the southeastern states it was found that 2.6 per cent of all farm owners owned 24.2 per cent of all farms. The planter and the landlord, then, are the entrepreneurs of this precarious economy; they are its directing element.[5]

Pre-Depression Poverty

As figures on farm production indicate, the land of forty acres and a mule farms too meanly on too small a scale. Moreover, in a society with the pyramidal class structure described above, no average based on size and physical production of farms gives an adequate picture of the various income levels. The averages for the period from 1924 through 1928, in the six states shown in Table 7.2, range between $743 and $1,060 net income, which is 25 per cent lower than the national level.

In 1929, a fairly prosperous year, nearly half of all the farms in the United States produced less than $1,000 worth of crops: in the major cotton areas this group included 70 to 80 per cent of the farms. The three states, South Carolina, Georgia, and Alabama, show the following average gross incomes per farm from 1929 to 1933:

1929	$1,456
1930	1,095
1931	740
1932	561
1933	766

This tabulation shows the characteristic fluctuation in farm incomes, the average gross income declining to 38.5 per cent of its 1929 level before it turned upward in 1933.

In these three states the average farm unit of cultivation consisted of 74.9 acres in 1929. Of this, 34.9 acres were in crops other than cotton. Eighty-five per cent of all farms reported cotton, and their average acreage in the crop was 15.7. Thus over 45 per cent of all crop land was given over to cotton. An average of 4.9 bales of cotton was grown per farm, with some 157 pounds of lint, less than a third of a bale of cotton to the acre. Cotton furnished 64.7 per cent of the cash income and 55.2 per cent of the gross income from farm crops. Averages for certain specialized cotton areas within these states show, on the whole, smaller farms, smaller acreage in other crops, higher percentage of acreage in cotton, with larger total values for cotton.

At prices unusual except in war time, the average of approximately five bales per operator could be expected to bring $250 to $400 gross cash income from cotton. Supplementary crops account for around 44 per cent (not more than $175) additional cash income in these three states for 1929. Livestock, except in the case of dairies and specialized farms, help but little to increase cash income, the main source of other revenue being swine and poultry products. Estimates on gross farm incomes from production, gathered by the Bureau of Agricultural Economics for use in index numbers, are not highly accurate and probably exaggerate their size.[6]

Figures of annual gross income per agricultural worker in the period between 1899 and 1927 probably depict the existing conditions more truly than average gross farm incomes. Even these, however, do not tell the whole story, since they include the earnings of laborers who were being paid $1.30 a day in the prosperous days of July 1929[7] along with the incomes of the large plantation owners. But they do demonstrate, clearly enough, the existence of pre-depression poverty in the agricultural areas of the Old Belt.

Careful studies as far back as 1899 show that the returns per farm operator in the Southeast are usually about half those of the rest of the nation. For ten southeastern states, Clarence Heer found gross agricultural incomes to range from 56.2 to 34.3 per cent of those for the rest of the country, depending on the basis of computation and on the year selected. Table 7.3 also shows the marked decline in income between the years immediately after the war (1919) and the period between 1924 and 1927.

Maurice Leven found the net per capita income for the population of the southeastern cotton states in 1929 to rank lowest in the nation[8] for both farm and non-farm incomes. The average for the whole area, as Table 7.4 shows, was $183; for the United States, $273. For the three states of Georgia, Alabama, and South Carolina, this average was only $139 per year.

Samplings of average incomes from the small Negro farms are indicative of even lower levels of economic adjustment. T. J. Woofter, Jr., found that Negro owner families on St. Helena Island averaged $420 a year income; Arthur Raper found the figure to be $339 for a sample group in Greene County, Georgia, and $438 for a similar group in Macon

TABLE 7.3

Annual Gross Agricultural Income per Worker, 1899–1927

Year	Basis of All Workers Employed			Basis of Adult Male Workers		
	Ten Southern States[a]	Rest of the Nation	Southern Percentage	Ten Southern States[a]	Rest of the Nation	Southern Percentage
1899	$189	$471	40.1	$334	$595	56.2
1909	318	925	34.3	648	1214	53.4
1919	1059	2569	41.2	1656	2993	55.3
1924	591	1582	37.4	925	1844	50.1
1927	609	1611	37.8	953	1879	50.7

Source: Clarence Heer, *Wages and Incomes in the South*, Chapel Hill, 1930.
a. Virginia, North Carolina, South Carolina, Georgia, Florida, Tennessee, Alabama, Mississippi, Arkansas, and Louisiana.

County. These figures include cash income and family living from the farm plus all money earned by members of the family working off the farm.

Population Pressure in the Southeast

Not only was the Southeast a region of established poverty before the depression, but its meager standards were also continually being threatened by the excessive pressure of a rapidly increasing population. The Old Cotton Belt is second only to the Appalachians in its high rate of natural increase. In every southeastern state except Florida the excess of births over deaths is greater than the average rate of increase in the nation. Frontier heritages, the absence of industrial pressure and urban patterns, and the low living standards of an agrarian culture dependent on the field labor of women and children go to make up an environment favorable to early marriages and large population increases. The birth-rate has been a response not so much to race and biology as to environment.

The birth-rate in 1929 was more than 20 per 1,000 in every state of the Old Belt. Moreover, the proved tendency toward under-registration of births in rural areas makes it probable that the region's birth-rate is from

TABLE 7.4
Per Capita Personal Incomes, 1929

State	Entire Population	Non-Farm Population	Farm Population
South Carolina	$261	$412	$129
Georgia	343	532	147
Alabama	331	527	141
Mississippi	287	530	173
Arkansas	311	503	185
Louisiana	438	603	186
Southeast[a]	365	533	183
United States	750	908	273

Source: Adapted from Leven, Moulton, and Warburton, *America's Capacity to Consume*, Brookings Institution, Washington, 1934, p. 173.
a. Computed by the Southern Regional Study. Includes 11 states.

10 to 20 per cent above reported figures. In Tennessee and Louisiana,[9] to take the most extreme cases, the registered births of 1929 are estimated to be approximately 74 per cent of actual births. South Carolina, Alabama, Mississippi, and Arkansas all have 50 per cent of their population classified as rural-farm, while only Louisiana, in our group, falls below 40 per cent. With death-rates somewhat above the national average, the Southeast still shows a rate of excess of births over deaths of more than 10 per 1,000 as compared with seven for the nation.

Since most of these states have only recently entered the registration area, the rate of natural increase for the decade 1920–30 cannot be calculated. A valuable index, however, is to be found in the number of children under five years of age per 1,000 women of childbearing age, as recorded in the 1930 census. This picture, presented by counties[10] in Figure 7.1, indicates that the six states of the Cotton Southeast rank below the Appalachians but well above the national average according to this measure of fertility. Although the mountain area contains a solid block of counties with more than 1,000 children per 1,000 women, the six states show only one case in this category, and that lies in the Ozarks outside the true cotton economy. The more significant comparison, how-

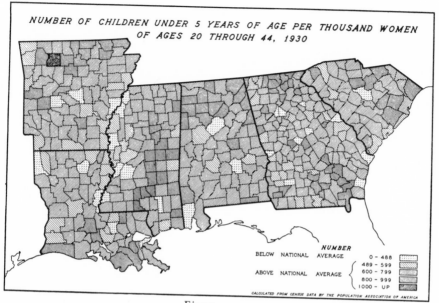

NUMBER OF CHILDREN UNDER 5 YEARS OF AGE PER THOUSAND WOMEN OF AGES 20 THROUGH 44, 1930

Figure 7.1

ever, is with the nation as a whole. Only 27 counties out of a total of 555 in the six cotton states fall below the national average of 488 children per 1,000 women of childbearing age. A number of these exceptions are found in the Delta counties of high Negro population, and this pattern is difficult to explain unless one presumes an undercount of Negro children; but all the other less-than-average counties, as might be expected, are those which contain substantial cities.[11] This measure does not particularly differentiate the specialized cotton areas from their surroundings, but the map does make it clear that the entire rural Southeast, of which they are a part, is a region of unusually high population pressure.

In the period from the beginning of the depression until 1932 the natural rate of increase continued to show gains. Birth-rates fell slightly in three states, Alabama, Mississippi, and Arkansas; remained stationary in Louisiana; and displayed slight gains in South Carolina and Georgia (Table 7.5). The increasing rate of growth during this time is largely due to the paradox of the depression, the falling death-rate.

Thompson and Whelpton have projected existing trends of natural increase to estimate the gain in population by 1960. While their figures are not regarded as realistic by either Thompson and Whelpton or the writer, they are presented to indicate the possible situation that might

TABLE 7.5

Population Gains in the Cotton Southeast since the Depression

State	Births per 1000 Population				Excess of Births over Deaths			
	1929	1930	1931	1932	1929	1930	1931	1932
Virginia	22.4	22.6	21.7	22.4	9.4	10.1	9.3	10.5
North Carolina	24.7	24.1	23.3	24.0	12.9	12.9	13.0	14.4
South Carolina	22.7	23.3	22.7	23.8	9.4	10.4	10.6	12.4
Georgia	20.1	20.9	21.2	21.9	7.9	8.8	9.9	10.9
Alabama	24.0	24.0	23.5	23.5	11.6	12.5	12.8	13.2
Mississippi	22.9	23.9	22.3	22.7	9.9	11.9	11.4	12.7
Tennessee	19.5	20.1	19.8	19.8	7.3	8.7	9.0	9.0
Louisiana	20.3	20.3	20.4	20.3	8.4	8.6	9.3	9.4
Arkansas	20.2	22.1	22.0	20.1	9.7	11.9	12.4	11.4

Source: Vital Statistics, Bureau of the Census.

result in the Southeast. With no internal migration, the whole Cotton Belt would gain about 10.6 million people, and the Southeast from three to nearly eight million, depending on the size of the area chosen. If one assumes, on the other hand, the continuation of rural-urban migration at the rate followed in the pre-depression period of 1920–30, the Southeast would gain little over one million people and the whole area less than two million.[12]

THE BOLL WEEVIL INVASION AND THE MIGRATIONS OF 1910–1930

The conjunction of poverty and population pressure in the Southeast led to internal migration long before the post-war period. It is estimated from state-of-birth data that some five million people must have left the Old South for other areas between 1865 and 1900. A recent crisis, the boll weevil infestation, has intensified the need for population outlets and caused the recent accelerated egress from particular sub-regions, as well as initiated the transition to the newer areas of the Southwest.

The Cycle of Infestation and Recovery

In the Old Cotton Belt a period of industrial prosperity resulting from the war activities of 1917–18 was continued into a period of agricultural

TABLE 7.6
Estimated Increase in Population of Southern States by 1960

Area	Assuming No Rural-Urban Migration	Assuming Rural-Urban Migration in Ratio of 1920–1930
Total Cotton Belt[a]	10,618,000	1,890,000
Southeast[b]	7,820,000	1,135,000
Cotton states of the Southeast[c]	5,393,000	1,070,000
S.C., Ga., Ala.	3,060,000	625,000

a. N.C., S.C., Tenn., Ga., Ala., Miss., La., Ark., Tex., and Okla.
b. Except Tex. and Okla.
c. S.C., Ga., Ala., Miss., Ark., La.

distress coincident with the boll weevil infestation and the deflation of farm prices. The years immediately after 1914 with its record crop saw acreage reduced and then prices increased in response to the opening guns of the war. Acreage expansion lagged behind rising prices. It was not until 1923 that cotton acreage passed the 1914 level, and it was not until 1926 that production forged ahead of that year. Unfortunately for the Old Cotton Belt, the impact of the boll weevil invasion was here deferred until the post-war period of deflation.[13] Thus the years of greatest insect damage, 1921 through 1923, coincided with the years of low prices, 1920 through 1922. From a high of 16 million bales in 1914, production fell to less than eight million bales in 1921. Moreover, this crop brought only 640 million dollars, the lowest total farm value since the economic shock resulting from the outbreak of the World War.

The boll weevil swarms crossed the Rio Grande at Brownsville, Texas, in 1892, and in successive waves advanced over the sub-regions of the Southeast. For several years the enemy claimed higher and higher tolls until, in some areas, cotton yields fell to less than 10 per cent of former levels. The decline in yields of lint from pre-weevil to post-weevil period has been estimated by Joseph A. Becker to range from 24 per cent for Arkansas to 47 per cent for Louisiana. Alabama showed a decrease of 31 per cent, South Carolina fell 35 per cent, and Georgia 43 per cent.[14]

Drastic cuts in cotton acreage usually lagged four or five years behind the drastic losses in cotton yields. In Louisiana the greatest loss in cotton acreage came five years after the first weevil infestation; in Mississippi and Arkansas, four years. Alabama's cotton acreage fell from 3,730,000 in 1912 to 1,977,000 in 1917.

The process of infestation and partial recovery tended to follow a clearly discernible cycle. The Georgia Piedmont, which furnishes an example of almost complete breakdown in the regional economy, may be analyzed in some detail for a record of the first stages of the cycle. From 1920 to 1925 Georgia lost 61,600 farms, 19.8 per cent of all farms in the state. The 70 counties composing the Black Belt lost 27.2 per cent of their farms. Further, the counties of greatest loss are all within an area enclosed by lines drawn to join Augusta, Athens, Atlanta, and Dublin. This region lies within the Old Plantation Piedmont, a tier of counties three and four deep lying just above the fall line. Although much of its land was near the margin of cultivation, the area had fared well with the cotton prices prevalent from 1917 to 1919, and had expanded acreage at a more rapid rate than the South as a whole. The area had but few cattle; pastures were not good; and erosion was taking its toll of the red clay hills. With few working owners, comparatively little wage labor, and a high proportion of tenants (one-half of whom owned no workstock), the region needed but the shock of weevil invasion to place it in the poorest competitive position of any area in the Old Belt.[15] Absentee landowners had turned much of the function of supervision over to the "time merchant" who provided living supplies to tenants at high credit prices. Such landlords, disinclined to check up on crops produced and the care of workstock, exacted a standing rent of an agreed number of bales of cotton, and encouraged the tenants to own their mules even if mortgages left them but a bare equity in the animals.

The weevil invasion, it is evident, fell heaviest on this type of farming. With crop failure, the tenants lost their mules to the banks, while owners, deprived of their rents, were unable to secure work animals even on credit. While the workstock declined, the croppers increased in number. Had the workstock of those owning no land been evenly divided among the landowners who had no horses or mules, there would have been 40 acres per animal in 1920 and 141 acres per animal in 1926. What happened, as a result, was that planters without workstock saw their acres go untilled, while tenants lacking animals were compelled to leave farming. The ruin of the banks completed the cycle.

These conditions were largely repreated in South Carolina and other areas. Because of the crop failure and price collapse, owners lost their lands and higher-level tenants lost their chattels. The latter's chances of employment then depended on the credit situation. At this juncture the failing banks, bankrupt landlords, and supply merchants were powerless to check the general economic disorganization. The lowest level of tenants were forced to migrate. Many white farmers found employment comparatively near home in the booming cotton mill villages of the Piedmont; but Negro tenants, pouring out of the Piedmont, Coastal Plains, and Black Belt areas of Alabama, Georgia, and South Carolina, were virtual refugees, seeking whatever haven they might find with kin and acquaintance who had gone to southern and northern cities.

After several years the farmers who remained learned the method of insect control best suited to their region; cotton yields picked up; acreage was brought back into cultivation; tenants migrated back into the region; and with the reestablishment of banks and the installation of federal production credit agencies the areas made a partial recovery. Recovery has been completed in the areas first infected, such as southern and eastern Texas and the Delta areas of Louisiana, Arkansas, and Mississippi. Alabama, Georgia, and South Carolina, however, in the period between 1920 and 1922 experienced the greatest disaster possible in the economy —the coincidence of low yields with the low prices of the post-war deflation. The extent of the loss can be realized only if it is recalled that these small crops were planted on large acreage at the high cost of production resulting from war conditions.

The initial breakdown and the lag in recovery for the areas of the Old Cotton Belt seemed to be due primarily to institutional factors rather than physical resources. This is to be seen in one of the paradoxes of the period. In these areas much of the good land is held in blocks of tenant farms by large owners who are heavily mortgaged. Other land is held by small owners who use family labor, and whose farms are often so poor that no agency will lend money on them. In the breakdown of credit facilities good farms, it has been found by Arthur Raper[16] and others, were abandoned by migrating tenants while submarginal lands remained in cultivation largely because their owners had stayed outside the credit system and had nowhere else to go.

The one area in which physical factors appear to have retarded recovery is the Alabama Black Belt. It has puzzled geographers that the Alabama Prairie had its cotton culture almost completely demoralized while the Texas Black Land, of the same general soil type, recovered from the infestation. The blame has often been thrown on the Negro tenants of the Alabama area, but in view of the rapid recovery of Delta areas with the densest Negro population in America, the charge seems unjustified. The most plausible solution of this puzzle that has been offered is found in an unpublished study by a native of the region.[17] He points out that the weevil thrives in rainy periods and suffers from intense heat. The best practice, then, is to force cultivation ahead of the weevil so that the bolls may get their growth before insects can puncture them for egg-laying purposes. Arnold demonstrates that, contrary to the geography of the Texas area, the two annual maxima of rainfall in the Alabama region occur during the planting and growing seasons. The black soils characteristic of limestone areas hold water like a sponge, and since the sun's heat must first evaporate the excessive rainfall the crop suffers from late start and slow growth.

For most of the area, however, the question was not so much recovery from the weevil infestation itself as from the economic and institutional disorganization left in its wake. Before many of the devastated areas could either recover or make the transition to family-sized farms capable of producing on different bases, they were met by the emerging competition of the Southwest.

The tremendous expansion in the Southwest waited until after the war for several reasons. Throughout the war period the price of livestock, the mainstay of the southwestern plains, remained high, thus placing the grass area under no temptation to resort to competing crops. By 1921 the farm price of beef cattle per hundred pounds had fallen from the 1917 level of $9.61 to $5.44, and the delivery price at Chicago from $15.15 to $8.20. After 1922 the Southeast, caught in the throes of weevil infestation, was unable to expand cotton production even in the face of rising prices. This situation gave the Southwest's grazing areas their opportunity. Between 1919 and 1924 a million new crop acres were plowed out of the Texas Staked Plains area alone. And when once put under the plow, such lands are rarely abandoned by cultivated crops, since they do not become reset in native grasses for many years.

Delimitation of Problem Areas

The history of the weevil devastation and the concomitant contraction and expansion in various cotton areas may be summarized in terms of farm losses and gains between 1910 and 1930.[18] Further, this analysis enables us to narrow our choice of problem areas and to estimate the migration of the period. Since each farm in the census represents a unit of tillage, the change in number of farms in any area corresponds to the minimum gains or losses of farm population. If the farm figure is multiplied by the average size of farm family, an approximation of the movements of farm population, except for the unestimated number of farm laborers, is obtained.

As Table 7.7 indicates, Kentucky, Virginia, and Florida are not "cotton" states. Within the ten remaining states the selection of homogeneous physical areas in which 25 per cent or more of the crop land is given over to cotton furnishes us 29 sub-regions which are outlined in Figure 7.2. These areas are delimited on the basis of common physiography, climate, and plant life. In the main, the various types of soil in each region are

TABLE 7.7
Ratio of Cotton Farms to All Farms in Southern States, 1930

State[a]	Total Number of Farms	Per Cent Classified as Cotton Farms
Mississippi	312,663	82.9
Alabama	275,395	80.4
Texas	495,489	70.5
South Carolina	157,931	70.0
Louisiana	161,446	69.6
Arkansas	252,334	69.2
Georgia	255,598	67.4
Oklahoma	203,866	42.3
North Carolina	279,708	27.6
Tennessee	245,657	27.3
Florida	58,916	9.5
Virginia	170,610	2.0
Kentucky	246,499	0.2

a. The devotion to cotton has been measured in the Type of Farming returns by the proportion of farms which draw 40 per cent or more of their total income from cotton.

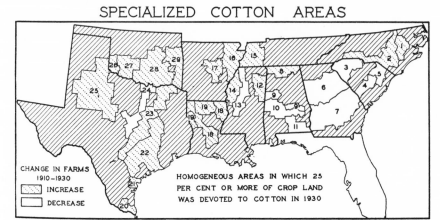

Figure 7.2

also fairly closely related as may be seen by reference to H. H. Bennett's map (Figure 7.3).[19] The change in number of farms within these various areas enables us to segregate the expanding and contracting areas of cotton production, and in addition affords an illuminating contrast between specialized and non-specialized areas of cotton production.

Figure 7.2 and the accompanying Table 7.8 show that the 29 specialized areas have a greater ratio of total changes (gains and losses combined) than the other regions of their states, 19.1 to 6.6 per cent; a greater ratio of gains in new farms in areas of net increases, 23.1 to 8.7 per cent; and a greater rate of loss in areas of net loss, − 12.3 to − 3.9 per cent. The actual and percentage changes show this was true for every state except South Carolina. Here the absolute destruction of the Sea Island cotton industry occasioned a great loss of farms and took the coastal area out of cotton production entirely. For the whole Belt the greatest losses are shown to have occurred in the Piedmont and Coastal Plains area of South Carolina, Georgia, and Alabama (Figure 7.4, Map A). Outside these states the only regions to show losses were the Mississippi Loessal Bluff and the Texas Fort Worth Prairie. In Alabama the losses from the Black Belt were somewhat compensated for by gains in number of farms in the Limestone Valley and uplands, the only cotton areas to gain in those three states of the Deep South. The greatest gains in percentage of farms are shown in Louisiana, Arkansas, and Mississippi. This, it must be remembered, is a gain in numbers; in acreage, the Southwest showed the greatest gains.[20]

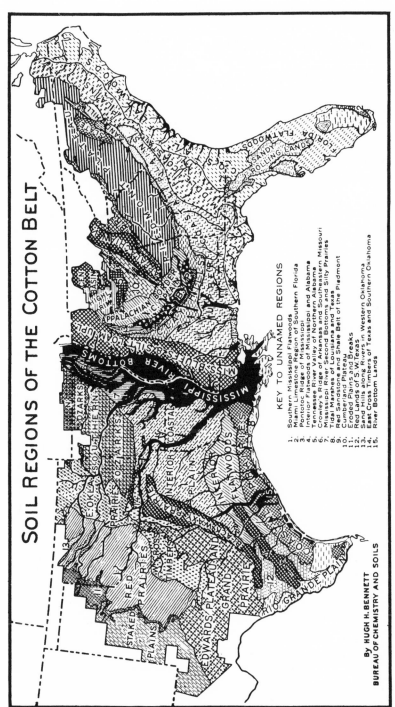

SOIL REGIONS OF THE COTTON BELT

KEY TO UNNAMED REGIONS

1. Southern Mississippi Flatwoods
2. Miami Limestone Region of Southern Florida
3. Pontotoc Ridge of Mississippi
4. Interior Flatwoods of Mississippi and Alabama
5. Tennessee River Valley of Northern Alabama
6. Crowley's Ridge of Arkansas and Southeastern Missouri
7. Mississippi River Second Bottoms and Silty Prairies
8. Tidal Marshes of Louisiana and Texas
9. Red Sandstone and Shale Belt of the Piedmont
10. Cumberland Plateau
11. Eroded Plains and Breaks
12. Red Lands of S. Texas
13. Sand Hills along Rivers in Western Oklahoma
14. East Cross Timbers of Texas and Southern Oklahoma
15. River Bottom Lands

By HUGH H. BENNETT
BUREAU OF CHEMISTRY AND SOILS

Figure 7.3

Figures on cotton production, as Table 7.9 indicates, also show that the regional shift to the Delta and the Southwest was associated with the boll weevil invasion and the price debacle of 1920–26. The four areas centered about the Mississippi, the Delta areas of Louisiana, Arkansas, and Mississippi, show real expansion—gains due to their rapid recovery from the weevil and the opening of new alluvial areas under federal flood control. Furthermore, these areas are not erosive, as are the neighboring Silt Loam Bluffs and the Piedmont. The latter was hardest hit, with a decrease of 50 per cent in size of crop between 1919–22 and 1923–26.

For the entire area east of the Mississippi the percentage of the total crop grown declined from 54.2 to 40.5 per cent from 1909–12 to 1923–26. In the years 1927–30 the Piedmont managed to regain some of its

TABLE 7.8

Total and Net Changes in Specialized and Nonspecialized Cotton Areas, Ten Cotton States, 1910–1930

	Changes in Number of Farms			Per Cent Changes		
State	Total State Areas	Specialized Areas[a]	Non-Specialized Areas	State	Specialized Areas	Non-Specialized Areas
North Carolina	25,983	20,878	5,105	10.2	21.6	3.2
South Carolina	− 18,503	− 7,381	− 11,122	− 10.5	− 6.4	− 18.4
Georgia	− 35,429	− 34,154	− 1,275	− 12.2	− 14.6	− 2.2
Alabama	− 5,506	− 5,222	− 284	− 2.1	− 3.8[b]	− 0.2[b]
Mississippi	38,281	30,055	8,226	13.9	21.1	6.2
Tennessee	− 355	2,566	− 2,921	− 0.1	3.7	− 1.7
Arkansas	27,656	27,183	473	12.9	36.2	0.3
Louisiana	40,899	31,787	9,112	33.9	40.9	21.3
Texas	77,719	43,660	34,059	18.6	18.7	18.5
Oklahoma	13,674	17,363	− 3,689	7.2	15.4	− 4.8
Total changes in number of farms in all areas (gains and losses combined	284,005	247,277[c]	76,266	11.6	19.1[c]	6.6
Net gains of new farms in areas of gain	224,212	187,006[c]	56,975	15.2	23.1[c]	8.7
Net losses of farms in areas of loss	− 59,793	− 60,271[c]	− 19,291	− 6.1	− 12.3[c]	− 3.9
Net gains of new farms in all areas	164,419	126,735	37,684	6.7	9.8	3.3

a. The specialized areas are the same used in the *Economic Status of American Cotton Producers*, Report of Farm Mortgage Conference.
b. If the expanding Limestone Valley (8) is transferred to non-specialized areas, the figures will be − 11.2 and 4.3 per cent changes.
c. *Gross* totals of the 29 specialized areas; if combined into *state* totals the figures would be as follows: total change, 220,249; net gains in areas of gain, 173,492; net losses in areas of loss, − 46,756. The percentage of change would be 17.0, 21.4 and − 9.6 respectively.

loss, but the Coastal Plains continued to decline. It is obvious then that the contracting areas of Georgia, South Carolina, and Alabama are the core of our problem zone. Not only does this section display the highest proportion of eroded soil, the densest pattern of tenancy, and the lowest standards of living, but it suffered the greatest weevil damage and has been the slowest region in recovering.

The delimitation of problem areas as associated with the land tenure system and migration is presented in the series of maps in Figures 7.4 and 7.5. While all farms in the areas considered increased 9.8 per cent, the

TABLE 7.9

Shift in Cotton Production by Regions, 1909–1930

Region	Percentage of United States Cotton Crop Produced in Period:			
	1909–1912	1919–1922	1923–1926	1927–1930
East of Mississippi[a]	54.2	47.0	40.5	43.7
West of Mississippi[b]	45.1	51.4	57.1	52.7
Total	99.3	98.4	97.6	96.4
SUBREGIONS:				
East				
Georgia and South Carolina Piedmont (3, 6)		9.6	4.8	6.6
Southeastern Coastal Plains (4, 5, 7, 9, 11)		9.2	7.8	7.6
Atlantic Coastal		18.8	12.6	14.2
Mississippi Delta[c] (14, 16, 17)		10.6	11.8	12.4
Total East		29.4	24.4	26.6
West				
Texas Black Prairie (23)		10.6	8.9	8.6
West Texas and Oklahoma (25, 26, 27)		7.5	10.7	9.7
Total West		18.1	19.6	18.3
TOTAL SUBREGIONS		47.5	44.0	44.9

Source: *Economic Status of American Cotton Producers*. Reprinted by permission.
a. Six states: N.C., S.C., Ga., Ala., Miss., Tenn.
b. Five states: Mo., Ark., La., Tex., Okla.
c. Includes Missouri area not shown on map.

PER CENT CHANGE IN FARMS 1910-1930

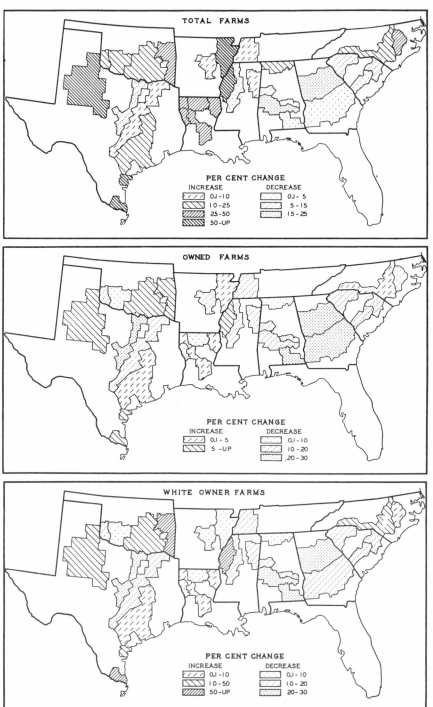

Figure 7.4

PER CENT CHANGE IN TENANT FARMS 1910–1930

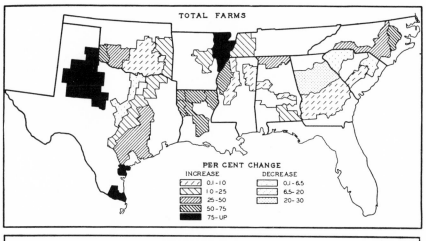

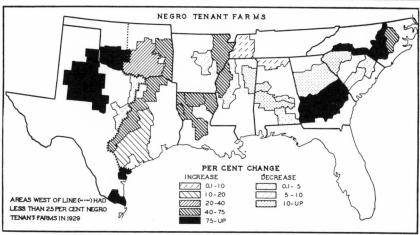

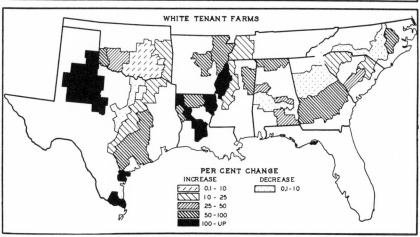

Figure 7.5

number of farms owned by the operators decreased 7.4 per cent. Only two areas east of the Mississippi showed a gain in owned farms: North Carolina Upper Coastal Plain and Piedmont (2), and the Mississippi Delta (14). Negro owners, who make up 4.8 per cent of total operators in all 29 areas, show slight gains in only four areas east of the Mississippi: (1), (9), (10), and (12). White owners form 24 per cent of all farm operators. The third map in Figure 7.4 shows high percentage loss of farms in this class in all areas except North Carolina, Mississippi Delta, and the Southwest. Here newly cleared land has contributed to increases.

It is evident that expansion in these specialized zones has been due to increases in tenant farms. This classification makes up 71.1 per cent of all farms in the areas and increased 18.8 per cent from 1910 to 1930. Decreases were shown in total tenant farms in only one area west of Alabama (24). Total tenants decreased in four eastern cotton areas: (3), (5), (6), and (10). Negro tenant farms account for 33.7 per cent of all farms in all areas, running as high as 60 to 80 per cent in special Deltas and Black Belts. Negro croppers comprise 19.6 per cent of all operators in these areas. Decreases in their number running from 3 to over 40 per cent indicate the major areas of distress and enforced migration: (4), (5), (6), (9), (10), (11), and (12). The Negro tenant has taken some part in the expansion of the Delta areas but has been largely left behind in the advance on the new southwestern areas. Here mechanized cultivation and Mexican casuals to the south have operated to exclude the typical cropper system. White tenants now make up 37.4 per cent of all operators in the areas, and white croppers furnish 14.1 per cent.

Most illuminating of all is the map of increasing white tenancy. Only *four* areas of decrease appeared before 1930: (2), (4), (10), and (24). These indicate emigration of tenants rather than the climb to ownership. The Cotton Kingdom has, in the main, moved deltaward and westward by the increase of white-tenant farms; often, it appears, by the infiltration of white tenants in the place of Negro tenants.

тHE CHANGING ECONOMY OF THE COTTON BELT

In its second major crisis, the Cotton Belt now faces failing markets with an accumulating cotton surplus that apparently challenges control. If the loss of world markets is to be visited in full force upon the Cotton Belt, the second crisis is capable of displacing even more population from the land. The immediate factors of change in the regional housekeeping of the Cotton Belt are: (1) the large increase in number of farms and the return of over a million people to the Cotton Belt, (2) the emergence of the Southwest as an area of low production costs, (3) the effect of the Agricultural Adjustment Act in its program to curtail the cotton surplus, and (4) the trends in the export cotton market. With the exception of southwestern competition they are all depression phenomena. In a field where much is controversy and prediction, evaluation of each of these will be held as closely as possible to the probable effect on the redistribution of population.

The Effect of the Depression on Agriculture

Changes in number of farms from 1930 to 1935 show in a gross way the effect of the depression on agriculture. There has been a large increase in the number of farms, amounting to 167,620 for the whole belt of twelve states. This increase is localized in the poorest mountain areas or on the sandy flats. The following map (Figure 7.6) indicates that the areas regarded as most hopeful in 1930 show losses, while those outside the main cotton areas tend to show gains. This reverses the trend of previous years for almost every state except Georgia, which continued to lose, and North Carolina, which continued to gain. The figures on rural-urban migration gathered by the Division of Rural Life and Population indicate that approximately a million and a quarter people have returned to the Cotton Belt since 1929. A comparison of Figure 7.6, showing increase,

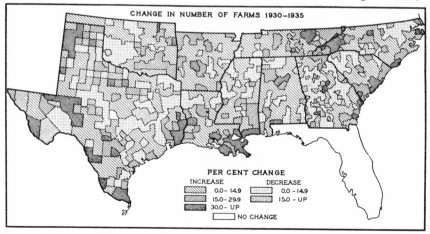

Figure 7.6

with Figure 7.3 shows that the increases are centered in the hilly and poor soil areas where high birth-rates are prevalent. The return of southern migrants working in northern industries has largely been to these sections.

The loss of farms is practically all accounted for by the decrease in cotton acreage. It will be noted that these areas coincide with regions in which cropper labor is most prevalent. When croppers are displaced or transferred to day labor, the tracts they once cultivated drop off the census list. In the new areas of the Southwest the increase in farms is much smaller than expected, due to drought.

Southwest versus Southeast

It has been suggested that in its attempted recovery from the economic and institutional paralysis left in the wake of the weevil, the Old Cotton Belt encountered stiff competition from the Southwest. Nevertheless, it must be emphasized that the latter area possesses agricultural drawbacks almost as great as those of the Southeast. Crop reporters of the Department of Agriculture found an 18 per cent crop loss from various natural hazards for the period between 1925 and 1930 (Table 7.10). Unfavorable weather conditions account for 22 per cent of the crop reductions, insects

TABLE 7.10
Reduction in Cotton Yields by Natural Hazards for the Cotton States, 1925–1930

| | Per Cent Reduction due to: | | | | | | |
States	Deficient Moisture	Excessive Moisture	Other Climatic	Plant Diseases	Boll Weevil	Other Insects	Total
Virginia	16.3	3.5	3.3	0.8	3.2	0.2	27.3
North Carolina	7.5	4.8	2.7	1.5	12.8	1.8	31.1
South Carolina	11.8	5.2	5.8	1.9	14.8	2.2	41.1
Georgia	10.7	4.8	4.0	1.5	11.0	2.0	34.8
Florida	5.3	4.0	5.9	1.2	9.3	6.3	31.4
Missouri	10.3	14.2	7.5	0.7	0.5	3.2	36.4
Tennessee	12.0	6.9	3.8	2.0	1.7	2.2	29.0
Alabama	8.0	4.5	3.3	2.5	8.8	1.7	28.8
Mississippi	8.3	4.5	2.8	1.5	9.7	2.2	29.0
Louisiana	10.0	5.2	5.3	1.5	11.5	2.2	35.7
Texas	17.2	3.5	4.2	2.9	10.3	6.2	43.7
Oklahoma	13.0	3.7	5.8	0.3	12.5	4.3	40.6
Arkansas	16.5	5.2	5.5	1.0	6.5	3.0	37.7
Weighted average	13.2	4.5	4.3	1.7	10.4	3.9	38.0

Source: *Economic Status of American Cotton Producers*, from records of the U.S. Department of Agriculture.

for 14.3 per cent, and the weevil for 10.4 per cent. After the Carolinas, Texas and Oklahoma experienced the highest weevil damage. Texas also suffered most severely from drought. In this five-year period the western region failed to show the advantages attributed to it. The three states with the greatest loss of crops from natural hazards—Texas, Oklahoma and Arkansas—are all in the Southwest.

Yet it cannot be denied that the area possesses notable advantages. Level lands, less tenancy, more mechanization, larger farms, greater natural fertility—all make for lower costs of production. Table 7.11 indicates very roughly that in the depression period the costs of producing cotton in the Southwest were, in terms of cash outlay per pound, only 49.0 per cent of Piedmont costs, and for net costs per pound of lint, 69.6 per cent.[21] The table is of value also in showing the low level (ten cents per hour) to which wages fell in the depression. Even at that low level, the total cost of production in the Piedmont was 12.2 cents per pound. West Texas shows costs of 8.5 cents per pound. If cotton were to sell at its cost of production in the Piedmont, the farmer in that region could expect a labor income of only 6.3 cents per pound, while the one in West Texas could expect 9.3 cents. The differentials in production costs between the two regions are in part due to the use of fertilizer in the Southeast. The consequent higher yield per acre, even in the disastrous year of 1924, minimizes to a certain extent the significance of this differential.

The question remains whether the Old Cotton Belt can compete with the Southwest. There are two main schools of thought concerning the future of Atlantic coastal areas. The more optimistic view holds that the physical advantages of the region have suffered little permanent diminution. The main task, accordingly, is recovery from the institutional and economic shocks of the weevil invasion. Another and perhaps more realistic view holds that with the emergence of the Southwest, the coastal region lost whatever comparative advantages it may have possessed in cotton production. The evidence now available, however, can permit no sound definitive conclusions.

Among the unpredictable factors in costs of production must be listed the much-discussed Rust cotton picker. If this or a similar machine should prove successful, it will lead to much lower cotton prices, larger farm units, and a tremendous exodus of tenants and laborers from the farms. The number of farmers who can secure a cash income from cotton will be greatly reduced. Moreover, the remaining producers will be centered largely in the level areas of the Southwest. Nevertheless, there is some possibility that small owners in the Southeast will continue to grow some

TABLE 7.11

Estimated Cost of Producing Cotton in Western Texas and Piedmont Section of Atlantic Coastal States

In Terms of Cost	Western Texas		Piedmont Southeast	
	Hours per Acre	Cost per Acre	Hours per Acre	Cost per Acre
Man labor before harvest	16.4	$2.05	60.4	$6.04
Horse labor prior to harvest	25.7	2.05	42.7	3.41
Man labor, harvest [a]	20.0	2.00	40.0	2.10
Marketing		.90		.52
Ginning		1.23		1.88
Fertilizer				7.00
Machines and equipment		.81		1.00
Taxes		.60		1.00
Miscellaneous		1.00		1.00
Interest on land and equipment		3.33		2.40
Total gross cost		13.97		26.35
Credit cotton seed		1.20		2.00
		12.77		24.35
Total net cost per pound lint [b]		.085		.122
Net crop outlay per pound lint		.029		.059

Source: *Economic Status of American Cotton Producers*, Confidential Report of the Farm Mortgage Conference. Data secured from correspondence with the Division of Farm Management and Costs, U.S. Department of Agriculture.
a. 400 pounds seed cotton at $.50 per 100 in Texas, 600 pounds at $.35 per 100 in the Piedmont.
b. Estimated yields: West Texas, 150 pounds lint per acre; Piedmont, 200 pounds per acre.

cotton by the use of unpaid family labor. Accordingly, the migrants will in the main be the tenants of the Southeast. Only to the few who can command sufficient capital to purchase or lease lands and operate large farms will accrue the benefits of the machine. In the event of mechanization, the need for diversification or for large-scale migration in the Southeast will be dramatic and insistent.

The Effect of Acreage Reduction

Before adjustments to competition of the Southwest could be worked out, the AAA was instituted and the acreage of southeastern farms was stabilized on an extremely low basis. In the hearings on the Bankhead Bill, Secretary Wallace stated that regulation on this basis, unless temporary, would impede the Southeast's attempted recovery. Whatever virtues the change from unrestricted production to government regulation of acreage and production possesses, the new system thrusts again into the limelight the problem of population redistribution.

The onset of the world depression saw the carry-over of American cotton mount to 13 million bales. In 1929 cotton sold for 18 cents a pound, but at its new low in June 1932 the farm price of cotton stood at 4.6 cents per pound. From 1928–29 to 1932–33 the gross farm income from cotton and cotton seed fell from $1,470,000,000 to $431,000,000, with the result that the average gross income per farm family engaged in cotton growing fell from $735 to $216. Distress and misery prevailed in every section of the Belt. Owners were threatened with loss of farms, and tenants were forced below levels of subsistence. These facts deserve to be stressed, for they are forgotten by many who criticize the measures of control that were to follow.

There is no need to recount in detail the application of AAA to cotton production. Its method of reducing the surplus by reducing production unfortunately tended also to reduce the demand for labor, already sharply curtailed by the depression. In an area of small farm owners this expedient would doubtless have served, since each farmer's reduced employment would be compensated for by rental and parity payments. In a tenancy region, however, while such a program affords larger returns to those continuing in production, it places an effective bar against increasing the number of people who can be adequately supported on the land.

This is all the more important in the South because in the first years of depression many cotton producers failed and many laborers and tenants were turned loose to shift for themselves. The freezing of cotton acreage under the quota system prevented the reentry of these displaced tenants into agriculture. Furthermore a vigorous controversy still rages as to whether the initiation of control measures did not occasion a second although smaller wave of displacement. The plow-up campaign was begun in the midst of the 1933 season and, it appears, reduced employment that year mainly for farm laborers, for whose protection no provision was made in the contract offered cotton growers. As the consequences of the 40 per cent reduction in acreage, with the corresponding reduction in bales under the Bankhead Act, became clear, provisions against net displacement of tenants were written into the 1934 contracts. Due to their wording and the difficulty of checking up from Washington, these contracts, it is held, were almost impossible to enforce.[22] Regardless of the time of displacement, it is clear that much of the rural relief load in the South has come from tenants and laborers who found their return to cotton production blocked by the control measures of AAA.[23] In December 1934, for example, there were estimated to be 118,000 families of "recent farming experience" on Texas relief rolls.[24] Nor can it be assumed that tenants displaced from farms, or all those who had left of their own accord and could not secure another farm because of the reduction program, were immediately placed on relief.[25]

Not only mounting relief rolls but also unaccustomed violence and the organization of sharecroppers' unions in plantation areas where gross farm incomes were more than doubled between 1932 and 1934, would indicate that the large benefits received by planters did not serve to lighten the general economic situation.[26] In addition, a definite shift from tenancy to farm labor has appeared in many of the plantation areas.

Moreover, the system of assigned quotas made no provision for farm youths growing to maturity who might normally expect to become tenants or small farmers. With the gates of industry closed against them, they can secure land to cultivate but no crop quota under the Bankhead and Kerr bills. From 11 to 12 per cent of the population in the six cotton states of the Southeast were 15 to 19 years of age in 1930. On the farms of the area approximately 70,000 males reach the age of 21 each year. Many of these would normally expect to secure positions as farm laborers, croppers, and tenants. The dilemma has been well stated by T. J. Woofter, Jr.:

> In the South, therefore, we have the strange spectacle of one government agency, the AAA, blocking the entry of displaced tenants and young adults to commercial agriculture and another agency, the Rural Rehabilitation Corporation, trying to replace them in subsistence agriculture. If, however, they are held to a subsistence economy, it would mean that a great segment of the farm population would be forced to a lower standard of living.[27]

Loss of World Trade

Possibly the most important single factor bearing upon the ability of the South to support its population is the changing situation in the export market. With the American price pegged at 12 cents by government loans and subsidies, export merchants cannot meet foreign competition, and the United States is placed in the position of holding the economic umbrella over the rest of the cotton producing world.

Over 50 per cent of American cotton has been regularly sold abroad, and, while the situation is still uncertain, it is doubtful whether this ratio can be maintained. For corresponding periods, August 1 to April 5, American cotton exports fell from 6,166,000 bales in 1932–33 to 3,637,000 bales in 1934–35. The United States has become a creditor nation in a world of unstable currencies and constricting tariffs. Instead of lowering tariffs in order to facilitate the sale of agricultural products abroad, the nation's present policies seem inclined to apply economic nationalism to agriculture as well as to industry. Barter agreements have so far proved abortive. Without sharing our crop reductions, foreign areas nevertheless participate in the rising demands and prices. Thus, for the first time since the Civil War, cotton production of foreign countries in 1933–34 exceeded that of the United States, 13,053,000 to 13,047,000 bales. In 1934–35 this margin was made real by a ratio of 12,896,000 to 9,731,000 bales.

Efforts to raise the cotton grower's standard of living are double-edged. By reducing the supply of products grown, these measures of control operate to keep out of production numbers of tenants and laborers at the same time that they raise prices for the operators who remain in production. Meanwhile, the cotton grower is threatened with the loss of his export market. Many students feel that in view of the uniformly low returns accruing to the great mass of cotton growers, the foreign market is hardly worth keeping if it must be retained by means of six-cent cotton.[28] There is much to support the view that this would mean either the bankr··· ·tcy of producers or the perpetuation of cheap labor for the sake of placing a cheap textile material in the channels of world trade. If the foreign market is to be lost, it must be released with the knowledge that it means the shift of more than 50 per cent of the Cotton Belt's agricultural population from their accustomed method of earning a living. Such a transition cannot be made overnight. It demands the best thought and energies that can be applied to an immense problem of regional reconstruction and redistribution of population. If under-taken, it should be with a full realization of the expenditure of time and money required, not as an unexpected by-product of the price-raising activities of the AAA.

There remains the possibility of subsidized cotton exports, suggested in a recent discussion of amendments to the AAA. Such a policy would involve an additional burden to the consumer, already paying for pro-cessing taxes. Moreover, subsidizing exports means economic dumping of the sort most likely to provoke retaliation. While the export subsidy is of doubtful value, it may nevertheless be visualized as a possible means of easing the situation in case of the sudden and complete loss of the world cotton market.

PROBABLE MIGRATION FROM THE OLD COTTON BELT

Although the farming population of the Old Cotton Belt has, in the recent past, participated in three large-scale migrations—to the cotton areas of the Southwest, to the growing mill towns of the Piedmont, and to the northern centers of industry—the region as a whole has retained much of its surplus population. The result has been subdivision of farms, higher tenancy rates, a gradually mounting cotton surplus, and a falling level of farm income dramatized by recurrent price failures. In the face of a changing agriculture, whether the point of emphasis be mechanical cotton picking, restricted acreage, or narrowed markets, it is this area which possesses the poorest equipment for survival, which will be able to support fewer and fewer people. Undoubtedly, therefore, industrial revival will see the resumption of internal migration.

Estimates of the magnitude of future migration, however, can be only tentative. In no sense can the discussion be as realistic as the study of the recent past in the Cotton Belt. If we had to deal with a clear-cut problem such as the failure of physical resources, we could compute data similar to those already presented. Instead, we are concerned with trends in changing markets and evolving agricultural processes which no one can predict, even as to the immediate future.

The attempt must be made, nevertheless, to estimate the upper and lower limits of probable migration. With unchanging objective condi-tions, one figure might represent the movement forced by agricultural displacement and might be termed necessary; while the other estimate might be recommended as desirable, in order to mitigate rural poverty and raise the standard of the southeastern population to nearer the national norm. With an uncertain future, the highest and lowest figures must be based mainly on the alternatives facing the Old Cotton Belt. The gravest calamity that might befall the region would be the loss of the world market;[29] at present, the happiest fate would seem to be the return of pre-depression conditions. Necessity and desirability enter both sets of computations, which must be regarded as a methodological assumption between whose limits the amount of migration will vary as conditions vary.[30]

In estimating a minimum figure of probable migration, the author has considered the smallest number called for in the event of the reestablishment of pre-depression conditions, as well as the minimum desirable for purposes of equalizing economic differentials between sections. Accordingly, a dual set of computations is given. Much of this minimum migration will represent the movement of rural youth, in O. E. Baker's phrase, "backed up" on the farm during the depression for lack of economic opportunity. Approximately two million rural youths in these six states will have attained the age of 21 between 1930 and 1940. It will be generous enough to estimate that with recovery, one-half of them will find employment on the farms, in the villages, and in the industrial centers of the area. In addition, it has been estimated that a million and a quarter have returned to the Southeast since the beginning of the depression. It has been shown elsewhere that they have returned largely to the worst areas. Accordingly, one-half to two-thirds of this group (depending on its age composition) will be included in any future migration.

If our estimate of minimum migration is to take into account any attempt to relieve rural poverty, it must be put at 2.5 million. This figure is based on the number of tenant cotton farms in the whole South, 1,120,000,[31] and on the assumption that one-half of the tenants are below decent living standards. Thus we have two appraisals of the lower limit of probable migration, according to which between 1.5 and 2.5 million people would have to leave the area in the ten years following recovery. The difference between the two allows for the absorption of rural migrants by an accelerated urban and industrial trend.

At the opposite extreme, the maximum migration would be required in case of loss of the world cotton market or in case of the mechanization of cotton picking. For the former contingency, a very simple device makes possible an estimate of necessary migration. There are slightly over 1.6

million cotton farms in the whole South. The loss of world cotton markets, it is safe to assume, would take at least half of these out of production.[32] These farms are returned by the census as units of tillage, not of
ownership. Accordingly, to multiply half of these farms by the average
size of the farm family (slightly over 4.5) will give us an estimated primary displacement of 3.6 million farm population, excluding hired farm
labor. It is notable that when the farm population is divided by the
number of farms, the average population per farm is 5.6. Whether the
excess represents mainly family dependents or hired laborers, another
800,000 persons must be added to primary migration. Thus, 4.4 million
people would be removed from agriculture. The amount of secondary
migration, although difficult to estimate, would also be large. If, as is
reasonable to believe, the failures are localized in vulnerable southeastern
areas, the secondary migration would include much of the population of
those towns and smaller cities which function as trade and service centers
for hinterlands of cotton production. Since the decadence of these centers
will react in turn on the metropolitan communities, no one can foresee
just where the line of ruin and forced migration may be drawn. Certainly
six to seven millions of primary and secondary migration is not too much
to anticipate.

But if six million of these migrants were to come from the six southeastern cotton states, the estimated movement would be equal to approximately 35 per cent of the total population, 63 per cent of the rural
population, and 86 per cent of the actual farm population. It goes without saying that a number of the abandoned cotton farms would lie in
states excluded from our calculations, notably North Carolina, Tennessee, Virginia, and Florida in the Southeast. Moreover, certain poorer
areas in eastern Texas and Oklahoma might be expected to suffer.

It is doubtful whether the success of cotton harvesting machinery
would greatly change the calculations here. There is no denial that with
such an innovation the transition would be more abrupt, and the localization of cotton production in the Southwest more complete. It must
also be admitted that the economies of the machine would at first dis-
place more workers. However, there is good ground for believing that
such a development, by lowering prices, would go far toward regaining
the world market for American cotton. In this case, the displacement of
American producers might be no greater than in the loss of markets
without mechanization. On this assumption, we shall leave the maximum

migration at six or seven million, although mechanization might increase the amount temporarily.

Since the lowest-level groups will necessarily be among the first to leave the region, our maximum estimate takes into account as well the class for whom migration is most desirable in order to raise their standards of living. In any case it would be absurd to consider adding to this figure on grounds of desirability if estimates of "necessary" migration point to a task so nearly impossible as the moving of six or seven million people.

ALTERNATIVES TO MIGRATION FROM THE SOUTH

Our estimate of a future migration ranging from one and one-half to seven million people was derived from the multiple assumptions of necessity and desirability, the success or failure of mechanization, the continuation or termination of present policies of acreage reduction, and, finally, the loss or retention of foreign markets. Even the more optimistic estimates deny the possibility of a Southeast economically capable of absorbing its surplus population in the future. The argument, therefore, requires a candid examination of the alternatives to migration.

The first to suggest itself is the continued industrialization of the South. The South has, in the main, gained its new industries by underbidding and undercutting industries already established in the East. As a result, its gains have largely been confined to light industry, notably textiles, where the lower costs of production, possible through cheap labor drawn from agriculture, enabled the Piedmont to attract part of the industry from New England. The depression put a temporary halt to this shifting, and the NRA codes for a while gave promise of permanently arresting it. With the abandonment of NRA and with industrial recovery, the southward movement may resume, but not in the ratio prevailing before the depression. The textile industry appears too over-expanded at the present to attract further capitalization, and in other branches of industry the progress of the South has not been so startling.[33] In heavy industry the area has Birmingham, but the Birmingham plants, it must be remembered, are largely subsidiaries of the United States Steel Corporation, and their output in relation to the national market is determined accordingly. The South may expect a continued industrialization, calculated to keep pace with its markets. But it is too much to expect the process of industrialization to continue at the pre-depression rate or to absorb the entire "surplus" population of the region.

Several new factors remain to be accounted for in the expected upsurge after depression. The lowered cost of hydro-electric power made possible by the TVA is expected by many to enable the area to repeat the process of attracting certain light industries. Barring legal and political difficulties facing the Authority, it seems safe to predict a measure of success from its efforts in this direction, especially in electro-chemical, electrometallurgical, ceramic, and cement industries in which power amounts to 10 per cent or more of the manufacturing costs. (It must be remembered, however, that the Tennessee Valley lies largely outside the area of the Old Cotton Belt, and has its own reservoirs of population to be tapped in the Cumberland and Appalachian Mountain areas.) A view shared by many experts is that the greatest means of improving the region's utilization of resources will be found in the development of chemical industries. Without going into detail, it appears that this possibility has more to offer in raising incomes of skilled and selected groups than in providing a large amount of employment.

The reverse may be found true in the cases where raw materials for the chemical industry can be produced on the farm. Many of these projected developments are too far in the future to be counted here, but one such project holds out some immediate promise. Dr. Charles H. Herty's success in making newsprint paper out of slash pine offers hope for the eventual development of a paper-making industry in the South. A carload of pulpwood processed in Canadian mills was used successfully by metropolitan dailies of Georgia for one day's editions in a recent experiment. The Southern Newspaper Publishers have agreed to contract in advance for the output of an initial mill to be established by private capital and government loans in a southeastern city.

With the gradual passing of the country's virgin timber stands, the South of the Piney Woods, many feel, is in a position to lead the country in the development of scientific forestry. The sun and rainfall of the region make native yellow pine the fastest growing tree in the United States. With slash and long-leaf pine producing naval stores, the South has the opportunity of developing a multi-level forestry that pays its way on four counts. In their early stages, young pineries can be used for grazing purposes. After that, thinning for poles and pulpwood clears the stand and pays handsome returns. When the slash and long-leaf pine reach a growth of 15 years, they can be worked for rosin and turpentine by improved methods for a period of 30 to 50 years without injuring their timber qualities. By that time the timber is ready for cutting and the process can be started all over again. No other section, it is felt, offers such varied returns from scientific forestry. Forests operated by sound business methods, with modern sawmills, paper mills, creosote plants, naval stores production, and wood-working factories of every description, could take the place of the old practice of "speeding up the cut" and moving away. Such a program would bring back into use millions of acres of the region's cut-over lands and offer a new resource basis for the support of population. Its introduction into present farming areas, on the other hand, would substitute an extensive for an intensive utilization of land. While forestry might be successful in raising incomes, it would, on the whole, provide less employment for the population than agriculture now furnishes in a given area.

GOVERNMENTAL POLICIES AND AGENCIES

Private industry is not likely to solve the problem of population redistribution in the Southeast. It is therefore worth examining the extent to which governmental policies may reduce the severity of future migration. Rural relief and crop reduction may be charged off to desperate need to meet desperate crises. The submarginal land program, subsistence homesteads, rural rehabilitation, and the proposed Bankhead Tenant Farm and Homes Bill are here considered simply from one point of view: How much can they serve quantitatively to reduce the necessity for migration out of the region?

The submarginal land program, it is to be hoped, can, over a long period, make many needed changes in the redistribution of population from poor to more fertile areas.[34] Basically, however, the southern problem is one of finding markets or alternative crops, and as this program will increase production, it will again bring to the fore the problem of farm prices.

Subsistence homesteads at present seem intended to relieve the congestion of urban unemployment rather than to solve the problems of an agrarian economy. In the South they have proved too few, too expensive, and too encumbered with bureaucratic management to offer much besides experimentation. At best, the number to be cared for by both programs is small compared to the total problem.

In many respects the rural rehabilitation program appears best adapted to reduce migration from the Southeast. It takes farmers from the relief rolls and uses rural relief funds to help set them up as self-supporting farmers. To select these people, to provide them with land, workstock, equipment, and seed, and to supervise their farming, has up to now proved a heroic task for the majority of the administrators of this program, many of whom were selected on the basis of social work qualifications. To provide a cash income for its clients and yet keep them from interfering with the cotton reduction program, rural rehabilitation attempts to place them on land with cash crop quotas. This means that the rehabilitation clients to a large extent replace the former quota owners who, it is presumed, have found economic opportunities elsewhere. Where no quotas are available for clients, they are allowed to grow two bales of cotton, tax free, but of course they receive no subsidy. From the viewpoint of the client, who starts on the lowest rung, this limitation is a distinct handicap; from the viewpoint of crop control, an extensive development of this program carries very real threats to the efforts at price stabilization.

The record of rural rehabilitation in the whole country for the year ending April 1935 may shed some light upon the extent to which the program can be expected to assist the South. For that period, 290,155 rural relief families were provided for by rural rehabilitation, leaving approximately 850,000 rural families receiving direct relief.[35] Of the 290,155 families, 212,712 were still listed on May 1, 1935, as clients of the Rural Rehabilitation Division. The difference of 77,442 families represents in a large part those who have returned to a self-supporting basis. The 212,712 families still receive loans or direct grants for the purchase of food, clothing, farm equipment, and improvements necessary to enable the families to earn a living.[36]

On the basis of five persons per family, there were 4,125,000 individuals living on farms who received direct relief in 1934–35; 1,450,000 who were removed from relief rolls; and approximately 383,215 who were presumably "rehabilitated." How many of these people had transferred to urban or transient relief rolls we have no way of knowing. Southern states showed the largest number of clients, Louisiana leading with 32,936 families, and Alabama next with 29,058. Moreover, if by any stretch of the imagination the program could be expected to provide a decent living for all relief cases capable of rehabilitation, there would still remain large numbers of poverty-stricken tenants, farm laborers, and small owners.

The proposed Bankhead Tenant Farm and Homes Bill has aroused further hopes in some quarters as an alternative to migration. Briefly, it differs from rural rehabilitation in its intention to select only the cream of tenants and laborers and to arrange for them to purchase farms, live-stock, and supplies at less than their usual rent and credit charges. Assuming final approval of the billion-dollar capitalization provided in this Bill, which has been passed by the Senate, it may be possible to estimate the extent to which such a reform, if successful, might relieve the pressure on migration. This estimate must, of course, depend upon an hypothesis. If the cost of farms were held to an average of $2,000 each, if no over-head were charged against the bonds issued, and if half the sum were spent in the Southeast, it can be estimated that 250,000 farm families could be settled on their own lands. This is a generous estimate, but in terms of population it would amount to only one and a quarter million. Obviously migration of some magnitude would still be necessary under the most optimistic conditions that at present can be envisaged for the South.

CONCLUSION

In conclusion it may be stated that the region's problem of low standards can, in the long run, be met only by the adjustment of (1) a decreasing rate of population growth to (2) an increasing utilization of regional resources with (3) redistribution of part of the population. The foregoing analysis indicates doubt as to whether any one of these three factors is at present operating to the benefit of the area. Furthermore, any change in the birth-rate of the population or any improvement in the economic life of the South is bound to take place very slowly. Migration remains the area's sole immediate recourse to soften the blow of lost markets or lift it from stabilized poverty in case of a return of pre-depression conditions. Even if a program of regional reconstruction larger than any yet contem-plated could be carried swiftly and effectively to conclusion, the nation and the region should plan for migration. If world markets are lost, it will be desirable, if not absolutely necessary, that six or seven million persons should migrate from the Southeast.

If a migration of such magnitude could be conceived, planning for it would involve an estimate of the skills and abilities of southern labor reserves, and of their opportunities for acquiring such skills. This last might necessitate certain changes in education whereby rural people would receive training to fit them for the transition to urban and industrial environment. In addition, there is the problem of the special disabilities and exclusions suffered by Negro workers. It is the general feeling that the Negroes are being pushed out of trades in which they were once proficient. If they are losing the apprenticeship in trades they once followed, it may be advisable to teach those trades in schools. Both white and colored groups should be provided training which develops flexible skills and adaptable personality, traits which may open the way to a choice of jobs in the more complex urban communities to which many of them, it now seems, must go.

Even with the best of planning, migration on any such scale might very well upset the national economy and prevent the restoration of prosperity. Certainly with seven millions wholly or partially removed from the consumers' market and pressing on the national labor market, it is hardly reasonable to envisage industrial recovery. The maximum figure, then, does not measure migration so much as the amount of regional poverty that might be expected to prevail. The point can easily be made that these figures can be put to their most realistic use as an estimate of the relief burden likely to fall upon the nation should the South lose the whole export cotton market.

NOTES

1. The general areas here considered comprise the southeastern states, in which cotton has long been grown. As the geographic and economic factors of the situation are further developed, the area for special consideration will be progressively narrowed.

2. This section was written before the Supreme Court's decision on the constitutionality of the AAA.

3. Whether this should be charged mainly to the system of tenure, to the caliber of the population, or to the lack of decent educational facilities, no one can say with confidence.

4. Since 1910 no census has returned statistics on the ownership of rented farms.

5. In 1900 in these states 56.9 per cent of returned farms were tenant farms belonging to 25.5 per cent of all farm operators. It was found that 15.9 per cent of all operators owned only one tenant farm; 7.3 per cent owned two to four rented farms, accounting for 18.5 per cent of all farms; while 2.3 per cent of all farmers were owners of five or more tenant farms. This group may be classified as planters. They owned an average of 9.9 farms and held 22.4 per cent of all farms listed in the area (*Census of Agriculture, 1900* 5:312).

In the Special Census of Plantations in 1910 in 152 counties in these states, farms were tabulated by five or more. There were found 19,019 plantation owners and operators listed as owning five or more tenant farms. In all they owned 177,373 rented farms. This gives each plantation owner an average of 9.3 tenant farms ("Plantation Farming in the United States," *Bureau of the Census Bulletin* [1916], 22).

6. A statistical difficulty is found here in that crops fed to livestock are counted twice, first as forage and second as value of livestock sold.

7. These workers were not boarded. Their daily wage was $1.20 in South Carolina, $1.30 in Georgia, and $1.40 in Alabama (*Monthly Labor Review,* September 1929, 173). The Southeast also shows the lowest rates of wages with board. During the depression the earnings of this class fell to 50 and 75 cents a day.

8. This situation has received official recognition in the president's order placing the states of North Carolina, South Carolina, Georgia, Florida, Tennessee, Alabama, and Mississippi in Region 4, with the lowest scale of relief wages—$19 a month for unskilled farm laborers to $40 for the same group in Region 1—centering in the North and West. For skilled workers the differential runs from $35 for the rural Southeast to $85 for the urban North and West.

9. T. Lynn Smith, manuscript.

10. The computations are through the courtesy of the Population Association of America.

11. It is possible that the figures overstate to an indeterminate but probably slight degree the effective fertility of counties from which there had been previous emigration, and understate it in those urban counties which had recently received migration, since young adults took part in the cityward movement to a greater proportional degree than small children. This point, however, would apparently not help to account for the low figures in the Delta counties, even those which had received a net migration, since the movement into such an agricultural area is mainly a family one.

12. These figures are taken and the table is adapted from the "Report of the Land Planning Committee," part 2, *Report of the National Resources Board* (1935), 97.

13. This was not the case in the Delta and western cotton areas.

14. Joseph A. Becker, "Effects of the Boll Weevil upon Cotton Production in the United States," *International Cotton Bulletin,* June 1924, 519–29.

15. The section which follows is largely based on O. M. Johnson, "The Old

Plantation Piedmont Cotton Belt," mimeographed preliminary report, Bureau A, U. S. Department of Agriculture, May 1930.

16. "Two Black Belt Counties in Georgia, 1910–1925," Ph.D. dissertation, University of North Carolina, Chapel Hill, 1931.

17. Fred Arnold, "Economic Geography of the Alabama Black Belt," M.A. thesis, George Peabody College for Teachers, Nashville, 1928.

18. The selection of the period 1910 to 1930 serves to show changes from a rather stable period before the migration set in to the onset of the depression. It avoids the period of war expansion in 1920 and the period of extreme contraction, if not under-count, in the agricultural census of 1925.

19. From the Bureau of Agricultural Economics. This passage rests also upon the work of the *Cotton Atlas* and the *Economic Status of American Cotton Producers*.

20. It is noteworthy that outside their cotton areas, Tennessee and Oklahoma showed a loss of farms.

21. Such figures on costs of production, however, are difficult to ascertain and probably unreliable except for purposes of broad comparison.

22. "A provision more hedged about by qualifying language could hardly have been drafted. It is not easy to imagine a case more difficult to prove than that a producer has not 'endeavored in good faith' to bring about 'insofar as possible' a reduction in acreage 'as ratably as practicable amongst his tenants'" (Paul W. Bruton, "Cotton Acreage Reduction and the Tenant Farmer," *Law and Contemporary Problems*, June 1934, 290).

23. "Before the AAA a great many landlords did allow their tenants to go on relief for at least part of the year as they did not feel that they could feed them. After the AAA superannuated or disabled tenants were allowed to go on relief and still live on the plantation, but for most part these were not participants in a regular crop agreement with the landlord" (Quoted by permission from a personal letter from T. J. Woofter, Jr., Coordinator of Rural Research, FERA).

24. *Texas Weekly*, 22 December 1934, 6.

25. It may be pointed out in passing that studies by Arthur Raper, of Georgia, and others indicate that variations between the practices of county administrators are an important factor in the admission of cases to relief rolls. Thus several Mississippi counties in 1933 closed relief offices and accepted no funds during cotton picking season, irrespective of the aged and the disabled on relief. In a low-wage area, habituated to chronic poverty and near-poverty among its lower level groups, the lack of professional standards in social work has often left the administration of relief policies to laymen and at the mercy of their prejudices (Walter Wilbur, "Special Problems of the South," *Annals of the American Academy of Political and Social Science* 176 [November 1934]: 49–56).

26. See Norman Thomas, *Plight of the Share Cropper* (New York: League for Industrial Democracy, 1934); and John Beecher, "The Share Croppers Union in Alabama," *Social Forces* 13 (October 1934): 124–32.

It is still too early to determine whether the marked decreases in relief in many of the cotton counties between 1934 and 1935 represent a reversal of this tendency or whether they are to be interpreted as the result of the change from a 40 per cent to a 25 per cent reduction in acreage.

27. "Southern Population and Social Planning," *Social Forces* 14 (October 1935):21.

28. One can sympathize with the present plight of cotton exporters and processors without accepting the view that what is best for them is best for the South. Their incomes are based on a percentage of the volume of turnover rather than of the total price returns.

29. In national competition, to what money crops can the South turn to replace its cotton and tobacco? To ask this question is to answer it. The area can supply local needs where costs of transportation and distribution are high; it can reduce the expense attendant upon commercial farming by producing much of its own supplies; but it cannot successfully invade the national agricultural market.

30. No one can be more skeptical of the validity of these devices than the author.

31. This represents 70 per cent of all cotton farms in the South.

32. If this figure seems excessive, consider that the Bankhead Act in 1934 has already withdrawn 40 per cent of the cotton acreage from production. The reasons why this did not result in a corresponding 40 per cent loss of employment lie, of course, in the special and not necessarily permanent factors of benefit payments and provisions for the partial retention of tenants and laborers.

33. Some indication of the relative importance of the industrial South in the nation may be found in the fact that out of 3,186 leaders taken from industry to serve on 364 code authorities, only 298 were from southern states. Of the 364 code authorities, there were 248 which had no southern representative whatever. The cotton textile code was the only one of major importance that contained a majority of southerners.

34. It is doubtful whether the program can do much for those farmers already located on fairly productive cotton lands.

35. Press release, Resettlement Administration, 17 July 1935.

36. An average of $101 per family had been spent by the agency in behalf of relief families to help them establish themselves on a self-sustaining basis.

8. Tennessee's War of the Roses (1940)

Not the most serious piece Vance ever wrote, this account of the political war between the Taylor brothers in post-Reconstruction Tennessee shows his deep, almost instinctive appreciation of southern folk culture—an appreciation that survived even the rationalist bias of his sociological training. Modern intellectuals might look down on the old-fashioned spellbinder, he notes, but those who took the trouble to understand could easily view such politics as a species of "folk art" which proved how "political democracy may sometimes function very well without being as dignified as its apologists indicate." Originally intended for the never-completed "Spellbinders of the Old South," the essay also illustrates Vance's abundant sense of humor.

Now that democracy is being abandoned everywhere else, we have in our curious way again made it the passionate hope and ideal of every American. In our rediscovered glory in democracy as a way of life, the question arises as to what we are going to do with the demagogues? If we accept our politics, warts and all, there's no denying that they are still with us. "Democracy," Herr Hitler has somewhere said, "is a henyard in which every chicken cackles."

Obviously in our present temper we are going to keep the democracy; and if we retain freedom of speech and party primaries, obviously we are going to retain the cacklers. For their own peace of mind, then, it is fitting that American intellectuals come to some ordered point of view about that peculiar product of American politics, the spellbinder.

It should be realized that no department of our communal life ranks higher than aesthetics; that no contemporary social science commands higher respect than anthropology; and that no group is more often discovered and rediscovered by our best thinkers than the folk. Why then should we not accept the spellbinder for what he is—a product of folk art as genuine as a cigar store Indian, the protagonist in a social ritual as authentic to the American scene as the snake dance was among the Hopi Indians.

From the *Virginia Quarterly Review* 16 (1940):413–24. © *The Virginia Quarterly Review.*

Once we came close to arriving at such a view. In the interim between periods of making the world safe for democracy and making democracy safe from the world, a musical comedy on the folklore of democracy romped its way to the Pulitzer Prize. For the folk idyl of American politics, however, examine the history of the Brothers Taylor of Tennessee. To admit that they were not great men and yet to retell their story in all its realism is sufficient to show that politics is often practiced as a folk art, and also to suggest that political democracy may sometimes function very well without being as dignified as its apologists indicate. For when the Brothers Taylor could not resolve social conflict, they mitigated it. That, in the post–Civil War welter of Tennessee, was no mean contribution.

The brothers' war in the Taylor family originated in fratricidal strife in the nation. The Taylor family came from east Tennessee, dark and bloody ground of the War for Southern Independence. Haters of slavocrats and lovers of the Union, the men of east Tennessee were led by their fighting Methodist parson, W. G. Brownlow, and their plebeian Andrew Johnson in a secession from secession. Nevertheless, the Unionists possessed enough neighbors of Confederate leanings to turn the whole region into a gory battle ground of guerrilla warfare. The war made Nathaniel G. Taylor, lawyer, politician, Methodist parson, and Whig Congressman from the old first district, a staunch Unionist and a Republican. It left his wife, the sister of Langdon C. Haynes, Confederate Senator from Tennessee, with her native sympathies. Thus was laid the foundation for those family differences which little brother Bob was later to explain on the stump, much to the discomfiture of brother Alf: "Take Alf and me, for instance . . . born of the same mother and nursed at the same breast—but Alf's milk soured on him and he became a Republican."

Thrice Congressman and once Governor, it was the fate of Republican Alfred A. Taylor to serve as the foil for his light-hearted younger brother, Democratic Robert Love Taylor, once Congressman, thrice Governor, and once United States Senator. Together Alf and Bob belong among the state's immortals, museum pieces of Southern politics and folk culture. Bob won the governorship, but in 1920, eight years after Bob's death, Tennessee elected Brother Alf, Republican politics and all, to the governor's chair. With Alf's death in 1931, the Brothers Taylor have assumed the proportions of a folk epic. Their sayings and their doings now belong with the state's cherished traditions, with split rail fences, spelling bees, old fiddlers' conventions, and good eating tobacco.

I

By the middle 'eighties in Tennessee conditions were ripe for the advent of a new type of leadership. Memories of civil strife had embittered the conflict between Republicans and Democrats, but the Bloody Shirt was receding into the background and the "damned Brigadiers" were losing their appeal as vote-getters. The common people, having followed Andy Jackson and then Andy Johnson until they could no longer stomach his out and out Unionism, now felt themselves without a leader. They remained within the folds of the Democratic party, but evinced no enthusiasm for its factional fights. The war had left Tennessee's great Whig party without a home. In east Tennessee, where there were few Negroes to raise the question of white supremacy, old Whigs felt no qualms in lining up with the new Republican party. In middle and west Tennessee, however, Reconstruction and the Bloody Shirt drove enough former Whigs into the Democratic party to give it a nominal majority, provided it could keep the peace. But the party was an amalgam of two factions. The Bourbons, led by Senator Isham Harris, whose coup d'état had thrown Tennessee into the Confederacy in 1860, stood for traditional Democracy of the Calhoun school, states' rights and low tariff. The newly acquired Whigs were industrialists and "New South" men, ready to admire Henry W. Grady, ready to develop Tennessee's resources and accept a high tariff. At times only the race issue kept this group from joining the Republicans. The basic warp and woof of the political fabric, the common folk of Tennessee, listened to the formulas of the Bourbons because they sounded less like Yankee doctrine, but showed their disdain for the factional fights that sporadically divided the party by "going fishing" on election day. And when they did, the Republicans invariably won.

Here is where Bob Taylor entered the picture. When his clear tenor arose in the hills of Tennessee, the common people recognized an authentic voice and began a stampede which the party leaders were never able to stem. Unwittingly enough, Brother Alf gave Bob his first push up the ladder of politics. In 1878 Alf was all set for the Republican nomination for Congress in the rock-ribbed first district when by some political tree shaking the plum was deflected into the open mouth of his rival, Major A. B. Pettibone. Enough of the inner party circle were disgruntled to let it be noised abroad that they were willing to vote for a good Democrat, if such an article were to be had. What was nearer poetic justice than for the Democrats to put up Brother Bob? In this stronghold of Republicanism, Bob told enough jokes, fiddled enough, and found enough Taylor sympathizers to edge in by the skin of his teeth. Thus, at the ripe age of twenty-eight, Bob gained admission to the bar, married a wife, and was elected to Congress. Two years later Major Pettibone repaired his fences and the Republican factions celebrated their reconciliation by retiring Bob to private life with great unanimity. In 1884, campaigning as presidential elector for Cleveland, Bob laid the foundations of a lasting popularity in the hinterlands of Tennessee.

By 1886 it was evident that the sovereign people were tired of factional fights and had already picked a candidate for the governorship. From the political rallies of the back counties reports came trickling in that delegation after delegation had been instructed for Our Bob. Not only were Democrats upset, but the Republicans grew perturbed. Meeting in convention three weeks before their rivals, they performed the surprising feat of nominating Brother Alf. One delegate let the cat out of the bag when he admonished the convention that this would mean the retirement of the strongest Democratic candidate. Democratic party organs agreed that to nominate Bob would perpetuate a "brothers' war," would be "unnatural and disgusting," "a contemptible farce," "a repulsive tableau." In more caustic vein one editor suggested that Father Nat be given the prohibition nomination, a younger brother, the Greenback nomination, and that the Taylor family hold a caucus to determine the next Governor. Nevertheless, after fourteen ballots, the convention nominated Bob and Tennessee's War of the Roses was on.

Nat Taylor said it was "a shame for them to nominate my boys to run against each other" and refused to cast a vote. His wife feared her sons would learn to hate each other, but the party moguls were troubled by no such considerations. They met and laid out a schedule of forty-one joint debates, beginning at Madisonville in east Tennessee. Both candidates were young and ambitious, anxious to justify their party's faith, and neither pulled his oratorical punches. The first debate calmed the fears of those who dreaded a fraternal wrangle or trembled to see the Taylor family wash exposed for political purposes. Bob set the tone: "I have a very high regard for the Republican candidate—he is a perfect gentleman, because he is my brother. I have already told him to come with me, and I would furnish him with crowds and introduce him in society. We are two roses from the same garden." With this phrase to set the final stamp of chivalry on the contest, Bob's supporters wore the white rose and Alf's the red throughout the campaign.

The joint campaign in those days partook of the nature of a social ritual. Its pattern and style had taken shape during a long period of development. From much participation in the ceremony the common folk came to regard its details as jealously and caressingly as any connoisseur views an object of art. With Bob and Alf it was in the hands of supreme artists in political ritualism, and their joint campaign established a new high for the delectation of all Tennessee.

At its best the pattern was as elaborate and highly involved as the ritual of the duel. At each town the candidates were met at the train; in his flower-bedecked carriage drawn by plumed horses, each led rival processions of banners and brass bands to the town's leading hostelry. At the disbanding of the processional each candidate made speech number one. After this he betook himself to one of the hotel's two entrances and shook hands with the sovereign people for some three hours. In the afternoon came a formal joint discussion with set speech and counter speech delivered, rain or shine, at the county fairground or on the courthouse square. At the banquet hall the campaigner, now going strong, unburdened himself of speech number three. For the final touch came a speech, lush and full of poetic sentiments, delivered from the hotel balcony in acknowledgment of the evening serenade. This was followed by the presentation of floral tributes by the ladies, bouquets of horseshoes, ships, fiddles, et cetera. But the end was not yet. The avid citizenry next crowded in the lobby to hear their champions fiddle. Here Bob, the poorer musician, was the center of attraction. With a grin on his face and a fiddle under it, his whole person fiddled from the top of his head to his toes. Not until the wee hours were the Brothers Taylor allowed to seek the rest necessary for an early start to the next scene of performance. Under a man-killing schedule, worked out jointly by the Democratic and Republican committees, this political circus continued for three months.

Bob and Alf plugged away seriously enough at their exposition of Hamilton versus Jefferson, but for the rest they romped through the joint campaign like a musical comedy team. After a verbal set-to of homicidal intensity, the two brothers would jolt off together in an old buckboard across a rugged mountain road, to sleep in the same hotel bed and to laugh over the ludicrous events of the campaign. Neither, be it said to their credit, violated the rule of Tennessee politics which reads, according to tradition: "Don't take yourself too damned seriously." Bob, taller with easy manner and bland face full of drollery, spoke with fluency and told anecdotes like a professional with a poker face. Alf, credited with greater abilities, hammered away on Hamiltonian doctrines and, when he told a joke, laughed with the audience. When their Memphis speaking date conflicted with Barnum and Bailey they changed the hour so that, according to one editor, the circus might draw a crowd.

So different from the usual political dialectics and appeals to Civil War prejudices did the swing around the circle appear that editors were torn between despair at its shallowness and admiration of its good nature. Bob, said one acrid editor, harking back to Dryden,

> In one revolving moon
> Was fiddler, statesman, and buffoon.

Alf, no doubt, had to exercise the more tolerance, for Bob's sense of the ridiculous was irrepressible. At Chattanooga each had exerted himself to write a suitable response to the inevitable serenade. Bob's turn came first. While Alf held reception for his henchmen within an earshot of the hotel balcony, he heard Bob's sonorous voice booming forth to the crowd below his—Alf's—speech. While Alf searched frantically for his manuscript, Bob's voice ceased, and Bob and his camp followers, bursting with pent-up laughter, pushed into the room and rolled on the floor before the astounded Alf. The crowd yelled for Alf, and in a daze the luckless aspirant floundered through an impromptu speech.

Alf had his revenge a few weeks later at Fayetteville. A crowd of dusty horsemen rode twenty-two miles from their rural fastness on Possum Creek to pay their respects to Bob. Ushered by mistake into Alf's room, they pledged their undying vows to Bob and hinted that their throats were dry from the ride. Alf sensed their error and his opportunity. Mounting a chair, he delivered a temperance lecture:

> O God! That men should put an enemy into their mouths to steal away their brains. Men, I would be frank with you. Before I would be instrumental in polluting your lips with one single drop of the hellish stuff, . . . I would give up the race entirely and allow Alf Taylor to be elected Governor of the Volunteer State.

Bob's partisans clumped down the stairs in disgust, leaving to Alf the gleeful task of informing his younger brother of their sudden conversion to the cause of temperance.

The campaign ended in approved éclat at Blountsville in northeast Tennessee. For hundreds of demonstrations before almost a million people, the two brothers had fiddled, handshaken, and orated the length and breadth of the state. For the last time they measured each other on the political platform. To the cheers of the crowd Alf declared, "I say to you now that after all these eventful struggles I still love my brother as of old, with an undying affection—but politically, my friends, I despise him." A few minutes later Bob concluded; and the War of the Roses was over. The electorate cheered and gave Bob a majority of 13,000.

II

Throughout his life Bob Taylor retained his power over the young voters and the agrarian masses. Popular with the people, unpopular with party leaders, Bob found he could use his influence to advance his interests and those of his "wool hats" only if he became a political boss himself. Unlike Tillman and Long, he lacked any passionate desire to wade to leadership through conflict. He was not a demagogue, he was not a self-seeking politician, he was not a reformer, and hence perhaps not a statesman, since he lacked the drive to leadership.

The rest of Bob's career serves to show the dualism in political leadership as between command of the party organization and command of the admiration of the sovereign voters. The factional leaders, Mugwumps and Bourbons, assembled in convention and prevented the endorsement of Bob's first term. They blocked his renomination for six long days, until the rustling of the grass roots forced them to give in on the fortieth ballot. Bob served out his term and retired.

But one honor to which Bob aspired his blessed red necks could not give him. Because Senators were elected by the state legislature, Bob's unparalleled popularity could not dislodge "King" Isham Harris or break the legislative caucus controlled by the two factions. Then followed a strange spectacle. The white-haired boy of state politics took to the lyceum platform while the party leaders, minus their greatest vote-getter, continued to peddle peanuts at the old stand.

The eve of 1896 found the party reverting to its accustomed factional chaos. Between fighting off the Populist revolt and actually counting out the Republicans in the election of 1894, the stalwarts had again run the ship on the shoals. Again the "sovereign people" came to the rescue. The grass roots began to rustle and county conventions were meeting early and instructing for Our Bob. Certainly the movement was not of Bob's making. He and brother Alf were off on a national lyceum tour, packing the opera houses with their replica of the War of the Roses, a lecture duet on "Dixie" and "Yankee Doodle." For the first time Bob was tasting financial independence and salting away for a rainy day. Indifferent to the nomination Bob refused to state his position on the issues of the day and was ignored by the leaders. Only the agrarians knew their minds and by acclamation the convention nominated a man not in the race. Again Bob served faithfully as Governor, and again he retired to the lyceum platform.

At last the time came when the State Executive Committee could no longer resist the demand for the man whose claims to represent the state had been so often and so mercilessly shelved by the politicians. It ordered a preferential primary binding upon the Democratic legislative caucus, and in 1905 Bob defeated the brilliant incumbent, Senator Edward W. Carmack. At last it seemed that the man who put harmony above ambition had retired to an arena where he might confine his unpruned rhetoric to sly digs at the concern of the high tariff bloc for the wages of the working man.

His last fight, the only battle he ever lost, was fought to rescue a party organization that deserved to lose. The Tennessee Democracy soon massed for a bitter fight over prohibition, and in 1908 Carmack, representing the statewide prohibition wing, was defeated by M. R. Patterson. Carmack assumed the editorship of the *Nashville Tennessean*, and when the Patterson organization, after unseating 150 delegates committed to prohibition, brought forth an anti-prohibition platform, Carmack repudiated the party platform, pointed the withering finger of scorn at Patterson's chief advisor, Colonel Duncan B. Cooper, and called for the election of a prohibition legislature. Colonel Cooper sent the editor a threat that if the Cooper name appeared again in the paper his life would be forfeit. The *Tennessean* the next morning carried Cooper's name in a short and bitter editorial. That afternoon ex-Senator Carmack was shot and killed on the streets of Nashville by Cooper and his son Robin. Held without bail, the Coopers were sentenced to twenty years imprisonment after a trial lasting three months. The day the Tennessee Supreme Court upheld the original verdict, Governor Patterson, without reading the decision and before Colonel Cooper left the capital, issued an unconditional pardon. From the shocked populace arose a great wave of indignation. Three judges charged that Patterson had sought to influence their decision. As candidates for reelection the judges refused to enter the primary dominated by the Patterson organization. Running as independent Democrats with Republican support, they defeated the regulars by forty thousand votes. When the Republicans named Captain Ben W. Hooper on a straight prohibition ticket, independent Democrats pledged their support and Union and Confederate veterans paraded side by side in token of harmony.

None too soon the machine halted in its rough-shod career. Three days before the independent Democrats were to meet, Governor Patterson, facing certain defeat, withdrew from the race; the regular Democratic committee resigned; and the new committee made the chairman of the Independents their own. For once the party bosses rather than the rank and file cast abroad for the Great Conciliator to mend the chaos they had made. Bob Taylor was drafted from Washington to run again for the governorship of Tennessee. No longer young, and in strange hands, Bob waited outside of the convention hall for the psychological moment to appear upon the platform and with the fiddle and the bow still the tumult. The moment never came, and fearing that the red necks might hiss him from the floor, Bob refused to enter the hall. The rural democracy, outraged by violence as much as by the urban liquor trade, had determined to destroy the machine control, root, branch, and spore. For the first time in his life Bob Taylor found between himself and his folk a great gulf. He did his duty in a hopeless contest. He stumped the state for the regulars on a platform that contained no mention of prohibition, he saw his agrarians roll up more than a 12,000 majority for Hooper, and he returned to the Senate to die before his term expired.

A mellow bassoon of a man was Bob, a great overgrown boy, generous with his time and money and furthest removed from our ideal type—the go-getter. It became the creed of those who watched this artist in folk-appeal at his work that Bob could win an audience without saying a word—just by the expression on his face. The story is often told of how Governor Taylor, with the audacity of a master of crowd-behavior, once turned a joint debate with the disaffected Populists into a revival meeting. After the party dialecticians had gotten in their soporific work, Bob rose to close the meeting. Working up to a great oratorical pitch, he suddenly raised his arms aloft and commanded: "Let everybody sing." Leading off with "We will seat Governor Cleveland in the presidential chair," he began to plead, "Come on back, boys, come on back." The power of that religious ritual asserted itself and the party deserters crowded up to grasp Bob's hand. Finally the old Populist chairman on the speaker's platform was observed to grow uneasy. He chewed on his tobacco and pulled at his whiskers. At last, unable to resist, he clambered to his feet, grasped Bob by the hand and declared, "By gosh, I'm coming back."

All in all, Bob takes his rank among the highest products of politics as a folk art before the blight of unbalanced budgets descended upon our fair land and the science of public administration put the expert of the desk ahead of the artist of the platform. All Tennessee was near enough to the frontier for the Brothers Taylor to represent an indigenous culture as true participants in a folk ritual and the cleavages in society were not so great that Bob or Alf had to play a part. Once, when an opponent spoke of Bob's supporters as "one-gallus fellows from the forks of the creek," the Governor took opportunity to slip out and discard one-half of his suspenders. Warming up in his reply, he asked permission to re-move his coat and was rewarded by plaudits: "Bob's a one-gallus man!" Admitting that he was a political tactician of no mean order, I wish to suggest that Bob also felt the inarticulate embarrassment of honest yeo-manry thus stigmatized by a tactless orator. "My blessed red necks," he called them to their faces, and they loved him for it. Steeped in the arts of folk appeal, Bob was the type of hero that politics once produced before class and economic conflict hardened all our attitudes. His like may never come again.

9. Human Resources and Public Policy

An Essay toward Regional-National Planning (1943)

Vance's wartime presidential address to the Southern Sociological Society dealt, appropriately, with the need for a federal population policy that would put an end to the waste of the South's human resources. The subject had been on his mind as he did the research for All These People *(not published until 1945). In the years before the war, the New Deal administration in Washington had in fact begun to respond to the plight of the South.*

More than anything else the future of the Southeast depends on the development of resources and capacities that are as yet largely unrealized. The region has natural resources and human resources. These forms of wealth are primary, but for their development they depend upon the building up of technological resources, institutional resources, and capital resources. The creation of these secondary forms of wealth as Howard W. Odum has pointed out are matters of organization, skill, and previous experience.[1] This is both an economic and a cultural task in which the nation is as vitally concerned as the region itself.

The decision of the course to be pursued and the goals to be sought are embodied in public policy. Public policy grows out of the great complex of social values held by peoples, is focused toward certain goals to be achieved, and finally comes to be embodied in certain social instrumentalities. This last phase enters the field of public administration and it is no doubt in the test of ways and means that many worthy policies may be shown incapable of immediate realization.

The present paper is not specifically concerned with action programs. It does seek, however, to determine the bearing of recent changes on the development and implementation of population policy in the United States. It grows out of the writer's research on the South's population problem,[2] and is based on two fundamental assumptions: First, that one of the value complexes of our society is the national interest in the development of human resources. Second, that the situation of the Southeast

From *Social Forces* 22 (October 1943): 20–25.

indicates that our policy toward human resources as well as natural resources will be formulated on a regional-national basis.

In making plans for our future development it is essential to decide in what direction the nation and the region are going. Better still, however, we should agree as to the place we want to go. Three questions are involved in this decision: (1) What do we want; (2) what do we have; and (3) what must we do to get from what we have to what we want?

If our desires did not exceed their realization, there would be little hope for progress in the area. We may begin with the future we want and then attempt to realize the distance between what is actual and what is potential and attainable, not tomorrow but in the reasonable future of ten or twenty years hence.

Actually, we shall not know how to appraise the resources we have unless we know what we want to do with them. We must know, as Erich W. Zimmerman pointed out, what kind of society we want to develop in this region before we can realize what kind of resources we possess. Natural resources are simply those aspects of the physical environment which men use to satisfy individual and social needs. Without man's control and direction, resources lie inert and unused. What people want and need thus determine not only what use they will make of inert nature; it determines what portions of their physical environment they will develop and what they will leave untouched.

This same point of view may be applied to the people themselves. In their hopes and aspirations, they furnish the purpose and direction of the ongoing processes of production. But in addition to serving as the goal of the productive process, the population must be regarded the main resource in its achievement. Their labor, their skill, and their thought furnish the means whereby materials are changed and made of use. Moreover, human resources themselves are conserved and developed as they are fitted into an on-going social process in which they may realize their productive capacities and provide for their needs and wants at the same time.[3] If this social mechanism is stalled at dead center, human resources will not lie inert like physical resources; they will deteriorate and waste away. To plan the future we want means more than the achievement of efficiency in the use of physical resources; it means the fuller development of our human resources.

In discussing the future we want for the Southeast, it should be possible to state a common goal so that we can see the subsidiary issues simply as means to an end upon which we are agreed. If our experiences with depression and war have meant anything, Howard W. Odum has pointed out, they have increased our determination to conserve, develop, and make more generally useful those two great sources of the good society, our natural wealth and our human wealth. If we were to make an all-inclusive statement of the regional goal that best fits with the long-time goal of national planning, it might well be a higher level of living for the great mass of the South's population. Unemployment, inadequate income, underconsumption, and inefficient use of natural and human resources are seen as the constituents of a low standard in a nation as richly endowed as America. "A modern nation," it has been pointed out, "can not avoid balancing its total production-consumption budget. This can be done at a low level with a great deal of unemployment, inefficiency, and suffering; or it can be done at a high level with full employment, high efficiency and a better life for all."[4]

For the total population, higher standards of living are required not only to save human resources from the deterioration due to malnutrition, poor housing, and the inadequate satisfaction of cultural needs, but to insure the level of activity necessary to keep the economic mechanism functioning. In the long run it must be realized that the nation can balance its budget and carry its fiscal burden only by stabilizing the national income at a high level—possibly in the case of the United States at approximately one hundred billion dollars annually. The attainment of such an income level would serve two functions. It would (1) greatly reduce the necessity for emergency expenditures and (2) raise the tax base. It would thus conserve our human resources by balancing consumption at a high level with the production necessary to insure full employment. In post-war planning the achievement of this goal seems the only thing likely to prevent the recurrence of a great depression.

The Southeast is a strategic area in this approach, for its population, suffering from real and concealed unemployment, low productivity, and low income, has a per capita consumption of the goods and services produced by our industrial economy that is lower than any region in the nation. Thus the region's need to balance production and consumption at high levels fits in with desirable national goals.

The hopes and aspirations which any people hold for their region as a part of the nation and the world are seen as the necessary major premise of any regional plan. The regional survey which furnishes the inventory of resources and capacities is the minor premise of the syllogism whose conclusion is the regional plan of development.[5] In this analysis, then, population policy is closely integrated with the future of our physical resources, and with the economic organization and governmental plans necessary to their fullest utilization and development.

THE FUTURE OF PHYSICAL RESOURCES

We may begin accordingly with some account of what we should expect from our natural wealth. It is something of a paradox to say that in the Southeast we need a fuller utilization of physical resources for the benefit of the present generation balanced with fuller conservation for the benefit of future generations.

It is a fuller, not a lesser, use of our physical resources that we must strive for in the Southeast simply because of our need to achieve a higher standard of living. It must be emphasized moreover that not full use but abuse is the enemy of conservation. Conservation is not to be defined as abstinence for the sake of posterity, but rather as living on a replaceable flow of goods instead of on stored-up capital. Thus stated the distinction is between the cropping and the mining of resources.

It is fortunate that in its large scale dependence on organic resources the agrarian Southeast is capable of developing what we may call a flow economy rather than a store economy. The annual increase of flocks and herds and the growth of crops, like the flow of water power, comes as an increment from the hands of nature without greatly diminishing its capital store. Food conservation practices may help to give higher yields for the present and yet conserve nature's capital endowment for the future. Mineral resources, however, must be regarded as a store, for a mine once rifled is not replaceable. The flow economy of organic life is also violated when resources of virgin forests, fisheries, and even soils are cleared out at one fell swoop.

Although it must be realized that these two concepts tend to shade into each other, the idea of utilizing a flow of energies and resources instead of rifling a store is valuable in distinguishing between the tendencies of a short-run and a long-run economy. Water power is accepted as a perfect example of the use of a flow of energy, but if a water power reservoir is allowed to silt up it becomes an example of the store economy, for it loses each year a part of its original capital of stored-up energy. The sign of a mine, it is said, is a hole in the ground, and the depletion of minerals is usually regarded as a good example of the store economy. With the rise of the junk man and the utilization of scrap, however, we are developing a continuous flow of resources in the field of metals to supplement the depletion of ores. While this process cannot extend to the conservation of coal and oil, the transition to the use of water power makes possible a greater use of energy in the long-run economy.

Plans for future development in the Southeast will thus attempt to provide for greater utilization and conservation by building up the resource base and thus increasing the flow of energy and resources. Restoration of soil fertility and further extension of soil conservation practices are necessary to provide a continuous flow of agricultural production; further extension of scientific forestry in private and public holdings is necessary to provide for the continuous production of timber resources. Those who plan for wildlife conservation realize that the stock of game will never again be large enough to admit of its use as an essential food resource. Here the problem is one of building up natural wealth to the point where the annual increase of game may be used for the recreation of hunters and fishermen. Scientific forestry, on the contrary, is not reduced to the assumption that we can have lumber only by depleting all the resources of virgin timber. Continuous operation of forest resources and multiple use appear entirely feasible. The South's greatest problem in the field of conservation of resources is that of soil erosion—a loss that if left unchecked will threaten the whole basis of the flow economy.

REGIONAL-NATIONAL POPULATION POLICY

From this view of our natural resources, we come to consider our population as human resources, actual and potential. While population in itself is to be regarded as both the ultimate source and beneficiary of all resources, there must obtain a balance between the physical and human resources. This balance has been called the man-land ratio.

The Southeast has a high birth rate, and the man-land ratio is higher than in any other region of our country. When population presses too heavily on a region and its developed resources, there is danger that it will encroach on its store of natural wealth and thus undermine the flow economy and progressively lower its standard of living. The development of higher levels of living through the correction of the man-land ratio in the Southeast calls for the formulation of a regional-national population policy.

Such a policy would find its basis in the unbalanced man-land ratio of the Southeast and would be related to population increase, internal migration, occupational mobility, and capital investment in basic land resources. Finally this policy must take account of social security as it affects the question of human resources in industry.

It is doubtful if our population policy has ever been completely laissez-faire. In our earlier period it was devoted to encouraging settlement and immigration. With the attainment of greater economic and demographic maturity it can be said that we adopted the policy of collective restriction of increases from without and individual restriction of increases from within. Our restriction of foreign immigration and our tolerance of birth control have carried the nation to the verge of stationary population, our urban population below replacement levels, and have left the Southeast the population seedbed of the nation—with higher increases than the region itself can accommodate.

This has brought us to the verge of a new development in policy. It is realized that as more attention is paid to child care and maternal health that deaths decrease, standards rise, and the birth rate falls. The public health service has been generally accepted as the means of bringing these advances to the general population. This new state policy was signalized when in 1937, the North Carolina State Board adopted as an optional part of the county health program, a contraceptive service for mothers too poor to afford family physicians. A survey in 1939 showed that the Southeast had 136 of the 166 public health contraceptive services then established in the United States. South Carolina and Alabama have since developed state programs endorsed by the State Medical Societies and administered by the State Board of Health. The development of such service in our analysis is to be regarded as the beginnings of a regional population policy in the area of highest fertility.

Regional variations in resources, productivity, wages, and income are so great within the nation and the region that we should not only expect but encourage the continued flow of both capital and labor. Here the development of national policy has come in the integration of the federal and state employment services in what amounts to a program of guided migration. Spontaneous population movements will continue but they need no longer be based on false information or no information. In addition, the FSA and the WPA have cooperated in experiments in subsidizing the migration of farm workers from overcrowded areas to areas of greater opportunity.

The crowding is the greatest and incomes are the lowest at the base of the occupational pyramid. Unless those near the bottom can climb to higher levels of skill and capacity, increased migration will simply serve to share the poverty with other regions with no benefit to the general welfare. Programs for developing the skills of oncoming youth have been developed in the NYA, in apprenticeship training, and in the upgrading procedures adopted in war industries. As new techniques are tested and applied we may expect raw recruits to increase their worth to prospective employers and to society at the same time. Obviously higher skills are needed not only in the industrial discipline, but in agriculture and forestry as well.

Finally we are led back to a consideration of our physical resources in terms of the long run implications of a flow economy. Since our man-land ratio is unbalanced on the side of too many men and too little good land, one corrective is to increase the quantity of good land. Land here must be understood in a very broad sense as practically synonymous with "nature." Hence capital investment in such things as soil conservation, terracing, increased fertility, better farm buildings, improved oyster beds, better orchards, disease-resistant species of crops, and purebred livestock is building up the land part of the ratio quite as much as capital investment in a drainage project, a coal mine or a hosiery mill. When capital is poured into the land side of the ratio it makes the man side relatively scarcer and hence more valuable.[6]

PUBLIC POLICY AND HUMAN RESOURCES IN INDUSTRY

It was in the quests for higher levels of income and higher standards of living, that the Southeast originally turned to industrial development. Regional variations in wages still exist throughout the United States, but the Southeast specially has come to be known as the region of the differential wage. There were many reasons, no doubt, for low wages in the Southeast, but presumably they derived from (1) inadequate capital equipment, (2) large population increases, (3) the pressure of labor seeking escape from an over-crowded agriculture, and the (4) population's lack of training in the industrial discipline.

In terms of balancing needed consumption with potential production, this tends to establish the balance at a low level, the lowest in the nation. The Southeast may not soon be able to change these conditions, but it can make up its mind whether under normal conditions low wages should be regarded as a permanent resource of the region.

This new attitude toward human resources is also made necessary by the fact that in our industrial life national policy has underwritten certain guarantees of social security that are threatened by the population pressure in the Southeast. In our effort to conserve human resources and maintain standards, the national policy has set up certain levels below which the Federal Power cannot and does not allow the states to fall. The Fair Labor Standards Act thus sets up minimum wages and maximum hours of work to which industries must conform, if their products are to move in interstate commerce. Programs of Social Security and Unemployment Compensation, together with Federal Aid to Public Highways, to Vocational and Agricultural Education, all set up minimum standards below which states must not fall.

Three corollaries as to future industrial development in the Southeast seem to follow from the assumptions behind the Fair Labor Standards Act. First, while standards affect only minimum wages they will in time come to be felt throughout the whole level of wages and skills. Secondly, if southern industry and labor are to gain access to national markets, they must in the long run be equal in efficiency and productivity to any in the nation. Third, southern firms on the margin of bankruptcy cannot long be saved from the consequences of mismanagement by recourse to the payment of substandard wages. When such firms fail, their laborers and their share of production will be taken over by more efficient firms in the region, if they can make the grade; outside, if they cannot. Higher standards, it is now generally recognized, offer industry its one hope of disposing of its product in mass markets once the war boom has passed. It is doubtful if the Southeast or any other region can present legitimate claims to stand in the way of the development of a national minimum wage.

There remains the problem of those who may face unemployment even at a high level of economic activity. In our national policy, the problems of those who grow too old to work, those who are temporarily unemployed, and those who for various reasons are unemployable are met in the program for social security. In this situation, as in the Fair Labor Standards Act, we can no longer depend upon the assumptions prevalent in classical economics as to the beneficient effect of unregulated supply and demand on unprotected units of labor. By action of the state, the political citizen is now an economic citizen with certain minimum rights of economic security underwritten by the state.

In the enactment of laws providing for unemployment compensation, old-age insurance, and the provision of relief and made work for the unemployed, we have abandoned laissez-faire economics for a return to an older conception of social policy. The wealth of the nation is pledged to a collective underwriting of the economic welfare of citizens at certain minimum standards. This, it must be realized, makes national-regional planning imperative in the economic sphere. Post-war unemployment is now accepted as a risk to our total national security, pledged as it is to this new program. To support insurance against unemployment on the part of the few requires a high level of employment among the many. To support old-age retirement funds for the increasing numbers of the aged will require a continuing high level of national income. These conditions are worth reviewing for they emphasize the stake that our national policy had assumed in underwriting high levels of employment, productivity, and total national income. With its solvency at stake in carrying out its guarantees of security to its citizens, the nation cannot proceed on the assumptions of the older economic order. It is no longer enough for the state to hope for continued employment and high national income; it must seek to plan for the achievement of these conditions.

The Southeast offers an especial problem in this field because two of its major groups, agricultural and domestic laborers, remain outside the guaranties of unemployment and old-age insurance. More than in any other region these two groups predominate in the economic life of the Southeast. The result was that in 1937 when the nation had 70 percent of its employed workers covered by old-age insurance, the Southeast had hardly half, indicating the predominance of agriculture in the region. Thus the Southeast had half of its employed women in covered occupations as compared to three-fourths in the nation—but less than half of its men workers were found in covered occupations as compared to 70 percent for the nation. The region with lower incomes is thus left with larger numbers to be provided for by the various forms of public relief which depend largely on the fiscal capacity of the states. For the region to reach and maintain a high level of income and security for its future workers ways must be found to extend to these groups the benefits of our social security program.

None of this discussion should imply that the Southeast will not continue its movement toward industrialization. It may suggest, however, that the means will differ somewhat from those once advocated. Artificial inducements to increased industrialization through municipal subsidies in the form of free factory sites, tax exemption, and outright subsidy have not proved their worth in the region. They are not needed in the war program and it is doubtful if they will long continue. Low wages, moreover, will come to count less than increased productivity. A certain normal growth of industrialization continued throughout the depression and was accelerated under defense and is no doubt to be expected in the future. The Southeast can reasonably expect to continue to process its raw materials in meeting the rising demand of its own regional markets. In certain products, it has shown its ability to manufacture for the nation, and, with further equalization of class freight rates, where these are shown to be discriminatory, it should have the chance to expand these markets. Increased facilities for financing regional industry and small business may be indicated here. This is likely to be needed in the post-defense period, for small business, unable to secure war contracts, has been hard hit by priorities and actual shortages of necessary materials.

The moot question of the South's industrialization, it appears, has created more controversy than any other phase of regional development. Here again we need a realization on the part of the nation and the Southeast that high standards of living, increased income and higher wages are necessary to balance our production-consumption budget at a higher level. Economic advance of the South is essential to further national progress. This will include greater technical capacity and higher levels of economic organization and resource use both in agriculture and outside. Further industrialization of the South in processing its raw materials and in utilizing its human resources is likely to continue and should be accompanied by a gradual rise in the purchasing power of labor through enforcement of Federal standards of minimum wages and maximum hours in all basic interstate industries.

Much controversy can be avoided in the future development of the South by the realization the region has to make no drastic choices on the all-or-none basis. We do not have to choose all-out-migration, all-out-industrialization, nor even all-out-diversification to the exclusion of staple crops. The principle to be served is one of balance. While we seek to improve agriculture, we shall also seek to make the best use of industry and of migration opportunities. The goal to be sought and the touchstone of development is higher utilization of resources and higher standards and levels of living for our total population, regional and national. It is these trends that the war effort has accelerated and it is these gains that post-war construction should seek to conserve.

NOTES

1. Howard W. Odum, *Southern Regions of the United States* (Chapel Hill: University of North Carolina Press, 1936), pp. 337–39.

2. Rupert Vance, *All These People: The Nation's Human Resources in the South* (Chapel Hill: University of North Carolina Press, 1945).

3. Erich W. Zimmerman, *World Resources and Industries* (New York: Harper, 1951), pp. 122–33.

4. *After Defense What?* National Resources Planning Board.

5. See Southeastern Regional Development Plan. Interim Report Southeastern Regional Planning Commission of the National Resources Planning Board (Atlanta, Georgia, November, 1941), 204 pp. Also John V. Van Sickle, *Planning for the South: An Inquiry into the Economics of Regionalism* (Nashville: Vanderbilt University Press, 1943).

6. I am indebted here to a paper by Albert S. Keister on the economic structure of the Southeast.

10. Regional Family Patterns

The Southern Family (1948)

This little essay is included here because it illustrates neatly Vance's ability to relate demographic patterns to a society's culture, and vice versa. His discussion of the South's new upper class contains an adumbration of his later concern for the maintenance of high culture in the region, most explicit in "Beyond the Fleshpots" (reprinted below).

Everything that can be said about the family in Western culture can be said with equal truth about many families in the southern United States. If we concentrate on certain characteristics of the family institution that have grown out of regional tradition and social structure, it is with the understanding that the similarities are both more obvious and more significant than the differences.

By tradition and the influence of its governing classes the family was more important in the South than in any other section, unless it was New England. Fertility remained higher, divorce rates were low, and the emphasis on kinship made family status and heritage a sure avenue to social rank. Outside of Louisiana and Kentucky this emphasis on family solidarity owed little to the teachings of the Catholic church. Among the upper classes its religious sanctions were largely those of the Episcopalian church; in other strata it was upheld by a Protestant puritanism that remained strong in rural communities.

Against the area's agricultural background the family tended to retain its economic unity and many of its functions. Its predominance maintained the private aspects of social life at the expense of the public sphere. A discerning social historian has written:

> In the decades after the Civil War the family was the core of southern society; within its bounds everything worth while took place. No one recognized to be a Southerner's social equal dined anywhere other than in his own house or in that of a friend. . . . This

From *American Journal of Sociology* 53 (May 1948): 426–29, by permission of the University of Chicago Press. © 1948 by the University of Chicago.

absorption in household affairs explained why strangers unacquainted with Southern home life found the social scene so dismal. They saw ugly main streets deserted after business hours, and noted an almost complete lack of public entertainment. The hotels were poorly equipped, the restaurants so drab and filthy that they repelled persons of good taste. Southerners who perserved the traditions of comfort and good manners seemed altogether oblivious to these conditions.[1]

As Simkins points out, the interminable visiting among brothers and sisters, the sheltering of elderly aunts and distant cousins, the seeking of favors from relatives in high places, and the innumerable tribal conferences whenever a daughter married or son changed employment, as well as the young people's emphasis on keeping count of "kissing cousins," all testified to a family solidarity approaching clannishness.

It has been said by several critics, and with some insight, that the emphasis on the family reflected the southerner's preoccupation with questions of social stratification quite as much as it showed his devotion to family ideals. The manner of family life, with whatever differences there may exist in total pattern or subtle sentiments, is closely related to the social structure prevailing in the area. Dynamic changes are playing on family life as they interact on this social structure and the norms and values which it represented.[2] Once visitors found "much talk about feminine honor and Southern virtue by those who tolerated a low age of legal consent for illicit relationships."[3] Now there is less talk and more attention to social agencies needed to deal with juvenile delinquency and broken homes.

The basis from which change, disorganization, and reorganization stem is the rural folk pattern of family life. There is as yet no adequate work on the rural family, although C. C. Zimmerman and M. E. Frampton have treated of the Ozark family. Most studies indicate the difficulties that the common folk have in finding in the family satisfaction for a multitude of desires—security, affection, sex, and improved living standards —while at the same time they are carrying the burden of involuntary reproduction.[4]

The size of the family will continue larger among rural people, no doubt; but fertility is declining, partly through a differentiation into what has been called "reflective" and "unreflective" family types. The area of involuntary reproduction is continually being narrowed by the spread of education, public health, and changes in status; but a major association with unreflective fertility seems to be found in the patriarchal structure of the rural family. The pattern of male dominance goes further than the purse strings. It conceals a sexual aggressiveness not found in the family based on companionship. Distinction between family types now appears to depend on whether the wife has had high-school education—a factor that may have some meaning for the companionship family. The distinction is often drawn between conceptions of romantic and companionship marriage. For the rural "common folk" the dichotomy seems to exist between the companionship and the patriarchal family, with a certain amount of realism pervading both in patterns of work, living standards, and sex adjustment.

Two major preoccupations of the rural family on this level determine the role of youth in courtship. The family sees little hope that the daughter will improve her lot by marriage, and the father is thus prone to disapprove of any suitor in her own stratum. The mother is more sympathetic but sees drudgery as her daughter's lot. If the father dominates, no boy that the girl is able to attract is likely to be made welcome at her home. Both parents are afraid the girl will "get into trouble with boys" and thus they attempt to restrict her contacts outside the home. The family exercises little control over the son's role in courtship; his troubles come from the girl's family. The conflicts which the girl faces increase her desire for independence and thus play a part in inducing her early marriage. After marriage the daughter is welcomed on a realistic basis, and both families will give what help they can to get the couple started in life.

In E. Franklin Frazier's brilliant monograph, the Negro family has received more careful analysis than any other family group in the United States. Its changing status may be measured against this same rural folk background. Its matriarchal form, its survivals from slavery, its continued struggle against dissolution, poverty, and limited education are replaced by middle-class standards among those achieving professional status. The break in domestic manners, sex, and family standards between upper and lower classes is as complete among Negroes as in any group in Western culture. Girls brought up in middle-class homes are shielded from contacts with boys whose behavior may be uncouth because of class origins.

Puritanical standards are less evident and sex behavior is less inhibited among the Negro folk groups. Nevertheless, without much statistical evidence, there are good "reasons to believe that miscegenation has declined and concubinage almost ceased to exist." The Negro's increased self-respect has operated with the avowed policy behind segregation, if not to interdict, at least to cast suspicion on, all heterosexual acquaintanceship across the color line. Violence is thus restricted, but occasionally sexual aggression brings indictments of white men for assault on Negro females. Increases in divorce, often taken as an index of family disorganization, represent an approach to stabilization among certain Negro groups. Legal arrangements take the place of informal domestic shifts, and the new family thus moves within the aura of community approval.

Preoccupation with the old agrarian aristocracy has kept students from giving more than casual attention to the standards under development by the South's new ruling class. J. P. Lichtenberger explained low divorce rates by the statement that "Southerners are traditional, romantic, chivalrous, and incurably idealistic."[5] The shift in control to men of commerce and industry left these older symbols without significant cultural content. Simkins writes:

> Merchants, bankers and industrial groups of the new South won economic power without achieving that social dominance which America in all areas outside the South accorded to business leaders. . . .
>
> The businessmen lacked distinction of their own; they were overshadowed by the more successful industrialists of the North whom they imitated in dress and economic concepts. . . .
>
> These self-made men did not know how to educate their sons to the responsibilities of wealth and did not always appreciate the importance of placing their daughters in exclusive educational and social circles. Family fortunes were frequently scattered through impractical marriages.[6]

A striking characteristic of the new upper-class southern society, as Simkins points out, was its almost complete lack of intellectual interests:

> Although members of the third generation of leaders were often college bred, they usually specialized in "campus courses," football and fraternities. They were induced by editors and professors to support museums and orchestras but displayed little understanding or enjoyment of these institutions. Theirs was the company of the perpetual Philistines to whom it meant social suicide to discuss intellectual or esthetic subjects.[7]

Upper classes are important because they embody the goals and values to which other groups aspire. While the South's new upper classes appeared unlikely to perpetuate old patterns of family life, they were not prepared to inculcate new ones. Stability and decorum proved of less importance, but the new roles of men, women, and children were not revalued in rational terms that the society understood. Except for the novelists like Ellen Glasgow, no one has depicted these conflicts in family standards. Since change, like the news, directs attention to problems rather than to long-time trends, it was noted that family disorganization increased and that Florida and Arkansas found it profitable to join Nevada as Meccas for quick divorce. Unconventional behavior, however, found no sanctions in an intellectual radicalism; family scandals were handled by lawyers in a manner befitting big business anywhere, but, like southern drunkenness, they were admittedly in the immoral pattern. Occasionally the point was made that upper-class youth were experimenting with the mores of chastity, just as the Negroes were beginning to accept them.

Less needs to be said about middle-class standards or the problems of the new industrial classes now rising in southern cities and mill towns. Patterns of the middle-class family are least divergent, for they represent largely the influence of general education and the acceptance of standards that prevail in urban culture. Among working-class families the problems of adequate standards, of working mothers, of juveniles on city streets, of member roles and family structure, differ in some respects from those in our great cities. Greater homogeneity of ethnic and cultural backgrounds reduces somewhat the incidence of family tensions as compared to problems faced by immigrant stocks. The smaller size of cities may give certain advantages in housing, etc., but they also afford fewer community and social case agencies for the adjustment of the problems of the underprivileged. The strain to improve family status through better education and the choice of marriage partners for youth and the competitive strain to improve living standards through application to the job are now characteristics of urban and industrial families everywhere. The patriarchal family is losing its character with the increased economic independence of women. With no large Catholic influence outside Louisiana and Kentucky, the resort to divorce is increasing in the South as elsewhere. And, as elsewhere, instability seemed to accompany the movement toward a more democratic family life.

NOTES

1. Francis Butler Simkins, *The South: Old and New* (New York: Alfred A. Knopf, 1947), p. 294.

2. Wilbert E. Moore and Robin M. Williams, "Stratification in the Antebellum South," *American Sociological Review* 7 (June 1942): 331–51; Rudolf Heberle, "Social Change in the South," *Social Forces* 25 (October 1946): 9–15.

3. Simkins, *The South: Old and New*, p. 292.

4. Margaret Jarman Hagood, *Mothers of the South* (Chapel Hill: University of North Carolina Press, 1939), pp. 108–69. Nora Miller (*The Girl in the Rural Family* [Chapel Hill: University of North Carolina Press, 1935], pp. 7–92) describes the role of the adolescent girl in eight types of southern rural families: dependent, mountain farm, coal mining, cotton farm, tobacco farm, potato farm, fishing community, and superior families. Gilbert W. Bebee, in *Contraception and Fertility in the Southern Appalachians* (Baltimore: Williams and Wilkins, 1942), pp. 56–85, found fertility higher because of uncontrolled conception and of marriage two years earlier than among women in the poorer classes elsewhere in the nation.

5. J. P. Lichtenberger, *Divorce: A Social Interpretation* (New York: McGraw-Hill, 1937), p. 117.

6. Simkins, *The South: Old and New*, pp. 285–86.

7. Ibid., pp. 291–92.

11. The Regional Concept as a Tool for Social Research (1951)

The symposium from which this article comes marked the high point of "regionalism" as a scholarly concern. Vance attempted here to place regional sociology in the context of area studies generally and to relate it to its parent discipline of sociology. As a summary of regional research and an explication of what regional sociologists had been doing for a generation, this article is unsurpassed. Vance's program for future research remained largely unrealized, as his interests and those of other "regionalist" scholars turned elsewhere.

It is a paradox that the development of regional analysis has paralleled the growth of world-wide communication and trade, the emergence of cosmopolitan culture, and the ideology of One World. The paradox has its explanation in the fact that the regional approach to social analysis has an integrative rather than a divisive function. Any practicing member of the social science fraternity who undertakes to use the regional concept as a tool for research will soon find, in Howard W. Odum's felicitous phrase, that the choice he has made is not that of regionalism *or* but regionalism *and*. The missing term is nation or world, for the region gains its significance only from its relation to a total structure. The relation that regionalism presumes to study is that of parts to wholes.

Without committing ourselves to either mechanistic or organic models, we must realize that the concept of a structure the elements of which are themselves smaller structures, is neither unfamiliar nor new. In philosophy Lucretius anticipated the atomic theory of physical structure, and Leibniz's treatment of the living organism as a plenum of organisms was an anticipation of cellular theory. In political science, federations from Ancient Greece to Modern Switzerland have given us examples of social structure whose component parts are similar structures.[1] No region can be defined except in relation to the total structure of which it is a compo-

From Merrill Jensen, ed., *Regionalism in America* (Madison and Milwaukee: University of Wisconsin Press, 1965 [1951]), pp. 119–40. © by the Board of Regents of the University of Wisconsin System.

nent part. No more can the reciprocal relation of function to structure be grasped apart from this theme of unity in diversity, familiar to Americans in the motto of their Federal Union, *e pluribus unum.*

Regionalism is thus a concept that cuts across many lines. Recent developments testify to the interest such ideas have aroused in the teaching and research programs of the social sciences. There have emerged a whole series of new programs, variously termed "American Studies" and "American Civilization," in which several disciplines, notably English and history, have converged to explore the literature and civilization of the United States and its different regions.[2] Richard H. Shyrock sees these programs as an attempt to repair the effects of specialization and the fragmentation of fields "which threatened understanding." The effort "to re-establish synthesis," he writes, "has taken various forms—from a return to the certitudes of the Middle Ages to the integration of our own complex scholarship. The study of American Civilization is one form of the latter process."[3]

The area studies developed during the war as a military necessity have been carried forward in the study of major world areas.[4] "All the social sciences, along with the functional study of languages, are brought together in area studies to promote a comprehensive understanding of a particular region, country, nation or civilization as a 'highly individual social and historical configuration in which all sorts of facts and events stand related in intricate and peculiar ways.'"[5]

Studies in both these fields are largely in the descriptive stage, and their theoretical and conceptual organization remains relatively undeveloped. Accordingly, it is not yet apparent how their attempts at synthesis are related to regionalism, although it is clear that both depend on areal and cultural concepts already developed in the contributions of geography and anthropology to regional analysis.

In the social science field one may note that the latest survey of American life, *Recent Social Trends* (New York, 1936), "took little notice of regional characteristics although its pages were full of data which invited a regional interpretation." On the other hand, there is a notable project in which specialists in the language, collaborating with specialists in social structure and geography, set out to develop a *Linguistic Atlas of the United States.*[6] Moreover, the work selected by specialists as the most noteworthy example of recent historical research was not conventional history at all but a regional monograph, showing in historical depth the development of civilization in a major area—the Great Plains.[7]

In 1936 the unilateral treatment of *Recent Social Trends* was corrected by one of its architects in a full-scale analysis which developed six major composite regions of the United States and documented the complex character of one, the Southeast.[8] "The Southeastern program is noteworthy," writes Julian H. Steward, "because of the conceptualization of the regional unit, and because it calls for a focus upon a particular problem for interdisciplinary collaboration."[9] The regional point of view was given official statement by the National Resources Planning Board in *Regional Factors in National Planning and Development* (1935) and reinforced by some baker's dozen of regional planning reports, all pointing to the close association of regional research and the planning movement. Few of these projects have developed complete and coherent regional theory, but all have served to show the contemporary interest in regionalism as a tool for research.

It is evident that we have many disciplines making use of regional units as a means of analyzing and understanding the phenomena with which they have to deal. Most of these uses of the regional concept have distinct value for social science research, and it is the purpose of this paper to glance at (1) the kinds of questions they undertake to answer, (2) the techniques used, (3) the basic logic common to this approach, and (4) the different levels of conceptual integration involved.

Several major questions arise: How is the concept of regionalism to furnish orientation for research in social science? What is a region? What frame of reference does regionalism employ? What point of view does it advance, and how does this point of view fit into the general background of social theory? What techniques are at its command, and what is the logic to be followed as the method of regional analysis is applied at various levels of explanation and interpretation? Consideration of these questions may well be preceded by a warning that standardization has not yet occurred in this field. Indeed it is doubtful that standardization is desirable at the present stage of regional analysis and theory. There can be no denial, however, that each specialist needs to know more about the developments made by his colleagues in the social sciences.

In political science the problem of relating parts to wholes is clarified by the fact that political entities have legal boundaries. In much of our social science analysis we deal with natural areas whose boundaries must be determined by research into the characteristics and functions of the regions under consideration. Given this advantage, history and political science have been able to specialize in the analysis of international and interregional relation in terms of formal structures and formal functions. By the same token, the social sciences are now proceeding to the analysis of cultural and economic phenomena where the basis has not been laid in formal political structures. "In both international and national affairs," Charles E. Martin has said, "regionalism has an office and a function. As a basis of consolidation and centralization, it integrates units within itself, and as a basis of decentralization, it forms units within the larger systems of administration and control."[10] Accordingly those who use regionalism as a guiding concept in research should never forget that when dealing with smaller units it has an integrating function. When considering relations to the universal system of which the area is a part, regionalism has a decentralizing function.

Once we abandon the formal boundaries set by political allegiance and the needs of internal administration, we are met with the question: What is a region?

What is a region? Geographers have variously defined the region as "any portion of the earth's surface whose physical conditions are similar"; as "distinguished by the use to which it is put"; and as defined by "an *ensemble de rapports* between man and the natural milieu." Sociologists have seen the region "as comprised of a constellation of communities"; as characterized by "a homogeneity of economic and social structure"; as a culture area, "an area whose people are bound together by mutual dependencies arising from common interests"; as "an area of which the inhabitants instinctively feel themselves a part." A Hindu sociologist, Radhakamal Mukerjee, points to the region as a psychological complex: "The region," he writes, "is a common and coordinate set of stimuli, eliciting a similarity of responses, habits and feelings which are reinforced by gregariousness and which are moulded and stabilized into a characteristic mental type and pattern of living."[11]

Manifestly, many definitions of the region reinforce each other. Points of view will vary by disciplines, but it is possible to have a general definition of the region as a unit of areal and cultural differentiation. Each region must differ from neighboring regions but must approximate a mode of homogeneous characteristics if it is to possess identity. As an objective entity and as a heuristic device for research, the ideal region will always be the composite region in which economic, political, and cultural identity is evident. Since part of this will inhere in the nature of the data and part will inhere in the purpose of the investigator, we are likely to have continued controversies about the structure and functions of specific regions.

In policy and planning, both practical considerations and the knowledge of people's attitudes will often determine the size and type of regions selected. Odum and Moore have suggested that in some such way as the astronomer's region is the space that can be explored with existing telescopes, so an administrative region must assure reasonable maximum distance for travel, organization, study, and administration. Obviously the choice and delimitation of regions is a function of the research to be undertaken or the public policy to be administered. Obviously, also, there are regions that will remain true regions regardless of whether any research is ever done or any administrative agencies ever set up with reference to their needs and functions.

Regionalism is thus a concept of many facets. Few areas of social science research have escaped its rays. To show its dynamic aspects and to relate it to history and social change, the region must be interpreted both as structure and as function, as process and product. It is not our commission to attempt a conceptual integration of the social science field. It would seem futile, however, to explore the logic of this approach except against the broad background of social theory.

Social research has on its agenda unfinished business—the task of providing an understanding of the society and the world in which we live. This, I fear, is a never-ending business, for society is forever changing beneath our feet and around our heads. No sooner does one generation lay claim to the understanding of its economic order, its political order, or its social order than the next generation reports that it has a new order—the old order has dissolved and resolved so that a new equilibrium and a new balance prevail.

Each generation of scholars is faced accordingly with the task of commanding its social life and its economic and political processes to stand still, as it were, so that they may be dissected and their structure and their organization presented in cross section. The social scientist today has come to realize the dilemma faced by the biologist of yesterday. The biologist found that the only still specimen was a dead specimen. The cross sections of his specimens gave him the structure of the animal, the icy perfection of anatomy; but when he wanted to determine the function, the physiology, he had on his hands for analysis "a living, breathing, pulsating riot." Society is no less dynamic. Certainly it took more than the dissection of cadavers to give us a knowledge of process; and yet how would Sir William Harvey have understood the circulation of the blood or the army surgeon William Beaumont the digestive processes of his half-breed, had they not known structure?[12]

The student of social theory accordingly can do no better, it would seem to me, than continually to remind himself that society exists both as process and as product. In the ongoing trend of society, the process is one of social change, but the end product is the development of social order. The energies of men are merged and channeled in a hundred different processes to result in a hundred different products. Structure is the product of ongoing processes, but structure itself becomes process as it goes over into function.

Regionalism as a research key is not to be understood apart from considerations of process, structure, and function. Regional structure is capable of analysis both as spatial pattern and as a facet of social organization. Its boundaries are both physical and cultural, and it is fortunate for the regionalist that, as Louis Wirth has said, the physical, economic, and cultural contours of the region usually coincide. It is characterized by "homogeneity of economic and social structure," for its order and organization have come out of the processes converging within the area.

This is also true for the structure of the larger unit. The nation is a fabric of regions, and it is the functioning of these interrelated structures that gives us the national life with its phenomena of regional-national balance and integration. Odum and Moore have developed the terminology for this interrelated regional structure. The term "region" denotes a composite major area which in America is a group of states corresponding both to a historic section and to a culture area. New England and the Midwest represent this type of composite societal region in American culture. For the minor area the term "subregion" is used. "Both of these are clearly differentiated from single purpose, isolated and specialized areas such as organizational or administrative units including districts, provinces, centers, zones, and the like." For subdivisions such as administrative areas the term "district" is suggested, while "zone" is also available.[13] Finally, it should be pointed out that studies of decentralization and of concentration, of international and national federation, of regional blocs and federations, are all studies of changing structure and function.

It is the contention of this paper that the potential role of regionalism as a conceptual tool for research has not been adequately understood in social science mainly for two reasons: First, its potential contributions have not been visualized against the background of general theory—an undertaking that must precede as well as follow the unfolding of regional analysis and theory.

In the second place, we have the problem of method and the logic of regional analysis. Regional analysis involves not one but several levels of attack developed along an ascending scale of complexity. It proceeds from the application, at an initial level, of simple techniques, to the development of complex theory at the highest level of integration. The remainder of the paper will discuss these four levels of analysis involved in regionalism as follows: (1) the delimitation of one-factor regions in the case of phenomena involving one variable, (2) the delimitation of complex regions, (3) the regional monograph involving the analysis and integration of the forces and processes acting in a complex region, and (4) the analysis of interregional relations.

The choice of single-factor regions follows logically from the choice of the problem to be studied. This method is valuable when one variable is involved and the main problem is to delimit component areas and show their relation to the whole. The analysis of such a universe in terms of a fabric of regions is simply an example of the convenience of studying the parts in order to understand the whole. This, I take it, is the only problem developed by those pragmatic specialists, the sales managers, in the following title which I lift verbatim from the December, 1937, issue of *Western Advertising*: "Regionalism Can Mean More Efficient Sales Volume, If Its Principles Are Rightly Applied."

We can begin with an illustration of what we call the first level of complexity in regional analysis. As an aid to understanding folk culture, anthropologists and sociologists might well note the country's distribution of rural house types as constructed by folk carpenters untrained in architecture.[14] Division of the nation into regions on the basis of one such trait or factor is a simple technique that represents the first use of the regional concept. In the same fashion, sales areas delimited by the United States Department of Commerce give the structure of wholesale and retail markets in the United States;[15] an account of the process involved in their relations would show how wholesale and retail trade function.

The second level of integration involves the regionalization of a universe on the basis of several variables or characteristics. The delimitation of complex regions may proceed by one of two methods, each having its own logic. One may (1) attempt to reconstruct the process by which a region has been built up out of its component parts, or one may (2) use statistical measurement to delimit areas homogeneous in certain economic, social, and cultural characters. The first method has been used in economics and ecology; the second has been developed as a cultural-statistical method.

How does this technique build up the subregion from its component units? An answer has been ventured at the theoretical level in economics by August Losch, whose *Die räumliche Ordnung der Wirtschaft* is promised an early English translation. Beginning with self-sufficing farmsteads equally distributed on a level plain of equal fertility, Losch follows the process as selected farmers, benefiting from the economics of large-scale production, make and distribute a product once made by hand on each of the self-sufficing units. As the product—bread, beer, or what you wish —is marketed to neighboring farmsteads, there appears the familiar scheme of hexagonal areas, each with a radius determined by the increasing cost of transportation. Losch here found three main types of economic areas that build up into regional constructs: (1) simple market areas, (2) nets of such areas, and (3) systems of nets. Such a subregion then is a system of nets; it integrates a complex of products and is thus a functioning organization rather than simply an areal structure. Finally, since in practice no such regions are themselves self-sufficing, their exchange with other regions will be mediated through central or port cities. Losch also tried to test his theoretical construct against actual situation in a fairly uniform area and selected Iowa for this analysis.[16]

In something of the same fashion, Walter Christaller developed his central-place theory of the growth of communities and their integration in regional organization. He applied his hypothesis to an area in South Germany and arrived at a hierarchy of subregions by communities of different size.[17] The astronomical perfection of this approach to the constellation of communities has repelled many students who feel that actual situations do not yield social geometry of such symmetrical proportions.

It was at the University of Wisconsin that Charles J. Galpin's pioneer study of Walworth County developed the concept of the "rururban" community with its constellation of farmsteads integrated around the trade and service centers.[18] Carried forward by J. H. Kolb and others, this method has not only served to delimit the farmer's community but has enabled us to understand how communities build up in cumulative fashion into subregions.

The integration of smaller regions into the structure of the large metropolitan region was largely the work of R. D. McKenzie and others. Again the process is largely economic in its ordering and function. C. A. Dawson has summarized the impact of these studies as follows:

In each physiographic region a major or gateway city emerges. The expanse of territory tributary to each city depends on transportation advantages, the resources of its hinterland and the stage reached in its development. Its life cycle of development links it in increasing intensity with a widening hinterland. If such a city has certain natural advantages in location and means of transportation it tends to become the center of a metropolitan region which extends beyond its original physiographic area. Meanwhile, the central city becomes increasingly the point of dominance about which its tributary hinterland develops its natural organization. Each of the region's subsidiary cities, towns, and village communities finds a more or less specialized place and functions competitively in the intra-regional division of labor. The most active agents in differentiating the function of subsidiary communities and integrating them with the center of dominance are the highly specialized institutions to be found in the latter. In the main all this takes place tentatively and selectively by means of the play of natural forces.

These metropolitan regions in turn compete with each other with regard to position and function. In such a struggle between giants the destinies of a region's subsidiary cities are involved. The region here competes as a unit through its gateway cities. In this fashion the whole of North America is in the process of being organized into a constellation of metropolitan regions. In the United States, New York and Chicago have come to play the role of super-centers of domination, integrating about them in a natural organization all outlying regions.[19]

In many instances, measures of common modes of life are taken to determine the structure of the region. This corresponds to the anthropologist's interest in the cultural areas of primitive societies. The logic here is fairly clear. "The fabric of modern society is composed," as C. L. Gregory writes, "of variable traits that are correlated among themselves." The approach of cultural areas thus is in terms of the culture complex, and the homogeneity of the region as contrasted with others is one of degree rather than of kind. Gregory has said that if no cultural trait were related to any other, a region would have to be determined by a single trait and thus would have no meaning except in terms of that trait.[20]

Regions are delineated in terms of statistical indices of important cultural, economic, or social conditions. Since these figures are gathered on the basis of administrative areas, such as enumeration districts, urban census tracts, minor civil divisions, and counties, the process is one of building up small political units into homogeneous subregions. We have discussed subregions organized and dominated by cities; it is fortunate that we can now draw examples from rural regions. Here the first important analysis divided the country into areas according to major types of farming.[21]

How important indices are selected and how they serve to delimit areas has been demonstrated with a rigorous statistical technique by Margaret Jarman Hagood and associates.[22] By applying correlation analysis to 83 measures of social and economic variation among Ohio counties, C. E. Lively and R. B. Almack had reduced the number successively to 32, to 16, and finally to 3 indices to which the 16 measures were related with correlation coefficients of .60 or above. The three indices were measures of rural fertility, average gross income per farm, and an index of the rural plane of living.[23] Hagood then applied the method of principal components (factor analysis) to develop homogeneous subregions on the basis of the selected characteristics. So that the counties of the subregions would be contiguous, latitude and longitude were introduced as two additional characteristics. The first-factor loadings were computed for the final series of measures on the 88 counties from a matrix of their intercorrelations. A composite index of subregionalization was formed by weighting each series with its first-factor loading. Counties grouped by class intervals of their values on this index then fell into contiguous subregions, with the exception of some six or seven counties containing large cities.

Arthur R. Mangus has made use of the technique developed by Lively and Almack to delimit two types of rural areas and subareas for the whole country. On the basis of farm indices he divided the country into 218 agricultural subregions and 32 general regions. When indices of industry and urban centers were admitted, Mangus found 106 strictly agricultural subregions and 158 agricultural-industrial subregions, which coalesce in 34 major areas. The general boundaries of the 32 major farm regions and 34 rural regions coincide with few exceptions.[24]

In a later paper Hagood applied this method of principal components to a test of the delimitation of groups-of-states regions in the United States as developed by Howard W. Odum. The results (shown in the Figure 11.1) can be interpreted as follows: Index values (numbers shown in circles) representing a composite of agricultural and population char-

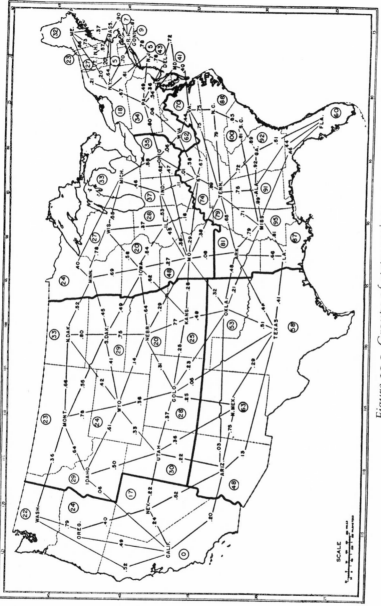

Figure 11.1. Groups-of-states regions.

acteristics were developed for the states. Then, in order to group states into regions, a correlation analysis was made, showing the similarity of each state to its neighbors. (On the map, the coefficient of correlation between a state and each of its neighbors is shown by the small numeral in the break of the line radiating from the center of the state.) Florida is far from resembling any neighboring state on these measures; but since this plan admits of no one-state regions, Florida by necessity falls in the Southeast. Missouri offers something of a problem but shows its closest resemblance to Illinois. West Virginia is found to have its closest attachment to the Southeast on the basis of agriculture and population. If we desire to separate the Northeast into two areas, the homogeneity of the New England States is clearly demonstrated by this method.[25]

It is fortunate that the regionalist has this rigorous technique at his command if for no other reason than to demonstrate that regions are not to be determined on the basis of whim and personal predilections. This is not to say that regional analysis is all statistics, or that only measured and counted phenomena fall into the picture. In the case of West Virginia, for example, the historical fact that the area "seceded from secession" during the Civil War was given sufficient cultural importance in Howard W. Odum's analysis to outweigh certain other characteristics for which statistical indices were at hand.

To show that statistics is not everything, let us turn aside for the moment to ask a question about local history. Why is it that local history, with its infinite attention to detail, has proved so deadly dull and so lacking in general significance? Shall we say that the local historian often fails to delimit a significant area and, lacking a subregion of determinate characteristics and problems, has no principle by which to integrate his treatment or to relate his local area to other areas? Discursive and un-pruned as it is, a book like Archer Butler Hulbert's *Soil: Its Influence on American History*[26] suggests how local historians, by combining several of their beloved counties into a natural subregion, might write history of distinctive value to social science.

The next level of complexity in research involves the analysis and integration of forces and processes acting within a region. The delimitation of regions may solve certain scientific problems, but often it is to be regarded as preliminary to this portrayal of a complex region in process. To be functional and dynamic, regional analysis must transcend the limitations of the traditional survey, regional or social. In the choice of data this research task is closely related to that of the preceding level. The

interplay and interaction of phenomena that create the regional *Gestalt*
—the concurrence of forces—should logically find representation in the
same indices that were used to delimit the area. The point at issue is
simple: Whatever factors are found to fuse together to give us the regional
economy, the regional culture, and the region's consensus of opinion—
these, obviously, are the factors which in the beginning should be selected
for use in drawing boundaries between regions. If this is regarded as
close reasoning, it may be given illustration. A market analyst might be
satisfied to delimit a network of trade areas in order to explain market
phenomena. To delimit an economic region, however, would demand the
use of multiple indices—indices representing the interplay of economic
forces. Once the analyst has determined the economic forces whose integration he hopes to depict in a regional monograph—for example, the
organization of physical production, of transportation, of distribution,
and of finance—he has also selected the indices to be used in dividing his
universe, in this case the national economy, into its component regional
units.

Early geographers sought to determine and catalogue the geographic
relationships and influences existing in a region. If enough could be catalogued, a satisfactory regional report could be prepared.[27] Contemporary
regional analysis seeks to show the region as a totality. This point of view
is well set forth in the eloquent statement of Vidal de la Blache:

> A country is a reserve of energies whose origin lies in nature but
> whose development depends upon man. It is man who, by moulding
> the land to his own purposes, brings out its individuality. He estab-
> lishes a connection between its separate features. He substitutes for
> its incoherent effects of local circumstances, a systematic concourse
> of forces. It is thus that a country defines and differentiates itself and
> finally becomes, as it were, a medal struck off in the effigy of a
> people.[28]

To present an integrated account of a region requires a dynamic rather
than a static approach and necessarily cuts across the traditional frontiers
drawn by our academic disciplines.

Preoccupation with regional structure and the task of defining regional
boundaries on the map tends too much to the impression that the region
is a fixed and static thing. This misapprehension is to be corrected in the
present level of regional study. Here the task of research is dynamic; it
aims at understanding the direction and redirection of a continual flow of

forces. In the transition to the demographic and industrial region, inert resources, for example, become a flow of goods. With the emergence of equilibrium in flow and interflow, the regional balance of population, regional balance of trade, and regional hierarchy of resources testify that the cultural and economic region has arrived. This flow may come from the hands of nature, but it leaves the region man-made. Streams and water power, men and communities, goods and transportation, trade and the regional balance of exports, population and migration—the region maintains its economic equilibrium and its social consensus by a continual flow and reflow of goods, people, services, and ideas.

Finally, the regional approach stands in contrast to the prevailing academic tradition. It brings phenomena into juxtaposition simply because they converge in a given spatial area or *Gestalt*, and from this juxtaposition it develops the relationships that aim at depicting the "integrated social system of an area."

Regional research, it must be remembered, became the core and culmination of geographic study simply by unifying phenomena around this principle. "It is the original role of geography," wrote Lespagnol, "to put in contact the facts which other sciences study in isolation." "Western science," writes Rudolf Heberle, "has been developed by specialization along lines of problem complexes or by abstraction and isolation of certain meaningful aspects of the chaotic reality. The social sciences are no exception to this principle. The aim is always the establishment of general principles, not the comprehensive knowledge of a concrete regional society."[29]

Disciplines are thus logical systems by which we focus our attention upon one complex of phenomena to the exclusion of others. But new and different relationships are seen in regional analysis. As Herberle says, "A certain familiarity with details in various fields of observation which can be achieved only for a limited regional area enables one to see connections, causal and others, which may escape the less initiated specialist who is accustomed to think within the framework of his particular discipline."[30]

With these considerations in mind, it is not surprising to find that few of our major regions have received adequate analysis. If the University of Chicago holds out, we bid fair to learn more about its city than was ever known of any other metropolitan region. I am tempted to say the same thing of Howard W. Odum and the Southeast. Certainly the complex regional case study is one of the highest products of the regional method. It does not, however, complete the ambitious task of regionalism.

Finally we come to the highest level of integration—the use of regionalism as the areal-cultural frame of reference for the comparative study of society. Here it is not enough to have specialized knowledge of single regions. This fourth level of complexity, therefore, embodies the goal to which, I take it, all our disciplines aspire—the creation of valid and significant theory of society and human behavior. This is the area of interregional relations. The task of constructing a social science on which we can stand is not going to be as simple as men thought a generation ago. Regionalism will contribute to the achievement, but at the moment it promises to increase rather than lessen the complexity of the task.

The emphasis falls on interregional relations—the comparative study of problems common to many regions, regional-national balance, and the processes of interregional adjustment and equilibrium. Regionalism can be advanced to this level of complexity only on the assumption that in the field of learning there is still a place for historical and theoretical scholarship. The goal is, therefore, to contribute to the development of a universal and general science of society and human behavior. The most useful theoretical model would seem to be the idea of a structure, the elements of which are themselves similar, if smaller, structures. The assumption is that such theory may be approached by the analysis of society's component units, the relations of functioning parts and wholes.

If one theory could be made to fit all conceivable areas and situations, there would exist no need for the comparative theory that regionalism promises at this level. But, fortunately or not, regionalism in one form or another seems destined to review—if not to undermine—all those theories that speculate about some sort of abstract man, abstract culture, or abstract economy. Theories developed in one culture area or in one stage must be tested against those developed about other areas or stages. In a slightly different context, John Maynard Keynes has sharply drawn the issue for economics: "The characteristics of the special case assumed by the classical theory happen not to be those of the economic society in which we actually live with the result that its teaching is misleading and disastrous if we attempt to apply it to the facts of experience."[31]

Interregional comparisons have made necessary new beginnings, and as these new departures are integrated and interpreted, they will lead to new levels of theory. It has been the contribution of world-area studies to force us to the realization that many of our universal generalizations apply only to Western culture. The comparison of different world areas means the comparative study of economic, cultural, and legal systems. In anthropology the results of a comparative approach to the study of cultural units are clearly evident. We have on the one hand those studies in which each separate culture is presented as an integrated pattern, a totality in which the significance of each trait and complex is determined by its relations to a functional whole. On another level we find that anthropology has solved for the time being the baffling question of intercultural relationships on the basis of cultural relativity—a neutral solution in terms of mores and ethics, displeasing to some but justified if the analyst himself is to escape the charge of ethnocentrism.

For the moment we must leave to the future the task of exploring the application of this point of view to international relations. In the study of our national life, it was the task of Frederick Jackson Turner to demonstrate the historical depths of this concept. This he did by showing the accumulated experience left in our cultural tradition by those two great complexes, the frontier and the section. Both the frontier and the section can be characterized as an area, an economy, and a type of culture.

In his studies of interprovincial relations, Turner, as Merle Curti points out, interpreted American political history in terms of a contest between economic and social sections:

> Below the surface of politics sectional groupings disclosed the lines on which new party issues were forming: rival sections made alliances, ententes, for no section could by itself determine national policy to suit its needs. . . . The existence of sub-sections within the larger sections complicated these interprovincial relations, often restrained sectional leaders and sometimes accounted for political straddling. National parties had their sectional wings, and party organization, also tended to diminish sectional antagonisms.[32]

Regional balance, as it is developed, will come out of the maturing of America's own political and economic experience with the frontier and the sections. The transition from an unsettled country marks the gradual change from the frontier process to social control. The intermediate stage in the transition is sectionalism; the ultimate stage may well be regionalism and regional-national planning. Under extreme laissez faire the frontier process carved human-use regions out of the differentiated area of newly settled territories. The frontier was a region in flux. The flow of population and the appropriation of regional resources proceeded apace in a process of extreme individualism, and the region did not appear until a degree of equilibrium was attained. In the self-contained economy of the frontier, the flow of population in a measure substituted for the flow of goods.

With the emergence of interregional trade and comparative advantage, and the coalescence of the economic interests of class groups now in possession of the region's resources of land, mineral rights, and industrial opportunities, the "sustentation region," in Giddings' phrase, becomes the section, conscious of the clash of economic interests within the nation. The section was a region smarting under economic penalties established in the national policy. The logic of sectionalism consisted in calculating the economic value of union and led more than once to overt separatist movements. Only once, however, has a sectional interest refused to accept peacefully its defeat at the polls.

Social control, hardly possible in the frontier flux, thus appears attainable when the flow and interchange of regional forces approaches equilibrium. Yet there is the danger that a frontier may remain a region in the raw material stage—contributing to national wealth and receiving little in return. The nationalization of business so vividly described by Ida M. Tarbell and others meant the localization of its returns in a few dominant areas. The historical acceptance of the income tax and the redistribution of these gains in the interest of national welfare marked the beginning of a shift toward regional-national balance.

What of the danger of sectional bias in the regional approach? It is customary to warn young scholars entering regional study of this danger, and it may be well to close this paper with a glance at the question. No doubt the problem has yet to be put in correct perspective, but I do not see that it differs essentially from the perennial problem of bias inherent in all social science research. To write of conflict and of war itself is not to advocate conflict. The historian of sectional conflict is not a participant; he is rather a recorder. We all live in regions as well as nations; for the scientist in the field, the problem is every whit as big as, but no bigger than, the problem of nationalistic bias in writing history. Some historians have passed the test; some have not. Can the reading public tell the difference between these attitudes, and does it respect objective history and reject chauvinism? Similarly with the analysis of class phenomena.

Then finally there is the saving honesty of the analyst who admits his value premises and yet refrains from a partisan presentation. The historian of a labor union can admit his sympathy with its aims and yet write honest, factual history. The critical faculty of the historian in treating the problem of sectionalism in his own area has been beautifully demonstrated, I feel, in Charles S. Sydnor's *Development of Southern*

Sectionalism, 1819–1848.[33] Similarly a regional monograph will of necessity be organized around the problems of a region if the work is to have unity and point. The author can show, if he likes, how much the realization of regional goals would affect other areas and other interests.

There exists one tendency to sectionalism, hardly on the level of social science, which has sometimes been allowed to flourish by default. This bias is more often shown in the treatment of the national economy, the national culture, and the arts than in analysis of the political process, where divergent interests are usually accepted for what they are—a basis of conflict. This point of view is found in the assumption that the designs, goals, and rewards of a dominant section are those of the nation itself. It is more subtle if it goes unstated; it grates harshly if the outlying provinces are explicitly called provincial. In the arts, for example, the artistic tastes or the artistic treasures peculiar to the metropolis are assumed to be those of the nation or for the good of the nation. This, of course, is precisely the point that should be argued, not assumed. The point of view is most sectional when it glosses over sectionalism or berates it.

In economics it is the bland view (so well exposed in Woodrow Wilson's *New Freedom,* 1913) which upholds monopoly under the guise of a theory of private enterprise—a theory which would stifle all private enterprise except that of monopolists. This type of sectionalism is sometimes accepted by good Americans who would recognize as sheer chauvinism its international counterpart—the assumption that the good of America is the good of all the world, whether the world wants that good or no.

It is no answer to this problem of sectional interest in sheep's clothing to state it in the familiar terms of the provinces against the metropolis. Ruralism against metropolitanism is not exactly the regional issue. We mediate our lives, our economy, and much of our cultural and artistic productivity today through cities. It is not a rural-urban issue, simply because each great region must finally develop its own regional centers and subcenters. Such regional capitals may well be artistic, literary, and cultural centers, as well as major livestock markets, cotton markets, and grain markets for the areas' economic production. An example of the danger to be avoided can be found in France. The extent to which Paris dominates the nation's artistic and intellectual life has reduced French provincial cities to cultural monotony. French travelers often remark on the economic and cultural rank of our regional cities as compared to those of France. Regional capitals need not be provincial. They should be regional, which to me means functional in relation both to the region and to the nation. The New York–Chicago axis will, I suspect, continue for some time to dominate, with occasional help from Hollywood, the financial, artistic, and cultural trends of our national life. As our great major areas pass from frontier, to sections, to regions, as they fill out their complex structure, they too will develop metropolitan centers and subcenters —centers which will realize their function and thus relieve the megalopolis of its centralizing tendency, thereby preventing "apoplexy at the center and paralysis at the extremities."

NOTES

1. Norbert Weiner, *Cybernetics: Or Control and Communication in the Animal and the Machine* (New York, 1948), p. 181.

2. Tremaine McDowell, *American Studies* (Minneapolis, 1948). The American Council of Learned Societies has a committee which brings together representatives of the disciplines concerned to consider mutual problems of research. The first issue of a new journal in this field, *American Quarterly*, published by the University of Minnesota, appeared in March, 1949.

3. Richard H. Shyrock, "The Nature and Implications of Programs in American Civilization," *American Heritage* (April, 1949). See also David F. Bowers, *The Princeton Conference on American Civilization: A Description and an Appraisal* (Princeton, 1944).

4. Robert B. Hall, *Area Studies: With Special Reference to their Implications for Social Science* (New York: Social Science Research Council, 1947). The Social Science Research Council has formed a committee on world-area research and has sponsored a large-scale conference on the problems involved. See Charles Wagley, *Area Research and Training: A Conference Report on the Study of World Areas* (New York: Social Science Research Council, 1948). The world areas here involved were Latin America, Europe, Soviet Russia, the Near East, Southern Asia, and the Far East. See especially Julian H. Steward, *Area Research: Theory and Practice* (New York: Social Science Research Council, 1950).

5. Werner J. Cahnman, "Outline of a Theory of Area Studies," *Annals of the Association of American Geographers* 38 (December 1948): 243.

6. Hans Kurath, *The Linguistic Atlas of the United States and Canada* (Providence, 1936).

7. Walter Prescott Webb, *The Great Plains* (Boston, 1931). See Fred A. Shannon's drastic critique, *An Appraisal of Walter Prescott Webb's "The Great Plains"* (New York: Social Science Reserach Council, 1940).

8. Howard W. Odum, *Southern Regions of the United States* (Chapel Hill, 1936).

9. Steward, *Area Research*, p. 66.

10. Charles E. Martin, "Regionalism as Illustrated by the Western Hemisphere," *Social Forces* 21 (March 1943): 272.

11. Radhakamal Mukerjee, *Social Ecology* (New York, 1945).

12. See Talcott Parsons, *Essays in Sociological Theory: Pure and Applied* (Glencoe, Illinois, 1949), especially chapters 1 and 2. Parsons also makes the point that, in analogy with biology, the structural approach is needed to insure completeness of the system—a point that fits in well with the regional-national approach.

13. Howard W. Odum and Harry Estill Moore, *American Regionalism: A Cultural-Historical Approach to National Integration* (New York, 1938), pp. 30–32.

14. This has been done by Fred B. Kniffen at Louisiana State University in a series of articles.

15. See the series of maps in Robert A. Dier, *Natural Areas of Trade in the United States* (Washington: Office of NRA, Division of Review, February, 1936).

16. August Losch, "The Nature of Economic Regions," *Southern Economic Journal* 5 (July 1938): 71–78.

17. Walter Chrystaller, *Die zentralen Orte in Suedendeutschland* (Jena, 1935).

18. Charles J. Galpin, "The Social Anatomy of an Agricultural Community," *Bulletin 34*, Agricultural Experiment Station, University of Wisconsin (Madison, May, 1915).

19. C. A. Dawson, in *Essays in Society* (Toronto, 1940), pp. 30–31, commenting on R. D. McKenzie's *Metropolitan Community* (New York, 1933).

20. C. L. Gregory, "Advanced Techniques in the Delineation of Rural Regions," *Rural Sociology*, 14 (March 1949): 59–63.

21. Foster F. Elliott, *Types of Farming in the United States* (Washington, Bureau of the Census, 1933).

22. Margaret Jarman Hagood, Nadia Danilevsky, and Corlin O. Beum, "An Examination of the Use of Factor Analysis in the Problem of Subregional Delineation," *Rural Sociology* 6 (September 1941): 216–33.

23. C. E. Lively and R. B. Almack, *A Method of Determining Rural Social Subareas with Application to Ohio*, mimeograph, *Bulletin No. 106*, Ohio Agricultural Extension Station (Columbus, January, 1938).

24. Arthur R. Mangus, *Rural Regions of the United States* (Washington, 1940). See maps, p. 4.

25. Margaret Jarman Hagood, "Statistical Methods for Delineation of Regions Applied to Data on Agriculture and Population," *Social Forces* 21 (March 1943): 287–97.

26. The complete subtitle continues: *With Special Reference to Migration and the Scientific Study of Local History* (New Haven, 1930).

27. K. C. McMurry, in Stuart A. Rice, ed., *Methods in Social Science: A Case Book* (Chicago, 1931), p. 234.

28. Paul Vidal de la Blache, *Tableau de la geographie de la France*, p. 8.

29. Rudolf Heberle, "Regionalism: Some Critical Observations," *Social Forces* 21 (March, 1943): 281–82.

30. Ibid.

31. John Maynard Keynes, *The General Theory of Employment, Interest and Money* (New York, 1936), p. 3.

32. Merle E. Curti, in McMurry, *Methods in Social Science*, p. 363.

33. This is volume 5 of *The History of the South* (Baton Rouge, 1948), forthcoming in ten volumes.

12. The Urban Breakthrough

in the South (1955)

Here Vance documented and discussed, for a general audience, the rapid transformation of the South from a rural region to an urban one. In the twenty years before he wrote, the proportion of Southerners living in urban areas had increased from one-third to one-half; in the subsequent twenty years, it increased to two-thirds. In fact, nearly all the trends discussed here have continued. (A significant exception, which no one would have predicted in 1955, is that black out-migration slowed, ceased, and has now reversed). Vance's interest in southern urbanization and its implications for the region's society and culture led him to edit (with N. J. Demerath) The Urban South, published about the same time as this essay.

The South in these latter days—if one may be allowed a figure of speech from the jet age—has been drawning nearer and nearer its supersonic barrier. Social changes have been coming thick and fast to Dixie in its most dynamic era. In fact there is a feeling that a "breakthrough" has occurred in the region's position and that from thenceforth the area is to be taken into account in all national development—social and economic.

This is a heady analogy and the people themselves are aware that change is in the air. A folk saying now going the rounds puts it thus: "Yankees coming South; Negroes going North; cotton going West; livestock coming East; money coming in." The South, in Werner Sombart's phrase, was never one of the "heartlands of Western Capitalism"; the amount of money coming in may be exaggerated. It should nevertheless be added that industry is still coming South and Southerners are moving cityward at an increasing rate. The breakthrough in the region may well be represented in the coming urbanization of the South. "The South is going to town" is a good slang phrase; it also happens to be literal truth.

In the last two decades, 1930 to 1950, urban population in the South has climbed from one-third to almost one-half the region's total. A recent Census publication, "Growth of Metropolitan Areas," found that the

From *Virginia Quarterly Review* 31 (1955): 223–32. © *The Virginia Quarterly Review*.

current rate of metropolitan development in the South is proceeding at a faster pace than the rate at which the North developed its larger metropolitan centers. For every three city dwellers in 1940, the South had four in 1950; for each five farm residents in 1940, just four remained in 1950. Today, in the words of Chicago sociologist Donald Bogue, "The South is moving rapidly toward an industrial and commercial economy which is organized around cities and metropolitan areas. This change in economic and social organization is requiring the South to redistribute its population in new patterns and to acquire new skills and take on new characteristics."

The Depression, the New Deal, and World War II so shocked and revitalized Southern economics that its agriculture and economy no longer follow traditional paths. The agricultural revolution which the South underwent was totally without precedent in the region. Mechanized agriculture and improved practices first developed in the North and West are now taking effect in the South. Hybrid corn and good pasture grasses are now developed for the South as for other areas. All this has meant a great exodus from agriculture. In 1930 the region had 5.5 millions employed in agriculture; by 1950 only 3.2 million.

The dominant psychology of the South is no longer agrarian; it is Chamber of Commerce. Modern metropolises, it is realized, organize our economic life; the South, it is felt, has been less advanced because it has been understaffed with cities. If the outlying areas of our nation are to partake more of the characteristics of the central core of power, wealth, and administration in this country, they must of necessity become more urbanized. Those Southerners who dislike life in crowded cities now realize that we cannot manage a complex economy without the development of metropolitan centers and functions. If modern man is to destroy his cities by A-bombs, H-bombs, or by any other means, he has calculated to destroy civilized life as it exists. Cities are valuable adjuncts to living and the South's advancing urbanization inevitably indicates an advancing region.

Regionalism which in the South began as an agrarian movement is accordingly becoming urban regionalism. To improve its agriculture has meant reducing the number of people involved so that the South now appears on the verge of taking the plunge which will mean a definite break with its past. The process is drastic; its causes compelling. Here meet the forces of industrialization, mechanization, and increased efficiency in agriculture, rural-urban migration, improvements in the social amenities, and the organization of Southern communities—in short the improved position of the South in the nation today. There is hardly a facet of our national life which will remain unchanged in the future urbanization of the South.

There are many questions we would like to ask about this important development. What, for example, goes on in the process of urbanization? As people move city-ward, what happens to their occupations, their birth rates, and the size of their families? What kind of people lead the movement? Who goes to the growing Southern cities, and who moves outside the South?

What kind of cities are growing up in the South today? How do they look from the inside? Are we simply moving rural poverty from the countryside to urban slums? Has the South developed any metropolitan centers capable of organizing and dominating its rural areas and small cities and of tying their production and trade in with that of the nation and the world?

And what is this new mode of life doing to the rural traditions and points of view inherited from an older South? How will the movement to cities change the class system of the South? What is its impact on the traditional pattern of race relations in the South? Do urban Negroes escape the paternalism of rural communities? Why do Southern cities have the highest crime rates in the nation? What is happening in Southern politics under urbanization? Are urban political leaders more liberal than the old agrarian leaders? Do the rural constituencies and legislators still dominate the growing cities?

With all the shocks and dislocations coming in the wake of urbanization, is the South doing any serious planning for its future? How far has the community organization movement advanced? What hope do the region's leaders see in city planning? Finally, what is happening to the South's rural communities and its many little towns? Is it really farewell to "Possum Trot?"

These are all heady questions—certainly beyond the ability of any one person to answer.

I

The urban South today is a region of small cities and it may remain so for some time to come. The point is that in its new status the South is generating cities large enough to carry on metropolitan functions. By 1950 the thirteen Southern states contained twenty-nine cities of 100,000 or more inhabitants. In its study of metropolitan areas, the U.S. Census includes the entire population centering around a large size city as integrated in its social and economic system. Of the nation's thirty-three metropolitan areas of 500,000 or more in 1950 the South had seven; Houston, 806,701; New Orleans, 685,405; Dallas, 614,799; Louisville, 576,900; Birmingham, 558,927; Atlanta, 671,797; and San Antonio, 500,460. It seems safe to predict that the first city in the whole South to reach a million population will be Houston, Texas. If Dallas-Fort Worth, some thirty miles apart, were counted as one concentration, this Texas giant would be the South's largest, reaching some 976,052 population. The high rate of metropolitan growth from 1940 to 1950 shows that the South will in the near future develop some four additional centers in the half-million category—undoubtedly Miami, now 495,084 population; Memphis, 482,939; Norfolk-Portsmouth, 446,200; and Tampa-St. Petersburg, 409,143.

In modern world economy what makes a city a metropolis? The answer is found in a city's ability to organize and integrate a hinterland so as to lead its production and trade into national and world channels. This is done in the performance of four functions: (1) the organization of the market, especially wholesale distribution; (2) the development of industry; (3) the organization of converging transportation and communication facilities; and (4) the maturation of financial organization.

We know that the first of the modern super-agglomerates—capital markets of the world—developed around the North Sea in London, Berlin, and Paris; a second for the Americans grew up along the New York-Chicago axis; and a third developed in the Far East dominated by Tokyo and Shanghai.

The South has grown up in the shadows of the great and none of its growing centers threaten to disrupt the lines of dominance and integration now well established in the national economy. But the South has been understaffed with cities. If it is to share in the nation's councils of wealth, power, and influence, it will generate regional capitals where economic leaders can operate with some degree of assurance. More than anything else the emergence of genuine metropolitan centers will attest to the region's movement out of the state of colonial economy.

Several methods have been utilized to rank the region's cities in order of magnitude of the four functions mentioned above. They show Atlanta in the Southeast, Dallas in the Southwest, to be second order metropolises—second only to national centers like New York and Chicago. Houston, New Orleans, Memphis, Louisville, and Birmingham appear as third order metropolises; while a long list of subdominants are found, namely: Richmond, Fort Worth, Oklahoma City, Miami, Charlotte, Jacksonville, Tulsa, Little Rock, San Antonio, Norfolk-Portsmouth, and El Paso. Important in determining these rankings are banking and fiscal resources as determined by position in the Federal Reserve system and as home of branch offices for major national corporations.

Gateway cities to the South have played an important part in the region's development. In the South lines of trade and control are mediated to New York by way of gateway cities like Baltimore, Louisville, and Cincinnati; in the Southwest via Saint Louis and Kansas City to Chicago and New York. Overnight sleeper jumps and air lines for the transport of key personnel show the importance of these lines of communication—well illustrated by the fact that while the Charlotte metropolitan area is the capital of physical production in cotton textiles, the center work of planning, designing, brokerage, sales, and finance is done from Worth Street, New York. The problems of center and periphery well illustrate the whole relation of the metropolis, its organization, its integration, and its control, to its hinterland and its satellite cities.

It is evident that Southern metropolises, no matter how rapidly they are now growing, will not replace the giants of the New York–Chicago axis. In all specialized functions they are sub-dominant to these super-metropolises—as in fact is the whole nation.

II

Urbanization, individual advancement, and economic progress in the history of the West have usually gone together. Urbanization means more than the movement of a population from country to city. It involves mass shifts in the occupations of a people since a function of migration is to place workers in position to climb that occupational ladder which leads from the agricultural to the industrial service and distributive rungs of the economy. Occupational mobility carries with it the rewards of increased income; and since these payments are made by the total economy as a going concern, it is not surprising to find that the conditions of individual advancement are also those of economic progress. The South now in its economic breakthrough is moving into the tide of this movement.

Colin Clark found in his world-wide study, "The Conditions of Economic Progress," that both economic efficiency and per capita income increased as the proportion of a nation's labor force engaged in primary economy, largely agriculture, decreased while the proportions in tertiary economy—service, distribution, administration, finance, et cetera—increased. The percentage engaged in secondary industry, that is, manufacturing, appears in the more advanced countries to rise to a maximum and then to stabilize. This maximum, Clark holds, was reached for Britain in the Census of 1901, France in 1901, Switzerland in 1910, United States in 1920, Germany in 1925; while in Austria, Italy, and Denmark the maximum had not been reached by 1940. In the United States in 130 years from 1820 to 1950 the proportion in agriculture declined from 72.3 to 12.5 per cent; those in industry increased from 12.5 to 33.7 per cent; while the services advanced from 15.3 to 53.8 per cent of the nation's total working force.

In this time schedule of transition the South, which had lagged some half century behind the nation, suddenly accelerated its movement into the main stream from 1930 to 1950. This trend has been studied by Lorin Thompson of the University of Virginia and his conclusions are well worth our summary. In the last twenty years the South's proportions in agriculture declined from 42.8 to 21.3 per cent as compared to a change from 14.6 to 9.0 per cent for the rest of the United States: in manufacturing the change was from 19.0 to 17.6 per cent in the South as compared to a shift from 32.4 to 28.3 per cent in the rest of the United States. Declines in manufacturing can be attributed to large increases in output per worker. Those employed in the tertiary level—trade, service, and all others—in the South increased from 38.2 to 61.1 per cent of the total, while in the rest of the nation they moved from 53.0 to 62.7 per cent. This statistic of approximate equality is the answer to those who have uncritically accepted industrialization as the one prime mover in the South's development.

The obvious fact is that the South in recent years has developed the forces auxiliary to industry and has strengthened its whole range of executive, professional, educational, and administrative services. Government and education have played a large part here.

Real increases in occupational skills in the South are further indicated by detailed analysis. Thus workers engaged in professional and technical occupations increased from 5.9 to 7.2 per cent of all workers from 1940 to 1950; managers, officials, and owners moved from 6.6 to 8.0 per cent; sales personnel grew from 5.2 to 6.4 per cent of the total. When other service workers are added, the South's proportion of workers in the third level of the economy increased from 28.8 to 37.2 per cent as compared to a shift from 43.7 to 45.0 per cent in the rest of the country. If we should add the region's skilled craftsmen, foremen, et cetera, to the third-level workers they increased from 36.7 to 48.8 per cent of the total.

Occupations showing losses prove equally satisfying to our main thesis. Laborers and unpaid family workers on farms fell from 13.6 to 7.7 per cent; while private household workers declined from 6.8 to 4.1 per cent. This last change is not welcomed by all the advocates of progress in the South, for in a period of rising incomes it is drastically reducing the amount of domestic service.

These changes have fallen with different impact upon what we may call two minority groups in the South. To women it has meant increased employment—a gain of 37.2 per cent in the South from 1940 to 1950— and an invasion of many fields of the services. Only among professional and technical groups have male workers increased faster than female workers. To the Negro the great shrinkage in agriculture has meant reduced employment, increased movement out of the South, and no large gains in services. Women move into white-collar work in Southern cities; Negroes move into urban industry outside the South.

In this rural-urban shift Southerners move into urban-centered occupations faster than they move into cities. Thus when Professor Thompson cross-tabulated the occupations people follow by their rural-urban residence he found, for example, that only 72 per cent of the employed living on farms actually work in agriculture, forestry, or fishing. A higher proportion of the South's rural non-farm dwellers are found to be working in manufacturing and construction, 33.2 per cent, than of the region's city dwellers, 27.7 per cent.

Some 3.3 million workers live in rural non-farm areas in the South. They are definitely associated with the secondary and tertiary levels of our economy. Only 12.7 per cent of this group now work in agriculture. Furthermore, the proportion of the urban employed working in manufacturing in the South, 19.9 per cent, is less than that of the rural non-farm people, 24.6 per cent. The South has developed a definite pattern of living in the open countryside and working in urban-centered occupations. Their way of life—with a difference—may be compared with that of millions of suburbanites who commute to our Northern and Eastern cities.

The maturation of the South's economy is definitely leading the march to urban centers. In this developing economy many rural residents commute to work in urban places and many enterprises including industrial plants are located in rural areas. There is a continual increase in the number of rural residents oriented toward urban-centered industries and employment, and the region is developing something of a balance between the efficiency of urban organization and the values of open country life.

The South has made its greatest progress along the road to urbanization in the generation of a limited number of cities with true metropolitan functions. The type of organization and control involved in the integration of a large hinterland around the metropolis is developing a new type of business-civic leader in our largest cities, devoted to aggressive expansion of the region's agricultural, industrial, and commercial life. The interconnection of leaders in the metropolis, the region, and the nation is often thought of in terms of what may be called the "Chamber of Commerce mentality." That it is more than this and that it makes for power and achievement is shown by Floyd Hunter, who studied a Southern metropolis in a recent book, well-named "Community Power Structure."

III

What of the future? While urbanization in our Western civilization has impressed some writers as a continuous and irreversible process, it is not safe to assume that the growth of cities will be eternal. For nations and regions there may well exist a ceiling above which the trend of urbanization will not ascend. Presumably in a given economy it would prove neither profitable nor rewarding for cities to exceed a certain size or proportion of the population. Obviously, no one can now delineate these limits for either the United States or the South.

Since the South has lagged some several decades behind urban growth in the nation, it will no doubt continue to grow cities that are bigger—if not better. In fact, to the extent that Southern cities take over functions previously carried on elsewhere, they might conceivably lower the ceiling on urban growth in the great city regions. With New York City as a prime example of a gigantic metropolitan district of over thirteen million, many can agree that some of the nation's metropolises might well stabilize their growth. It is reasonable to assume that in the new South cities of lower density and size can satisfy the requirements of metropolitan function, meet the test of economic organization and yet support a mode of life that will give greater accessibility to the open country, green trees, and fresh air. To a people reared in the agrarian tradition the city of smaller size and denstiy should come as a benefit—not a disaster. Such a balance of the urban and rural ways of life has often been advocated and but rarely attained. In the meantime, the South is experiencing a new sense of power and achievement in what may turn out to be the most important American development in the mid-century—the social and economic "breakthrough" in the South.

13. Regionalism and Ecology

A Synthesis (1956) [with Charles M. Grigg]

Regional sociology had from the outset a special identification with Howard Odum and his colleagues at Chapel Hill: in fact, it hardly existed at all outside their sphere of influence. In this paper, presented at a professional meeting in 1956, Vance and Charles Grigg tried to show how the concerns of the North Carolina group could be related to what was going on elsewhere in sociology under the label of "human ecology," an area in which Vance was a recognized authority. It may be significant that this effort explicitly to link regional sociology to other bodies of sociological theory took place only after Odum's death in 1954. Odum had attempted single-handedly to develop a theoretical structure for regionalism, and the idiosyncratic result had little impact on sociology as it was developing elsewhere.

The theories and concepts, the basic analyses and conclusions of ecological and regional science seem so near and yet so far from some common center that many specialists in the field must have wondered whether a synthesis is possible.[1] It would appear as though a "geological fault" had early developed between regional and ecological study. Although this unresolved hiatus still survives in the discipline of sociology, it is not the result of a deep and bitter controversy; if so, the points at issue would have been laid open and thus recognized as problems for investigation. Actually, it appears as though the gap exists by virtue of avoidance: ecologists are careful not to tell regionalists of their shortcomings and regionalists are careful to reciprocate. There has been a minimum of cross criticism and thus of cross fertilization. The problem of synthesis has gone by default.

Science, we know, is advanced by those who examine the likeness and differences of varying concepts to see where they touch and where they conflict. Certain basic notions in conflict can be discarded; others in harmony can be integrated and accepted as pervading principles. Ecological and regional studies come naturally by their related but divergent ideas,

From *Research Reports in Social Science* 3 (August 1960): 1–11. Reprinted by permission.

for they were developed out of investigations, concepts and analyses from varied fields: field studies in biology, surveys in geography and in demography, in community analysis, in the delineation of culture areas, in the political history of sectional development, and so forth. It is surprising that they possess the unity they have now.

I

Ecology traditionally deals with community—the urban community—usually a large metropolis in process of expansion. Regionalism develops the homogeneous culture area as a component part of the national society and, like the section, self-conscious of its economic interests and its political loyalties. Both ecological and regional phenomena can be examined from the point of view of (1) structure, (2) of process and (3) of content. Both disciplines are firmly based on the study of differences and they make use of all the statistical techniques and measurements of variation. "The fabric of modern society"—and we add of community also—"is composed of variable traits that are correlated among themselves."[2] The approach to differentiated areas is thus in terms of a culture complex and, as C. L. Gregory has said, if no culture trait were related to any other, "a region would have no meaning except in terms of that trait."

When we confront regionalist with ecologist, synthesis, as we suggested, can be sought for in the concepts of (1) structure, (2) process and (3) content. Following biology, human ecology has developed a sequence of processes, for example, invasion, succession, etc., to a high order of relevance in studying urban dynamics. Comparable suggestions have been made in the transition from frontier to section to region. A tentative verdict might well be made here that while no battle over theory is joined in this issue, no fruitful synthesis appears in the offing. Process had not meant much heretofore to regional analysis, but there are indications (Bogue, Hawley studies of under-developed areas) that process of concentration and decentralization of population in and around metropolitan centers not only appears in regional patterns, but that these processes are comparable on an inter-regional basis.

In depicting the content, cultural, economic and political, of ecological and regional areas, both disciplines have made notable analyses. Both are concerned with the variations in socio-economic conditions they find in their basic units; and here the argument is joined over cultural content—

that is, the substantive findings of regionalism and ecology. Regions have different cultures drawn from geographic, economic and political diversities, they develop continuity, aspirations and political attitudes. To the ecologist, urban culture now appears so standardized and all-pervasive that these traits are differences of accident, not essence, so that the very content of regionalism, some feel, will fade as metropolitan organization advances. This view is carried to its logical conclusion when some sociologists visualize the diffusion of urban traits and personality throughout the rural hinterland, so that the rural-urban continuum gradually becomes a faded spectrum. The final act in this view is the passing of regionalism. Any method of implementing it, they contend, will revive an otherwise outmoded and discarded sectionalism.

Ecologists, on the other hand, also have their differentials in the urban pattern—the mosaic of natural areas. When examined, these variations appear to be the survivals of ethnic differentials not yet assimilated to American life and acceptance. Southern cities, except of Negro-White areas, often lack the Ghettos and little Sicilies of Northern and Eastern areas. Opponents of ecology make the same critique: the phenomenon is due to the peculiar accidents of American immigration—not to the essence of ecological process. So much for the conflict over cultural content. Here issues are joined, and resolution may be in the offing. Will it provide synthesis, or will one view vanquish the other?

Viewed in this context, the basic rift between ecologists and regionalists appears to be another manifestation of the divergence between an urban and a rural sociology. Homogeneous regions are usually agricultural and rurally oriented; the communities studied by ecologists are invariably great metropolises. Nor can it be said that this break between urban and rural has been bridged by the good empirical and statistical analysis. While they offer some support to the hypothesis of convergence among regions and natural areas, they demonstrate the heterogeneity of urban and rural. The conclusion appears obvious: no synthesis of ecology and regionalism can be carried through by statistical analysis of content or of socio-economic variations between metropolitan and rural areas; the differentials are simply too great. Such areas do not merge. Thus in Lively and Almack's *Regionalization of Ohio*, Margaret Jarman Hagood and others were able to incorporate the seven large city counties only by weighting the factor loading with indices of latitude and longitude. In the census delimitation of economic areas for 1950—the best controlled analysis yet made—Donald J. Bogue working on good regional and economic principles developed two fundamentally different types of areas: about 148 metropolitan and 293 non-metropolitan areas. Variation between the two in social and economic traits was so great that contiguity apparently offered the only principle for merging.[3]

This leaves structure—the basic element in area study and the forte of both regionalist and ecologist—as a basis for synthesis. Here the rationale is not homogeneity but functional interrelation. Somewhere in between intra-metropolitan ecology devoted to its mosaic of natural areas and the homogeneous region is found the analysis of inter-community ecology. The regionalist can participate in this because he sees the region developing as a constellation of communities. The ecologist sees this as the study of inter-metropolitan dominance and integration— what R. D. McKenzie called the "new city regionalism." This, McKenzie wrote, "differs from the regionalism of former times in that it is the product of contract and division of labor rather than of mere geographic isolation."

Excellent work in this field has been done in depicting the genesis of a region and the development of its dominant and related communities as they have organized the new economy. C. A. Dawson, for example, traced the development of a Canadian pioneer zone as the Peace River District developed gateway and subdominant communities. On the West Coast R. D. McKenzie traced the growth of the Puget Sound Region, using the principles of both ecology and regionalsim in the analysis.

II

Can the powerful apparatus of statistics also be used to test the validity of this explanation? The Southeast as analyzed by Howard W. Odum is accepted as a distinctive region, and its component subregions were delimited in 1930 in 27 homogeneous areas by T. J. Woofter. The Southeast is also undergoing rapid urbanization. Both metropolitan dominance of hinterlands, and the integration of metropolises serve to organize regions. Since homogeneous and metropolitan regions are concerned with the spatial aspects of culture and economic organization, it would seem that such a structure can be synthesized as a constellation of communities.

In order to test the theoretical scheme outlined above—changing structure of a region—the 976 counties composing the eleven Southeastern states were used. The variable which we have chosen to test our thesis is the rate of population change for each of the two ten-year periods, 1930–1940, and 1940–1950. The question which needs to be answered is, which one of our spatial models best explains the change in county population during each of these two periods?

The first of the two spatial models to be used is that of T. J. Woofter in which he arranged the 976 counties in the Southeast into 27 homogeneous and contiguous subregions. Woofter's primary consideration was to incorporate the largest combination of factors which displayed the largest homogeneity within a land area characterized by certain geographic and physiographic features. The two major considerations of Woofter's classification and indeed of the concept of homogeneous regions are that the similarity of social and cultural traits is related to geographic characteristics, and second, that these land areas should be contiguous.

Table 13.1 indicates the rate of population change when Woofter's classification of the 976 counties is used as our universe. These 27 subregions vary in size from four counties to one with 122 counties. From the table it is clear that in the period 1930–1940, the subregional delineation did not point up a large amount of diversity between the subregional breakdowns. Also, all of the regions showed a positive rate of growth; and the range was not too great. However, in the period 1940–1950, the variation between subregions has increased, with several showing population losses, and some with high population gains. The range in the latter period was greater than in the period 1930–1940.

It is quite evident that the subregional delineation obscures the effect of urbanization on the differential rate of population growth. In other words, the "within" variation could be quite large due to the fact that these subregions do not consider the effects of urbanization. In an agricultural society, where large concentrations of population are at a minimum, social and cultural characteristics are closely related to geographic and physiographic considerations. But with the rise of urban centers, the bases for regional delineation also change. The second spatial model represents the changing base of regional delineation. It emphasizes the increasing importance of metropolitan centers in the changing pattern of regional delineation. It is the change from social and cultural characteristics being closely identified with certain geographic areas to form the natural area to a region composed of a number of metropolitan centers, each influencing to a varying degree its hinterland. This concept of regional analysis stresses diversity, the division of labor, the ordering of the

TABLE 13.1

Mean Rate of Increase in the Southeast of Woofter's
Twenty-Seven Subregions for the Two Decades,
1930–1940 and 1940–1950

Subregion	1930 to 1940	1940 to 1950
Atlantic Tidewater	5.13	17.40
Black Belt	3.86	− 3.69
Blue Grass	4.44	1.00
Blue Ridge	13.72	1.53
Bluffs	6.80	− 2.82
Citrus Vegetable	18.67	35.14
Cotton Piedmont	9.38	10.30
Cumberland Mt. Region	15.86	− .10
Delta	8.62	6.14
Gult Coast Region	11.33	2.61
Interior Plain	5.44	− 5.08
Mining	13.00	6.89
Muscle Shoals	7.62	− .07
Northern Cotton and Tobacco	10.38	12.84
Northern Piedmont	13.38	27.08
Ozark	4.66	− 8.21
Red River	10.50	2.00
Rice-Cane	17.31	6.19
Ridge (Interior)	8.26	− 9.11
Semi-Tropical	42.44	52.00
Shenandoah Valley	11.00	13.20
Southern Cotton and Tobacco	3.57	− 1.87
Tennessee Valley	15.28	13.62
Tobacco Cattle	7.54	− 5.36
Tobacco Piedmont	7.31	8.36
Vegetable, Citrus	3.50	20.75
Gulf Tidewater	11.28	29.17

Source: Computed from basic data.

hinterland in a consistent pattern, and reflects the size and function of the particular metropolitan center. Thus the region becomes a constellation of communities, each with its own orbit of influence, rather than a group of natural areas, stressing homogeneity of social and cultural characteristics as well as physiographic features.

The rise of metropolitan centers within the Southeast in the last twenty years represents one of the most important changes within the region. In 1930 there were 29 such centers with a total population of 3,637,000. In 1950 there were 40 such centers representing a population of 5,732,608. This is an increase of 59 per cent in the number of people now living in metropolitan centers over this twenty-year period, and an increase of 40 per cent in the number of such centers. Another factor in the changing base of the subregion is the increase in the number of metropolitan centers over 100,000 during this period. In 1930 there were 13 centers over 100,000 with a total population of 2,583,146 and in 1950, 20 metropolitan centers had over 100,000 representing a total population of 4,256,964. This is an increase of 65 per cent.

In the period under consideration we have the phenomenon of a rapidly urbanizing region. The question then becomes one of whether these centers have changed the basis of regional delineation.

The second spatial model represents a region composed of a constellation of communities, each with its own hinterland of influence. This model can be conceptualized in two steps.

Step one: All counties with a city over 50,000 were designated as central counties. Where two adjacent counties had cities over 50,000, they were combined to make one central unit.

Step two: Radiating from these central units in concentric circles were the counties within the hinterland of each of these central units. Counties in tier one were those counties which included the Metropolitan Center. Tier two were those counties contiguous to the county in tier one. This procedure was followed until the hinterland of one metropolitan center coincided with that of another. When the hinterland of two metropolitan centers met and there were counties which would fall into the same tier in either hinterland, they were allocated to one with the largest central city.[4]

This method of delineating the hinterland of the metropolitan centers makes it necessary to survey these centers at intervals to determine whether other cities have reached the lower limit of population. Every ten years, we allocated the counties according to the number of new cities which reached the lower limit of 50,000 population. This was done for each ten-year period, thus reflecting the dynamic aspect of population growth and development within the region.

For the period 1930–1940, the metropolitan centers which were present in 1930 were used as the basis for dividing the 976 counties in the region. In 1930 there were 29 counties containing a city of 50,000 or over. The region was then divided in 29 metropolitan centers, and all the counties were allocated to one of the 29 hinterlands as indicated previously. In our study the use of tiers as a measure of distance is important because it is the similarity in tiers which forms the basis for comparison with the homogeneous subregions. As mentioned earlier, it is the assumption that these metropolitan centers order their hinterland in some consistent pattern along a continuum of distance whether measured in miles or in tiers and that there will be a similarity between all metropolitan centers by tier distance from the central county.

Table 13.2 presents the mean rate of population change by tier distance for the period 1930–1940. Also the table shows the comparison of the

TABLE 13.2

Mean Rate of Population Change by Tier Distance, Counties within the Orbit of Central Cities of 100,000 Population and Over, and Counties within the Orbit of Central Cities between 50,000 and 99,999 for the Period 1930–1940

Tier Distance	All Counties	Central City over 100,000	Central City between 50,000 and 99,999
Tier 1	16.1	18.5	14.2
Tier 2	11.1	14.5	8.1
Tier 3	7.5	8.2	7.0
Tier 4	6.6	7.0	6.4
Tier 5	8.2	8.2	8.2
Tier 6	11.9	11.0	13.1
Tier 7	10.6	10.3	13.3
Tier 8	10.5	10.5	—

mean rate of change by tiers of metropolitan centers by size 100,000 and under and over 100,000 population. During this period there was little differentiation when the region is analyzed by metropolitan centers. Even when we look at size of metropolitan centers and break out the larger one (in over 100,000) little difference is found between tiers.

To analyze population change for the period 1940–1950, all cities with 50,000 or more population in 1940 were used as metropolitan centers and then all counties were allocated to the hinterland of one of the 32 metropolitan centers. It should be noted that this represents an increase of three in the number of metropolitan centers which emerged over the ten-year period. During this period greater differentiation is present between tiers. When size of central city is controlled, two patterns of population change are seen. In the centers over 100,000 there is a consistent pattern of decreasing rate of population change with the central county having the highest rate of increase and the second having the next largest. It might also be stated that the smaller centers have decreasing influence at the periphery of their hinterland, for it is in these counties that the mean rate of population change is positive as contrasted with

TABLE 13.3

Mean Rate of Population Change by Tier Distance, Counties within the Orbit of Central Cities of 100,000 Population and Over, and Counties within the Orbit of Central Cities between 50,000 and 99,999 for the Period 1940–1950

Tier Distance	All Counties	Central City 100,000 and over	Central City between 50,000 and 99,999
Tier 1	32.7	33.9	31.8
Tier 2	13.4	20.9	6.6
Tier 3	1.9	5.7	− 2.0
Tier 4	− .6	.3	− 2.2
Tier 5	− 3.1	− .9	.6
Tier 6	1.3	− 4.5	8.2
Tier 7	− 4.4	− 3.4	6.3
Tier 8	− 13.8	− 13.8	___

the larger centers in which these counties represent the highest rate of population loss.

From a descriptive point of view, it seems fairly clear the the Southeast is emerging from an agricultural into an industrial society. During the past twenty years there has been a rapid increase in the number and size of metropolitan centers within the region. In the period 1930–1940, it is not clear which approach is most effective in understanding population change. However, in the period 1940–1950 the concept of the region as a constellation of communities orders population change along a continuum of distance in a meaningful way. This is particularly true if we control the size of metropolitan centers. This raises the question as to whether we can test the relative importance of each of these two concepts in explaining the variation in population change.

It would appear from the descriptive data given that the metropolitan region provided the most effective means of analyzing population change in the latter period. However, it would strengthen our case if some statistical model could be used to test the relative importance of these two constructs over time.

The model used was that of analysis of variance with two criteria of classification. With this model a test of the relative contribution of each of the two classifications for each of the periods can be moded.

The procedure for selection of the sample was that all of the counties were cross-classified by the two criteria and then those cells which had sufficient numbers selected. From this cross-classification, N size was selected at random from those originally in the classification.

For the period 1930–1940 the interaction was tested; and as it was not significant, it was pooled with the within mean square variance and from this the remaining "F" ratios were computed. The subregional classification was significant at the .01 level, whereas the "F" ratio for the classification by distance from metropolitan center was less than one. This result is not surprising in view of the limited number and size of the metropolitan centers in the region at this time.

For the period 1940–1950 the interaction was again tested; and as it was not significant, was pooled with the within mean square variance. There was for this period a reversal in the trend of the "F" ratio in that the classification by tier distance from a metropolitan center was significant at the .01 level and the classification by subregions was significant at the .05 level. Again this is not surprising in that during this period there had been an increase in the size and number of metropolitan centers in the region.

The results of these two tests in addition to the description of the growth of metropolitan centers within the Southeast confirms our theoretical model in that in an agricultural society the homogeneous subregion is the most appropriate spatial model to use. However, with the development of cities, the spatial model has to be modified to allow for the effect of large metropolitan centers on the region. The most appropriate model then is one which attempts to express the relationship between the center and its hinterland. This relationship can best be expressed in some measure of distance. In this study tier distance was used.

The preceding analysis serves to indicate the importance of the organizing metropolitan nucleus in the integration and coalescence of subregional areas. This research lead is now well founded in the literature and generally accepted. It may suggest one bridge for the gap between urban ecology and the regionalism of homogeneous areas. Regions, it is shown, vary not only because of the degree of urbanization; they also vary by virtue of the nature of their cities and the network patterns in which they are integrated.

Obviously, it requires more than an empirical test of the relations among subregions and metropolitan areas to yield a theoretical synthesis of ecology and regionalism. Our synthesis, therefore, is neither full nor complete enough to portray all the rich detail of either the regionalist's or the ecologist's area. Social change of an undeveloped area as it emerges into the modern economy will present the emerging urban patterns we have discussed. Regional analysis of this change, however, will demand much more descriptive detail and a wider grasp of culture content than can be given in our statistical analysis. Variation and differentials accordingly will continue to be the criteria of ecological and regional studies, while the region will of necessity add the political factor. Regions may never become as standardized in culture and behavior as our great cities. Interaction and interdependence, however, is the essence of synthesis, and here our hope lies.

NOTES

1. This is a paper read at the Fifty-First Annual Meeting of the American Sociological Society, September 9, 1956.

2. C. L. Gregory, "Advanced Techniques in the Delineation of Rural Regions," *Rural Sociology* 14 (March 1949): 59–63.

3. Donald J. Bogue, "Economic Areas as a Tool for Research Planning," *American Sociological Review* 15 (June 1950): 409–16.

4. Charles M. Grigg, "Demographic Change and Subregional Analysis, 1930–1950: A Study in Emerging Urban Dominance in the Southeast." Ph.D. thesis, University of North Carolina, 1952.

14. The South's Image and

the American Dream

Notes for a Fourth of July Oration

out of Season (1958)

The Lamar Lecture at Georgia Wesleyan College gave Vance the opportunity to express his views on the political and economic implications of urbanization and industrialization. It is fitting that five years later he received the University of North Carolina's Thomas Jefferson Award, given annually to the faculty member "whose life and work is in the best tradition and spirit of Thomas Jefferson."

It was said of the German sociologist, Georg Simmel, that he "took his students down a pit into the mine"; he was not a teacher; he was an "inciter". Just about the time one felt he had reached a conclusion, Simmel had a way of raising his right arm and with three fingers of his hand, turning an imaginary object so as to exhibit another facet. A lecture by Simmel was a creation at the moment of delivery.

From childhood memory I recall an American ritual in an age of innocence. From our town all the inhabitants went out on a summer day to a rural grove, the band played, we had a picnic on the grounds, and the speaker of the day delivered a Fourth of July oration. He presented the American dream and the lights of oratory played on the facets of this symbol and image. I doubt if anyone here under the age of thirty ever attended a Fourth of July celebration. With this symbol before us, I should like to give my remarks a subtitle. Let us call it: Notes for a Fourth of July Oration out of Season. As we revolve the facets in the light, who shall tell which is image and which is reality?

Every social institution, we are told, consists of a concept and a structure. The structure is the way the institution is organized, the way it is built to get its work done. The concept is the basic ideal which the insti-

From *The Lamar Lectures* (Macon: Georgia Wesleyan College, 1958). Reprinted by permission.

tution is to carry out. Thus we can say in our secular society that the structure of the family is basically a legal contract, but the concept is that of affection. Where love is, family members rarely worry about their legal rights. When affection has languished, husbands and wives may prove violation of the contract and sue for divorce.

If we had to look for the structure of our American union, we would look to the Constitution where the framework for our Federalism is laid down. But if we seek for the basic concept of our American heritage we will find it in that document which dates the birth of the American nation and antedates the writing of the Constitution. It is the Declaration of Independence which embodies the hope of the American Dream and the challenge to its survival. In a world which denied these "truths" on every side, Thomas Jefferson of Virginia had boldly written: "We hold these truths to be self evident: that all men are created equal; that they are endowed by their creator with certain inalienable rights; that among these are life, liberty, and the pursuit of happiness." These cryptic and inspiring words now belong to the ages along with the historic watch-words of the Great Enlightenment, the slogan of the French revolution, *Liberty, Equality,* and *Fraternity.*

Certainly here is the basis of the American Dream, ". . . that dream of a land in which life should be better and richer and fuller for every man with opportunity for each according to his ability or achievement," as James Truslow Adams wrote, ". . . the dream of a land in which each man and each woman shall be able to attain to the fullest stature of which they are capable and to be recognized by their fellows for what they are, regardless of circumstances of birth and position."

But equality? There's the rub! It was John Randolph of Roanoke, Virginia's eccentric aristocrat, who said: "I love liberty; I hate equality." To this, Jefferson's doctrine seemed to answer, "Equal rights for all; special privileges for none." Without this much equality there can be no liberty.

Ideas of equality came naturally in the New World. Both the Pilgrim Fathers and those who settled Virginia were largely of middle class origins. Of the members of the Virginia House of Burgesses in 1662, no less than 43, Dixon Westor tells us, had reached these shores as indentured servants.

ECONOMIC BASIS OF JEFFERSONIAN DEMOCRACY

Every man is entitled to his interpretation of Thomas Jefferson—one of the great men of all times. Jefferson, we are told, had wished to have the trinity of inalienable rights read *life, liberty, and property*, but was unable to suggest how government could underwrite a guarantee to the right of property. Basic to Jefferson's ideal of equality was his doctrine of the individual ownership of productive property.

He believed in economic independence as a foundation of our system of individual freedom and political liberties. The political independence of the citizen was to be based on his economic independence. Then he would vote his own best interest instead of being voted.

This independence was best based on the ownership of productive capital; it is best found in the independent farmer, the small shop keeper, the small businessman. As for the wage hands of industry, Jefferson once said that the city mobs added no more strength to the body politic than sores to the body physical. And as for factories and workshops, he once hoped that they would stay in Europe.

Jefferson's political democracy won; his economic basis for it passed away. Our ideology is that of Jefferson; our economic structure is that anticipated by Alexander Hamilton. This is one of the essential contradictions in American life today.

America made its transition from an agrarian to an industrial order. Now our economic support consists in being hired for salary or wages by an organization in command of capital, able to make a profit from our services or fire us. Few of us own sufficient productive capital on which to use our labor to make us independent. Most of us have jobs to which very slender property or tenure rights adhere.

The political position of the South has been largely that of the farmer, the small business man, the owner of productive capital.

In areas long dominated by large industrial corporations, this is an anomaly for the Jeffersonian approach to political democracy and economic security has largely passed away. Increasingly, men have given up the idea of small business. When small farm owners leave the land they expect to be salary or wage earners all their lives. Expecting to be laborers all their lives, men organize to make their jobs secure—if they can, to make them better jobs.

To the South of Jefferson, this is not agrarian democracy, rather it is something alien and apart. Once democracy was economic individualism in political action—every tub on its own bottom—every farmer and shop keeper voicing the philosophy of little business. But under Mark Hanna labor voted for the full dinner pail, their employer's interest in the gold standard and high tariff. While the South could always be counted against Wall Street, it has rarely been found on the side of organized labor. The South had the mentality of small property and the farthest to the left it ever went was Populism—the radicalism of the right.

Jefferson's dream did not come to pass. Instead of a nation of shop keepers and farmers, we have developed a great industrial system—a nation of giant corporations and hired wage earners.

We never attained equality of station in life. We never will. We have cherished Jefferson's political democracy; we have lost the economic basis on which he hoped to see it built.

THE MORAL BASIS

But there is also a moral basis for the American dream. The values system imparts worth to the person regardless of social status. In his historic statement of man's equality before his creator, Jefferson built on the fundamental religious beliefs of both Catholics and Protestants. All souls are of equal worth in the sight of God. This is probably the one sense in which Jefferson accepted the doctrine. In the moral world this shows in the intrinsic worth ascribed to persons as persons. This includes the equal right of all persons to inviolability, respect and accountability. Here, as the sociologist E. T. Hillier stated it, is the core of the democratic principle.

1. Inviolability of the person: morality forbids degradation or profanation of the person. This includes freedom from physical or mental or moral damage. It also extends to the protection of property rights.

2. Respect: this includes the deference of one person for another in matters of self-feeling—that is, each person is to be regarded as a social self, not as a convenience or thing.

This is shown by courtesy, "face"—recognition of feelings and sensibilities. The law which gives redress against insult, indignities, slander and libel shows the extent to which self-feeling is a publicly recognized value.

3. Accountability and responsibility: morality and law invest each person with accountability. Each person is viewed as a free agent conscious of his intentions, capable of choice and self-direction and thus able to

decide on his actions and accept the consequences. Accountability pre-supposes initial self-direction and thus the largest amount of freedom consistent with the freedom of others. Equality in personal accountability allows one to undertake difficult tasks and to take the consequences of success and failure. We all have equal rights here, though we may lack equal ability to succeed. This leaves little room for pity, since pity imputes lack of ability on the part of the person to participate. Here is the inherent individualism of the American Dream.

In religion, personal accountability had its roots in teachings of individual's responsibility for his own salvation, for his choice of right or wrong.

In economics, "individualism" includes the right to make a profit; this was also part of the drive for equality. In their dependent status, serfs, minors, and defectives have limited accountability and their property must be administered for them.

Inviolability, respect and accountability are in the *mores*—the foundations of a single status society, where all are equal in moral responsibility. Each person is to count for one; each is viewed as an unique and irreplaceable value. All souls are of equal worth in the sight of God. Imbedded in Christianity, this view has been the basis for our democratic social order.

THE AMERICAN DREAM AS POLITICAL FACT

I have said the American Dream has its basis in morals and religion but that we can not expect to see it carried out in our economic life. We can now ask what this heritage came to mean in our political life.

First, we can say the drive for equality was carried on by the unequal. Not merely the common man but men of great natural gifts and abilities, men like Franklin, Adams, Washington, and Patrick Henry, were regarded as inferior to English lords, generals and governors—some of more limited gifts and abilities. That is why the American Revolution was led by natural aristocrats like Washington and Jefferson throwing in their lot with the common people. The great benefits of liberty, freedom, and equal opportunity were not conferred as free gifts by kings and nobles upon the common people; they were won in a fair fight. And the characteristic expression of this drive for equality came to be stated in Jacksonian democracy: "I am just as good as anybody else, if not a darn sight

better!" Americans have supported the dream of equal rights, not because they were content to be equal or average with everybody else, but
because many wanted a chance to see if they weren't better than most.

In our political life we voice this demand for equality and claim:

1. *Equal rights as citizens*: One man, one vote—with every man
counted as one, no more and no less. This does not mean we are equal in
political influence or power.

2. *Equal status before the law*: Equal right to stand before the bar of
justice and plead our cause. Equal right to sue and to be sued on the basis
of the rightness of our claims. Equal right to the presumption of innocence until the evidence indicates guilt. These are the claims of the American Dream in our legal system. And when they are not attained, we then
claim the right to strive for them until they are attained.

3. *The abolition of privileged classes*, of a hereditary aristocracy, and a
landed and titled nobility was an ax at the root of tyranny. It did not
make Americans equally smart, equally beautiful, or equally well-to-do.
This was not intended and could not be. Nor did it make men equally
devoted to the public weal or equally competent in civic duty.

With the passing of the principle of nobility and aristocracy, the problem of who are to be the social *elite* was simply put on a new basis. Social
standing became a matter of achievement rather than birth; the pressure
was to win status by hard work rather than bask in the enjoyment of an
inherited station in life. Hence the emphasis in America on symbols of
achievement. We ask about a man: What does he do? We even ask how
much is he worth, meaning how much money has he made; and the material possessions are often accepted as a short way of translating his
achievement into figures we can understand.

The American Dream is the hope for political man in a political democracy, but it is also the dream of a better life in terms of this world's goods.
This is an area in which America has achieved greatly, taking its stand
among the richest nations of the world. In this great achievement we
have created and accented inevitable differences in wealth and property.
If this be true—and it is true—why then have we continued to talk in
terms of the American Dream of equality?

UPWARD MOBILITY IN THE AMERICAN DREAM

I believe there is one answer to this question and it is simply this: America
has always been able to visualize a better tomorrow. In terms of the

equality of opportunity, fathers have seen better chances for their sons than they have ever had. In America there have been more people going up the social elevators than there have been coming down. It is not universal equality which gave America its tradition of classless democracy. Rather it is the rate at which people have been able to climb upward. Every father has expected his son to secure a better education, follow a higher calling, to have a better chance than he did. Throughout our history blue collar men have become white collar men and white collar men have become starched collar men, until in our informality we took off these symbols of dignity. This is the land of Horatio Alger, "Bound to Rise."

Eldridge Sibley has identified three important factors that have operated to make the group climbing the social ladder larger than the one coming down: (1) technical progress, (2) immigration, (3) the differential birth rates of the masses and the classes. To these we can add a fourth: (4) organization of the worker.

1. Our great *technical progress* has continually reduced the proportions engaged in the physical labor of producing and handling material goods and consequently increased the number in services, clerical, and professional occupations. As science, inventions, and machinery decreased the amount of physical labor, workers went into white collar occupations. In 1870, 30 percent were in services, now over one-half are in services and distribution; yet we produce much more material goods per capita.

2. The effect of *foreign immigration* has undoubtedly served to accelerate the upward mobility among native-born Americans. Before the immigrant could rise in the scale himself, he made a large contribution to the native-born American's chance of rising in the world. From 1900 to 1915, almost 14 million immigrants entered the United States; almost all were poor and unskilled. Thus, of 642,724 immigrant workers admitted during the year ending June 30, 1914, 603,378 stated they were engaged in manual occupations. Many of these, no doubt, began by taking lower occupations than they had followed in the Old World. To maintain the same percentage distribution of blue and white collars, many Americans must have risen; to increase the proportion of non-manual workers, more must have risen. It would seem that upward circulation resulting from migration at the bottom must have equalled the volume resulting from technical progress. After immigrants served their apprenticeship, they—or rather their children—began to rise.

3. *Differential fertility.* The migration from heaven has operated to

produce the same results as migration from Europe. Low birth rates of the well-to-do have produced what has been called a social vacuum within the upper classes. Into this vacuum, gifted children of the lower class moved, aided by free public education. Around 1930, 80 percent of the babies born were children of manual workers. Manual workers, however, represented less than 70 percent of the population. An annual shift of over 160,000 persons from "blue collar" to "white collar" status was required to make up the failure of the people in the upper occupations and educated classes to reproduce themselves. This is not necessarily a bad thing. It has given the gifted children of other classes a chance to rise.

4. *Organization of Workers.* The movement of individuals up the class ladder has not been the only response in the push for equality. Equally important has been the upward mobility of entire classes. It is as though someone had said: "You don't need to climb the social ladder. Just stand where you are and push. This whole floor is going up." Such in fact is the philosophy of the labor movement: "We are not leaving our jobs to become bosses; we intend to make our jobs better." From 1870 to 1954, those self-employed declined from 40 percent to 13 percent of our total working force. But this loss in ownership has not meant the destruction of the middle class.

In the same period, salaried workers increased from 6.6 percent of the working population to 30.8 percent. And we have every reason to believe that the wage earners who remained stable around a proportion of 56 percent of all occupations have had about one-half of their numbers moved up into a new middle class. How can we say this? For one thing, more than half of the working class have now risen into the middle income category. Thus 58 percent of the 15.5 million families making between $4,500 and $7,000 in 1953 were not headed by white collar workers at all, but by manual laborers. Moreover, 37 percent of the families with after-tax incomes of $7,500 and over were headed by manual workers. Seniority rights, paid vacations and insurance benefits show how far the new groups have gone toward middle class status. The guaranteed annual wage will have the effect of striking down the distinction between the wage earner and the salaried employee. And whenever dial-watching employees decide to wear jackets and slacks to work instead of blue jeans, the last symbolic distinction between wage earner and salaried employee will have disappeared.

Education also shows how blue collars have become middle class. Once high school education was a middle class monopoly—one that paid off in income and prestige. As late as 1941 white collar men had had an average of at least 12 years of school completed, while no level of manual worker averaged more than 8.6 years. In 1950 a comparison of the 25–29 year-old males showed a much narrower range—11 to 10 1/2 years for most manual workers as compared to 12 and a fraction years for white collar workers.

IMPACT ON EDUCATION

Finally, our educational system reflects this ideology of equality. Who shall be educated? Our concept of education has in Robin Williams' terms alternated between two models: the Jeffersonian model which would open the race to everyone yet eliminate all but the best from the final heats, and the Jacksonian model which would provide education at all levels for anyone. The way we attempt to follow both models has helped make us one of the most educated peoples in the world and at the same time to cast doubt on the quality of the education we achieve. As compared to the European system, there is pressure in the United States to graduate all students from high school, to admit all high school graduates to college and to permit college students to continue in college as long as they wish. And whenever the feeling arises that equality of opportunity is being diminished, education will be called upon to accelerate the processes of upward mobility.

Among Europeans, only the very able are allowed to continue and education tends to assume a class structure. In Britain, until recent reforms, only 15 percent of the primary enrollment went on to high school, and only 3 percent to the universities. In France, less than half the youths of high school age are in school; in Italy, only 7 percent of those beyond 14 years of age are enrolled in any school. At what seems to us a cruelly young age, school children are given fierce competitive examinations which determine who shall have the advantage of higher education. Those who fail will become the "trades people" and the working class.

We have spread education further and diluted it more. The issues involved reach as deeply into our society as the doctrine of equality itself. There is the comparison duly noted by a widely-read columnist, Kathleen Norris. In Europe, small boys under parental pressure with "dull little pencils and heavy little heads" do eight hours of homework over the weekend to pass qualifying exams set by the National Ministry of Education. Our columnist asks: "Who really learns most, who learns the things that are going to fit him for living with his fellow creatures and contributing to the general job of life? The stooped, anxious little foreigner, with his piled books and his smudged penciling, or the sturdy small boy in your family, who has learned some lessons from books, but more from ball fields, gym, scouts, swimming pools, movies, comics, TV, the weenie roast at the beach and the soda counter in the drugstore?"

Finally, in America there is the drive to make professions out of what the Europeans regard as trades. The American insurance salesman, the mortician, the realtor, and the auto salesman is open to the conviction that higher education will elevate his calling to the level of a learned profession. He also wants to be taught how to attract and serve the customer. The real argument, whether they realize it or not, is even more subtle. In a middle-class nation, people in these occupations have need of education so that in manner and style of life they can deal with the people they serve. Our doctrine of equality tolerates neither subservience nor "lower-class manners" from white collar occupations. Even janitors, one of the last lower-class holdouts, have succumbed to this doctrine. They are beginning to call themselves "maintenance engineers."

WHAT IS THE ETHICAL PROBLEM?

And finally what of our claims versus our achievements in equality? It has long been an observation of continental writers, especially the realistic French, that the English seem a hypocritical people, not because their behavior is so degraded, but because their claims are set so high. American democracy has taken this same risk and has encountered similar indictments. So true is this that we hear suggestions that we stop and take stock lest the ethical wares displayed on our shelves be shopworn.

Have we overpromised our children, our citizens, and the next generation on what we can deliver—or rather, on what they can achieve? Shall we lower our claims? Put our ideals in storage? Obviously there is one test of a social system that can be made before it is abandoned—that of success. As long as more social elevators go up than down; as long as each generation finds itself—or feels itself—advanced beyond the last, the system meets the pragmatic test.

There is another sanction to a functioning social system. Do the people find satisfaction in the attainment of the ideological goals they profess, and do they experience feelings of guilt when this attainment is thwarted or blocked? Do the American people still feel pride in achievements that spring from the equalization of opportunity? This question answers itself in spite of the sardonic comment that no pride equals that of the self-made man in his creator. I would say that the billions plowed back into philanthropy and educational endowment in the United States represents the impact of our great wealth, the incidence of our tax structure, and one more thing: the gratitude of people who have achieved under this system. Read some of the indentures to this great storehouse of public gifts.

As for guilt, we probably have too much of it on the part of one group —those who fail in our regime of assumed equality. If men actively believe that the system functions, that "where there is a will there's a way," then those who fail can have no one to blame but themselves. Margaret Mead suggests that there is an initial condition inserted into the mother's simplest kiss for her child that "I will love you only if you achieve as much as other people's babies. I can't love you if you don't."

The myth of equality unfortunately leaves little hope for self-respect for failures. We are almost in the position of having to assure some people that, in spite of free public schools, we do not really provide the equal opportunity we talk about. Or shall we inform them that their IQ's are so low that they never really had a chance?

The order of equality is basically a belief system. As such it has its hazards. We know there is a natural order of things assumed to exist in the physical world and in the social world, there is an ideal scheme of values that we would hope to see realized. Everything ideal, as Santayana said of Aristotle, has its basis in nature and everything natural has its ideal extension. In spite of science, however, the natural order of things is never completely understood; and in spite of our ethical tensions, the ideal scheme of things is never realized. The doctrine of equality remains in American life a bridge as it were between earth and heaven—a bridge between reality and the dream.

15. The Sociological Implications of

Southern Regionalism (1960)

In 1959, George Tindall chaired a symposium on regionalism for the Southern Historical Association, with contributions from William Hesseltine, Cleanth Brooks, and Rupert Vance. Vance's contribution was, for the most part, a backward look at regional sociology, almost a eulogy, in striking contrast to the optimistic tone he had taken only a decade before. The movement's successes had, ironically, been its undoing. Vance assumed, rather uncritically, that the cultural convergence of American regions would soon follow their economic and demographic convergence. In suggesting areas for continuing study, he touched on the problems of southern cities and industrialization, mentioned Appalachia as a subregion largely bypassed by the South's development, and had some interesting things to say about the nascent civil rights movement, as it was then taking shape.

The regional approach to the analysis of society possesses a stark reality which affects every interpretation we undertake. Power and administration, social consensus and policy determination are inseparably linked to area, that is, to units of territory. In the localization of resources, of industry and finance, the economic order parallels the political from the concert of great nations to their component elements in provinces and states.[1] If territorial groups did not exist, political organization logically would have to create them in order to function.

Thus, sociological regionalism arrives as it were after the *fait accompli*, a territorial distribution of wealth and resources, of political powers and representation, of consensus and decision. Spread over a national domain as wide as the United States, this array of forces joins local interests to make regional consciousness a necessity.

But before the national state developed, there were locality groups, call them tribes, clans, or what you will. For a long time the attitudes and values of these groups, in short their culture, represented a fixed and pro-

---

From *Journal of Southern History* 26 (February 1960): 44–56. © 1960 by the Southern Historical Association. Reprinted by permission of the managing editor.

vincial thing. Such groups were kith and kin, no doubt; as communal and regional groupings they were in Howard Odum's term, the *folk society*.[2]

The sociologist, insofar as he has contributed in this field, has related these regional factors in order to build up a total complex.[3] That is to say, he has gone from geography to modes of livelihood, to the folk, to political interests to develop as it were the formula that Le Play, the French pioneer in social science, called *place, work, folk*.[4] The sociologist has done less to relate regionalism to his own field of interests.

The sociologist develops his specialty, I take it, around the social group as his basic concept. Groups converge and are organized around interests. Society itself is viewed as a group of groups in co-operation and in stress and tension, in short in adjustment and balance.[5] The first group any social scientist is likely to meet is the territorial group. Here politics, history, and regional sociology appear to be firmly based and rightly concerned with sectional and regional phenomena. The historian who writes the running account of regional history is, I think, the least vulnerable. The political scientist dealing with formal organization and distribution of powers has a clearly defined field. The sociologist studying groups and cultures in their less informal aspects takes certain risks, if he wishes to explore regional phenomena. When diverse interests and attachments crisscross each other, regional alignments are not necessarily the paramount interests in a modern nation. Since society is a group of groups in a national context, the regional group comes to be but one of many alignments demanding loyalty of the people.

Indeed, it seems safe to say that many clashes of interests that might well be fought out on a class basis are by the very demands of political representation fought out in terms of sections and regions. Political parties are the conflict groups designated to carry on this fight; in the national arena the strife is mitigated, rather than intensified as the Founding Fathers feared. In our system of representation, states rights have, as F. J. Turner suggested, furnished the shield for sectional ideologies.[6] If class and sectional interests are the food that partisans feed upon, it must be remembered that it is the business of political parties to win and integrate support on a national level. As D. W. Brogan put it in the Weil lectures at North Carolina:

> Sectional loyalties spontaneously created by geographical and powerful traditions, as in New England, have been tamed by the national party system. Thus the most easily identifiable section, the South marked off by climate, by its basic economy, by the special

character of its population, black and white, has been, except for a brief interval, kept national by the party system. It was not at all accidental that the first steps on the "Road to Reunion" were taken by the political parties, specifically by the Democratic Party.[7]

What I have been emphasizing up to now is that (on a different level) the sociology of regionalism faces up to the same general problem encountered in the politics of federalism—where federalism exists. Heretofore, regional sociology has been much better at taking in other people's washing, relating its contributions to those of geography, economics, political science, and so forth than it has been in relating regionalism to its own domain, that of general sociology. Thus in the future, regionalism could well be remembered in studies of the South where regionalism appears pertinent but be left out of general sociology where it would appear to have less bearing. This of course handicaps sociologists in the writing of regional analysis, for it appears to limit them to special interests, notably those of the South or of the West as in the notable work of Walter Prescott Webb and Morris E. Garnsey.[8]

There are two facets here. First, regional analysis, the survey of regions, relates the data of one discipline to that of others because the phenomena occur within the same area. Cultural-statistical data patterned by groups of states furnished H. W. Odum's approach to this analysis.[9] Regionalism, however, is an ism; that is to say, it embraces policies and advocates programs. In the heyday of the New Deal its program embraced national-regional planning.[10] As a social movement, composed of organized and unorganized groups, such phenomena offer substantive material for sociological study. Short of goals, plans, programs, conflicts, groupings and regroupings around regional interests, the sociologist would seem to lack the kind of material he nowadays finds easily at hand in race relations, in social class, and in many other clashes of interests. Furthermore, since the region's major demand is not territorial autonomy, since its interest is participation in the processes that distribute the goods of power, wealth, and cultural amenities within the nation, its claims are made within the context of nationalism. To demand independence, it must generate its own nationalism.

So much for what must be a purely academic question—the discussion of disciplines and their legitimate subject matter. As one of the practicing regionalists of the late lamented 1930's I came not to bury regionalism but to praise it. I am prepared, however, to say with King Pyrrhus concerning certain regional developments, "Another such victory and we are all undone." Briefly, the trend toward the convergence of regional and national status has dulled the edge of regional claims and reduced the drive of regionalism as a social movement. To the extent that this happens, regional analysis lacks data or grist for the mill.

In Italy, for example, certain differences between north and south have been notable. With the industrial progress of north Italy, these two areas have drawn further apart within the last fifty years. In the United States in the same period regional differences, as Floyd Saville shows, have steadily diminished.[11] Indeed, given a continuation of this trend, economic differences can become comparatively unimportant in the foreseeable future. Changes are bringing the area close to national development and characteristics. The last three decades—Depression, New Deal, World War II, and the New Prosperity—have meant more for growth in the range and variety of the South's interests—agricultural, industrial, financial, political, and cultural—than any previous fifty-year period.[12] The region now appears to be moving from a one crop economy and politics to a diversified South more integrated with the nation. Only in its racial composition and attitudes does a major historical difference carry the great weight of the past into the future.

At the time of his death in 1954 Howard W. Odum was engaged in rewriting *Southern Regions of the United States*. It was to carry the subtitle The South at Mid-Century, and the theme was the convergence of economic and social trends as the South approached closer to equalization and participation within the life of the nation.[13]

It is not just that these trends are converging and give promise for the future. Many of the basic conditions that gave rise to regional disability and difference have simply evaporated on our doorsteps. In the field of public health, we appear to have lost track for example of hookworm, pellagra, and malaria. I lose my students when I discuss these things, just as I lose them when I talk about the depression. Many of the pertinent demands of the regional movement in the thirties have evaporated in just this way. The New Deal has been dealt; what is the fighting all about? As the affluent society crosses the Mason-Dixon line, the regionalist of the 1930's turns up as just another "liberal without a cause."

Does this represent the failure of regionalism as a social movement, or does it represent success?[14] Are the regionalists dismayed over the passing of inequalities and the further equalization of opportunity? Did we claim a vested interest in our disabilities so great that we fear to see them removed? Are we enamored of being Economic Problem Number One? Were there rewards to be gained from this position? If so, those rewards are disappearing, and our stance is no longer appropriate.

Cultural differences are lessening along with the shift in economy. Running through all regional characteristics of the South have been the contrasting strands of the rural and urban styles of life. The sharp decrease in its farm component has had the greatest influence in changing the South's style and its regional outlook. This shift is upon us in the South; its impact remains to be assessed, but we can be sure that regionalism— Southern brand—will be different, and it will be less. It is a smart saying now current in the metropolis, "There are no more hicks left"—a cynical epigram to be sure. To this I would add in summation, "Such as they are, they most resemble urban hicks." This convergence of different value systems in the attainment of common American goals in the middle-class style of life is important. In Southern life it means a lessened dependence on nature, a greater dependence on man-made artifacts and mechanisms.

Of the many changes now converging on the South, urbanism is the symbol—not the efficient cause. Industrialization, social mobility—the shift from agricultural to mechanical and white collar occupation—mean that more people live in proximity to each other at focal points where transportation, communication, and the mass services converge.[15] Those who do not migrate to these focal centers have the urbanizing cultural forces beamed in their direction—services that run the gamut from pre-mixed biscuits and precooked rice to television's mass pabulum of horse operas and soap operas. Once, like Vermont, we in the South too had unique rustic personalities—somewhat cross-grained at times. Today we have mass culture and minds, and the only way a man and his family can remain "hayseed" is to be brought up in a mountain cove with communication cut off by land, sea, and air.

Sociologists learn at an early age to be tough minded, and I am not here to shed any tears. The South has been understaffed with cities, and its metropolitan functions of organization and management have heretofore been performed outside the region. Men now work together, plan and administer in the collective life of our larger communities. "If the outlying areas of our nation are to partake more of the characteristics of the central core of power, welfare, administration and finance in this country, they will of necessity become more urban and more metropolitan."[16] Like you, I am sometimes dismayed by the manifestation of the "Atlanta spirit,"[17] but I am also dismayed when I perceive how the rural counties live off Atlanta's largess, hang on her coattails, keep her in the strait jacket of a medieval electoral system. Certainly, I wonder if the Chamber of Commerce is really as powerful as it is claimed or is as aggressive as it should be.

Agrarianism flourishes as much as it does in our area simply because staple crops are subsidized, held in mid-air as it were by quotas, bounties, soil banks, governmental stock piling of unwanted and unused commodities. Whether this can be maintained until the last unneeded agrarian goes to work for Du Pont or Burlington Mills, thereby contributing his transfer to the urban industrial complex and assuming his rightful burden of contributing to the support of the economy, we do not know.

As urbanization and metropolitanism increase, the South will relocate its centers of strain and conflict. Today they are inter-regional in competition for the rewards of industrialization and an increase of material comforts in the American way of middle-class life. Tomorrow the lines of stress will have moved to the center of the South's growing cities. Inner conflict will replace regional and sectional striving to the extent that we must balance and adjust the clash of interests at home; as indeed we are beginning to realize, among classes, groups, workers, unions, and organizations caught up in the great transition, pushing claims once unheard of in the *status quo ante*. We can preview our problems by studying the metropolitan conglomerate that now stretches from Boston to Washington. While the South will never attain this expanse, new troubles, new expenditures, new drains on budgets, energy, and patience come with increasing industrialization, increasing responsibility—even with increasing prosperity. We have asked for these gifts in pushing for regional equalization. The future will be less Southern, less regional, certainly less traditional, thus bringing the South nearer the national mode. The case of the Magnolias versus the Bulldozers in C. Vann Woodward's phrase will furnish nostalgia and literary artistry. Can we hope it will humanize the South's transition?

The Southern Appalachians, it would appear, is the one area that has not kept up with recent advances of the South; at least, that was the assumption of certain Southern scientists now engaged in a survey of the region. In order to demonstrate the different culture that comes from rural areas, an opinion and attitude survey on matters of social import was set up to sample the population ranging from the mountain coves through the rural and small town areas to the big cities of the region. The returns are now being tabulated, and regionalists may be disappointed to learn that the differences between extremes appear to be much less than most of us had anticipated.[18] In education, in health and medical care, in economics and livelihood, in civic duty and politics, in family life and what they hope for their children, the rural mountaineers come very close to the urban dwellers of Chattanooga, Knoxville, and Asheville, who by our account should closely resemble the national mode of thought. In the area of morality and even more in the area of religion, the rural Appalachians show greater differences, but here they are not as great as expected. The impact of all this admittedly is difficult to determine. The meaning for regionalism, however, seems pretty clear. In areas where isolation and poverty once limited participation in national thought patterns, education and communication have brought the regional culture nearer to national modes. These people are now repeating the national credo. Who are we to contend that they do not understand what they are saying? The study also gives evidence of the great numbers who have migrated out of this area and of the improved economic condition of many who remained. Even in the culture of our rural Appalachian mountains, we can no longer expect to find the regional opinions and attitudes which once prevailed. In belief systems, in matters of old time religion, in matters of faith, where the success patterns and the pragmatic ways of life do not intrude, these people remain closer to the early verities.

There is a literature of knowledge which makes us aware of the transition we have discussed; there is also a literature of high artistry which develops its symbols and its tragedy out of these materials. Here the South has long passed beyond the local colorists. The South now produces writers who rank with the most creative of the age. How do these two trend lines coincide in Southern regionalism today? Undoubtedly, our articulate intelligentsia, artists, writers, and occasional college professors find difficulty in coming to terms with the South's new ruling class. What we meet here is the problem posed by the transfer of function from one ruling class to another. The plantation elite have been succeeded by an industrial elite. William Faulkner with his attitudes toward the Compsons and the Snopeses illustrates the artist's problem in this tragic tension.[19] The former agrarian elite is to be dealt with in terms of high tragedy; the new industrial ruling class in comparison is vulgar, if not obscene. Its leadership and responsibility lost, the agrarian aristocracy is presented as the very type of decayed aristocracies. At the height of their power, however, the Ante Bellum Elite showed no weakness to the Abolitionist; they were seen as powerful—"right forever on the scaffold, wrong forever on the throne." In the transition from agrarian to urban-industrial society, functions are lost and functions are gained. It takes three generations, it is said, for families to learn to live with wealth; it probably takes more, if we can judge from Charleston and Mississippi, for families to learn to live without accustomed wealth. The ruling classes that lose their functions and their basis for being become fit subject for Tennessee Williams and William Faulkner; stress and strain, nostalgia and loss furnish the materials for high tragedy. And as always along with the great go the pretentious. What Southern writers give us here is the portrait of "trained incapacity." The phrase is Thorstein Veblen's, but the literary artistry is that of Chekov. The South today, if we read our greatest artists, is a landscape of *Cherry Orchards*.

If the old elite has lost its function, the new ruling class has not yet assimilated its role. The business man is not expected to be a figure of tragedy; he is not heroic; he is not yet a figure of respect. In fact, in much of our fiction he is not treated as a figure of humanity. Shall I risk a summary verdict and say that our new elite is given the literary treatment the abolitionist once gave the slave holder? The new *Uncle Tom's Cabins* are being written by Southern intellectuals about the ruling class to whom our Chambers of Commerce and State Planning Boards look for salvation. Admittedly the literary regionalist viewing the highest achievement of art also illustrates the dilemma of transition faced by regional sociologists.

The Southern regionalist today is not "a rebel without a cause." He is not in rebellion; and the more material dimensions of his cause appear to be on the way to achievement. But what of the place of the Negro in the discussion of Southern regionalism? His position shows the weakness faced by a strong social movement that lacks a basis in locality. The Negro is not a regionalist, and he lacks the territorial basis for nationalism. The Negro does not seek independence; what would have suited the Confederates does not suit him. Marcus Garvey saw this as a psychological deficiency and tried to fill it with his spurious African movement. The Negro movement converges around no sectional or regional interest, for his section is a battleground, not a homeland but a base of operations. He fights a battle for equalization in which his group lacks any kind of territorial basis except that of the Negro community. The community is

Negro, however, only if it represents the segregated community—a proposal that the Negro is in duty bound to oppose. Thus when Communist propaganda once advocated the organization of an autonomous Negro state, the proposal fell with a thud and was abandoned in the Party councils.

The Negro's interest, then, must be racial; and yet this is forced upon him, for he would in certain respects prefer to lose his identity. Some of his leaders, for example, go so far as to ask that the returns on the Negro not be enumerated in that category by the census.

Not a regionalist and in rebellion against the mores of the majority South, the Negro is yet a Southerner.[20] I was once forcibly reminded of this when I told an audience of Negroes that in possessing the right of mobility they had the cherished American right to migrate to improve their status. To a man, it seemed to me, the audience took the position that the right to give up what they had and to abandon the fight where they lived was the right of refugees and therefore not much of a right at all. In a way that seemed to me to make them Southerners all over again and regionalists of a sort, and with this view those in the audience were inclined to agree.

Theoretically, a sociologist might conclude here that given the rights of his common humanity, the cause of the Negro would rejoin the cause of the human race, and the racial interests as a stimulus to group cohesion would disappear. At present I would have to regard this view as a fallacy. Compared with the total population, the Negro is poor and thus underprivileged. His interest accordingly is also a class interest, and this agitation the Negro leaders must control, for that avenue leads back to the Communist propaganda from which they happily managed to escape in the 1930's.

The strategy of the Negro movement, then, like that of the regionalist is found in the drive for equalization. While the Negro seeks the equality of opportunity and treatment that, it seems to me, falls within the strategy that Thomas Jefferson organized for the rights of mankind, their appeals are limited to national power, to the federal government and the Constitution. The movement lacks a home basis outside the segregated Negro community. The anomaly of the conflict then consists of the territorial basis of group organization, the very strength of regional movements. As the Negro fights to lose identity, the regionalist struggles to maintain his identity.

So much for the region's minority. What shall we say about the majority group in this issue? We can, of course, agree with Ulrich B. Phillips's dictum that the Negro's presence and the reaction to that presence has been the unifying theme of Southern history. In agreeing with so obvious a statement, I doubt that we now advance the argument very much. To the extent that this means that much of what is distinctive in Southern culture has its origin in racial interaction, for example the dance (graceful, ungraceful, and disgraceful as James Weldon Johnson once put it) and music, secular and sacred, spiritual, blues and jazz, we must, of course, all agree.

But if we are to reach the conclusion that the unifying principle of a revived Southern regionalism is to come out of resistance to the Negro's drive for further equality, I would demur and on good grounds. This is sectionalism—a sectionalism that could block the regional goals I have discussed. When Dr. Samuel Johnson said that patriotism is the last refuge of a scoundrel he was not being critical of patriotism but of scoundrels. Patriotism is not the last movement a scoundrel would embrace; rather he could wear that mask and play the role when he could get by in no other part. If regionalism should become the last refuge of an anti-Negro rights movement, it will to my mind no longer be regionalism.

As a social movement regionalism is devoted to the maintenance of balance, both in the acceleration of and in the adjustment to social change. In economic development, industrialization, and all that goes with it, regional forces and leaders have pushed toward integration with the national economy. As they succeed, regional differences are blurred, but regional identity remains. Regionalism like individualism claims a right to maintain identity—to defend and to cherish a certain autonomy in cultural values, a style of life, certain attitudes regarded as Southern.[21] This autonomy takes nothing from the national life; it may in fact enrich our national range and variety. It is to be found in our national motto, if we may be said to have one—*e pluribus unum*—the one from the many.

NOTES

1. The other system proposed for representation, the soviet based on occupational groups, makes use of areas for administration. For the relations of regionalism to political science, see James W. Fesler, *Area and Administration* (University, Ala., 1949) and Vincent Ostrom, "The Political Dimensions of Regional Analysis," Regional Science Association, *Papers and Proceedings 2*

(1956): 85–91. See also, for economics, papers by Walter Isard and Morris E. Garnsey with discussion, ibid., pp. 13–51.

2. Howard W. Odum, "Folk and Regional Conflict as a Field of Sociological Study," American Sociological Society, *Publications* 25 (May 1931): 1–17; "Folk Sociology as a Subject Field for the Historical Study of Total Human Society and the Empirical Study of Group Behavior," *Social Forces* 31 (March 1953): 193–223; George L. Simpson, Jr., "Howard W. Odum and American Regionalism," *Social Forces* 34 (December 1956): 101–6.

3. For a multiple approach to regional research, see Rupert Vance, "The Regional Concept as a Tool for Social Research," in Merrill Jensen, ed., *Regionalism in America* (Madison, Wis., 1951), pp. 119–40.

4. P. G. F. Le Play, *Les Ouvriers européens* (Paris, 1855, 2nd ed., 6 vols., Tours, 1877–1879). A sympathetic account of the Le Play school is found in Pitirim Sorokin, *Contemporary Sociological Theories* (New York, 1928), pp. 63–98.

5. Alvin L. Bertrand, "Regional Sociology as a Special Discipline," *Social Forces* 31 (December 1952): 132–36.

6. Merle Curti, "The Section and the Frontier in American History," in Stuart A. Rice, ed., *Methods in Social Science* (Chicago, 1931), pp. 353–67.

7. Dennis W. Brogan, *Citizenship Today: England, France, the United States* (Chapel Hill: University of North Carolina Press, 1960).

8. Webb, *The Great Plains* (Boston, 1931) and *Divided We Stand* (Austin, Tex., 1944); Garnsey, *America's New Frontier: The Mountain West* (New York, 1950).

9. Howard W. Odum, *Southern Regions of the United States* (Chapel Hill, 1936); Odum and Harry E. Moore, *American Regionalism* (New York, 1938).

10. U.S. National Resources Committee, *Regional Factors in National Planning and Development* (Washington, 1935), *The Structure of the American Economy* (1939), *Industrial Location and National Resources* (1943). Between 1936 and 1943 this agency and its successor issued thirteen Regional Planning Reports and twenty-two Drainage Basin Committee Reports.

11. Floyd Saville, "Sectional Developments in Italy and the United States," *Southern Economic Journal* 23 (July 1956): 39–53.

12. Though the literature on regional convergence has not been brought up to date, it is too extensive to be reviewed here. Samplings would include John L. Fulmer, *Agricultural Progress in the Cotton Belt since 1920* (Chapel Hill, 1950); James H. Street, *The New Revolution in the Cotton Economy* (Chapel Hill, 1957); Calvin B. Hoover and B. U. Ratchford, *Economic Resources and Policies of the South* (New York, 1951); Harriet L. Herring, *Southern Industry and Regional Development* (Chapel Hill, 1940); U.S. Office of Business Economics, *Regional Trends in the United States Economy* (Washington, 1951), and *U.S. Income and Output* (Washington, 1958); Victor R. Fuchs, "Changes in the Location of United States Manufacturing since 1929," *Journal of Regional Science* 1 (Spring 1959): 1–17. The theme of regional-national integration is presented for six U.S. regions in six special articles in the *Collier's Encyclopedia 1957 Year Book*, William T. Couch, ed. (New York, 1957), pp. 647–68.

13. Under a grant from the John Simon Guggenheim Memorial Foundation

this analysis is being carried forward by George L. Simpson of the University of North Carolina. Odum's own hopes for regionalism are reflected in his "The Promise of Regionalism" in Merrill Jensen, ed., *Regionalism in America*, pp. 395–425. For an estimate of Odum's own contribution to regional-national integration, see George B. Tindall, "The Significance of Howard W. Odum to Southern History: A Preliminary Estimate," *Journal of Southern History* 24 (August 1958), pp. 285–307. For Odum's bibliography, see Rupert B. Vance and Katherine Jocher, "Howard W. Odum," *Social Forces* 33 (March 1955): 203–17.

14. Thus Walter Prescott Webb's "The South's Call to Greatness," *Texas Business Review* 33 (October 1959): 1, 6–8, may be viewed either as a recantation of *Divided We Stand* or as the triumph of regional development.

15. Rupert B. Vance and Nicholas J. Demerath, eds., *The Urban South* (Chapel Hill, 1954).

16. Rupert B. Vance, "The Urban Breakthrough in the South," *Virginia Quarterly Review* 31 (Spring 1955): 223–32.

17. The symposium of which this paper is a part was given at a joint session of the Southeastern American Studies Association and the Southern Historical Association at Atlanta, November 13, 1959.

18. The administrative director of the Southern Appalachian Studies is W. D. Weatherford, of Berea College, Berea, Kentucky. The research director is Thomas R. Ford, of the University of Kentucky, under whose editorship the finished study will be published by the University of Kentucky Press. Earl Brewer, of the School of Theology, Emory University, is director of religious research.

19. Louis D. Rubin has discussed Faulkner's work in this context with somewhat different conclusions in an unpublished paper before the Southern Sociological Society at Gatlinburg, Tennessee, April 7, 1959.

20. Both sides of this thesis are presented by L. D. Reddick in "The Negro as Southerner and American," a chapter in *The Southerner As American*, ed. Charles G. Sellers, Jr. (Chapel Hill: University of North Carolina Press, 1960).

21. C. Vann Woodward, "The Search for Southern Identity," *Virginia Quarterly Review* 34 (Summer 1958); 321–38.

16. Social Change in the

Southern Appalachians (1965)

John Kennedy's political debt to West Virginia and the subsequent
focus of national attention on the problems of Appalachia were
reminiscent of Roosevelt's debt and attention to the Deep South a
quarter century earlier. A number of scholars, Vance included, had
already begun an Appalachian regional survey—a natural project for
researchers accustomed to examining problems of development in
regional terms. This assessment of the southern mountains and the
area's resources and problems is an example of the kind of work that
Vance was doing at the time—essentially the application of regional
sociology to a marginal subregion. Vance had been aware of the
special problems of Appalachia at least since his early work on
subregional variation within the South. This essay makes an appro-
priate companion piece to his article "The Old Cotton Belt" of thirty
years before.

The Southern Appalachian Region, it is sometimes said, comprises the
backyards of some seven southern states. In the brief compass of this
book it was not possible to present all the subregional components that
make up the South. For several reasons, however, the Southern Highlands deserve their own accounting. They are different, but this analysis
is not presented as a portrait of quaint customs and surviving folklore.
Rather, when the problem of continuity and change is examined, the
serious question arises as to how and on what terms the region will be
able to follow the South in its thrust to get back into the mainstream of
American economic and cultural life. Examined in terms of its attitude
toward industrial change sweeping over the rest of the South, the region's
stance seems to partake more of a heritage from the frontier than from
the Civil War. Social change has not dealt kindly with certain parts of
this area.

Analysis of the Appalachians, we find, is no longer regarded as an aca-

From John C. McKinney and Edgar T. Thompson, eds., *The South in Continuity and Change*, pp. 404–17. © 1965 by Duke University Press, Durham, N.C.

demic exercise in delimiting subregions and subcultures; it has become a problem of social action and policy. "End the cycle of poverty," economic redevelopment, and the attempt to prevent large parts of the areas from becoming a back eddy of American life represent aspects of current policy. The present chapter, if unable to present sure solutions, will nevertheless be written in concern with what is unique and urgent about the region.

If the Appalachians are here presented as a problem area, it is only to point out that great variations exist. Cities in the area are like cities elsewhere in the United States, except that their slums are populated by recent migrants from the mountains rather than by Negroes and Puerto Ricans. The Great Valley is surrounded by mountains, but it stands out as one of the richest agricultural areas in the country. The truly mountainous areas, those over 2,000 feet in altitude, no longer offer serious problems. Scenery of pure beauty, often penetrated by magnificent highways, stretches across these highlands, and areas like the Great Smoky Park and the famous parkways have few or no permanent inhabitants left —only touring customers. Nevertheless, the Appalachian problem areas remain, mainly in the lower reaches of hills and dissected plateaus as we shall see. Vigorous studies of these areas have documented the problem.[1]

ONE

Without committing ourselves to geographic determinism, we can point out that the Southern Appalachians, as a part of the Eastern Mountain system running from the Laurentians of Canada to Alabama and Georgia, have the highest peaks and the most sharply dissected plateaus east of the Rockies. Beginning from the east, (1) the Blue Ridge Mountains comprise the highest ranges; (2) the Central Division has four valleys with alternating ridges; and (3) the Western Subregion consists mainly of three dissected plateaus, the Allegheny, the Northeastern Cumberland, and the Northwestern Cumberland areas.[2]

In its unfolding analysis the extent of this subregion has gradually been narrowed. From the first important survey, that of John C. Campbell in 1910,[3] to the Appalachian survey of 1960, the region as depicted shrunk from 210 counties of 112,000 square miles to 190 counties of approximately 80,000 square miles and 5,600,000 population. This includes the six metropolitan areas formed by the cities of Charleston and Huntington, West Virginia; Roanoke, Virginia; Asheville, North Carolina; and Knoxville and Chattanooga, Tennessee.

It is agreed in our country's history that differing geography has gone along with differing types of settlement. Regional distinctions soon gave the Southern Tidewater its primacy with an aristocracy based on tobacco, rice, and indigo. The rest was back country, for the supremacy of the Piedmont was to be delayed until industrialization approached its zenith in the twentieth century. The image we have of the mountains is that of a frontier with "no indication that the people were shuttled into the mountains nor that they were of inferior stock." When D. H. Davis studied the mountain region for the State Geological Survey of Kentucky in 1928 he reported: "The stock is in all probability, in a large part, the same as that of the Kentucky Blue Grass [region] but it has been modified by long isolation in an area of lesser opportunity."[4]

TWO

The fluctuating trend lines of social change and continuity in these mountains are as baffling to the analyst as those of our national life—partly because they are inextricably intertwined. As it moved out of the frontier period, it must have required some time for the nation to realize that the mountain people were likely to be left isolated and underprivileged in the change. For a time good hunting, pasture on the free range, subsistence agriculture, and homespun living were adequate rewards. Finally, the breakdown of isolation made possible the comparison of regional and national standards of life. When the Great Depression introduced relief and public works in the 1930's, the application of federal standards made half the population in certain Appalachian areas eligible for relief —and this without any lowering of the customary "live-at-home" and "do-without" economy.[5]

As economic recovery proceeded, it became evident that the economic status and thus the social adequacy of the region would depend largely on its ability to participate in the nation's urban industrial complex. Any analysis along this line will point out the great diversity of the region in terms of (1) what communities have lost in economic competence and (2) what they never had.

Before 1900 most adult workers were employed in agriculture. Today (1960) two-thirds of the population live in rural areas but this figure exaggerates the region's social continuity with the frontier. Only 55 per cent of the employed who live on farms now work in agricultural occupations. Less than one-ninth of the employed males are farmers and farm managers. More persons work in industry than any other branch of economy, but manufacturing employs only 21 per cent of the people. In 1957 the average number of miners working daily was 122,243—a drop of 40 per cent in six years. Now less than one-eighth of the working force in the area, the mining force continues to decline.

Without laboring the details, certain clear-cut conclusions are evident. (1) Coal mining is a sick industry, ruinous of men and natural resources of stream and soil. The worst areas in the Appalachians, the Kentucky Cumberlands, certain West Virginia areas and northern areas as in Pennsylvania, consist of stranded coal communities. With the finest reserves of bituminous coal, expected to last 1,000 years, with the chance of reaching again some of the peak years of physical production, the industry will never re-employ its stranded workers. Until the workers move out and the abusive practices of strip mining are abandoned these many coal camps have little hope beyond dire poverty.[6]

Much of (2) mountain agriculture has been subsistence farming— strictly limited in resources and furnishing very little cash income to the farmer's family. The mode of national agriculture today is one of extended operations, requiring capital and access to well-organized markets. Agriculture in the mountains can be improved and more commercial crops can be grown but only for fewer farmers cultivating larger acreage. Land is limited; slopes are steep; more lands should be put back into forests; and more people will be pushed off the farms. Subsistence farming today is an occupation in which no self-respecting parent should want to rear his children. Everytime the health authorities issue a new directive that fluid milk must be carried to market in glass-lined refrigerator trucks instead of milk cans, more hill farmers go out of the dairy business. Mountain agriculture produces few commercial staples, gets few subsidies for cutting back production—they underproduce not overproduce —but pays the increased prices for grain for feeder calves and hog production. Few government programs have been designed for this type of farming, and it is evident that many offer no hope at all for the mountain farmer. It seems safe to say that mountain agriculture is not only the stepchild of nature; it is the forgotten stepchild of the United States Department of Agriculture.[7]

The mountains have the finest (3) national and state forests left in this country and more land can be reforested. Lumber production, however, has passed its peak and the new program is one of conservation and reduced yield with public and private employment in scientific forestry. The larger areas in corporate and private ownership must be given the same treatment, if timber is to remain a continuing resource. The frank truth is that not a large number of people are required "to watch trees grow." If a sizeable labor force is employed in speeding up the cut, they will have neither trees nor their employment very long! The United States Forestry Service and certain private owners are doing a magnificent work, but they offer no great hope of re-employing a population of any size.[8]

This analysis leaves (4) industrialization as the main hope of a reinvigorated Appalachia. There is a distinct industrial belt in the Appalachians as the survey showed; manufacturing employment has increased at a faster rate than in the nation; the region's cities generate markets and employment for their hinterlands.[9] The crucial point here is the amount of capital investment required to furnish employment for an industrial worker at a decent annual wage. If the farmer requires some $15,000 to $25,000 invested capital in land and equipment to furnish an annual return of $5,000 to $7,500 on his labor, the industrial worker depends on an equal or greater amount of capital investment—an investment that may be lost unless there exists access to a good market for the product. This usually means a national market. Every area in the country, it appears, is in competition with other areas for industrialization and for access to markets. All communities in the United States want to further industrialization and good, sound commercial agriculture, but since the localizing factor is anchorage to resources which may be developed and processed on the site or near it, industrialization has many choices of where to alight in its movement over the country. To expect corporate industry to function as a relief program to bail out stranded communities in the Southern Appalachians is futile. To attract national corporations and to break into competitive markets, areas must offer special advantages. This is a fair statement of what any region faces in competition in the national picture. It is also a fair statement of what other parts of the South have accomplished.

THREE

We can be more specific and more statistical. Agriculture and coal mining are the sick industries of Appalachia; the new hope is to be found in industrialization and urbanization. Of the 5,672,178 people enumerated in the subregion in 1960, one-third lived in some 157 urban places; two-thirds were still accounted among the rural population. The metropolitan centers have been listed; while not large by national standards, they include some 25 per cent of the region's population. In all there were only 13 cities of 25,000 population and over; 42 cities had from 10,000 up to 25,000 people. Over half the nation's working force are now employed in the services, distribution, the professions, etc., the so-called white-collar trades, located in urban centers. It is here that the great middle-class standard of living is developed and spread throughout the population. These occupations are hardly affixed to any specific source except that they represent central operations in and related to the urban complex. Here transportation, finance, and marketing tend to equal resources in importance.

All over the South great advances have been made by participating in the nation's industrial goals, adjusting commercial agriculture, and creating centers for the increased emphasis on the expansion of social and institutional services—educational, clerical, and professional. Here it is generally felt that portions of the Appalachians have not kept up with advances in the South. No part of the country needs these improved institutional services more; and certainly serious efforts must and will continue to be made toward reorganization of the area's basic economy.

To basic economic pressures, the inhabitants of this area have reacted by taking out-migration as the avenue of escape and self-help. From 1940 to 1960 almost 2,000,000 more people have left Appalachia than have settled there. A loss of 13 per cent from 1940–1950, and 19 per cent from 1950 to 1960, was balanced by a rate of natural increase—the excess of birth over death—of 21 and 16.2 per cent in 1940–1950 and 1950–1960 respectively. Kentucky lost over 500,000 by out-migration and West Virginia over 600,000 during this twenty-year period. The greatest out-migrations left the Cumberland and Allegheny Plateaus: 28.3 per cent in 1950–1960; the next greatest loss was from the Blue Ridge area: 14.7 per cent; the least from the Great Valley: 8.7 per cent. From 1940–1950 the six metropolitan areas gained 10,518 by migration; from 1950–1960 they lost 137,684. The only metropolitan area to show gain was Roanoke, Virginia.[10]

When the 190 counties were classified on the basis of major occupations, the regions' hard-pressed economies were easily identified. Mining counties had approximately 40 per cent loss by net out-migration; agricultural areas with mining and manufacturing lost 23 to 25 per cent. Only state economic areas characterized by manufacturing and mixed agriculture, or manufacturing and commercial showed gains, 8.3 and 5.4 per cent respectively from 1950 to 1960. Where population numbers have been maintained, it must be assigned to the natural increase, and here the trend is downward. Migration has a double effect. It removed a disproportionate number of people in the younger working ages and it reduces future population increase by the number of children these people would have had in their home communities. Here we are faced with an interesting question. If changed conditions have forced this amount of out-migration, what changes have they induced in mountain attitudes?

FOUR

The older regional studies, more concerned with causation than social change, emphasized social continuity in the mountains. They looked back to physical limitations, and from physical resources and crude modes of making a living, the analysis moved forward to consider institutional adjustments and the attitudes of the people. Thus mountain isolation, which began as a physical limitation enforced by rugged topography, became mental and cultural isolation which causes people to remain in disadvantaged areas and resist the changes that would bring them into contact with the outside world. The effect of conditions thus becomes a new cause of conditions, but the cause is now an attitude, not a mountain. If we devote attention to religion in the mountains, we find it an effect of conditions under which people have lived. Not only is it an effect of conditions under which people live, but the particular attitudes of religion may then operate to perpetuate these conditions. Thus if hard lives have given rise to fatalism and fundamentalism, these attitudes may operate to perpetuate original conditions. The change from fatalism to the social gospel may actually go over into engineered change in breaking through limiting physical conditions. Since mountains are not likely to be moved, the new regionalism proceeds on the assumption that men can be moved.

How resistant to change are the mountain people in their sentiments and beliefs, the way they feel the world is, and should be, ordered? In a field survey the opinions and attitudes of a representative sample were secured. In attempting to measure the extent and influence of individualism and self-reliance, of fundamentalism and fatalism, the survey showed that attitudes are changing. The aspirations of our national life have penetrated the mountains and the people visualize a more equitable future for their children. They are now willing for them to leave the region in the search of a better life. In the main the population accepts the necessity of welfare and relief; they feel that the government should do more, but hesitate to give their support to the raising of taxes for these goals. They now recognize the advantage of group action, but think of government as "they" not "we." While they may not have yet reached the level of responsible organization for self-help, the people, as the survey showed, present a greater hope of improved social organization.

The much-criticized fundamentalism no longer appears as an obstacle to progress, for the people have assimilated much of the social gospel along with the belief in the ability of education and science to improve their lot. Professor Thomas Ford calls his analysis the passing of provincialism. While present attitudes show no passive acceptance of the *status quo*, they do not indicate that the people themselves yet know how to lead the way to change.[11]

Special attention was devoted in the Appalachian survey to the attitude of community leaders selected from interviews with the people themselves. The persons named as leaders—379 were interviewed—were considerably ahead of the total population in education, property ownership, income, and age. Half were regarded by the criteria of the study as belonging to the region's upper class. The leaders were definitely ahead of the people, activists and progressive, pushing for change and development, receptive of national values and contacts. Although named by the people, they were not of the people in modal attitudes and opinions. Nevertheless, to find the professional and propertied people of the area with these new attitudes gave an indication that this can hardly be called a traditional society. Here is one indication that feasible plans and programs, if developed, will have the support of the community leaders. This whole trend of attitude toward change increases from the rural through the urban to the metropolitan populations.[12] Admitting it has required a long period for these attitudes to develop, the question now remains: Can the new attitudes clear the ground for a changeover in the more depressed areas of the Appalachians?

FIVE

Change has been abroad in the land and the Appalachians are far from being a stagnant enclave. Population growth has tended to stabilize; nearly two million people have migrated elsewhere in the last twenty years. Since 1939 manufacturing employment and production have increased more rapidly than in the nation. Unprecedented aid from outside the region has pushed the development of new highways and of water resources as in the TVA. Schools have been improved; more students attend schools and for longer periods. Programs of public assistance, while inadequate, have developed to mitigate the harsher aspects of poverty. While change is by no means absent from the region, the nation has advanced at a more rapid rate, leaving the Appalachians still under a disadvantage. Moreover, certain areas like the Kentucky Cumberland have encountered serious damage. Schools have improved but it is less easy to repair the educational damage already inflicted on maturing populations.[13]

In public policy it is ofttimes easier to agree on basic goals than to reach consensus on how the goals may be attained. In the case at hand, the determination of objectives has been especially compelling. The Appalachians problem areas show no tendency to go away if they are simply left alone. However, since they also show little tendency to depress the normal trend line of our national prosperity, it has been suggested that they can be accepted as chronic pockets of poverty, and thus safely disregarded in the ordinary plans of business and government. The fallacy of this argument "is that it ignores the enormous human and social cost of the depressed areas and the danger to national policy in letting them fester." The continual wastage of human resources in depressed areas has thus been called "a social crime, an economic absurdity and a political menace."[14]

In the present climate of opinion, and with the resources of an affluent society, it may surprise some to find that it will prove less difficult to secure budgets for the development of Appalachia than to determine how best to use these budgets. In the problem of induced social change we have two main questions to answer: What is the strategy of regional development in an area like this? What type and kinds of social organization already exist and what others can be developed to carry through this strategy? Just as we have glanced at the new researches and the new knowledge developed about the Appalachians, let us recount the appearance of agencies and organizations devoted to redevelopment. Then we shall follow through by looking at the problem of strategy and tactics.

The Appalachians have long been the center of missionary and extension activity by private groups and agencies. Health services were first taken to the mountains by the Frontier Nursing Service. Nurses who rode horseback to deliver the babies of mountain mothers were the first to bring modern maternal and child health services to remote areas. Practically all of the national denominations have supported missionary activity in the area; and before the era of public schools, many staffed and supported a mountain academy. Berea College remains a fine example of an institution especially adapted to mountain culture and needs.

Recent events converging on this area have served to make induced change regarded as a social necessity. From the Southern Governors' Conference to President Lyndon Johnson's attack on poverty many agencies, governmental and private, are at work on plans for the region's development. The Conference of Governors of the Appalachian States issued an initial call for action at its meeting in Annapolis, Maryland, in May, 1960. The group sponsored an economic report, and agreed on programs of increased highway facilities, the development of water resources, and improved education.[15] On May 21, 1961, President Kennedy signed the Area Redevelopment Act—a measure to help stranded rural and urban communities overcome chronic unemployment by a series of studies, projects, and programs to be financed by grants-in-aid. The Area Redevelopment Administration was established in the Department of Commerce and given a sizeable budget with promise of other funds to come.[16] In the meantime, conditions became worse and the program of surplus foods was developed in order to feed hungry people in certain stranded communities. Much of the Cumberland Plateau of Eastern Kentucky, many of West Virginia's counties and other regions of the Appalachians were designated as redevelopment areas under the new act.

Certain other plans can also be pointed out. In West Virginia a group of core counties, organized under the combined Extension Services of the State University, have embarked on a program of development proposed and guided by core county committees. Under a grant from the Kellogg Foundation, the University of Kentucky is carrying integrated extension services to the thirty counties of the Cumberlands in an attempt to hasten redevelopment. The idea is to stimulate certain communities by offering these services, to encourage them to inventory their needs and work toward alleviation. The governor of North Carolina and his advisors organized a program entitled, "End the Cycle of Poverty in North Carolina," secured the support of the Ford Foundation and other groups, and established an agency embarking on a program of upgrading and developing an educational program geared to the undereducated. While this is mainly devoted to vocational education it involves an upgrading of all education. Other projects can be mentioned in various stages of development.

With administrative machinery at hand, with seed capital in sight, with favorable climate of public opinion, we come to a most important question: What alternatives should be set up and what choices will have to be made in the attempt to develop physical and human resources in a program of induced social change in the Southern Appalachians? The Appalachians and the nation have come to a point where they must ponder policy. Do we have any guide lines in such a program of deliberately breaking the trend line of continuity with tradition and embarking on a program of hastening social change?

Certainly, if this region or any other is to be more fully developed, it must be agreed that the program for its development will take place in the context of national growth and development. Not all areas in need of advance are equally capable of it. What America wants is the equitable and desirable development of physical and human resources. It appears, however, that inevitably a Spartan decision may have to be made. When the potential physical resources of a given area do not furnish a basis for further development, the resources to be conserved are the people themselves and their development must be put foremost. This conclusion means that for certain areas, the conservation and development of the human resources of the Appalachians must proceed elsewhere. Whether they know it or not, parents in the region should no longer rear their children to go into subsistence agriculture. And if only one-sixth to one-tenth of the males growing to adulthood in the mining camps can expect to find employment in the mines, these facts must be faced in the necessity for outward movement. Large contingents of mountain youth must be prepared to migrate to strange cities to engage in new trades and crafts, and the institutional agencies of the region must give them all the aid they can in this difficult adventure.[17]

In America, people have always moved in an effort to better themselves —this is the way America was settled. Sometimes they made mistakes, but it was these movements that settled the country and balanced the economy. Such migrations will continue as our changing agriculture and the shifting Appalachian populations show. But it now seems that these movements can be guided and speeded up for the benefit of the people and for the nation. The development of growing pockets of poverty must be prevented wherever they threaten to occur. This is hard doctrine for any American community and one service of the subsidies of the Area

Redevelopment Administration is to test the chances for redevelopment of certain problem areas. Once satisfied that these communities are unsuited for industrial development, other plans can be made that will get the support of community forces.

It would be well therefore to develop a sense of urgency about the problems of the Appalachians and its people. Many subregions will aid in carrying forward induced social change. The metropolitan areas and the Great Valley especially can be further developed. Other urban centers will develop important functions. Certain areas are severely limited in their opportunities and here social institutions, geared to a culture of poverty, have not only failed to solve these problems but have contributed to their perpetuation. Many people cannot and do not realize what has happened to them and what goes on in the great world outside. In such situations the schools have failed to provide the youth with the knowledge and skills required for high-income employment. Local agencies operating in an atmosphere of poverty in which expenditures beyond a bare minimum are luxuries cannot make the capital investments necessary for cultural and economic development. Here the rule is to conserve and develop the human resources. As the people move to new opportunities, it will be realized that with its crowded industrial and urban areas, the nation stands in need of open spaces for recreation and refreshment. It is here that many of the Appalachian areas will find their better utilization.

Once certain areas are opened up to the development of the natural beauties of water, lakes, and forests, there will be a reorganized basis of support and a new social structure for an emerging economy and culture. A better life for fewer people has proved necessary in national agriculture; it is overdue in the mining areas of the mountains; it can extend through the depressed areas of subsistence agriculture. Where resources are limited, population pressure great, and failure endemic, outward movement will continue and should be aided and accelerated. If we are to confess to sentiment in this situation, we must be sentimental about people—not about territory. The value to be served is the better preparation of oncoming youth to take their place in American life, wherever they choose to go.

The Appalachians are located in one of the more advanced and dynamic countries of the world. Many natural processes work for change—growth, expansion, migration, and readjustment. It seems safe to contend that continuing readjustment and much shifting within the area will, over a period, enable the Appalachians to support as many people as they now have and at higher levels of accomplishment. Planning procedures accelerate certain processes here, retard others there, take up the slack elsewhere. This is a national challenge and the nation and the region have the resources, the skill, and the organization to bring it to pass. Here in induced social change we have a new approach, a new type of program, and a new urgency in its accomplishment.

NOTES

1. Thomas R. Ford, ed., *The Southern Appalachian Region: A Survey* (Lexington: University of Kentucky Press, 1962), is the best overall analysis. Mary Jean Bowman, and W. W. Haynes, *Resources and People in East Kentucky* (Baltimore: Johns Hopkins Press, 1963), is an excellent survey sponsored by Resources for the Future. Harry Caudle, *Night Comes to the Cumberlands: A Biography of a Depressed Area* (Boston: Little, Brown and Co., 1962), is an excellent account by a journalist who is also a native of the area.

2. The U.S. Department of Agriculture, *Economic and Social Problems of the Southern Appalachians*, Misc. Publications 205 (Washington, D.C.: Government Printing Office, 1935), chapters 7, 10–15.

3. John C. Campbell, *The Southern Highlander and His Homeland* (New York: Russell Sage Foundation, 1921), pp. 10–18.

4. D. H. Davis, *Geography of the Kentucky Mountains* (Frankfort: Kentucky Geological Survey, 1928), pp. 157–58.

5. Ford, *The Southern Appalachian Region*, p. 5.

6. Ibid., pp. 103–14.

7. Roy E. Proctor and T. Kelly White, chapter 6 in ibid., pp. 87–101.

8. Ibid., pp. 115–18.

9. Ibid., chapter 8, gives an excellent account of the development of manufacturing in the region.

10. J. S. Brown and G. A. Hillery, chapter 4 in ibid., pp. 54–78.

11. T. R. Ford, "The Passing of Provincialism," chapter 2 in ibid., pp. 9–24.

12. Ibid., pp. 24–29.

13. Ibid., pp. 289–90.

14. Melvin R. Levin, "What Do We Do with Depressed Areas?" *Iowa Business Digest* (April 1960): 1.

15. Maryland Department of Economic Development, *The Appalachian Region* (Annapolis, 1960).

16. Public Law 87-27, 87th Congress, p. 1, May 1, 1961; Area Redevelopment Act Report of the Committee on Bonding and Currency, House of Representatives, 87th Congress, March 22, 1961.

17. See discussion in chapter 19, Ford, *The Southern Appalachian Region*, pp. 289–99.

17. The Changing Density of Virginia's Population

Urbanization and Migration (1965)

An example of Vance's more purely demographic work, this essay examined a number of trends still continuing, as they could be seen in the 1960s in one of the South's most heterogeneous states. Although the bulk of the essay was strictly descriptive, in the closing paragraphs Vance displayed his awareness of the human realities behind the statistics he analyzed so skillfully.

It may aid in our analysis of Virginia's changing pattern of people on the land to suggest that this country was presettled, settled, and is now being resettled. The United States was presettled by a process of dispersion in which pioneers appropriated vacant lands—vacant, that is, except for hostile Indians, who could hardly be expected to approve of the proceedings. It then achieved agricultural settlement by farmers who filled the land up to a certain maximum density attainable by a handicraft agriculture. In the main, the first two essays have dealt with Virginia's part in these proceedings.

The first stage—presettlement—was ended for the United States when the Census Bureau in 1880 announced the disappearance of the frontier as represented by a density of six or fewer persons per square mile. Agricultural settlement was led by the covered wagon and the homesteader. It appears to have reached its maximum just before mechanization and scientific practices in agriculture began to push farmers off the land.

Essays 1 and 2 indicate that Virginia as our first settled colony is not too clearly represented by this summary treatment of what was essentially the westward movement. The country has long been in the process of resettlement by convergence and concentration in large cities and metropolitan areas. Virginia is caught up in this third movement—one that

From Roscoe D. Hughes and Henry Leidheiser, Jr., eds., *Exploring Virginia's Human Resources* (Charlottesville: University Press of Virginia, 1965), pp. 35–53. Reprinted by permission.

can best be viewed in terms of the state's participation in major national and regional trends.

URBANIZATION AND THE DENSITY OF SETTLEMENT

The distribution of people over the land—the pattern of settlement—has a useful index number, that of population density. Like the size of the community, this appears to be a function of urbanization, which in turn can be regarded as a function of the complexity of the economy—its economic distance from the frontier, if you please. It is also seen as a function of the extent to which population is retained in rural areas; this is a process which may be uneconomic, as witness portions of the Southern Appalachians.

The extreme range of population distribution in space—from high concentration at one end to sparsity of settlement at the other—in this country is surprising when one begins to study it. In 1960 our urban population amounted to almost 70 percent of the country's total. It was concentrated in slightly more than 1 percent of the United States' land area.

Obviously in America we huddle close together. The degree to which we huddle together decreases as the size of the community decreases—a thing to be expected. For cities of a million or more, population density in 1960 was 13,865 persons per square mile; between communities of a hundred thousand and a million population it was from 4,000 to 6,000 persons per square mile; in places of 2,500 to 5,000, the lowest range of urban communities, it was 1,446. In the urban fringes of settlement, areas just outside the city's legal limits, it averaged 1,781 persons per square mile; but in the rural territory of the United States we now have an average settlement of only 15 people per square mile.

In its simplest aspects urbanization is seen as a concentration of people in restricted localities followed by the multiplication, the expansion, and the fusion of these concentrations. So far, this process has shown no signs of abating. The farm population now represents only 7.7 percent of the nation's total, and the nation is still trying to cut back surplus agricultural production. Many people who own or cultivate farms today do not live on them; contrariwise many who live on them do not work there or on any other farm. Specialists in the United States Census Bureau long ago told us that the residential and occupational categories in the farm population are not to be confused. This caution must be held in mind continually.

So far we are not able to predict a ceiling to the growth of metropolitan areas in the United States. We tend to see their growth as a function of the complexity of the economy as it moves from an extractive to an industrial stance with highly technical and professional services. Without efficient production in the agricultural sector and without that technology on the urban side which enables people to work and live in large concentrations —technology that enables us to purify and store water, dispose of wastes, and tranport and preserve food—our great concentrations would not prove feasible. It is remarkable that Rome and other cities of antiquity partially solved many of these problems.

Our country began its census count with an average of 4.5 people per square mile; it counted 50.5 in 1960. From 1910 to 1960, a half-century period, the population density of the coterminous United States increased from 31 to 60 persons per square mile. In Virginia it increased from 51 to approximately 100 persons per square mile.

In regard to urbanism, Virginia resembles a man who, after spending his boyhood in rustic haunts, in his maturity becomes enamored of city life. In 1900 the state had only 27 urban places; in 1960 there were 76. In 1900 Virginia had 300,241 people living in places of 5,000 inhabitants or more; in 1960 there were 1,730,576 inhabitants in cities of 5,000 and more, and 1,249,847 lived in places of 50,000 and over. Only 4.1 percent of the state's population live in hamlets of under 1,000 up to 2,500, but 40.2 percent live in other rural territory.

At the first United States census, taken in 1790, Virginia had four settlements of urban status: Alexandria, 2,748; Petersburg, 2,828; Norfolk, 2,959; and Richmond, 3,761. In contrast, North Carolina as late as 1840 contained no population center worthy to be called urban. Arkansas, Mississippi, Tennessee, and Florida territory kept it company. Other Virginia cities reached urban dimensions—2,500 population—rather late: Fredericksburg, 3,308, and Lynchburg, 4,630, in 1830; Portsmouth, 6,477, and Winchester, 3,454, in 1840. Roanoke jumped from 699 population in 1860 to 16,150 in 1870. In 1870 Charlottesville first attained urban status with 2,838, as did Danville with 3,463. Waynesboro, a hamlet of 856 in 1900, did not become urban until 1930 with 6,226. Martinsville also entered urban circles with 3,368 people in 1930. Williamsburg, Virginia's colonial capital, had a population of 1,344 in 1790. It did not attain urban status until the 1910 census, with 2,714. Restoration and all, the city had not climbed above 8,000 in 1960.

In 1960 Virginia, 55.8 percent urban, had 76 places of 2,500 population and over; in its rural areas it had 187 places from 1,000 to 2,500 population. On the highly urban side, 9 of its cities were 50,000 and over; and the state had, of course, 6 metropolitan areas. Figure 17.1 provides an overview of population concentration as it existed in 1960. For the record it can be said that since 1962 the state has had 34 independent cities and 96 counties. Some of these cities are rather small in population.

In the higher density of urbanization, Virginia's procedures—while they baffle the outsider with their independent cities—allow the student to develop the range of urban density easily. It runs from 5,013 in the town of Norton to 304,869 for Norfolk.

Virginia's over-all density now exceeds that of any other Southeastern state and is approached only by North Carolina, which has a density of 92. Since Virginia is only 55.8 percent urban, as compared to 74 percent for Florida, 75 percent for Texas, and 67.7 for the whole West South-Central Division, it is evident that the state also has retained a fairly high density in its rural population. In this characteristic, however, it is exceeded by North Carolina, which supports a density of 92 with a population that is only 39.5 percent urban.

Differences in county density of population are shown for the state in Figure 17.2. Variations in 1960 ranged from 7.7 persons per square mile in Highland, a mountain county largely uninhabited, to 6,808 in Arlington, a suburb of Washington. Figure 17.2 indicates that Virginia in 1960 had 16 counties rather sparsely populated with a density of less than 25, 44 counties with 25 to 49, 25 counties with 50 to 99, and 13 counties with over 100 persons per square mile.

As Table 17.1 shows, almost two-thirds of Virginia's counties fail to attain half the average density of the state, 50 persons per square mile. Those counties with a density of less than 25 had only 3 percent of the state's population and averaged less than 8,000 people per county. The 13 counties with a density of 100 and over included the 10 counties in metropolitan areas and contained 64.5 percent of the state's people. Counties with 25 to 50 people per square mile had an average of slightly over 14,000 people and contained 15.6 percent of the total population. Counties with a density from 50 to 100 had an average of 23,604 population and contained 14.9 percent of Virginia's people (Table 17.1).

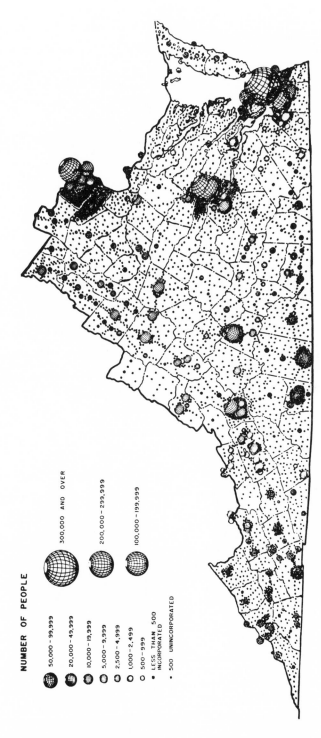

Figure 17.1. Distribution of Virginia's people, 1960 (courtesy of Agricultural Extension Service, Virginia Polytechnic Institute, Blacksburg, Virginia).

NUMBER OF PEOPLE

300,000 AND OVER

200,000 - 299,999

100,000 - 199,999

50,000 - 99,999
20,000 - 49,999
10,000 - 19,999
5,000 - 9,999
2,500 - 4,999
1,000 - 2,499
500 - 999
LESS THAN 500
INCORPORATED

500 UNINCORPORATED

Figure 17.2. County density, Virginia, 1960.

TABLE 17.1

Virginia's Pattern of Density by Counties, 1960

Categories	Under 25	Population per square mile 25 to 49.9	50 to 99.9	100 and over
Number of counties	16	44	25	13
Total population	119,010	618,852	590,091	2,638,996
Average county population	8,000	14,065	23,604	203,000
Percent of state's population	3.0	15.6	14.9	64.5

Source: Computed from U.S. Bureau of the Census, *U.S. Census of Population: 1960, Virginia*, vol. 1.

MIGRATION AND POPULATION GROWTH

In the main, the counties of low density will continue to lose population and those of higher density will grow and overflow into contiguous areas. With due allowance for unique events to come, it would seem that the trends which prevailed from 1940 to 1960 are setting the pattern for Virginia's future development.

Figure 17.3 shows how Virginia's counties shared population gains and losses from 1940 to 1950. It allocates the state's gain of 641,000 population from 1940 to 1950, a 23.9 percent increase, among its subregional areas. In the war period the natural increase of the state's population amounted to 67.5 percent, leaving a net inward migration of 208,157 to account for 32.5 percent of the gains.

More people moved from one place to another from 1940 to 1950 than in any other ten-year period in Virginia history.[1] The impact of World War II shifted population, and while some results were temporary, most of the migrations, it appears, advanced trends already established. The war decade confirmed the emergence of four new metropolitan areas. Although some 208,000 persons net moved in from other states, the tremendous shifting within the state seems to have been equally important. Workers moved into defense centers. The Hampton Roads area gained 153,000 persons from 1940 to 1944. In the decade from 1940 to 1950, 173,000 persons moved into this concentration. The continuation of the cold war meant that these centers retained a large share of the wartime gains. Virginia's overflow settlement from Washington, D.C., was to remain permanent, and the Richmond metropolitan area gained 13 percent by migration. Figure 17.4 shows very clearly the emergence of Virginia's

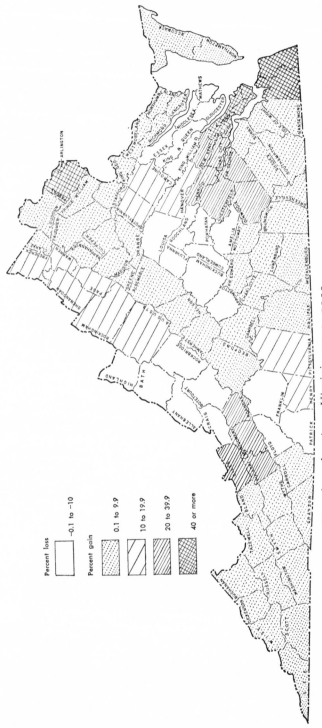

Figure 17.3. *Population gain and loss by subregions, Virginia, 1940–1950.*

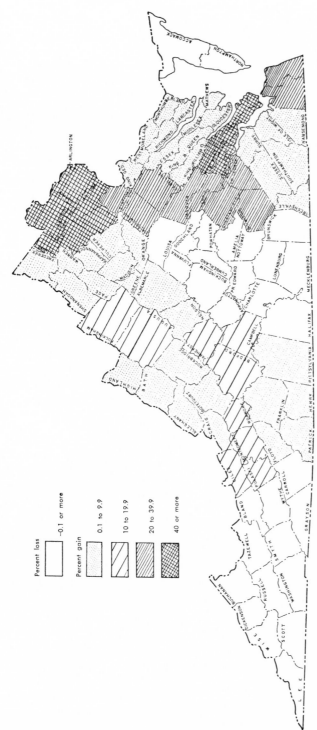

Figure 17.4. *Population change by subregions, Virginia, 1950–1960.*

"Urban Corridor." Continuing losses in rural counties with their unbalanced economies are evident in both Figures 17.3 and 17.4.

From 1950 to 1960 losses were concentrated in the Eastern Shore and
the southwestern and south-central areas (Figure 17.4). Is it not surprising to find that in spite of a population increase of 19.5 percent in the
decade there were five subregions which had fewer people in 1960 than
in 1950? They include the Eastern Shore, Central Piedmont, Central
Southside, Central Southwest, and Cumberland subregions.

Along with these areas were a number of other subregions whose gains
fell below those of natural increase, showing that they lost by migration.
In addition to the five areas named above that lost population, the James
–New River Highlands, the Blue Ridge Piedmont, the Roanoke-Radford
Area, the Western Southside, the Midwest Piedmont, the Northwest Piedmont, the Upper Shenandoah, the Southern Tidewater, and the Northern
Neck, as shown by Figure 17.5, all lost by net outward migration. Then
follow certain areas whose migration gains were low. This includes the
Lower Shenandoah, the Middle Peninsula, and the Richmond and Southside Hampton Roads areas, with net inward migrations of from 0.1 to 9
percent. The Roanoke-Radford area, which showed net inward migration in the 1940's, returned to outward migration in the 1950's.

Figure 17.5 points up the importance of recent migrations. Virginia's
population continued to grow with 1950 to 1960 showing an increase of
618,214 persons, or a percentage gain of 23.9. Of this, 95.4 percent,
Lorin A. Thompson concluded, was due to natural increases—the excess
of births over deaths within the state.[2] Just 4.6 percent was due to net
inward migration. Nevertheless, urban areas continued their gains over
rural territory, as shown in Figure 17.5, a fact which indicates the large
amount of economic readjustment which went on within the state. The
"population scramble" continued the trend of people to huddle together,
but those rural areas which failed to attract industry still sent their people
elsewhere. Figure 17.5 shows the extent to which migration gains were
concentrated in the Urban Corridor: the Washington area and contiguous
counties gained more than 20 percent by migration, with the Hampton
Roads and York Peninsula areas in the next highest rate.

GROWTH OF VIRGINIA'S METROPOLITAN AREAS

The American people are now moving into metropolitan areas, and Virginia as something of a statistical microcosm of the nation is following

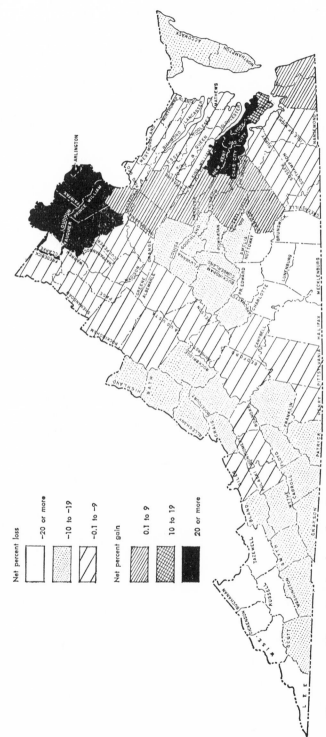

Figure 17.5. Net migration by subregions, Virginia, 1950–1960.

these trends. The movement to cities and out to the periphery is creating new patterns of life and work as expressed in changing densities of population. In the last census year the United States had 212 standard metropolitan statistical areas, containing about 62.7 percent of our total population. Virginia's six metropolitan areas did not fall far behind this national average; they contained 61 percent of the state's population.

Urban strips, it appears, grow by proximity, the fusion of contiguous areas. Thus we are hopefully told by chambers of commerce that Los Angeles will soon become a linear settlement extending for 200 miles up and down the Pacific Coast. A second conurbation is springing up, stretching from the New Jersey coast westward through Pittsburgh to Chicago with a trend toward the formation of one enormous more-or-less integrated urban strip.

On the East Coast people will not have to wait for this development. The one which most affects Virginia has already occurred. By 1960, 32 million people, one-sixth of the population of the coterminous United States, lived in 33 metropolitan areas, stretching from Boston to Washington, D.C., Maryland, and Virginia. Included are 43 separate cities and hundreds of ringing suburbs.

Differing from the Southeast of which it is a part, Virginia thus appears to be the North of the South, or rather the entering wedge of the metropolitan North extending southward. Of the 2 million population in the metropolitan area of Washington, 1,238,000 live outside the central city, in Maryland and Virginia. The central city lost 4.5 percent in population in the last decade while the outside areas gained 87 percent. Of this total, 539,618 live in Virginia (Table 17.2). Metropolitan Washington in Virginia consists of the counties of Arlington and Fairfax, with the cities of Alexandria and Falls Church and suburban areas extending farther into Loudoun and Prince William counties. All are in the corridor.

Table 17.2 serves to show the strength of metropolitan development in the state. Over 2 million of the state's nearly 4 million people lived in six metropolitan areas of Virginia in 1960. Of Virginia's 2.2 million urban population, 1.7 million live here, leaving 471,538 urban dwellers scattered elsewhere throughout the state. But of the state's 1.8 million rural people only 287,251 are found in the metropolitan areas, leaving 1.5 million ruralites in the remaining part of the state. Further growth can be expected to spread outward from Virginia's metropolitan areas.

It is here that we may begin to demarcate Virginia's urban strip— the Urban Corridor, well-named and analyzed by Lorin A. Thompson. Some twenty counties stretching from the banks of the Potomac through

TABLE 17.2

The Population of Virginia and Its Standard Metropolitan Statistical Areas, 1960

Metropolitan-nonmetropolitan residence	Total	Urban.			Rural total
		Total	Central city or cities	Other Urban	
The state	3,966,949	2,204,913	995,423	1,209,490	1,762,036
In SMSA's:	2,020,626	1,733,375	995,423	737,952	287,251
In Virginia's Corridor					
1. Washington, D.C., in Va.	539,618	479,072		479,072	60,546
2. Richmond, etc.	408,494	336,436	219,958	116,478	72,058
3. Newport News—Hampton	224,503	208,874	202,920	5,954	15,629
4. Norfolk—Portsmouth	578,507	521,623	420,645	100,978	56,051
Outside the "Corridor"					
5. Lynchburg	110,701	62,618	54,790	7,838	48,083
6. Roanoke	158,803	124,752	97,110	27,642	34,051
Not in standard metropolitan areas	1,946,323	471,538		471,538	1,474,785

Source: Computed from the Bureau of the Census, *Population: 1960, Virginia*, vol. 1.

Petersburg, Hopewell, and Richmond to Northside and Southside Hampton Roads with Newport News, Norfolk, and Portsmouth contained 2,077,504 Virginia people in 1960 as compared to 1,889,445 for the rest of the state.[3] Of the 2 million in the corridor, only 18.5 percent lived outside its four metropolitan areas. The corridor has 1.7 million of the state's metropolitan population leaving 270,000 in the Roanoke and Lynchburg areas (Table 17.2). From 1950 to 1960, 236,000 whites and 10,142 Negroes moved into the corridor while outside the corridor the state had a net migration loss of 145,500 whites and 71,546 Negroes. Between 1940 and 1950, 81 percent of Virginia's population growth was in the corridor; from 1950 to 1960, 91 percent.

THE SLUMS AND THE PROBLEM OF URBAN CONGESTION

Present problems of urban congestion, exemplified in the great megalopolitan strips, go beyond the dimensions of increasing density, as serious as this may become. Congestion affects the quality of environment and of the population itself. People who once made an acceptable adjustment to a simple agriculture—one which no longer exists as a going concern— move to cities and face adjustment to a complex environment. Since Virginia is entering this transition ahead of many Southern states, it will be helpful to glance at urban structure as it is now developing. Cities grow around central business districts in something resembling a series of circles. Here the trend is toward decentralization by reason of the growth on the urban periphery of new shopping centers which can furnish parking areas for retail trade. This movement is clearly related to the growth of rings of city suburbs which is treated later in this essay.

The central problems of urban congestion and substandard environment are tied up with those areas which we have come to call "city slums." Slums can be defined as areas which specialize in providing substandard accommodations to those who cannot make an adequate adjustment to city life. People who are pushed out of agriculture approach the city more or less as rural refugees, entering the lowest level of urban rents and services. Typically these are areas, not of second-hand housing but of tenth- and twentieth-hand housing. Typically also, the slums are ringed around the central business district and represent, as it were, the port of arrival of the less-fortunate migrants. Dilapidated housing is not repaired because in the natural course of expansion business concerns will occupy these run-down residential areas. In Northern cities such areas have received successive waves of foreign immigrants, and many have now become Black Belts harboring a displaced Negro peasantry from the South. Virginia lacks the foreign component in its slums, but its place is taken by the poor-white farmers and the Negro families whose opportunities in the new environment remain restricted by their lack of education and urban skills. In these areas are found the problems of poverty, delinquency, and unemployment which make the slums the slums. This remains true for the area, for as fast as families can improve their standards and living conditions they desert the slums to occupy better neighborhoods. The continuation of slums is then to be explained in part by the continued migration to cities of people who hope to "better themselves."

Slums, however, are not to be explained by any one factor; they represent the convergence of many conditions of inadequacy, those which exist among the people as well as those in their environment. No over-all solution appears to be in sight, and considered from this point of view the wonder is not that urban slums continue to exist. The puzzle, in fact, is that they do not expand at a faster rate to disable more of the oncoming generation than they do. It must be kept in mind that at no time do a majority of slum dwellers fail to receive an education, take to delinquency, or even land on the welfare rolls. In short, dwellers in city slums are not outcasts or rebels against society; they are more often a working-class group of the less skilled. Individual improvement, as we have said, does not improve slums; individuals who achieve simply leave these areas for better neighborhoods. Only if the stream of poor migrants to the cities were to stop, could the city draw its breath and face up to the problem of urban renewal. Even then our real-estate interests would be faced with the question, To whom do we rent our substandard housing? The other side of the coin is found in the suburbs, which represent largely middle-class groups of skilled, white-collar workers and the business and professional classes. We shall discuss this later in the essay.

THE SUBURBAN TREND

Virginia's urban strip development, bending eastward to the coast as it does, stands in notable contrast to major population growth in the rest of the Southeast. Here the great advance in industrialization and urbanization has occurred along the Piedmont Crescent, paralleling the Southern Railway—the South's "Golden Street"—as it curves south and westward through the Carolinas and Georgia, ending at Birmingham. The northern end of the Crescent can be located in Virginia, beginning at its upper point in the Lynchburg metropolitan area and passing through Danville.

Coastal areas in North Carolina, and to some extent those of South Carolina and Georgia, resemble dead-end territory when compared to Tidewater Virginia with its development. Virginia of the early colonial settlement holds its rural people better, and some of its suburban settlement is now devoted to restoring old mansions.

What feeds this pattern of increasing settlement and how does the settlement spread? It requires more than the analysis of density patterns to explain this.

People who are moving urbanward to participate in the center work of our economy no longer find it necessary to live in the urban core of metropolitan centers. The metropolitan trend is generating a new migration —a movement out of the inner city into its fringes. Every large American city is now surrounded by rings of suburbs. So great is this trend in certain parts of the country that the suburban dweller who moves out in search of green trees and grass finds that he has run out of open country. Real-estate developers creating new subdivisions are beginning to find that the suburbs of one metropolitan center thrust into the suburbs of the next.

Virginia is participating in this multiplicity of changes, a kind of three-fold movement as I see it, in which certain shifts swallow up the effects of others. For this reason it will not be safe for those who view the metropolitan trend as all-encompassing to predict the depopulation of rural areas. Urbanization and metropolitan movements are now serving to repopulate certain rural areas. First, agricultural areas give up their population to feed the movement into cities, leaving the land to be consolidated into mechanized farming for controlled markets. The population moves into the central core of settlement in our cities. This trend cannot long continue, however, because in its second stage the urban core passes its optimum density and proceeds to expand. The third trend, the suburbanization movement, passes far beyond the city limits and proceeds to repopulate contiguous rural areas standing in the path of suburban expansion. Thus it appears that Virginia's rural counties in the corridor will gradually be repopulated. Note, for example, how four-lane highways between two cities draw open-country settlement. All this is hastened by the population explosion, in which the middle classes, having decided to do their duty by posterity, now have four children instead of two.

It is hardly necessary to describe our suburbs. They are populated by a homogeneous middle class whose values have been inimitably put by a popular song which states that the houses and children all look alike, the children all go to the university, and all are made of "tickey-tackey." Virginia has retained certain values of rural life from its early settlement, and the fine custom of restoring old homes and watching boxwood grow obviously reduces the amount of tickey-tackey. The cutting edge of the suburban movement has been called the "rural-urban fringe," the initial phase that represents the city taking over the countryside. It also represents the "I'd rather do it myself" aspect of the suburban movement. Out beyond the developers, who are continually laying out new settlements and counting up the profits inherent in subdividing farms into residential lots, these new pioneers move in. As shock troops of the rural-urban fringe, they take advantage of rural electrification, of oil-heating systems and septic tanks, to settle down among the farmers. Such a pioneer begins by putting his children on the bus and sending them to a consolidated rural school; his wife engages a butter-and-egg man to deliver produce at home. In the end it costs just as much as it did to live in town and pay city taxes, but the new homesteader could not have known that in the beginning.

Finally the farmers give up the struggle, sell out to the subdividers, move away, and join the urban job hunt. The farmers' daughters and sons are now attending the urban high school with its social functions. The rural-urban fringe has accomplished its transformation and is simply another suburb—inconveniently located further out. Parents either drive the youngsters into the city now for necessary social functions, or they buy the second and third car demanded by the children of the affluent society. Such is the confluence of suburbanization and the population explosion in Virginia's changing population density.

NOTES

1. Sara K. Gilliam, in *University of Virginia News Letter*, Feb. 1, 1956.

2. Lorin A. Thompson, "Virginia Population Change: Age and Color, 1950 and 1960," *University of Virginia News Letter*, June 15, 1961.

3. In addition to the metropolitan areas, three subregions are involved: the Northern Piedmont (4 counties), Fall Line area (4 counties), and the York Peninsula (4 counties). They had a population of 326,382, mainly rural and small town (Lorin A. Thompson, "Recent Population Changes in Virginia," ibid., Feb. 15, 1961).

18. Beyond the Fleshpots

The Coming Culture Crisis in the South (1965)

In this essay, written at the height of southern white resistance to desegregation, Vance chided his fellow Southerners for not living up to his expectations. In a personal digression—about as close as he ever came to autobiography—he discussed his own affection for the South, and for his adopted state of North Carolina, in particular. He held out North Carolina's support for the beaux arts as an example to the newly-rich industrial and commercial classes of the South and suggested that some of the monetary returns of the South's economic development might well be reinvested in the region's cultural development—an echo of a theme sounded almost half a century earlier by H. L. Mencken.

> And the children of Israel said unto them, "Would to God we had died by the hand of the Lord in the land of Egypt, when we sat by the fleshpots, and when we did eat bread to the full; for ye have brought us forth into this wilderness to kill this whole assembly with hunger." Exodus 16:3.

Like the children of Israel, the people of the South have undertaken a Journey. The South is on the way to a Promised Land. By day we follow a pillar of cloud and by night a pillar of fire. The pillar we follow is a vision of economic parity with the nation—the nation, you recall, with the highest standard of living in the world. It is to the credit of the altogether charming Henry W. Grady that when he developed his myth of the New South he turned the vision of his countrymen from an unattainable past to the future. And when it became evident that nostalgia for magnolia blossoms and Grecian porticoes led back to Egypt and slavery, the pillar of fire led straight to partnership with Northern capital in business, commerce, and industry, where all would eat bread to the full.

Not all belief systems are realized, but the myth of the new South is

From *Virginia Quarterly Review* 41 (Spring 1965): 217–30. © *The Virginia Quarterly Review*.

coming to pass before our very eyes. There *is* a land of milk and honey; the South in due course can expect to sit by the fleshpots; and Southern leaders can rightfully feel that the Mason-Dixon line no longer constitutes an iron curtain against the Affluent Society.

Here is one myth that the statisticians can establish with figures on per capita income. Personal income in the South rose from $368 per capita in 1929 to $1,820 per man, woman, and child in 1963, a figure that if apportioned out among an average family of five represents today an annual average income of $9,100. These figures mean that personal income per capita in the South rose from 46 per cent of the non-South per capita in 1929 to 51 per cent in 1940, to 69 per cent in 1963, a gain of twenty-three percentage points in thirty-four years.

Projecting these trends to 1975, Professor Howard G. Schaller of the University of Indiana is able to visualize a per capita income of $2,422 (in 1963 dollars) in the South, thus reaching 79 per cent of the national per capita. At the rate at which the South has been moving since World War II, Schaller estimates it will require a half century for the South to overtake the rest of the country in the matter of income per person. This, it must be pointed out, presumes that not only will industry continue its movement southward, but that Southerners will continue to migrate outside the South at prevailing rates. The point here is quite simple. In the main these migrants are people who realize the need to better themselves. By the very act of migrating, people with the lowest income raise the South's average and by the same token bring down, only temporarily we hope, the average of the areas to which they migrate.

The recent rediscovery of poverty undoubtedly means that more federal money will go into the Appalachian region and the attack on poverty will apply to the Negro. All these subsidies, too, will help to raise income in the South. One might stop and think a little: what should the government do about these benefits if finally, fifty years from now, the South turns up as well off as anybody else?

I

In the midst of world change we cannot overlook the fact that the American South has repeatedly been summoned to embark on social upheaval. In this situation, we sought to declare a moratorium on cultural values until the region obtained the capital to implement whatever values represented Southern culture. This was a decision we would make at a later date—after we had the cash in hand.

Few publicists have projected as clearly as did Henry W. Grady the course of history, "a history as it were without a country of its own." As "one of Howard W. Odum's boys" I was accustomed to delivering occasional homilies throughout the South advocating economic development. Invariably, I was asked by someone in the audience if I thought materialism was enough. What should the South seek to do with its economic achievement? Invariably, I tried to shrug off the question. Sometimes, referring to our own fortunate status in the South's middle classes, I countered with the old African proverb: "Full-belly child says to hungry-belly child, 'Be of good cheer.'"

If the choice of culture goals were open ended, Grady's Utopia would not really represent choice. This was shown by the quick collapse suffered by the Agrarians when they presented their point of view. Grady's Utopia was simply the means to an end. The end remained undefined, even when stated as the "Southern way of life." To choose magnolias and Greek porticoes was to pay deference to a certain aristocratic quality in antebellum life, but the definitive consideration against the return to the land of Egypt was given by an old slave, speaking for more than one of the groups concerned. Asked if he repined for the security of his master's plantation with its assurance of three meals a day, he scratched his venerable white head and answered: "No, there is a kind of looseness about this freedom that I admire." Finally, far too many well-meaning Southerners have proved so timid that they allow the Southern way of life to be publicized and defined by the Ku Klux Klan and members of the suddenly respectable Citizens' Councils in their own terms. The South, be it remembered, is the one section in the country where a man can gain a reputation as a liberal thinker by declaring without equivocation that the public schools should remain open to the public.

It has now been five years since William H. Nicholls, economist though he is, attributed the slow pace of Southern economic development to non-economic causes. In "Southern Tradition and Regional Progress" he contended that the South must make its choice between maintenance of the Southern tradition and further economic development. It cannot have both. In this hampering tradition Nicholls included: (1) the constricting effect of dominant rural values; an agrarianism which holds our cities in thrall; (2) the region's rigid social structure; (3) its undemocratic political structure; (4) the weakness of social responsibility, especially for the education of its people; and finally (5) the debilitating effect of the South's tradition, which enforces conformity of thought and action.

For whatever Ellen Glasgow meant by it, that genteel conservative wrote in "The Woman Within" that she could never remember a time when "the pattern of society as well as the scheme of things had not seemed false and even malignant." Elsewhere she wrote: "For as long as the human race remains virtually and perhaps essentially barbaric, all the social orders invented by man will be merely the mirror of his favorite imperfections."

Furthermore, as Nicholls might have said, but didn't, the Southern tradition is calculated to prove that single-mindedness is no unmitigated blessing. In agriculture, the one-crop system, cotton; in politics, the one-party system, Bourbon democracy; in industry, another one-crop system, textiles; in religion, the one true church, Bible Belt Protestantism; for Utopia, the one salvation, industrialization by Northern capital; in cultural values, the one great phobia, racism; in progress, the one great goal, economic parity and the fleshpots.

Feeling as he did about Southern cultural values, Nicholls could easily have reversed his dialectic. What good would it be for the South to achieve economic parity if it retained the Southern tradition in its rigid orthodoxy? This, it seems to me, is the Southern equivalent of the scripture: "What does it profit a man if he gains the whole world and loses his own soul?"

Discussing this same problem, Dean Hugh Holman contends that Southern culture produces a double image. He writes:

> Approach it however you will, you will find that the heart of the Southern riddle is a union of opposites, a paradox. Calm grace and raw hatred. Polished manners and violence. An intensive individualism and intense group pressures toward conformity. A reverence to the point of idolatry of self-determining action and a caste and class structure presupposing an aristocratic hierarchy. A passion for political action and a willingness to surrender to the enslavement of demagogues. A love of the nation intense enough to make the Southern fighting man notorious in our wars and the advocacy of interposition in the defiance of national law. A region breeding both Thomas Jefferson and John C. Calhoun.

Once the region was assured that it could care for the body, it was time to look to the care of its soul. The results, it must be pointed out, were not encouraging. After my little homily on progress, ministers often asked: "What is the South's greatest need?" Unconsciously, perhaps, I always tried to avoid the answer they hoped for: "A revival of religion." Had I known how soon these same ministers would be met by the crisis of the sit-ins and the pray-ins, I am sure I would have been more charitable.

Howard W. Odum had suggested a culture creed for the South. Sectionalism would give way to regionalism; regionalism meant regional-national equilibrium and the return of the South to the mainstream of American life. It never caught on. The public imagination was not supplied with a picture of a South that was to be; and Grady remained as the regional equivalent of Mark Hanna's full dinner pail, the bribe that held the working man in the Republican party a full half century before. And so—when the final crisis of desegregation hit, the South no longer stood hitched; the fleshpots were not enough; and no respectable position had been prepared to which a people could repair in comfort and in self respect. The crisis of culture was on; and the Supreme Court of the country was the advance agent of Communism.

The realization will come hard to our people but let us face it: it is precisely this Southern way of life that the rest of the country and probably the rest of the world are getting "sick and tired of hearing about."

Much of our economic progress has come from federal bounty—the grants-in-aid and subsidies that have helped to bail out distressed agriculture and distressed areas. It is time for somebody to ask the damaging question: "Is there any reason why the nation should subsidize resistance to national goals?" This is the real issue behind the demand for Federal aid with no Federal controls. Everybody is willing to admit that inspection of Federally subsidized highways is necessary to enforce standards and prevent corruption; but it comes as a real "outrage" when in the Civil Rights Act the Federal government actually steps out and asks of the recipients of its bounty whether they intend to obey national legislation. "Give us our money; don't ask us what we intend to do with it."

In one of her inimitable New Yorker cartoons, Helen Hokinson had one of her portly club ladies say to the clerk in a bookstore who has evidently offered her a Southern novel: "I feel sorry for Mississippi, but I don't want to read about it any more." By now let it be said that the lady probably no longer feels sorry for Mississippi. Recently, the usually imperturbable head of our FBI in a press conference so far lost control as to speak of Mississippi as a landscape of swamps, water moccasins, and red-necked sheriffs, all equally noxious.

In the great tradition of settling for nothing but the best, the eminent critic, Sir Herbert Read, denies that capitalism is capable of producing a great culture. He supports Eric Gill's battle cry: "To hell with culture as a thing added like a sauce to otherwise unpalatable stale fish." If culture belongs to the past, the art of the future, Read contends, will spring from a democratic society, not from the servile products of commercialism where, as G. K. Chesterton said, "writing on the backs of advertisements is called journalism." "We have frequently printed the word Democracy," wrote Walt Whitman in "Democratic Vistas." "It is a great word whose history I suppose remains unwritten because that history has yet to be enacted."

The theme of Read's book is especially germane to the Southern problem. Either our region will resolve its culture crisis in due time or be prepared to renounce the Southern way of life as one of the major neuroses of our times. We have volunteers self-appointed to suggest our way of life and what do some of the most vocal suggest? Racism, white supremacy, get rid of the Negroes, go back to the Utopia of the Nazis, dynamite a few more churches, keep Martin Luther King in jail, make this a white man's country and it will be God's country. None of this seems as pathetic, however, as the quiet desperation of that gentlewoman who wrote: "Every Sunday our rector preaches on integration. If I have to make a choice, I have decided to give up Christianity."

II

Is there anything going under the name of culture which will serve to set new goals for an emerging South? Oddly enough, there is. It is, to be straightforward about it, not culture as the anthropologists define it, the total way of life of a people, but culture as it is defined by humanists— art, literature, music, and the fine arts.

In an address at Amherst, honoring Robert Frost, President Kennedy proposed a new goal for the nation:

> I look forward to an America which will not be afraid of grace and beauty, which will reward achievement in the arts as well as reward achievements in business and statecraft . . . which commands respect not only for its strength, but for its civilization as well.

"Every man," Shakespeare has Hamlet remark, "hath business and desire." We have just suggested that the region attends assiduously to the rewards of business. What do we desire? Beyond the fleshpots where does the horizon lie?

On May 24, 1964, the first citizen of the South to become President of the United States since Zachary Taylor, more than a hundred years ago, said in an address at the University of Michigan:

> For half a century we called upon unbounded invention and untiring industry to create an order of plenty for all our people. The challenge of the next half century is whether we have the wisdom to use that wealth to enrich and elevate our national life, and to advance the quality of our American civilization.
>
> Your imagination, your initiative, and your indignation will determine whether we build a society where old values and new visions are buried under unbridled growth. For in your time we have the opportunity to move not only toward the rich society and the powerful society, but upward to the *Great Society.* . . . It is a place where the city of man serves not only the needs of the body but the desire for beauty and the hunger for community. The Great Society is a place where every child can find knowledge to enrich his mind and to enlarge his talents.
>
> It is a place which honors creation for its own sake and for what it adds to the understanding of the race. It is a place where men are more concerned with the quality of their goals than the quantity of their goods. . . . It is a challenge, constantly renewed, beckoning us toward a destiny where the meaning of our lives matches the marvelous products of our labor.

What would be required if the South, to the great amazement of all, were to turn from preoccupation with its peculiar navel, the Southern way of life, to the pursuit of high culture? Talent, an economic basis sufficient to furnish markets, rich patrons to underwrite artistic projects, and general good taste. And the greatest of these is taste.

If admission to the Great Society depends upon the development of an élite, the South, let it be said, has developed a remarkable outpouring of literary talent. It could have come as a surprise only to the non-reading public in the South to learn from the London Times Literary Supplement of September 17, 1954, that "The literature (of the South) . . . has solidly established itself as the most important, the most talented, interesting and valuable in the United States." There will be no attempt at a roll call here. The risk of omitting major figures is simply too great.

The greatest of these was William Faulkner. It is clear that Mississippi never quite understood the point that Faulkner was making—and a fortunate thing, too, for it left him unmolested. Out of the agony of his early reception Tom Wolfe wrote as true a word as artist ever uttered, "You can't go home again." John Gould Fletcher, the poet, did go home again to his native Arkansas, wrote a notable history of the state, and killed himself. So did Clarence Cason of Alabama after writing "90° in the Shade," and W. J. Cash after the publication of "The Mind of the South." But the South is still the place where an unknown woman in an unheard-of Alabama town can write a book like "To Kill a Mockingbird" and not only produce a novel of distinction, but furnish the vehicle for a motion picture of significance.

So profuse has this display of talent become that we have a kind of witticism: "It is a sad day in the South when a Southern novelist or journalist does not win the Pulitzer Prize." In Robert Penn Warren the South produced a talent that won the prize both in the novel and in poetry.

Frankly, I think the problem goes deeper than the development of talent. In its search for economic achievement the South has created a new class, men of wealth and power. What sight is more shocking than to see a man of wealth who doesn't know what to do with his money? Already our region is facing the problem of the *nouveau riche*. Here we have a good old American prescription of long standing. We have long said to our newly rich: "Get some culture and get it quick." As long as our newly rich have nothing better to do than to harass the few distinguished universities the South has produced, to buy radio time to try to turn back the clock, to prove that they are economic Neanderthals by boring into the Republican party and trying to destroy it with racism, who needs them?

It takes three generations, we are told, to produce culture among the new rich. The South should develop a function for its rich, for they are desperately needed. This function should go beyond that of reinvesting their capital in economic development of the South, as desperately as this is needed. The South needs patrons of the arts.

I am reminded here of the saying of Joseph Kennedy, notoriously a hard man with a buck: "It's not how much money you make, it's how good a family you raise." I am not suggesting here that the Southern rich should be impressed into careers of public service. Many are not ready for this, although we have had notable exceptions. If the rich are to escape the clutches of the Birch Society; if they are to be worth their salt to the region in which they have prospered; if they are to acquire a sense of worth: there are functions which even the new rich can perform. Let them become patrons of the arts. There are symphony orchestras to be supported in our larger cities; we could establish more little theaters; we need art museums; we would even appreciate having people who can support our universities financially without trying to dictate their policies.

In the South, our literature resembles the work of Leo Tolstoy and the great Russian novelists; it is for catharsis and the purging of guilt. No wholesale call to sackcloth and ashes will be issued, however, for any part of the region. William S. White, one of the most perceptive of our working columnists, has written in compassion of "the anguish of that large part of Mississippi which wants to do right in a world it never made." The key to the situation in Arkansas, Alabama, or anywhere else does not involve a call for public repentance in any form or fashion.

Recalcitrant Southerners need only to learn one uncomplicated lesson from history. It is they, not the rest of the country, who must now learn how to "live with people who are wrong." As George Lundberg, the sociologist, has pointed out, we suffered religious wars until Protestants and Catholics learned this lesson. Coexistence means simply this: that so far, Communists and members of the free world, as much as they dislike it, are both engaged in learning how to live with people who, they know, are wrong.

Nuclear war is not at stake here; perhaps not even the American way of life. But what about our way of livelihood as members of a unified American economy? Here I am glad to say a good word at last for the fleshpots and the pillar of fire that leads on to the land of milk and honey. In Mississippi, the state's largest organization of businessmen, The Mississippi Economic Council, has just issued a remarkable manifesto. It reads in part: "We recognize that the Civil Rights Act of 1964 has been enacted by Congress as law. It cannot be ignored and should not be unlawfully defied."

In the crisis of culture I am reminded that there follows a crisis of personal identity. When professional Southerners claim a higher loyalty, I think of Dr. Samuel Johnson's crisp dictum: "Patriotism, Sir, is the last refuge of a scoundrel." For certain persons Southern patriotism is to be feared; it has proved to be not the last but the first refuge for the scoundrel. One recalls the brave words of Nurse Edith Cavell, before she faced the German firing squad: "Patriotism is not enough." In the crisis of culture, there is a great temptation to renounce one's Southern citizenship;

to commit, as it were, some symbolic act of treason—or better still, counter-treason. But my Southern citizenship is purely mythological; there exists no headquarters to which I might forward a resignation or signify renunciation.

I am reminded, however, that the state of North Carolina is a legal entity and that there must exist some procedure by which I might renounce my citizenship. This, I hasten to say, I will not do—in all integrity, I cannot. This strange adopted state of mine is not rich as states go. It carries many nicknames and has endured many humorous slurs from that early time when William Byrd wrote his "History of the Dividing Line": "The Rip Van Winkle of the states"; "The vale of humiliation"; "The militant mediocrity"; "The living proof that God loves the common people because he sent so many of them here."

It was at an alumni dinner of the University of North Carolina that I heard the late, great Spencer Love of the Burlington Industries rise to his feet to say that he wished to comment on academic freedom and, since his remarks were critical, he wished to address them to the faculty. The faculty, he said, put up a great fight for academic freedom, and then made very little use of it. Where, Mr. Love demanded, are the new ideas that should lift their heads above the dead level of conformity? Where do we find the disturbances and the agitations that follow people of talent who have the freedom to think and like to make use of it? Could it be that the faculty has taken out operators' licenses in fields in which they had no intention of operating. If the faculty knows anything that we out in the state haven't heard, for goodness' sake, let us hear it.

At this point in his discourse a fellow alumnus was heard to grumble, not under his breath: "Sure, Spencer Love can afford to talk like that; he's filthy rich. What about us little businessmen who can barely hang on by our teeth and toenails?" Then and there I decided that the only way the University of North Carolina could get rid of me was to fire me.

My reason for making every effort to maintain my citizenship goes further. In the search for culture the commonwealth has stepped forward to become the patron of the arts. This may have begun with the development of three outdoor dramas calculated to purvey a modicum of culture to the summer tourists as they wend their way across the state. But in North Carolina a state symphony orchestra travels by buses from one end of the state to the other giving concerts to school children—concerts at which the meaning and content of symphonic music is carefully explained. Leonard Bernstein does it better, but he does not depend for his support on a state legislature. The legislature has endowed and maintains a state art museum—one of high standards, and one to which owners of valuable collections are glad to bequeath their treasures. The state has just established a center for the performing arts—a little Juilliard, a conservatory of fine arts in the backward South.

For its oncoming geniuses the state conducts special summer schools for children of talent—schools where these children may study what they like, go at their own pace, and have fun while they do it. For children of lesser gifts, the state is engaged in developing learning institutions where new techniques and experimental work are devoted to children from what one calls the homes of the "culturally deprived." The governor whose term of office has just expired went up and down the state talking about excellence in education to the school children until some turned to their parents in despair, crying out, "Aren't we ever going to get to look at television?" North Carolina applied to the Ford Foundation and became the first state ever to receive a state grant from a major foundation to tackle the problem of the poor and the culturally deprived. Governor Terry Sanford has just ended his term of office, and all over the state one can imagine he hears the people breathe a collective sigh of relief as though they say, "Maybe we can relax and rest a little from this culture kick." One almost has the feeling that in some way the state heard about the Great Society and tried to sneak in before the gate was open for general admission.

Let us leave, however, the note of local patriotism. State subsidy of art in the European manner, a strange phenomenon to find in any American state, leaves the question of culture for the South unresolved. The problem, as Sir Herbert pointed out, is not one of a democratic society *plus* culture; it is the more serious problem of a *democratic culture*. The wife of an invited Harmsworth Professor of American History at Oxford, asked what her husband did, replied: "He teaches American history." "Is there any?" came the surprising response from the British dowager. The response reminds one of the old question of the twenties: "Do you believe in prohibition?" Liberals always divided this question into two: "Do you believe prohibition exists?" and "Do you believe it ought to exist?" To both questions, they gave an unqualified negative.

Authentic reasons can be listed for the hope that a Southern culture of the future will come into being: talent, a basic commitment to democratic society—once it is admitted that Negroes, too, have rights—, sufficient wealth to provide patronage and economic support, and an emphasis on excellence in education that might some day be extended so far as to include appreciation of the arts.

Two figures serve as symbols of our hope: Jefferson and Whitman. In his inimitable style, President Kennedy spoke of the Nobel prize winners as "The greatest array of talent ever assembled around this board since Thomas Jefferson dined alone at the White House." Communism has yet to produce the equal of Jefferson—philosopher of democracy, man of a dozen authentic talents, "the ornament of the age and of the country in which he lived," as Jefferson himself said of Benjamin Franklin. We have also that other ideologue of democracy, Walt Whitman, Jefferson set to poetry, "our democratic poet exemplar," who wrote:

> I speak the password primeval, I give the assign of democracy.
> By God, I will accept nothing which all cannot have their
>   counterpart of on the same terms.

19. Education and the
Southern Potential (1966)

Broader than its title indicates, this chapter is a summary of the economic and social transformation through which the South had passed. It closes with a discussion of the role of education in developing the human resources required by the changed situation. Vance's lament for the absence of "think tanks" like the Institute for Advanced Studies in Princeton or the similar center in Palo Alto was unduly pessimistic: a decade after he wrote this, the National Humanities Center was established at the North Carolina Research Triangle Park, a few miles from Chapel Hill.

The future of the South today depends more upon the development of capacities and resources which now remain unrealized than upon anything else. The region has natural resources and human resources in good supply, and it has set itself to the task of their utilization and development. These sources of wealth are basic, but their release and development depend upon building up institutional resources, technological resources, and the accumulation of capital, or financial resources. Howard W. Odum was fond of pointing out that the creation of these secondary forms of wealth are matters of skill, organization, previous experience, and the ability to make the right decisions at the right time. As stated by Lancelot Hogben: "The material resources of man's environment, the biological resources of social personnel, and the social resources of organization and institutions are all we have for developing the wealth and welfare of nations."[1] This development is a complex task, and one that can easily go by default. It is to be viewed as a sequence of interrelated processes in which the mobilization of the common will for the task depends upon the democratic participation of the whole community. Certainly, conservation and development of human resources are every whit as important for the economic future as the processing of natural resources.

From *High Schools in the South: A Fact Book* (Nashville: George Peabody College for Teachers, 1966), pp. 7–22. Reprinted by permission.

The purpose of this chapter, which serves to introduce basic educational and school conditions, is to point out certain economic developments that have affected the utilization of human resources. Important aspects of economic activity can be found all over the South: shipping in the Norfolk and Gulf Coast areas; production of power and aluminum in the TVA area; heavy industry in Birmingham; textiles, rayon, and nylon in the southern Piedmont; refining and chemical industries plus synthetic rubber in the oil producing areas; pulp, paper, lumber products, minerals, and the processing of metals throughout the region.

In a nation that is developing and maintaining a more complex economy, there are many reasons to believe that the South has basic resources for further industrialization. Some of these include:

1. Proximity both to the already highly industrialized areas of the Northeast and Middle States and to potential developments in South America
2. A climate, growing season, and type of land which allow a great variety of plant life and diversified types of agriculture ranging from truck, fruit, livestock, and tree crops to already developed staples such as cotton, sugar, rice, and tobacco
3. Mineral resources of coal, iron, oil, gas, sulphur and nonferrous minerals, with stone and building materials of all kinds
4. Adequate transportation facilities in the highly developed railroad network, public highway systems, and rapidly expanding air routes
5. Comparatively low land and site costs as compared with some congested areas
6. A large group of basically sound and capable people, in need only of more adequate training, education, and services to become a skilled labor supply
7. A large potential group of consumers for all economic goods and services, awaiting only better productive organization to become the country's best new market.

As Erich W. Zimmermann pointed out, natural resources are potential, not absolute.[2] Resources are not to be estimated in terms of their existence but of their availability. The degree of technology, the efficiency of economic organization, the availability of capital, and the existing social demand—not the inert existence of minerals underground—determine whether these natural resources are to be made available for us. Nothing is done, nothing can be done, apart from the skills, the needs, and the demands of men organized in group effort.

In our economic scheme of things, human resources count twice, for human beings serve as both means and ends in the productive process. Man, as an agent of production, must be regarded as the greatest of all resources, for it is his intelligence and labor that give shape and form to all the useful aspects of our environment and discover new ways of utilizing its materials. Among all resources, human talent and energy rank the highest. But man is also the end, the raison d'être, of the productive process. Production exists for consumption, and mankind is the ultimate beneficiary of all production. Thus, man, the paradox, is at one and the same time the end and goal of the economic process and part and parcel of it, the chief instrument and means towards its attainment. Obviously, how well he fits into the productive scheme determines in the main how well he will be rewarded in the range and variety of his consumption. Thus the first advice that technical experts give to the leaders of the underdeveloped nations is to set up an educational system and put it into operation. No modern economy is possible without it.

In agriculture, efficiency has been increasing and a labor force too large for its task has consistently overproduced its market. Accordingly, any discussion of a region's use of human resources must be related to the area's agricultural background. The South is and can expect to remain an important agricultural area of the United States for a long time to come. Some of the problems to which the region has adjusted and must continue to adjust include:

1. The loss of soil resources by leaching and erosion
2. The gradual loss of a large share of the world's cotton and tobacco markets (In volume of production, the region is well equipped for world competition, but not at the low level of prices now prevailing.)
3. Continued need to adjust to agriculture's decreased capacity to employ people at former rates or at an adequate standard of living
4. A continuing solution, through increased migration from plantation type farms, of the numbing effects of tenancy on the South's agriculture
5. Further changes in the terms of trade, in which the South has traditionally exchanged cheap goods for dear goods
6. A resolute and measured approach to the inadequacy of the

South's educational programs and facilities to prepare children to meet needed changes, rural and urban, required by new occupational patterns

7. The South's lack of capital and economic organization to finance needed developments in new fields
8. Further improvement in the industrial mix, currently dominated by the region's concentration on low value industries
9. The location within the South of a major problem area where the rate of economic growth has fallen behind the nation's advance.

THE SOUTH'S HUMAN RESOURCES

Any discussion of the South's potential can well begin with its human resources. In the great depression, Gerald W. Johnson wrote: "The central irony of the era is the fact that if we have overproduced anything in this country what we have overproduced is Americans."[3] In national recovery, the agricultural South has faced this problem of overproduction to a greater extent than other parts of the country. The great majority of counties in the South had two or more farm youths entering working age for every elderly male leaving agriculture, either by death or retirement.

As of April 1, 1963, the population of the United States was estimated at 188,643,000 people—a far cry from the 3,929,000 population reported in the first Census taken in 1790. This represents an increase of 4,700 per cent in the population in a hundred and seventy-three years. An electric population chart on display in the main lobby of the Department of Commerce in the nation's capital shows what this means in terms of population growth. When this report was written the mechanism of the recorder was set to show an average of:

1 birth every 7 ½ seconds
1 death every 18 ½ seconds
1 in-migrant every 1½ minutes
1 out-migrant every 23 minutes

Taken together, these components give the United States a net gain of one person added to the population every 11 seconds. The South is contributing more than its share to this national population growth.

Accepting the U.S. Census definition of the region, the South had some 55 million people in 1960, approximately 31 per cent of our total population.[4] It also had the second largest population increase from 1950 to 1960, a growth of 16.5 per cent as compared to an 18.5 per cent increase for the nation. The West led all other regions, with an increase of 38.9 per cent. (See Table 19.1.) Florida led the South with an increase of 78.7 per cent. Forty-one million infants were born in the decade 1950–1960; of these, 13.6 million were born in the South. Subtracting the 4.4 million deaths, the South had a natural increase of 9.2 million, a rate of 19.6 per cent as compared with 16.7 per cent for the nation. (See Table 19.2.)

The South is no longer regarded as the "Seed Bed of the Nation." The great gap between the birth rate in the South and the non-South is in the process of closing. In the great depression, the difference between the South's fertility and that of the rest of the country reached as high as 15

TABLE 19.1

Population Change, United States Regions and the Southeast, 1950–1960

	1960	1950	Change	Per Cent Change
United States	179,323,175	151,325,798	27,997,377	18.5
Northeast	44,677,819	39,477,986	5,199,833	13.2
North Central	51,619,139	44,460,762	7,158,377	16.1
West	28,053,104	20,189,962	7,863,142	38.9
The Census South (17 states)	54,973,113	47,197,088	7,776,025	16.5
U.S. except Southeast	142,429,381	119,542,071	22,887,310	19.1
Southeast (11 states)	36,893,794	31,783,727	5,110,067	16.1
Southeast except Florida	31,942,234	29,012,422	2,929,812	10.0
District of Columbia	763,956	802,178	− 38,222	− 4.8
Delaware	446,292	318,085	128,207	40.3
Maryland	3,100,689	2,343,001	757,688	32.3
West Virginia	1,860,421	2,005,552	145, 131	− 7.2
Alabama	3,266,740	3,061,743	204,997	6.7
Arkansas	1,786,272	1,909,511	− 123,239	− 6.5
Florida	4,951,560	2,771,305	2,180,255	78.7
Georgia	3,943,116	3,444,578	498,538	14.5
Kentucky	3,038,156	2,944,806	93,350	3.2
Louisiana	3,257,022	2,683,516	573,506	21.4
Mississippi	2,178,141	2,178,914	−773	——
North Carolina	4,556,155	4,061,929	494,226	12.2
South Carolina	2,382,594	2,117,027	265,567	12.5
Tennessee	3,567,089	3,291,718	275,371	8.4
Virginia	3,966,949	3,318,680	648,269	19.5
Texas	9,579,677	7,711,194	1,868,483	24.2
Oklahoma	2,328,284	2,233,251	94,933	4.3

Source: U.S. Census, Advance Reports, *General Population Characteristics*, PC(A2)-1, March 31, 1961, for the United States, and the same series for each state.

births per 1,000 population. But in the rise of middle-class fertility during the great "baby boom," the South's rural families continued to decrease their fertility so that the nation and the South converged at a birth rate of approximately 25 per 1,000 in 1959. A higher fertility rate in the South at the present time is mainly because of the high birth rate of the Negro population.

The important news about the South in the period in which it was entering a more complex stage of industrialization was the migration of its people. From 1940 to 1950, the South lost over 2 million population by out-migration, a net loss of almost 5 per cent; from 1950 to 1960 the loss was about 1.4 million or 3.0 per cent. (See Table 19.2.) Omitting Delaware, Maryland, Virginia, Florida, and Texas—the only states which gained by net migration—the other twelve southern states had a total loss of 3.5 million people to areas outside the region. The record of Florida is so distinctive as practically to mark it off from the remainder of the South. During this decade, Florida gained 1,617,000 population by net migration, a rate of gain which amounted to over 58 per cent of its 1950 population. Both West Virginia and Arkansas lost over 22 per cent of their population by outward movement.

Migration trends within the South, involving a massive move from rural areas to cities, are equally important. This rural exodus has been greatest in back country areas and among the Negro population. Thus, 751 counties—practically all rural—lost population, compared to 621 counties, mostly with urban centers, which gained in the period. Among the South's cities of 10,000 to 100,000 population, 379 gained while only 33 lost. Of the South's 78 metropolitan centers (cities of 50,000 or more plus their suburbs), only two lost population.

In many areas throughout the South, abandoned farm dwellings testify to the fact that the rural southerner, in his struggle for livelihood, has had to change his base of operations from the farm to the city. Consolidations and reconsolidations of schools testify to the continuous adjustment that education has had to make to shifting population trends. In all, population movements are bringing the South closer to the nation in its racial and rural-urban composition.

It is estimated that since 1940, over three-fourths of the region's migration losses have been due to the outmovement of Negro population, a trend which dates back to World War I. (See Table 19.3.) Dr. C. Horace Hamilton has shown how migration has continued over the decades, leading to a loss of 2.4 million whites and 5.4 million nonwhites from

TABLE 19.2
Components of Change in the Population, United States and the
Southeast, 1950–1960

	Net Change		
	Number	*Per Cent*	*Births*
United States	27,997,377	18.5	40,947,000
Census South	7,776,025	16.5	13,611,000
Southeast	5,110,067	16.1	9,184,000
Southeast except Florida	2,929,812	10.0	8,269,000
Delaware	128,207	40.3	101,000
Maryland	757,688	32.3	684,000
District of Columbia	− 38,222	− 4.8	206,000
West Virginia	− 145,131	− 7.2	474,000
Alabama	204,997	6.7	851,000
Arkansas	− 123,239	− 6.5	470,000
Florida	2,180,255	78.7	915,000
Georgia	498,538	14.5	1,031,000
Kentucky	93,350	3.2	766,000
Louisiana	573,506	21.4	885,000
Mississippi	− 773	a	639,000
North Carolina	494,226	12.2	1,156,000
South Carolina	265,567	12.5	675,000
Tennessee	275,371	8.4	850,000
Virginia	648,269	19.5	946,000
Oklahoma	94,933	4.3	520,000
Texas	1,868,483	24.2	2,442,000

Source: U.S. Department of Commerce, Bureau of the Census, *Current Population Reports,*
Series P-25, No. 227, April 26, 1961.
a. Less than 0.1 per cent.

1880 to 1960.[5] (See Table 19.4.) Negro population growth remains practically static in half the states in the South, while increasing greatly in the
rest of the nation. If this trend continues, over half of the Negro population will come to live in the North, West, and the East; and the South

| Deaths | Natural Increase | Net Migration | |
		Number	Per Cent
15,610,000	25,337,000	2,660,000	1.8
4,431,000	9,180,000	− 1,404,000	− 3.0
2,995,000	6,189,000	− 1,080,000	− 3.4
2,644,000	5,625,000	− 2,697,000	− 9.3
37,000	64,000	64,000	20.1
246,000	438,000	320,000	13.7
86,000	120,000	− 158,000	− 19.7
172,000	302,000	− 447,000	− 22.3
277,000	574,000	− 368,000	− 12.0
161,000	309,000	− 433,000	− 22.7
351,000	564,000	1,617,000	58.3
319,000	712,000	− 214,000	− 6.2
283,000	483,000	− 390,000	− 13.2
262,000,	623,000	− 50,000	− 1.9
206,000	433,000	− 434,000	− 19.9
334,000	822,000	− 328,000	− 8.1
188,000	487,000	− 222,000	− 10.5
302,000	548,000	− 273,000	− 8.3
312,000	634,000	15,000	0.4
206,000	314,000	− 219,000	− 9.8
687,000	1,755,000	114,000	1.5

may expect to have only about 12 to 15 per cent of its population Negro in the not too distant future. Three southern states lost over 30 per cent of their Negro population by migration in 1950–1960; four more lost over 19 per cent; and five lost over 10 per cent. (See Table 19.5.)

TABLE 19.3

Population Change, United States and the Southeast, White and Negro, 1950–1960

	White		Negro	
	Number	Per Cent	Number	Per Cent
United States	23,682,103	17.5	3,826,894	25.4
Southeast	4,445,794	19.0	613,979	7.4
Southeast except Florida	2,568,864	12.1	336,894	4.4
Alabama	204,018	9.8	654	0.1
Arkansas	− 85,804	− 5.8	− 37,852	− 8.9
Florida	1,897,830	87.6	277,085	45.9
Georgia	436,646	18.3	59,834	5.6
Kentucky	77,993	2.8	14,028	6.9
Louisiana	415,032	23.1	156,779	17.8
Mississippi	68,914	5.8	− 70,751	− 7.2
North Carolina	416,164	14.0	68,668	6.6
South Carolina	257,617	19.9	7,214	0.9
Tennessee	217,496	7.9	56,273	10.6
Virginia	560,888	21.7	82,047	11.2

Source: U.S. Census, *Advance Reports*, Series PC (A2), for the U.S. and each state.

In 1960, six states had a population of over one million Negroes. The state with the largest Negro population was no longer a southern state, but a northern one—New York. During the decade, New York rose from sixth in rank of Negro population to first. Illinois rose from tenth in rank to sixth; Texas, from fifth to second; Louisiana, from seventh to fifth. During the same period, Georgia and North Carolina dropped from first and second, respectively, to third and fourth, while Mississippi's rank in Negro population dropped from third to eighth, and the number of Negroes in that state declined over 70,000. Alabama fell from fourth to seventh, while California's Negro population almost doubled during the decade, raising its rank from fifteenth to seventh place.

The Census figures show that the Negro is not only a part of the current migration, but that he follows the prevailing population trends and, with remigration, is becoming more widely dispersed throughout the nation. Thus, as stated above, while the Negro population in the United States increased by 25.4 per cent, in the Southeast it increased by

TABLE 19.4

Net Migration to and from South by Race and Decade, 1870–1960 (in 1,000s)

Decade	Total South			Southeast (11 states)		
	Total	White	Nonwhite	Total	White	Nonwhite
1870–1880	11	82	− 71	− 304	− 205	− 99
1880–1890	− 411	− 328	− 83	− 515	− 405	− 110
1890–1900	− 143	52	− 195	− 849	− 537	− 312
1900–1910	− 274	− 77	− 197	− 872	− 605	− 267
1910–1920	− 1,088	− 566	− 522	− 1,219	− 642	− 577
1920–1930	− 1,576	− 704	− 872	− 1,704	− 778	− 926
1930–1940	− 756	− 349	− 407	− 651	− 188	− 463
1940–1950	− 2,135	− 538	− 1,597	− 1,878	− 365	− 1,513
1950–1960	− 1,405	52	− 1,457	− 1,080	+ 381	− 1,460
Grand totals	− 7,777	− 2,376	− 5,401	− 9,072	− 3,344	− 5,727

Sources: (1) Compiled by C. Horace Hamilton from Lee, Muller, Brainerd, and Easterlin. *Population Redistribution and Economic Growth in the United States, 1870–1950*; Methodological Considerations and Reference Tables. Philadelphia: American Philosophical Society, 1957. (2) 1940–1960: U.S. Department of Commerce, Bureau of the Census. Current Population Reports, *Population Estimates*. Series P-25, No. 247, April 2, 1962.

TABLE 19.5

Net Migration to and from the Southern States by Color, 1950–1960

State	Total		White		Nonwhite	
	Number	Rate	Number	Rate	Number	Rate
Total 17 southern states	1,404,000	− 3.0	+ 52,000	0.1	− 1,457,000	− 14.1
Total 11 southeast states	− 1,080,000	− 2.9	− 328,000	− 1.2	− 1,459,000	− 16.3
Total 6 non-S.E. southern states	325,000	− 1.8	+ 381,000	2.4	+ 3,000	0.1
Delaware	+ 64,000	20.1	+ 58,000	21.0	+ 6,000	14.6
Maryland	+ 320,000	13.7	+ 284,000	14.5	+ 36,000	9.3
District of Columbia	− 158,000	− 19.7	− 213,000	− 41.1	+ 54,000	19.2
Virginia	+ 15,000	0.4	+ 84,000	3.3	− 70,000	− 9.5
West Virginia	− 447,000	− 22.3	− 406,000	− 21.5	− 40,000	− 35.0
North Carolina	− 328,000	− 8.1	− 121,000	− 4.0	− 207,000	− 19.2
South Carolina	− 222,000	− 10.5	− 4,000	− 0.3	− 218,000	− 26.5
Georgia	− 214,000	− 6.2	− 9,000	− 0.4	− 204,000	− 19.2
Florida	+ 1,617,000	58.3	+ 1,516,000	70.0	+ 101,000	16.6
Kentucky	− 390,000	− 13.2	− 374,000	− 13.7	− 15,000	− 7.6
Tennessee	− 273,000	− 8.3	− 216,000	− 7.8	− 57,000	− 10.7
Alabama	− 368,000	− 12.0	− 144,000	− 6.9	− 224,000	− 22.8
Mississippi	− 434,000	− 19.9	− 110,000	− 9.3	− 323,000	− 32.7
Arkansas	− 433,000	− 22.7	− 283,000	− 19.1	− 150,000	− 35.0
Louisiana	− 50,000	− 1.9	+ 42,000	2.4	− 92,000	− 10.4
Oklahoma	− 219,000	− 9.8	− 192,000	− 9.5	− 26,000	− 13.0
Texas	+ 114,000	1.5	+ 141,000	2.1	− 27,000	− 2.7

Source: U.S. Bureau of the Census. *Current Population Reports*, Series P-25, No. 247.

only 7.4 per cent; and in the Southeast without Florida, the increase was only 4.4 per cent. The Negro has become more urban than the white population and has benefited greatly from improvements in health, resulting in the lowering of his death rate. Since there has been an unexpected rise in birth rates, the Negro population is increasing at a faster rate than the white population.

THE SOUTH'S CHANGING ECONOMY

The struggle of the people to improve their standard of living has been a long one. For most of its history, the South's basic economy was agricultural, limited to the production of a few staple crops—cotton, sugar, tobacco, and rice, supplemented by a subsistence economy based on Indian corn, truck gardens, and pork. In the midst of one of the world's most industrialized nations, the South began with the simple processing of its raw materials of cotton, sugar, lumber, pitch, and tar products. The region has now developed a more diversified manufacturing economy. As industrialization has grown more complex, distribution and services have become important economic endeavors.

The first result of this process of economic development was to reduce the number of workers attempting to gain their livelihood in agriculture. The 5.6 million workers in southern agriculture in 1930 had been reduced by 1960 to 3.4 million by crop controls, by government programs and diversification, and by mechanization and scientific advancement. Mechanized farming and improved practices, first developed in the North and Midwest, are now taking effect in the South. Hybrid corn, good pasture grasses, purebred livestock, and deep freeze storage are accepted developments in southern agriculture. Larger farms, greater yields per acre, fewer persons dependent on farming, a great decrease in tenancy, and a trend toward mixed farming incorporated with livestock production characterize the region. A reduced farm population now finds a better living.

American farmers, including those in the South, are among the most efficient in the world, a fact which has contributed heavily to the decline in agricultural employment. The more food each farm worker produces, the more workers are set free to move to the cities and participate in the industrialization of the region. Accordingly, there has been a "squeeze out" in agriculture; a pull into industry; a drift of workers out of the

South; and a movement of industries southward. The net result of this shift can be summed up in the rising trend of per capita income in the South.

Even in the depression, it was evident that the South was going to move forward industrially. During the depression years, 1929–39, the nation's manufacturing work force declined 6.6 per cent; but in the Southeast there was a gain of 6.3 per cent. This amounted to an increase of about 100,000 industrial employees. Most of this, as George Simpson showed, represents the continual movement southward of the textile industry.[6] As a result, by 1939 the Southeast contained 14.3 per cent of the nation's manufacturing workers as compared with 12.5 per cent in 1929. This fact was reflected by relative gains in personal income. In 1929, per capita income in the Southeast was 52 per cent of the national average; by 1940, it had risen to 58 per cent.

The period of World War II brought a surge of growth to the region. From 1939 to 1947, manufacturing employment increased by 588,000 workers, a gain of 43.3 per cent. Salaries and wages increased by 237.5 per cent. These increases were supported by almost an identical rate of increase in the value added to products by manufacturing. The result was another rise in per capita income, which increased in this period from 57 per cent of the national average income per capita to 68 per cent in 1947.

A continuation of the trend toward higher wages, increased capitalization, more industrial units, and a better rounded industrial structure, with greater value added by manufacturing, characterized developments in the post-war South. There was an increase of more than half a million employed in manufacturing from 1947 to 1956 in the Southeast. These workers in 1956 received $8.3 billion in salaries and wages—more than double the amount received in 1947. Their work also added over $17 billion to the value of the product, again more than double the 1947 figure. Discounting changes in dollar value because of inflation, this gain, nevertheless, represents a real breakthrough. The national increase in employment in manufacturing in 1947–1956 was 20.2 per cent; for the Southeast, it was 26.4 per cent. Comparable increases in value added by manufacturing were: 87.7 per cent for the United States and 97.2 per cent for the Southeast. In salaries and wages, the percentage increase was extremely large: 104.2 per cent for the region, 94.2 per cent for the nation.

Possibly the best single measure of economic advance is found in the trend of per capita income. Personal income data developed by the Department of Commerce since 1929 enable us to make regional comparisons.[7] Per capita personal income in the Southeast rose from $368 in 1939 to $849 in 1946 to $1,820 in 1963.[8] This means that the region's proportion of the non-South per capita income rose from 46 per cent in 1929, to 69 per cent in 1963—a gain of 23 points in 34 years. Howard G. Schaller used these figures to project a gross national product of $924 billion in 1975.[9] With personal incomes of $693 billion, this would mean about $3,066 national per capita income for the United States. Projecting the region's trend, he arrived at an estimate of $2,422 per capita income in the South, 79 per cent of the national average. At present rates, Schaller estimates it will require half a century for the South to attain equality with the rest of the nation in income per person.

Using techniques developed by Edyn Dunn of Brookings Institute, Schaller was able to divide the economic changes governing income gains into three components: (1) gains resulting from the overall growth of the national economy; (2) increases resulting from changes in the South's industrial mix; (3) and gains due to the effect of regional shifts within industries. Table 19.6 shows the change in incomes for southeastern states between 1948 and 1962. The South's industrial mix was unfortunate and this cost the region about $4 billion income. The region's share of industries, however, increased sufficiently to account for a gain of over $7 billion. Thus, income in the South grew by $3 billion more than would be expected from national growth alone. Only Florida and Virginia benefited from improvement in the industrial mix and thus advanced in all three factors. North Carolina benefited most from national growth and was second to Florida in increasing its regional share of new industries.

Each southeastern state, however, was able to increase its proportionate share of the nation's industry. George Simpson pointed out how the industrial mix of the Southeast has been enriched since 1947.[10] Once dominated by a cotton industry in the gray-goods state, the South moved into lumber, furniture, and tobacco processing, with crude pig-iron production in Birmingham. Today, however, the area has moved further into paper, chemicals, hydroelectric power, electrical machinery, electronics, steel and aluminum production, and oil refining. Of these industries, the largest increases have been in transportation, pulp, paper, chemicals, and machinery. The South's less favored industries—food, textiles, apparel, lumber, furniture, and tobacco—accounted for only 35 per cent of all manufacturing employment increases in the Southeast between 1947 and

TABLE 19.6

Components of Change in Participation Income, the United States and the South, 1948–1962 (millions of dollars)

	Total Change	National Growth	Changes due to	
			Industry Mix	Regional Share
United States	173,667	173,667		
South	29,778	26,538	− 3,929	7,169
Virginia	3,954	3,106	184	664
West Virginia	589	1,876	− 638	− 649
Kentucky	1,867	2,283	− 589	173
Tennessee	2,457	2,546	− 226	137
North Carolina	3,681	3,140	− 872	1,413
South Carolina	1,615	1,523	− 386	478
Georgia	3,360	2,633	− 312	1,039
Florida	5,907	2,421	337	3,149
Alabama	2,126	2,178	− 384	332
Mississippi	1,015	1,348	− 479	146
Louisiana	2,335	2,169	− 50	216
Arkansas	872	1,315	− 514	71

Source: Howard G. Schaller. "Changes in the Southern Economy," paper read at Charlotte, North Carolina, December 9, 1964. To be published in forthcoming volume *The Manpower Revolution in the South* (Raleigh: Agricultural Policy Institute, North Carolina State University).

1958, although they made up over two-thirds of the total in 1947. At the other end of the scale, the hard industries, metals, machinery, transportation, and instrument industries—sectors which accounted for only 12 per cent of the region's manufacturing employment in 1947—accounted for about 33 per cent of the new growth. Finally, the federal government, which has pioneered in both the TVA and Atomic Energy in two great installations at Oak Ridge and the Savannah River, has added the Redstone Arsenal in northern Alabama, Cape Kennedy in south Florida, and the new Space Complex around Houston, Texas.

Proof of the enrichment of the southern industrial mix is to be found in the decline of textiles from 29.4 per cent of total manufacturing employment in 1947 to 22.4 per cent in 1958. This has meant a loss of 25,000 workers in textiles. Moreover, the textile industry in the South has reorganized, and the trend is now toward greater diversification with new mixtures, new fabrics, and new products. Since 1929, the excess capacity created in cotton textiles by World War I has been liquidated. The industry lost more than 16,000,000 spindles, while the market, as measured by population, increased more than 50 per cent and income increased much more. Symbolic of the improved textile picture in the region is the passing of the mill village, with its housing sold to the workers, and the rise of a concern like Burlington Mills to a position of national prominence as a leading producer of new fabrics.

North Carolina, Georgia, Tennessee, and Virginia remain the most industrialized states in the Southeast, in that order, as measured by employment in manufacturing. Louisiana has the best industrial mix as measured by value added by manufacturing—some $10,000 per worker. Florida has shown the highest rate of development of any region in the Southeast, with an increase of 101 per cent in manufacturing employment between 1947 and 1957, mostly in the more productive segments of manufacturing.

THE URBAN SOUTH

The Southeast is the least urban of all our large regions; but from 1950 to 1960, it passed the halfway mark, going from 43.0 to 51.6 per cent urban. In the Far West, 81.5 per cent, and in the Northeast, 78.4 per cent of the people dwell in cities. The nation is now 70 per cent urban.

Urbanization, individual advancement, and economic progress have usually gone together in the history of the West. Urbanization means more than the movement of a population from country to city. It involves mass shifts in the occupations of a people, since a function of migration is to place workers in a position to climb that occupational ladder which leads from agriculture to industry, services, and distribution. Occupational mobility carries with it the reward of increased income. Since these payments are made by the total economy as a going concern, it is not surprising to find that the conditions of individual advancement are also those of economic progress. The South, now in its economic breakthrough, is moving into the full tide of this movement.

The South is moving rapidly toward an industrial and commercial economy which is organized around cities and metropolitan areas. This change in economic and social organization is requiring the South's population to redistribute itself in new patterns and to acquire new skills and take on new characteristics. A recent study by Donald Bogue found that, at the current rate, metropolitan development was proceeding at a faster pace in the South than the rate at which the industrial North developed its metropolitan centers.[11]

What makes a city a metropolis in today's economy? The answer is found in a city's ability to organize and integrate a hinterland so as to lead its production and trade into national and world channels. This ability is characterized by the performance of four functions: (1) the organization of retail and wholesale markets, especially wholesale distribution; (2) the development of industry; (3) the organization of converging transportation and communication facilities; and (4) the maturation of local financial resources and organization.

Several methods have been utilized to rank the nation's cities in order of magnitude of the four functions mentioned above. They show Atlanta for the Southeast and Dallas for the Southwest as second order metropolises—second only to national centers like New York and Chicago. (See Table 19.7.) Houston, New Orleans, Memphis, Louisville, and Birmingham appear as third order metropolises; while a long list of sub-dominants is found, including Richmond, Fort Worth, Oklahoma City, Miami, Charlotte, Jacksonville, Tulsa, Nashville, Little Rock, San Antonio, Norfolk-Portsmouth, and El Paso. Important in determining these rankings are banking and fiscal importance, and position as the homes of branch offices for major national corporations.

Gateway cities to the South have played an important part in the region's development. In the South, lines of trade and control are mediated to New York by way of gateway cities like Baltimore, Louisville, and Cincinnati; in the Southwest, via Saint Louis and Kansas City to Chicago and New York. Overnight sleeper jumps and airlines for the transport of key personnel show the importance of these lines of communication, well illustrated by the fact that while the Charlotte metropolitan area is in the center of physical production in cotton textiles, the base for planning, designing, brokerage, sales, and finance is Worth Street, New York. It is evident that southern metropolises, no matter how rapidly they are now growing, will not replace the giants of the New York-Chicago axis. In all specialized functions they are subdominant to these supermetropolises, as, in fact, is the whole nation.

While the urban South is characterized by small cities, the region is generating cities large enough to carry on metropolitan functions. By 1950 the thirteen southern states contained twenty-nine cities of 100,000 or more inhabitants. Of the nation's 33 metropolitan areas of 500,000 population or more, as defined in 1950, the South had seven, none reaching to a million population. By 1960 these seven cities had grown to the following sizes: Houston, 1,243,758; New Orleans, 907,123; Dallas, 1,083,360; Louisville, 725,139; Birmingham, 634,864; Atlanta, 1,017,188; and San Antonio, 716,188. The first city in the whole South to reach a million population was the "Great Giant of the Gulf," Houston, Texas. If Dallas-Fort Worth, some thirty miles apart, could be counted as one concentration, this Texas giant would be the South's largest, reaching over 1,600,000 population. The high rate of metropolitan growth from 1950 to 1960 gave the South six new centers in the half-million category: Miami, 935,047; Memphis, 674,583; Norfolk-Portsmouth, 578,507; Fort Worth, 573,215; Tampa-St. Petersburg, 772,453; and Oklahoma City, 517,833. Thus, the region had 13 out of the nation's 54 metropolitan areas of a half-million and over in 1960. (See Table 19.7.)

The new industries in the South employ less unskilled labor and require more capital and more technical knowledge than those industries that formerly dominated the region. Accordingly, in both agriculture and industry, the battle for efficient production is now being waged in the fields of engineering, technical services, management, distribution, and finance. This means, in short, that more southern workers have moved from blue-collar to white-collar occupations and have been forced to acquire better skills and become better educated. To hold these gains, a fast pace must be maintained; to make more gains, the process must be stepped up. Thus, while the proportion of workers in manufacturing remains fairly constant, around 20 per cent, those employed in the third level of the economy, in such auxiliary forces as trade, distribution, technical, professional and other services, increased from 38 per cent to well over 50 per cent of the total work force between 1930 and 1960. Along with increased services came the greater employment of women, who now comprise some 30 per cent or more of the South's labor force. Negroes forced out of agriculture have benefited least from this shift, and many have had to find their best employment opportunities outside the region. Nevertheless, the shift of the Negro to southern cities closely follows that of the white working force. In the main, it is clear that the Negro males have not improved their position in the labor market. White

TABLE 19.7

Major Cities in the South, Ranked by Metropolitan Function

City	Rank Score on Metropolitan Function 1950	Rank Score on Size 1950	U.S. Rank 1960	Population of Metro. Areas 1960
Second-Order Metropolises				
Atlanta	9.91	6.67	24	1,017,188
Dallas	9.71	6.38	22	1,083,360
Third-Order Metropolises				
Houston	8.10	7.43	17	1,243,158
New Orleans	7.36	6.77	28	907,123
Memphis	6.62	5.67	39	674,583
Louisville	6.43	6.18	36	725,139
Birmingham	5.94	6.07	43	634,864
Subdominants with Metropolitan Characteristics				
Richmond	5.34	4.83	63	436,044
Fort Worth	5.24	5.00	50	573,215
Oklahoma City	5.02	4.81	58	511,833
Miami[a]	4.90	5.71	25	935,047
Charlotte	4.80	4.11	82	316,781
Jacksonville	4.79	4.70	61	455,411
Tulsa	4.60	4.40	64	418,974
Nashville	4.59	4.79	58	463,628
Little Rock	4.54	4.09	120	242,980
San Antonio[a]	4.48	5.75	37	716,168
Norfolk–Portsmouth[a]	4.42	5.28	48	578,507
El Paso	4.38	4.12	83	314,070
Subdominants				
Tampa–St.Petersburg	4.18	5.26	32	772,453
Chattanooga	4.11	4.38	90	283,169
Knoxville	3.84	4.88	60	368,080
Shreveport	3.62	4.00	91	281,481
Mobile	3.54	4.29	71	363,389
Savannah	3.46	3.87	133	188,299
Corpus Christi	3.30	3.94	119	221,573
Montgomery	3.25	3.79	127	199,734
Baton Rouge	3.25	3.90	114	230,058
Austin	3.19	3.92	124	212,136

Source: Rupert B. Vance and Nicholas J. Demerath, *The Urban South* (Chapel Hill: University of North Carolina Press, 1954).

a. Miami because of its resort function and San Antonio and Norfolk–Portsmouth because of military installations probably rank somewhat higher than their basic metropolitan function would place them. They are essentially subdominants. Port cities, by this method, usually rank lower than cities doing "center work."

women have made the greatest proportionate gains. The number of Negro males in the labor force decreased by 13.3 per cent while that of Negro females increased by 15.4 and white females by 110 per cent from 1940 to 1960. (See Tables 19.8 and 19.9.)

The major effect of industrialization, therefore, is found in the great shift in the distribution of labor. At no point, however, has any highly industrialized nation anything like the majority of the labor force employed in straight manufacturing. The tremendous increases in output

TABLE 19.8

Changes in Employment Status and Occupation of the Labor Force of the Southern States of the United States between 1940 and 1960

Employment and Occupation	Number in 1000s 1940	Number in 1000s 1960	Per Cent Change	Number in 1000s 1940	Number in 1000s 1960	Per Cent Change
	White Male			Nonwhite Male		
Total labor force	9,220	10,741	16.5	2,746	2,319	− 15.5
unemployed	1,095	465	− 57.5	351	169	− 51.9
Total employed	8,126	10,276	26.5	2,395	2,151	− 10.2
Professional	395	1,024	159.2	37	63	72.8
Farmers	1,868	738	− 60.5	621	154	− 75.1
Managers	808	1,298	60.6	23	32	37.2
Clerical	948	1,470	55.1	28	83	196.4
Craftsmen	1,032	2,106	104.1	87	185	112.6
Operatives	1,288	1,969	52.9	260	477	83.5
Private household workers	11	6	− 45.5	65	17	− 73.3
Service workers	360	412	14.4	204	272	33.3
Farm laborers	867	304	− 65.0	570	246	− 56.9
Other laborers	495	538	8.7	489	493	0.8
Not reported	53	412	677.4	12	128	952.3
	White Female			Nonwhite Female		
Total labor force	2,378	4,985	109.6	1,342	1,546	15.4
unemployed	320	226	− 29.4	143	117	− 18.2
Total employed	2,058	4,759	131.2	1,199	1,430	19.3
Professional	322	668	107.5	53	107	101.9
Farmers	49	34	− 30.6	46	15	− 67.4
Managers	103	226	119.4	7	14	100.0
Clerical	640	1,958	205.9	11	67	509.1
Craftsmen	17	55	223.5	1	6	500.0
Operatives	434	807	85.9	60	123	105.0
Private household workers	161	160	− 0.6	697	638	− 8.5
Service workers	214	539	151.9	106	297	180.3
Farm laborers	76	46	− 39.5	199	69	− 65.2
Other laborers	16	20	25.0	10	13	30.0
Not reported	28	245	775.0	8	80	900.0

Sources: U.S. censuses of population of 1940 and 1960. 1940: Vol. 3. *Labor Force*, Pt. 1, U.S. Summary, Tables 4 and 63. 1960: U.S. Summary, *Detailed Characteristics*, Tables 251 and 257.

per worker in the factory system feed economic growth, produce material comforts and luxuries, and release workers from primary employment to occupations in the third level of the economy. More people are shunted into research, planning, management, clerical, and technical services. The changes in occupational groups from 1940 to 1960 show what this means to the South. Losses in this period among farmers and farm laborers ran from 30 to 75 per cent of the 1940 employment, depending on race and sex. Gains were found in the great increases in professional and technical workers, managing officials, clerical and sales people, and craftsmen—for whom employment gains ranged from 37 to 160 per cent. The South, then, is moving toward an economy in which education,

TABLE 19.9

Changes in the Per cent Distribution of Employed Persons in the Southern States by Occupation, Sex, and Race, 1940–1960

Occupation	Per Cent Distribution 1940	Per Cent Distribution 1960	Difference 1960–1940	Per Cent Distribution 1940	Per Cent Distribution 1960	Difference 1960–1940
	White Male			Nonwhite Male		
Total employed	100.0	100.0		100.0	100.0	
Professional	4.9	10.0	5.1	1.5	2.9	1.4
Farmers	23.0	7.2	− 15.8	25.9	7.2	− 18.7
Managers	9.9	12.6	2.7	1.0	1.5	0.5
Clerical	11.7	14.3	2.6	1.2	3.9	2.7
Craftsmen	12.7	20.5	7.8	3.6	8.6	5.0
Operatives	15.9	19.1	3.2	10.9	22.2	11.3
Private household	0.1	0.1		2.7	0.8	− 1.9
Service workers	4.4	4.0	− 0.4	8.5	12.6	4.1
Farm laborers	10.7	3.0	− 7.7	23.8	11.4	− 12.4
Other laborers	6.1	5.2	− 0.9	20.4	22.9	2.5
Not reported	− 0.6	4.0	3.3	0.5	6.0	5.5
	White Female			Nonwhite Female		
Total employed	100.0	100.0		100.0	100.0	
Professional	15.6	14.0	− 1.6	4.5	7.5	3.0
Farmers	2.4	0.7	− 1.7	3.8	1.0	− 2.8
Managers	5.0	4.7	− 0.3	0.6	1.0	0.4
Clerical	31.1	41.1	10.0	0.9	4.7	3.8
Craftsmen	0.8	1.2	0.4	0.1	0.4	0.3
Operatives	21.1	17.0	− 4.1	5.0	8.6	3.6
Private household	7.8	3.4	− 4.4	58.2	44.6	− 13.6
Service workers	10.4	11.3	0.9	8.8	20.8	12.0
Farm laborers	3.7	1.0	− 2.7	16.5	4.8	− 11.7
Other laborers	0.8	0.4	− 0.4	0.9	0.9	
Not reported	1.3	5.2	3.8	0.7	5.6	4.9

Sources: (1) *U.S. Census of Population,* 1960. U.S. Summary, *General Social and Economic Characteristics.* PC(I) IC. Table 88. Also the corresponding state census reports. (2) 16th Census of the United States, 1940. Vol. 3. *The Labor Force.* U.S. Summary, Table 63.

professionalization, technical services, and skills are of the essence. This represents the raison d'être of the "permanent revolution"—a drastic change which demands the maintenance of a complex culture with highly developed technical and institutional resources.

Here, then, are the reasons behind the recent growth of our cities. Those who read history with attention will remember that the industrial revolution as it took place in England was a painful process. As the Russian and Chinese versions of the permanent revolution have been engineered, they have repeated this painful process with only the overtones that dictatorships can add. Peasants were forced off the land, agriculture was squeezed, famine was used as a weapon while industry was being developed, so that a wholesale transfer of the nation's working force could be made to the industrial sector. The South is accomplishing this same process, not by force, but by the use of economic incentives. While the shift does not involve coercion, it can be said that strain, nevertheless, exists in the economic necessities which push people from the land into the factories and on into the service industries.

The first prototype of industrial discipline and the strains it creates is found in the modern factory. In scientific management, time and motion studies have developed as methods of measurement so that the optimum possibility of each worker can be calculated like any material means of production. As a result, the discipline of the plant and the mechanization of the work are made congruent. In its extreme range in mass production, natural individual rhythms are subordinated to the pace set by the conveyor belts. The punching of time clocks, the docking of workers for absenteeism, and large scale layoffs have all come to constitute the new discipline whereby rural workers have been made over into factory operatives. To the workers, this is the "stretchout" and it has been responsible for as much unrest as any one fact in industry. The initial phases of the discipline attending southern industrialization had to do with the manual labor force. The second and third states go over into the higher demands of the academic discipline in the training and education of the new working force to enter clerical, technical, professional, and allied services. How far automation will carry this trend no one knows. Accordingly, the test of the South's ability to make its full commitment to the permanent revolution will be found in the higher rankings and more complex functions of its educational services and institutions. As manual labor is mechanized, more people are due to make large scale shifts from agriculture and machine-tending to clerical and semiprofessional services.

Most of these people will go to live in our cities. To succeed where they are going, they must go further in our schools than did their fathers.

The educational status of an earlier generation can be presented in the nationwide data on rejection rates for mental deficiency and illiteracy per 1,000 registrants for Selective Service, November 1940–December 1944. These figures have been accepted largely as a measure of educational deprivation. It will be noted that with registrants ranging from 18 to 45 years of age, the 45 year old in 1940 would have been of school age during the period from 1900 to 1910; and the 18 year old registrant in 1944 would have been of school age from 1932 to 1942. Thus, the draft group represents an entire generation within itself, and includes the present population age groups of 40–70.

Ginzburg and Bray found that the white rejection rates for this earlier generation were over five times as great in the Southeast and Southwest as in the Far West: 52 and 54 per 1,000 as compared to 9 per 1,000.[12] A preponderance of the high rejection rate was in the Appalachians and in the Cajun country of Louisiana. Regular rejection rates, the highest for whites in the country, were as follows in the Southeast: Louisiana, 55 per 1,000; Virginia and Arkansas, 59; North Carolina, 62; and Kentucky and Tennessee, 64. These were equalled outside the Southeast only by New Mexico, Arizona, and Texas with 50, 53, and 63 per 1,000, respectively. A high concentration of rejection rates appeared in Indian and Spanish-American populations also. Regional rates of rejection for Negro populations ran over 200 per 1,000 for seven Southeastern states: Alabama, Arkansas, Georgia, Louisiana, Mississippi, North Carolina, and South Carolina. These rates were over four times those found for Negroes in the states of New York, Pennsylvania, Indiana, Iowa, Ohio, and the states of the Far West and Northwest, where rates were 36 to 52 per 1,000.

EDUCATIONAL PROGRESS

We know that along with technical advances have gone sustained advances in the educational level of the South in recent years. These factors have been mutually supporting, and progress by either has speeded the other. Improved support, increased enrollments, rural school consolidation, and state equalization funds have led the attempt to bring the South closer to the reality of a high school education for all able to benefit therefrom. Public education has made especially memorable advances during the post-war period. The number of pupils in average daily attendance increased by well over a million; yet the Southeast managed simultaneously to make substantial gains in financial support. Between 1949–50 and 1963–64, for instance, current expenditure per pupil in average daily attendance increased from $134 to $319 in the Southeast, a gain of 138 per cent as compared to a national growth rate of 121 per cent.

The effect of the general rise in the level of education is seen in the changing social characteristics of the people. The number of persons with no schooling has been greatly reduced, so that they now number only about 3 per cent of the general population and are confined in the main to the older generation. A full elementary school education is now the accepted standard and represents the average for the population over 25. Numbers with some high school and college education have increased from 40 to 50 per cent, so that now about 34 per cent have obtained a high school education and 15 per cent of the population over 25 have attended college. While the Negro still has about one-third the proportion of college and high school graduates, this difference decreases as the older generation, with its limited opportunities, is replaced by the younger. The Negro is continuing to decrease the gap by climbing the educational ladder at an increasing rate.

In emphasizing the South's potential in the further development of its human resources, we point directly to education and the institutional resources necessary for such development. The region began its advance with a campaign for universal education; it is now in the process of shifting to an emphasis on excellence in education. To some this may mean raising educational standards to new heights, forcing the least qualified entirely out of the educational process. The lack of realism in this view should be pointed out.

The design by which the members of the oncoming generation find their position in life can be compared to climbing an occupational pyramid. Rewards go to those who climb to the highest positions on the pyramid and are able to retain their positions. Here, the task of the school is evident; it motivates students to scale these heights and helps them acquire the skills needed for achievement. To complicate the matter, the pyramid of occupations is changing before our very eyes, narrowing at the base and broadening at the top. There is less room at the base for the unskilled, while the room at the top has increased for those with talent and ability sharpened by technical and professional training.

This leads us to point out that the region is engaged in developing new institutional resources for improving the quality of its personnel. Thus, beyond the high school, vocational education takes a new turn with the development of special institutes to fill the region's great need for technicians. Special summer schools for gifted children are now held in several southern states. Talented children set their own pace, and come to realize what talents they have. In similar fashion, learning institutes are now developing for the culturally deprived. New techniques are tried out and evaluation is made of new ways of learning. Kindergartens are being established, aimed at improving the early cultural experience of children whose home backgrounds offer them no motivation or help on the road to learning. Finally, the community college movement, designed to get more students into the college experience, will bring junior colleges to local communities. It is well known that more students will attend college if they can live at home. Education can be provided at more reasonable costs at these nonresidential colleges. Whether or not these students can go on to universities will depend upon the extent to which they can take advantage of two more years of education.

The cornerstone of the system remains the university. Certain state and private universities furnish strong professional, graduate, and undergraduate training, so that the South is better able to man and direct its new developments. Nevertheless, it is entirely fair to say that the South is attempting to participate in the permanent revolution without possessing universities of the highest rank. A recent study of graduate education for the Carnegie Corporation judged that no southern university was to be found in either the top twelve of the nation or in a second group of ten. Only six of the South's universities—Duke, North Carolina, Texas, Tulane, Vanderbilt, and Virginia—have as yet achieved membership in the Association of American Universities. Beyond the level of graduate training, a new pattern in American intellectual life has been the emergence of centers for advanced study, such as the Institute for Advanced Study at Princeton and the Center for the Study of the Behavioral Sciences at Stanford University. There is no comparable institution in the South and none in sight.

As much as the South needs and desires economic advancement, its leaders have not limited their goals to the material. Along with education, the region has also developed cultural aspirations. Once called "The Sahara of the Bozart," the South has developed a literature of worldwide importance, well represented by the achievements of Ellen Glasgow, Thomas Wolfe, William Faulkner, Tennessee Williams, Allan Tate, Robert Penn Warren, and James Agee. Warren is the only person who has won the Pulitzer Prize in both fiction and poetry. It has become something of a witticism to say that it is a sad day in the region when a southerner doesn't win a Pulitzer Prize in the novel or in journalism.

No comparable renaissance in music, painting, and sculpture has developed; but the growth of libraries, museums, symphony orchestras, and little theatres among the new cities of the South has in its way been quite remarkable. In some states, lacking wealthy patrons, the legislature has become a patron of the arts. For example, North Carolina supports three outdoor symphonic dramas during the tourist season, a state art gallery, an institute for training in the performing arts, and a symphony orchestra which travels all over the state bringing concerts to the citizens and school children alike. Culture for the people is a worthy goal to be added to the educational process. For all its disabilities, it seems safe to say that the South is not being "dragged screaming into the twentieth century."

NOTES

1. *The Retreat from Reason* (London: Watts and Company, n.d.), p. 66.

2. *World Resources and Industries*, revised ed. (New York: Harper and Brothers, 1951).

3. Gerald W. Johnson and Rupert B. Vance, *All These People* (Chapel Hill: University of North Carolina Press, 1945).

4. Those who work in this field have a choice of the regions they delimit. Thus, the Census South contains 17 states and combines three Census divisions: the South Atlantic States, the East South Central, and West South Central divisions. The Southeast contains 11 states, omitting Texas and Oklahoma as well as the border states of Delaware, Maryland, West Virginia, and the District of Columbia. Table 19.1 has a listing of the states in the Census South.

5. "The Negro Leaves the South," *Demography* 1 (1964): 273–95.

6. Unpublished manuscript, carrying forward Howard W. Odum's analysis of Southern Regions into the 1960s. In files of the Institute for Research in Social Science, University of North Carolina, Chapel Hill, 1963.

7. U.S. Department of Commerce, *Survey of Current Business* 44 (April 1964): 15–23.

8. U.S. Department of Commerce, *Personal Income by States Since 1929* (Washington: Government Printing Office, 1956).

9. "Changes in the Southern Economy," in *Manpower Requirements and Human Resource Adjustment* (Raleigh: Agricultural Policy Institute, Series 15 [May, 1965]), pp. 1–14.

10. See note 6, above.

11. "Population Distribution and Composition in the New South," in *The New South and Higher Education* (Tuskegee Institute, Alabama: Department of Records and Research, 1954), pp. 3–4.

12. Eli Ginzberg and Douglas W. Bray, *The Uneducated* (New York: Columbia University Press, 1953).

20. The South Considered as an Achieving Society (1967)

A symposium on research needs marked the opening, in the mid-sixties, of Duke University's Center for Southern Studies. Vance's contribution was a discussion of the mutual effects of regional culture and economic development. Gordon Blackwell commented that the regional approach, as Vance used it, combined "the theory and methodology of cultural anthropology, demography, economics, geography, history, the humanities, political science, social psychology, and sociology." He added, "I trust I have not been offensive by leaving anybody out!"

At a meeting of the Southern Historical Association in Atlanta in 1959, attention was given to the state of Southern regionalism. Among the considerations advanced at the meeting we may note the following: (1) The section had gathered to praise regionalism, not to bury it. (2) But as the South advanced in economic status, the rationale of Southern regionalism was receding. Along with King Pyrrhus regionalists might say: "More such victories and we are undone!" (3) Regionalism was never taken up as a movement by the people; it remained the preoccupation of certain university scholars. (4) The deal is dealt, we were told. Shall we proceed to the next deal?[1]

Now that we are greeting the establishment of a new Center for Southern Studies at Duke University, let us show no hesitation to follow Mark Twain and say that the report of the death of regional studies has been greatly exaggerated. In Atlanta some contradictions seemed in evidence: the movement had never caught on; and it was to be abandoned because it was succeeding.

We are under the obligation to make what use we can of historical perspective in terms of our national and regional trends. The American Civil War has had its centennial; the first hundred years since emancipation has had its commemoration; and now for a hundred years since

From Edgar T. Thompson, ed., *Perspectives on the South: Agenda for Research*, pp. 59–70. © 1967, Duke University Press, Durham, N.C.

Appomattox Court House the South has been pursuing the trend line of a developing economy. Only since 1920 has the pursuit seemed real. The value of economic development, "putting first things first," slowly gained acceptance in the South, but two world wars, high postwar productivity, and Keynesian economics were required to make these values operative. With the analysis of the gross national product, measurement of the phenomenon of economic development for regions has become possible. Empirical analyses of components have been plentiful, and I do not propose to read them into this record. Rather we shall seek to discuss inter-relationships; to ask whither we are trending; and mayhap to apply what we can of theory and speculation to research in probable developments in the South. And if it seems impossible to keep values out of the account, we may adopt the virtue of frankness and admit a perference for progress. In considering the complementary interaction between quantity and quality in periods of development, one can hardly escape the assessment of values.

It is the assumption of this paper, then, that the South can be viewed as following along certain lines of development which may or may not reach culmination; that such movements are fairly general phenomena in historical times; and that they have suggested strategy and tactics for research in the transition of an ongoing society. To follow through on such leads bespeaks the efforts of several varieties of social scientists and of humanists, an undertaking congenial, I would assume, to the purposes of the university's new institute. May I in speculative fashion draw on certain assumptions to suggest contiguous areas of ignorance which the research of the future should be able to explore? (1) Here the course of economic development sets the model; (2) the trend line of social process opens up neighboring problems; and (3) the unfolding of new culture in literature and the arts will be related.

I

We lack the trained imagination to realize the great gulf which separates the mentality of underdeveloped societies from that of today's complex economy. Let me cite a parable which I hope will suggest the distance our region has traversed in a century. On certain islands of the Pacific the natives, contemporary primitives comparable to those of the Old Stone Age, were caught up as observers on the fringe of World War II. As transport ships and freight airliners landed with shipments of materials, the natives uttered the cry "Cargo!" and rushed to the harbor to earn porters' wages in unloading inexplicable riches. For this the natives developed their own set of explanations, which anthropologists came to call the "Cult of Cargo." Observing the mass of paper work involved—bills of exchange, bills of lading, invoices, receipts checked and counterchecked, signed and countersigned—they reached an explanation. Desirable cargo was summoned out of the sky and out of the ocean's vastness by marks which white men made on pieces of paper, marks which could not be resisted and which only white men had mastered and understood.[2]

Democracy having been introduced in the islands, one candidate, we are told, mounted his campaign with the promise to teach his people the magic of cargo, to show them how to make the marks that summoned goods from across the ocean and from out of the sky. I like this parable. The one thing wrong is that the natives' procedure would start at the top and work its way downward; so far we haven't learned how this is done. One might well ask how the common man was to understand the poverty which gripped the South in the years following Appomattox or understand the wealth-producing qualities of the new industrialism arising in the Northern United States. There is a textbook test of an underdeveloped economy which is often cited—if over one-half of the occupied males work in agriculture the country may be put down as underdeveloped.[3] As late as 1920 slightly over 50 per cent of the Southern total labor force worked in agriculture; by 1960 it was 10.4 per cent; today, it is less.[4]

Industrialization represents a commitment to the improvement of material well-being and the conditions of life as a goal of public policy and private endeavor. In poorer countries outside the West, economic development appears to certain groups well-nigh unobtainable. It calls for drastic changes that include both intended and unanticipated consequences. The acquisition of the skills required in the performance of modern types of economic activity and the deep-seated acceptance of the attitudes and beliefs appropriate to industrialization are to be seen as the problem of the commitment of a society's labor force to a new social discipline.[5] In England's Industrial Revolution no social change, it seemed, could be more drastic than the acquisition of the new industrial discipline. Russia repeated the process with variations that only a totalitarian state could introduce. In the South we are in the midst of the strains, the tensions, and the achievements that accompany the industrialization which is a pervasive feature of modern life. Leon Trotsky called this "the permanent revolution." Great as the tensions are, greater are the rewards; survival lies in no other direction. As the South shifts from an agrarian to an industrial economy, it mechanizes, reorganizes, in fact, "industrializes" its agriculture. Other economies have threatened the agricultural basis of their existence in the transition. The South, along with other regions, has gained efficiency and stored up surpluses of its staples at the same time that it has liquidated small-time agriculture. This should not blind us to the plight of the Negro and poor-white working forces, many of whom have faced liquidation of the only skills they have learned since Appomattox.

The commitment of the working force is exceeded by that of certain Southern leaders. Floyd Hunter, fresh from studying community power structure in Southern cities, wrote:

> Southern leaders, particularly those in the institutions of business and politics, are convinced that organized efforts on a large scale are necessary to (1) improve agriculture, and (2) to expand and build up new commercial and industrial enterprises. This is seen as "putting first things first." The general agreement from the top down is that nothing must stand in the way of these laudable aims.[6]

Add the pursuit of (3) expansion and excellence in education, however visualized by the educational and political forces, in a movement that extends all the way from public schools to the universities. Finally, the political leaders have united in (4) the support of social security goals. "All major Southern institutions are busily engaged in defining their value systems in terms of progress and development," Hunter wrote in 1954. "They all have the forward look and optimism is abroad in the land."[7]

Many analyses have been made of regional per capita income and deservedly so, for it constitutes the one index of economic achievement and reward. Per capita income in the South was about 46 per cent of that in the rest of the nation in 1929; in 1960 the South's share approached 70 per cent. Professor Howard G. Schaller has developed projections of the South's per capita income which indicate that in fifty years the region will attain equality with the United States per capita income, if the present rates continue. This calculation includes the proviso that migration out of the South also continues at present rates.[8]

Industrialization ran a full course in England, in Japan, and in communist Russia without much importation of capitalization. Japan, we might recall, developed its industry under state socialism and then turned it back to private owners. W. W. Rostow, studying international economic development, holds that underdeveloped countries subject to the thrust of initial capitalization and industrialization reach a take-off stage after which economic growth is self-sustaining.[9] The South's access to capital and the extent to which it has benefited as a component region of the world's richest nation are now very clear.[10] The South's development, however, does not automatically follow from this trend. In Italy's economic growth, the industrial area of Northern Italy has pulled further away from the problem-ridden South, progressively widening the differential.[11]

I have no intention of presenting economic growth as an impersonal, spontaneous evolutionary force. It represents, in fact, a resolution of forces, a merging of the energies of individuals and groups, pushing, striving, wanting, claiming, deciding, struggling, and achieving. To the desire for cargo is added a certain know-how. It is notable that when social psychologists like David McClelland and J. W. Atkinson came to study the achieving society, they took economic development as the prototype and motivation (defined as realized, conscious need to achieve) as the rational component.[12] Undoubtedly the riddle of achievement remains to be riddled; but if the equation were to be written, it would look something like this: IQ (talent) + motivation + opportunity = achievement. We leave to our research people in social science the consideration of how one gets back and forth from individuals to collectivities, from corporate groups to growing cities and achieving regions. Nor does one have to attribute sainthood, superhuman energies, or extraordinary intelligence to businessmen to place a value on the achieving society thus defined.

Given the assumption that economic progress will push through to a plateau of achievement, can the change carry other aspects of regional society and culture along with it? Under one assumption, our region has wanted all things needful and required only the resources to meet the required budgets. Under another assumption, the Southern public has wanted economic development so badly that it was willing to give up certain regional traits and attitudes which stood athwart the line of advance.

In 1959 a student of the South's economy attempted to come to grips with the question of the impact of non-economic factors on development. W. H. Nicholls of Vanderbilt University devoted his presidential address before the Southern Economic Association to the impact of the Southern tradition on economic progress. In 1960 he published *Southern Tradition and Regional Progress*, stating his firm conviction that the South must choose "between its traditions and progress."[13] Nicholls filed a bill of particulars and the list was a formidable one. Urban and industrial development, he said, run counter to: (1) the persistence of agrarian values, (2) the rigidity of inherited social structure, (3) an undemocratic political structure, (4) the weakness of social responsibility, especially in regard to public education, (5) a forced conformity of thought and behavior, behind which lurked the threats of violence and anti-intellectualism. Nicholls' evidence was familiar to students: the agrarians were taken more seriously than they deserved; racism, while not given the center of the stage, was everywhere in evidence. In Howard W. Odum's terms, the South had turned from regionalism to sectionalism.[14]

One reaction to Professor Nicholls' thesis pointed to the disastrous effect on the life and livelihood of the common man, if tradition should block development. The conflict of values involved was evident in another view: how tragic for the nation and the region if the South carried through to become new-rich and purse-proud only to use its wealth to underwrite its peculiar doctrines. Apparently it was Nicholls' hope that the issue would force a choice and that Southern leaders would be forced to choose development over the implementation of tradition in closed schools and massive resistance. Political compliance, where subsidies and benefits were concerned, was also seen as tied to Southern development. If the region held out its hand for the benefits of equalization funds and railed against the new regulations, it was seen to take the position of saying to the federal powers: "Give us our money and don't ask us what we intend to do with it."

II

Different institutions and different organized ways of doing things have different impacts on the trend of events. We have followed the economic trend closely; others may point to the trend line of compliance and the new federalism in our political structure, to the generating of new social traditions, or to the talent-releasing power of education. These are the variables of social change and it behooves us not to announce conclusions, but to seek tactics and strategy for the long pull. To my mind this means that in research we must turn to the legitimate use of theory.

Certain bodies of older theory do not attempt to explain all phenomena before analysis; rather, they suggest where to look and what questions to ask.

Let us begin by asking if there exist general propositions applying to such social elites as: (1) business leaders, (2) engineers and technicians, (3) political groups and leaders, (4) scholars and research scientists who face change and the demand for change. We do not propose technical answers; we seek rather the general characteristics of social situations. We begin with the assumption that social change involves a learning process—individual, collective, and interactive. A society, a group, an individual is confronted by X: an emergency, a crisis, a research problem demanding solution, or at minimum a choice of alternatives, one which may involve public opinion. Such a stimulus arouses a circular reaction, a focus of group attention. A change of direction may follow if the crisis brings forth an invention, an innovation, a research solution, or a new choice of policy. No response or an inadequate response defers the process, which then becomes cumulative. How the crisis is met depends on certain complex conditions which we may state simply.

> 1. The general level of group culture furnishes the basis for response. Machine retrieval of the stored information in "knowledge banks" has shown how much we expect from the culture basis. Thus in the classic case wartime radar could not have been developed had we lacked any one of a score of previous inventions.
> 2. The achievement of mastery is dependent on what can quite simply be called the character of ideas in circulation. Thus, the attitudes of the Catholic church and the economics of Lord Keynes greatly affect the chances of innovation to meet economic or population crises.
> 3. Much depends on the presence of extraordinary individuals in the group. No one should be called on to define genius, but one might say that even Einstein became what he was because of the training he had before he took charge of his own education. It may be entirely possible that many technicians and professional men operate up to the limit of their best training and no further. If so, they are still men of talent.

The elite, the inventors and innovators of our society, thus create new patterns of action, new mechanisms for their achievement, and new ideologies for their justification. If they are problem-solving, such patterns are spread abroad by diffusion and communication, a process as it were of social learning, meeting opposition even as Gabriel Tarde showed in his account of social imitation.

Innovations and inventions come to be incorporated in the social traditions of the group, and the powerful norms of society move in as sanctions. Fortunately, bad laws are occasionally subject to repeal and new science itself is subject to re-evaluation. The final step is taken when elements of the cumulative culture are incorporated in the corpus of knowledge, and are then transferred to the formal curricula of the schools. By the inculcation of new elements in the minds of the young, society establishes a process of intergenerational diffusion, thus molding a new social heritage. Here in simplified form—from the works of Gabriel Tarde, W. I. Thomas, Charles A. Ellwood, Florian Znaniecki, W. F. Ogburn, and Arnold Toynbee[15] is what every young native of Borneo should know about cargo. This represents, of course, a process in which the South is now far advanced.

The interrelations of (1) economic development, (2) changing social conditions, and (3) achievements in the fine arts and the humanities will offer materials for analysis for generations of scholars to come. Certainly the humanities are not to be neglected. Stewart Udall writes: "It is the artists and men of ideas who have done and will do the most to determine our national purpose, to fix our national character, and to shape the American legacy." Nor can the developing South avoid the verdict stated by President Eisenhower's Commission on National Goals: "In the eyes of posterity the success of the United States as a civilized society will be largely judged by the creative activities of its citizens in art, architecture, literature, music, and the sciences." One does not have to contend that the arts will remain in total dependence on the marketplace to visualize the impact of Southern development on the humanists.

Problems of interrelations between these areas will call forth suggestions whereby theory may guide further efforts. Alfred Weber gave statement to one such formulation as early as 1935 in his *Cultural History as Cultural Sociology*, and he returned to the theme in 1951 in *Principles of Historical and Cultural Sociology*.[16] Again we are concerned with hypotheses which have not yet been processed into conclusions. Life to Weber was fundamentally historical in process and the student should face up to this question: What is our place in the stream of history? Here explanations are to be sought in cultural science, not in natural science.

Certain it is that if we are to have social dynamics, they must come from the energies and propensities of individuals interacting in groups, however structured.

In the historical process Weber points out a social process, a culture process, and the process whereby civilization accumulates and is integrated. The last may be treated first. The products of civilization are transferable across cultural boundaries and they are cumulative, adding to the stockpile of technology. More than anything else the process represents the idea of development as progressive, unilateral, and irreversible. The civilizational process used to exploit nature's resources reaches culmination in the development of technology and the natural sciences. It is this process, dominated by considerations of utility, rationality, and purpose, which pushes toward a unified civilization—not culture—the world over. Culture is superstructural and ideational. In the culture process as Weber defines it, the main uniformity is not accumulation, but unique creativity. Products of high culture represent a synthesis of the world and the mind of individual personalities, uniquely talented. Expressed in art, religion, and philosophy, they furnish no predetermined patterns that we can deduce, no universally valid and necessary criteria except those of taste, no generally applicable laws to relate this creative process to other processes. Such creations, being unique, do not easily transfer from one period or one culture to another. In a work like Dante's *Divine Comedy* we have the epitome of an age and the creative expression of a unique talent, phenomena that cannot be understood without understanding an age.

Both are associated with the social process, which Weber sees as creating a network of interpersonal relation and a *social* heritage. The events of the social process are found in the struggles, the conflicts, and the competitions of the folk: the formation and organization of families, tribes, classes, groups, and nations. The social process then consists of specific events, giving rise to general patterns of social structure and tradition. We see society as a group of groups, all in complex interrelation and interaction. It can be viewed as a hierarchy of groups ranging from the national society downward. Regions, as we see it, merit inclusion here, since a region represents a group organized around an interest—in this instance the interest of locality, on a larger scale than that of community. The interrelation of such processes if explored should, in future studies, serve to guide and to challenge our understanding of regional structure and change.

Finally, it is interesting to note that in 1964 Professor Nicholls visualized a new shift in the South's development:

> The non-economic factors which historically have shackled the South's economic progress are at last in full retreat. The recent sound and fury emerging from the South can easily be misunderstood. It clearly represents the death throes, not the renaissance of those Southern traditions which are inconsistent with the region's industrial-urban development. In the process, the South is finally creating the environment needed for it to achieve full economic parity with the rest of the nation.[17]

Thus, in Weber's terms he sees the civilizational process as dominant and economic development as the locomotive of social change in the South.

III

For much of the last century the South pursued the goals of quantity—not enough jobs, not enough capital, not enough goods, not enough services, not enough schools, certainly not enough money. None but the few well-to-do could pursue a search for quality. Before the region could ask of anything: "Is it good enough?" it had to ask: "Is there enough?" This chapter has been written with a future reference, seeking out a context and framework for research to come. As the South turns to the achieving society it must face the transition from the goals of quantity to quality in its culture and demography.[18]

Again, economic development points the trend. From the opening wedge of the poor man's industry—cotton textiles in the gray goods stage, to new fabrics, new mixtures, and high styling; from unassembled kitchen tables and chairs in High Point's new industry to the reproduction of antique furniture—industrial development has moved to higher quality of product and the attainment of a new industrial mix. The movement to quality has involved the abandonment of a certain element of quantity production. From its excess capacity in 1929, the textile industry has lost six million spindles.

In wartime, industry moved South, not because Southern workers were cheap, but because they were of higher quality than those then available in industrialization elsewhere. In this process Southern workers were found capable of higher skills, and the movement has continued.

In education the first need was schools for the masses. This movement is now being expanded to bring high school training within the reach of all able to benefit thereby. Technical institutes and community colleges will add two years of education, while Southern colleges and universities face the problem of expanding their capacity. Southern Negro youth now have a better chance of getting college training than white Englishmen.[19]

Throughout the whole range of occupation the South's working force is rapidly being upgraded. Domestic servants, farm laborers, and the unskilled drop out of the statistics decade by decade. Skilled operators, foremen, technicians, clerical workers, salesmen, managerial and the professional and semi-professional workers show large scale increases, many over 40 to 50 per cent in the last two decades.

In the long run, population growth may well come to mean fewer people, better prepared. The demand for high quality manpower has brought the small family pattern to the region's expanding middle class. As the family seeks more training for its children, it limits its numbers. Even the baby boom, now declining, is thought to represent the middle-class family's reactions to better chances for their better educated children. Changing occupational distribution is bringing more components into the Southern middle class, thus affecting demographic structures. Rural fertility continues to decrease, and there are now indications that the non-white birth rate is turning downward.

Finally, in economics, improved product meets with better taste in an expanding market, raising the question of a better appreciation of the products of high culture and a more favorable climate for creative talent. Here the dominance of the marketplace and the mass media has led to the conflict between mass culture and high culture which apparently exists throughout the world. The South might well stabilize its population increase as it meets new demands for quality in its culture, social conditions, and demography.

Interaction between processes now ongoing in society, civilization, and high culture furnish materials for manifold studies of a region in the midst of things to come. Challenge and response, however viewed, are moving across the South in its approach to the achieving society.

Transition and social change, it is apparent, do not issue from apathy nor has the South, whatever it has been, been a center of apathy. While the South has been called a history without a country of its own, it can no longer be called an underdeveloped society. It, too, has heard the cry "Cargo!" and the region now knows whence cargo comes. The South is also a participant in the revolution of rising expectations. Whatever achievements this particular province has tasted, they have but whetted the appetite of people and leaders. Like Oliver Twist, the South extends its cup and pronounces that fateful monosyllable, "More," and it adds what Oliver would never have dared, "And Better."

NOTES

1. "The Status and Future of Regionalism," *Journal of Southern History* 26 (February 1960): 22–56.

2. Peter Worsley, *The Trumpet Shall Sound* (London: MacGibbon and Kee, 1957); J. Van Boal, "Erring Acculturation (Case of the Cargo Cult)," *American Anthropologist* 62 (February 1960): 108–21, esp. pp. 108–11; "Explaining Cargo Cults," *Hibbert Journal* 62 (April 1964): 151–53.

3. William Peterson, *Population* (New York: Macmillan, 1961), p. 466.

4. William H. Nicholls, "The South as a Developing Area," in Avery Leiserson, ed., *The American South in the 1960s* (New York: Frederick A. Praeger, 1964), p. 28.

5. See A. F. Feldman and W. E. Moore, "Moot Points in the Theory of Labor Commitment in Developing Areas," S.S.R.C. *Items* 14 (December 1960): 1 ff.; also the committee's *Labor Commitment and Social Change in Developing Areas* (New York: S.S.R.C., 1961); and "The Meaning of Discipline," in H. H. Gerth and C. W. Mills, eds., *From Max Weber: Essays in Sociology* (New York: Oxford University Press, 1946), pp. 253 ff.

6. Floyd Hunter, "Community Organization: Lever for Institutional Change?" in R. B. Vance and N. J. Demerath, eds., *The Urban South* (Chapel Hill: University of North Carolina Press, 1954), p. 252.

7. Ibid.

8. Howard G. Schaller, "Changes in the Southern Economy," in *Manpower Requirements and Human Resource Adjustment* (Raleigh: Agricultural Policy Institute, Series 15 [May, 1965]), pp. 1–14, esp. p. 5. On Southern development in general, see J. J. Spengler, "Southern Economic Trends and Prospects," in J. C. McKinney and E. T. Thompson, eds., *The South in Continuity and Change* (Durham: Duke University Press, 1965), pp. 101–31; also chaps. 6–10. See also Clarence Danhof, "Four Decades of Thought in the South's Economic Problems," and part 2 in M. L. Greenhut and W. T. Whitman, eds., *Essays in Southern Economic Development* (Chapel Hill: University of North Carolina Press, 1964), pp. 7–68, 169–358. A good reference on regional growth is H. S. Perloff et al., *Regions, Resources and Economic Growth* (Baltimore: Johns Hopkins Press, 1960).

9. W. W. Rostow, "The Take-Off into Self-Sustained Growth," *The Economic Journal* 66 (March 1956): 25–48. Also his *The Process of Economic Growth* (New York: Norton, 1956).

10. Joe S. Floyd, "Trends in Southern Money, Income, Savings, and Investment," in *The South in Continuity and Change*, pp. 132–44.

11. Lloyd Saville, "Sectional Development in Italy and the United States," *Southern Economic Journal* 23 (July 1956): 39–53.

12. David McClelland, *The Achieving Society* (Princeton: Van Nostrand, 1961), esp. chaps. 1–3, 5–8, and 10. Also J. W. Atkinson, "Determinants of Risk-Taking Behavior," *Psychological Review* 64 (November 1957): 359–72.

13. The volume was published by the University of North Carolina Press.

14. Howard W. Odum, *Folk, Region and Society: Selected Papers* (Chapel Hill: University of North Carolina Press, 1964), pp. 173–91.

15. Gabriel Tarde, *Social Laws*, trans. H. C. Warren, Jr. (New York: Macmillan, 1899); William I. Thomas, ed., *Source Book for Social Origins* (Chicago: University of Chicago Press, 1909); Charles A. Ellwood, *Cultural Evolution* (New York: Century, 1927); William F. Ogburn, *Social Change* (New York: Viking, 1956 ed.); Florian Znaniecki, *The Social Role of the Man of Knowledge* (New York: Columbia University Press, 1940); Arnold J. Toynbee, *A Study of History*, abridged by D. C. Somervell (New York: Oxford University Press); vol. 1 (1947) covers vols. 1–6; vol. 2 (1957) covers vols. 7–10 of the original.

16. Alfred Weber, *Kulturgeschicht als Kultur-Soziologie* (Munich: R. Piper and Co., 1950). *Fundamentals of Culture-Sociology: Social Process, Civilization Process, and Culture-Movement*, trans. G. H. Weltner and C. F. Hirshman (New York: WPA and Columbia University, 1939).

17. In *The American South in the 1960s*, p. 40.

18. State studies are few, but the Virginia Academy of Science with the support of the Virginia Chamber of Commerce sponsored an analysis of the state's population structure. See Roscoe D. Hughes and Henry Leidheiser, Jr., eds., *Exploring Virginia's Human Resources* (Charlottesville: University Press of Virginia, 1965). Chapters 4 to 9 treat occupations, skills, fertility, and physical and mental health, in the attempt to assess "the productivity and creativity" of Virginia's people.

19. Richard L. Wilson in "The U.S. Isn't as Sick as We Think," *Look*, February 8, 1966, p. 39. The original calculations were done by C. A. Anderson of the Department of Education, University of Chicago.

21. When Southern Labor

Comes of Age (1968)

This introduction to a special issue of a Labor Department periodical is another illustration of Vance's talent for summarizing research findings for a general audience. In it, he briefly and clearly abstracted some research of a kind which is often boring, when not obscure.

It is becoming increasingly difficult to write about the South in any new and pertinent fashion. Labor and its status in the region, however, remains a topic of perennial controversy and permanent interest. This is not the first time that the *Monthly Labor Review* has featured the topic nor is it likely to be the last. The editor has assembled contributions of such worth that I was greatly pleased when he asked me to provide a brief introduction. My function, as I see it, is to make certain informal comments of my own and to indicate how the contributed articles tie in with each other.

The contrast between South Italy and the Southern United States serves to point a moral. In the remarkable resurgence of Italy after World War II it is noted that economic development in North Italy has pulled further away from the underdeveloped South, increasing a differential that was already stultifying.[1] In the United States it can hardly be maintained that the highly developed regions, the Northeast and the Midwest, have failed to maintain their rapid pace. The point is that for recent decades, in an economy in which communities have to move fast just to stand still, both the Southeast and the Southwest have mounted and sustained more rapid growth rates than the remainder of the country. It is from these trendlines that the *Review* can project the coming of age of Southern labor.

The one adequate measure of labor's economic status and a region's productive power appears to be personal income per capita. Here it should be permissible to cite a pertinent calculation in addition to those furnished in the *Review*. Professor Howard G. Schaller of the University of Indiana has calculated that per capita income in the South, as a percentage of per capita income in the rest of the Nation, rose from 46 percent in 1929 to 51

From *Monthly Labor Review* 91, no. 3 (March 1968): 1–4.

percent in 1940 to 69 percent in 1963—a gain of 23 percentage points in 34 years.

Projecting these trends to 1975, Professor Schaller was able to estimate a per capita income of $2,422 (in 1963 dollars) in the South, thus reaching 79 percent of the national figure. At the rate at which the South has been changing since World War II, Schaller estimated that it would require a half century for the region to overtake the rest of the country in the matter of income per person.[2] It is against this background of change that this issue of the *Review* is written.

INDUSTRIALIZATION AND CHANGE

No Nation, and no regional component, escapes its history however much it may hope to overcome it in time. The South has been called a history without a country of its own. In no sector has *The Burden of Southern History*, in C. Vann Woodward's title, been heavier than in the region's labor experience. The South, the one major section of a democratic country that lacked a free labor system as late as 1865, was not rescued from its problem by emancipation. The Negro freedman found precarious refuge in an inefficient system of share tenancy based on cotton, where he was joined by poor whites, and together they built up an immense labor reserve that has not been liquidated to our own day. Our contributors cite this unskilled labor reserve in agriculture both as a source of Southern differentials and as a manpower resource inviting further development.

It is not surprising to find that Southern leaders have opposed the imposition of national standards in the Federal minimum wage laws and in the Equal Pay Act of 1963 before the South's economic development is completed. Competent economists, such as Marshall R. Coldberg, have sometimes supported this view.[3] Joseph J. Spengler has pointed out that the South may require an increase in the number of rural growth points at which to locate new manufacturing in order to take advantage of lower living costs.[4] H. M. Douty, however, is able to point to a wide range of wage differentials which should appeal to mobile industries for some time to come.

In the wake of the South's search for quick industrialization in the 1920's came a reputation of being biased against labor. A recent historian, George Tindall, has given pertinent exhibits of the period. A steel executive extolled the South as "the greatest, best, and cheapest labor market in the United States." "Strikes unknown," a chamber of commerce proclaimed. "Under no more than reasonably fair treatment of its help," a Kiwanis Club of North Carolina explained, "every factory or branch of industry is certain to be able to secure adequate, satisfactory, and contented labor."[5]

Broadus Mitchell, historian of *The South's Industrial Revolution*, wrote: "The workers are being offered on the auction block pretty much as their black predecessors were and their qualities are enlarged upon with the same salesman's gusto. Native whites! Anglo Saxons of the true blood! All English speaking! Harmoniously satisfied with little! They know nothing of foreign-born radicalism! Come down and gobble them up!"[6] "In booster rhetoric," summed up George Tindall, "the patient docility of the Saxon churl became almost indistinguishable from that attributed to the African."[7]

Labor unionism grew feebly before the 1930's. The hostility of Southern men of business toward unions conformed to their philosophy of quick development and was cherished as though it were a magnet to attract migrating capital and industry. F. Ray Marshall shows the extent of the Southern differential in union organization. Certain Southern firms and certain segments of industry, it is reported, have found a most effective way to ward off union organization. They pay the national wage scale and meet union standards with the obvious pitch: "What need have you to organize and pay union dues?"

The higher that Southern development goes in technology, skills, and participation in national corporate enterprise, the greater will be the importance and the amount of union organization. So true is this that those who carry on the old fight against unionization will become suspect as reactionaries who align themselves against progress. The South, however, remains more hospitable to craft unions than to the new industrial unions.

AN ERA OF DEVELOPMENT

Our contributors rightfully have avoided limiting themselves to a review of history, preferring to examine the South as it is today and comment on its future. All share the conclusion that, whatever its national role, the South no longer represents an underdeveloped economy. If one had to date the crossover, it might well be placed in the census decade between 1910 and 1920. As late as 1920 slightly over 50 percent of the region's labor force worked in agriculture (the textbook case for underdevelopment). By 1960 it was 10 percent: today it is much less.

BASIS FOR DEVELOPMENT

The South's older complaints emphasized its position as a colonial economy, subject to exploitation by national corporate interests. The new analysis emphasizes its access to capital and points out the extent to which the South has benefited as a component region in the world's richest economy. W. W. Rostow, studying international economy development, holds that underdeveloped countries subject to the thrust of initial capitalization, industrialization, and expanding markets, reach a take-off stage after which economic growth is self-sustaining.[8] Articles in this issue by William Stober and Robert F. Smith indicate that the Mason-Dixon line no longer constitutes an iron curtain against the affluent society. Changes in industries and occupations in the Southeast and Southwest, they are able to show, resemble each other yet exhibit regional differences. Whether the two regions will move into Rostow's stage of high mass consumption in the 50 years assigned remains dependent on the state of agriculture. Pertinent here is the changing status of farm labor as discussed by Walton Jones.

As the South secures the capital resources required to develop its natural resources it encounters a basic fact of life and labor, the problem of its human resources. Today U.S. manpower is in short supply while 3 million Americans remained unemployed as of January 1968. In growing Southern cities, as throughout the Nation, help-wanted ads ask for teachers, engineers, doctors, policemen, pilots, toolmakers, physicists, journalists, middle-management executives, machinists, computer programmers, and mechanics—in brief, jobs that are critical and for which skills are necessary.

E. E. Liebhafsky is able to present the demographic projections of the Southern labor force in terms of its numbers by age, sex, race, rural-urban residence, and migration. That Negro men are underemployed while Negro women are overemployed tells us something about tradition and heritage, Southern and Negro. Since human resources depend on institutional resources for their highest development, James Whitlock and Winfred Godwin are able to show how far the South has gone in providing secondary and higher education and how far the region needs to go. The influence of present manpower programs on the projected future of Southern labor is assessed by Professor Vernon Briggs. All show the familiar differentials against the South; all suggest that these differentials demand a differential rate of growth in favor of the region. They suggest that the region may find this rate difficult to maintain unless full equalization is achieved in expenditures for education and manpower development.

As much as the region has done to improve higher education, its universities are rarely rated above second class levels. Not a single Nobel Prize winner has done his work at a Southern university and none teach there now. To staff its business and universities with talent of the highest rank, the South must send many of its sons outside to win scientific, engineering, and doctorate degrees, and then try to lure them back. In a field closer to skilled labor, however, the South is now setting the pace in vocational education. In public occupational education, as Herbert M. Hamlin prefers to call it, the 13 Southern States now have 281 area schools in operation to provide technical training for persons past high school age. As Hamlin shows, along with the region's community junior colleges this trend represents two important movements: (1) the attempt to attract industry by providing it with trained employees and (2) a laudable endeavor to improve the earning power of its native white and Negro workers.

Special national projects like Oak Ridge, the Savannah River Project, and military installations, have forced increased manpower demands on the South in terms of both quantity and quality. A fresh and enlightening account of the impact of manned space flight installations on Southern communities has been prepared especially for this issue by Mary A. Holman and Ronald M. Konkel. The way these programs have upgraded skills, changed local mores, and improved facilities in such communities as Huntsville, Ala., Brevard County, Fla., and Hancock County, Miss., is nothing short of astounding. That they are capable of shocking certain communities out of the age of the "Southern Cracker" is literal truth. That the communities themselves rise to their responsibilities is equally amazing.

SOUTHERN LABOR

When one comes to consider the status of the worker and his job, the South conventionally remains the home of nonunion labor, the differential wage, racial discrimination, and the lower standard of living. While

Ray Marshall is able to show that the South has about 14 percent of its nonagricultural workers organized, as compared with 30 percent elsewhere in the country, there are some industries in which the region has a good union record. No one can predict, but the gap between the North and South should continue to narrow as national corporations move South bringing their union contracts with them. The South will have to increase union membership to 3 million to reach the national proportion by 1972 and an increase of 1,455,000 will be needed to maintain its 1964 proportion of 14 percent organized.

Southern promoters, it appears, have always cherished Southern wage differentials as an important part of their sales talk. H. M. Douty, however, is able to show that earnings in the South exceed those in the rest of the country in at least three groups: pulp and paper, industrial chemicals, and synthetic fibers. In eight others, wages reach at least 90 percent of the national rates, including textile and hosiery. Increasing diversification, better industry mix, needed investments in education and training, and greater capitalization will bring the region nearer to equal pay for equal work. But as Mr. Douty points out, wage structures change slowly and no drastic reversals can be expected without lower birth rates and further liquidation of the agricultural labor reserve.

Emory F. Via writes that Negroes feel that job discrimination in the South is pervasive and racial. It is true that more Negroes hold new and better jobs but they get a disproportionate share of low status jobs and unemployment. While improvement is planned and demanded in the region's new Human Relations Councils, it appears too soon to project improved trends.

Any résumé of the South's condition will point out that with 28 percent of the U.S. population, the South draws 22 percent of the Nation's personal income. One fourth to 30 percent of all Southern families and individuals can be classified as poor compared with 15 percent of families in other parts of the Nation. Helen H. Lamale and Thomas J. Lanahan feel that these conditions, too, will alter but that changes in income and standards of living will be slow. The most beneficial change in terms of statistical average would come from improvement in the Negro's employment and occupations.

Along with the economy, scholarship about the South, as this issue makes clear, is achieving maturity. Shortly after the editor laid plans for the specialized issue of the *Monthly Labor Review*, 1967 saw the appearance of two definitive studies of Southern labor: The Twentieth Century Fund's *The Advancing South: Manpower Prospects and Problems* and F. Ray Marshall's *Labor in the South*. It is eminently fitting that the present issue should contain contributions from authors involved in both while the books themselves are reviewed by one of the country's leading journalists, Ralph McGill of the *Atlanta Constitution*. Whether one casts his glance forward or backward, he must conclude that the region is going in the right direction and at a fairly brisk pace. That it may be a half century or more before inequalities are resolved, if ever, is one of the considerations that make regional analysis important. When Southern labor comes of age, the term New South will also reach maturity. If and when, the term should be retired and moved to the storage files of history.

NOTES

1. Lloyd Saville, "Sectional Development in Italy and the United States," *Southern Economic Journal*, July 1956, pp. 39–53.

2. Howard G. Schaller, "Changes in the Southern Economy," *Manpower Resources and Human Resources Adjustment* (Raleigh: Agricultural Policy Institute, May 1965, Series 15), pp. 1–14.

3. Marshall R. Coldberg, "Southern Economic Development: Some Research Accomplishments and Gaps," in Edgar T. Thompson, ed., *Perspectives on the South: Agenda for Research* (Durham: Duke University Press, 1967), p. 18.

4. Joseph J. Spengler, "Southern Economic Trends and Prospects," in J. C. McKinney and E. T. Thompson, eds., *The South in Continuity and Change* (Durham: Duke University Press, 1965), p. 127.

5. George B. Tindall, *The Emergence of the New South, 1913–1945* (Baton Rouge: Louisiana State University Press, 1967), pp. 317–18.

6. Broadus Mitchell, "Flesh Pots in the South," *Virginia Quarterly Review* 3 (Fall 1927): 169.

7. Tindall, *Emergence of the New South*, p. 318.

8. W. W. Rostow, *The Process of Economic Growth* (New York: Norton, 1956).

22. Region (1968)

When a new encyclopedia of the social sciences was prepared, its editor naturally turned to Vance to write the entry on the concept of the region. While not as comprehensive as his article "The Regional Concept as a Tool for Social Research," Vance's entry represents his last look back at a topic that had occupied his attention for forty years. It is significant that he saw "regionalism's" future, if it was to have one, in the study and solution of the problems of underdeveloped countries—societies resembling in many ways the South of his youth.

A region is a homogeneous area with physical and cultural characteristics distinct from those of neighboring areas. As part of a national domain a region is sufficiently unified to have a consciousness of its customs and ideals and thus possesses a sense of identity distinct from the rest of the country. The term "regionalism" properly represents the regional idea in action as an ideology, as a social movement, or as the theoretical basis for regional planning; it is also applied to the scientific task of delimiting and analyzing regions as entities lacking formal boundaries.

Official status is given to regions in the statistics of countries like the United States, where the national census groups states and counties in statistical and economic areas. In the international sphere, a region may consist of a group of national states possessing a common culture, common political interests, and often a formal organization. Thus the Scandinavian countries, the Benelux nations (Belgium, the Netherlands, and Luxembourg), and, in the Western Hemisphere, the Organization of American States (OAS) are true regional groupings (the OAS consists of North and South American states, with the exception of Canada).

In tracing the history of territorial integration, historians have placed little emphasis on ethnically or culturally homogeneous regions, tracing rather the cycle of conquest, aggregation, and empire building, and its antithesis of sectionalism, revolt, self-determination, and movements for national independence. In the Hellenistic world and during the Pax Ro-

From David L. Sills, ed., *International Encyclopedia of the Social Sciences*, 13: 377–82. Reprinted with permission of the publisher from the *International Encyclopedia of the Social Sciences*, David L. Sills, editor. Volume 13, pp. 377–82. © 1968, Crowell Collier and Macmillan, Inc.

mana larger cultural structures appeared—empires brought together by force. It was not until after the interregnum of feudalism that smaller political structures, in the form of modern nations, finally emerged from such empires. Regions thus appeared when national territories grew to large size, incorporated new domains, and began to adopt federal forms of government. In a highly centralized country like France, the origins of regionalism can be traced back to differences between historic provinces; it also represents a movement toward decentralization.[1] In modern Italy and Germany unification laid the basis for regionalism—a trend accented by the increasing importance of economic differentials. Russia as the Union of Soviet Socialist Republics faces most of the problems of ethnic, economic, and sectional differences. In Great Britain regionalism verges on localism, for it goes beyond the traditional differences between England, Ireland, Scotland, and Wales, extending to the imponderable distinguishing characteristics of such subregions as Wessex, Sussex, and Yorkshire, which have been best portrayed in literature. In its extreme form, regionalism may result in separatism. Regions involved in such conflict are commonly referred to as "sections"; and sectionalism may culminate in self-determination, secession, and independent nationalism, as it did for the Irish Free State. If the movement is crushed, the section may again assume the status of a constituent region, as did the South after the American Civil War.

As concepts utilized in social science, region and regionalism appear at some midpoint between the community and the nation. Whereas formal boundaries delimit the jurisdiction of political units, if basic regions are to be delimited, social scientists must concern themselves with social realities—demographic and economic. Regionalization is thus a heuristic device undertaken to advance analysis, planning, and administration; it is a common thread that runs through studies of regionalism by diverse disciplines. Regions can thus be regarded as building blocks making up the structure of the larger sociocultural area. The term "subregion" is usually applied to the next unit in descending order, but analysts also use such terms as tract, precinct, center, zone, district, and province.

Region and regionalism are topics common to all the social sciences, and contributions to theory and method in this area have come from both the physical and the social sciences, including biology. Certain evolutionary biologists, for example, hold views at variance with most psychologists about the man-land relationship. Any exegesis of regionalism is likely to prove a gloss on Aristotle's dictum that man is a political animal. To this is added the corollary that man is by nature a territorial animal. To agree, however, that all behavior patterns observed in man's political and societal structure are potential in human nature has not proved sufficient to satisfy the more ardent social Darwinists. The association of fighting and rage responses of insects, rodents, birds, and mammals (especially the higher apes) with the defense of territory against invaders of the same species has been demonstrated in a series of biological studies. Man, by species, evolution, and survival, it is contended, has fixed and retained these drives. In the present revival of conflict theory, a work such as Robert Ardrey's *The Territorial Imperative*[2] represents a return to the instinct hypothesis—in this instance, a supposed compulsion to hold and defend territory. Citing recent biological studies, Ardrey bases his theory of the "territorial imperative" on the hypothesis that lower species have an instinct to defend definite and precise boundaries. He then extends this hypothesis to explain the foundation of the national state, patriotism, and the universal prevalence of war. Few psychologists or social scientists now welcome a return to the instinct hypothesis as an explanation equally applicable to the varied phenomena associated with localism, feudalism, nationalism, sectionalism, regionalism, and community spirit. To many the jump from animal instinct to human social organization is made by ignoring much of the work done by students of social structure.

Thus the areal approach to the analysis of society poses a stark reality underlying many of the interpretations made by social scientists. According to economic analysis, the primitive "sustentation area," anchored to the soil and water complex, set boundaries to social interaction and thus both aided in developing social types and, by forcing inbreeding, developed physical types among the inhabitants. In modern society, power, administration, social consensus, and policy determination appear inseparably linked to areas. Moreover, in the localization of resources, industry, and finance, and in the tie-in of lines of transportation to economic centers, the economic order parallels the political at all levels—from the international level to that of the component elements of states and provinces. If territorial groups did not exist, political organization would have to call them into being in order to function. The sociologist develops his specialty around social groups; these groups converge and are organized around interests—locality being a major interest. Society itself is seen as a group of groups. The territorial basis develops as a major social interest at any group level, and below the national level this interest can be seen as focusing on the section or the region. As other interests, such as those of social class or occupational group, gain importance, the regional interest may recede.

Contributions of the geographers.

Geographers provided the initial impetus to regional studies. Rigorous and precise analyses of areas are to be found in the works of physical geographers, who are devoted to the integration of the findings of such specialities as climatology, physiography, soil science, and ecology. Geography set the mode of analysis early for differentiating world regions, as exemplified by the work of the French human geographers Paul Vidal de la Blache[3] and Jean Brunhes. The point of view of the new cultural geography was well stated by Vidal de la Blache in 1903:

> A region is a reservoir of energy whose origin lies in nature but whose development depends upon man. It is man, who, by molding the land to his own purposes, brings out its individuality. He establishes a connection between its separate features. He substitutes for the incoherent effect of local circumstances a systematic concourse of forces. It is thus that a region defines and differentiates itself and becomes as it were a medal struck off in the effigy of a people.[4]

It was natural that geography, with its emphasis on the analysis of land forms, should have proceeded from the natural to the cultural landscape. Dynamic assessment of the interaction of life forms and their habitats was first applied to biotic areas of indigenous plant and animal life and later to human-use regions seen as basically economic. Areal analysis was thus held by some to be a function of the new ecology—plant, animal, and human. The full turn was made when culture and technology were given rein in the modern power complex, and, following G. P. Marsh, the regional phenomenon was viewed in terms of man's role in changing the face of the earth.[5]

REGIONAL STUDIES

Like the concept of space in philosophy, region as an idea general to all the social sciences has suffered from vagueness and thus from a too easy identification with any and all territorial units. The regional concept will contribute to the social sciences only if greater precision is introduced in its use. Recognizing this need, the Committee on Regionalism of the Association of American Geographers has distinguished between two types of regions—uniform and nodal. Uniform regions are homogeneous throughout, whereas nodal regions are homogeneous only with respect to internal structure or organization. The structure of the nodal region has a focal area, and the surrounding areas are tied to it by lines of circulation—communication and transportation.[6] Uniform areas prevail when the physical environment is the important factor and agriculture is the prevailing mode of economy. Nodal regions appear with increased technology and the growth of large-scale transportation, wholesale distribution, finance, and manufacturing; in such regions metropolises perform the central work of the economy. An analysis of homogeneous regions and focal center areas, using the 67 metropolitan regions of the United States, showed almost no agreement between the boundaries of the two types of regions.[7] Nevertheless, it seems clear from the same study that the uniform region and the nodal region concepts present equally valid and important ways of viewing the structure and processes prevailing in an inhabited territory.

The next problem in need of analysis concerns the interrelations between these regional units. According to one viewpoint, the structure of national societies has developed as a complex of metropolitan regions, each consisting of its own constellation of communities. This view has been variously supported by, for example, N. S. B. Gras, an economic historian; Robert L. Dickerson, the British geographer; and R. D. McKenzie and Donald Bogue, American sociologists. As metropolitan areas expand, they may eventually form a continuous urban-strip region. This type of region—called the "megalopolis"—has been analyzed by Gottmann in his study of the 43 contiguous metropolitan areas stretching from Boston, Massachusetts to Washington, D.C.[8] Such an area makes new problems for the regional analyst. For example, the intense competition of closely placed centers points to the lack of regional unity. Moreover, it is difficult to assign hinterlands to these metropolises, when they are viewed as nodal regions. Because of the high population density of the megalopolis, its components stand in need of regional-urban planning of a type as yet undeveloped.

Von Thünen's work on the isolated state put location and spatial analysis in the forefront of accepted economic theory.[9] Walter Christaller developed central place theory, a type of analysis which, strangely enough, had been undertaken by Charles Galpin in his work on rural communities in Walworth County, Wisconsin.[10] The "place-work-folk" formulation of Le Play and the "valley section" of Victor Branford and Patrick Geddes brought social organization and advanced planning into the analysis of regional relationships. Culture area studies, carried forward under the leadership of Clark Wissler, utilized the location of physical and social traits to reconstruct regional cultures and their diffusion. Wissler's work on North American Indians was supplemented by Melville Herskovits' culture area analysis of indigenous Africa.[11] Regional studies, cultural in the best tradition, are also found in the work of the American geographer Carl O. Sauer and in Isaiah Bowman's analysis of "pioneer belts."[12]

It should be pointed out that the logic of regional study contravenes that of orthodox science: "Western science has been developed by specialization along lines of problem complexes or by abstraction and isolation of certain significant and meaningful 'aspects' of the chaotic reality. The social sciences are no exception to this principle. . . . The aim is always the establishment of general principles, not the description of a single concrete society."[13] In regional analysis, phenomena are studied and related simply because they converge within a given area to affect the economy and culture of the particular societies. The regional survey, however, proceeds beyond a catalogue of traits into the analysis of an interacting system. Since causation cannot always be made explicit, such surveys often remain more descriptive than systematic—a fact which does not deny their usefulness.

Regional studies can be placed along an ascending scale of complexity, depending on the level of integration of variables. First, regions may be delimited on the basis of one variable: for example, the laying out of market areas and areas of wholesale distribution. Second, regions may be delimited on the basis of a complex of related variables, thus coming closer to cultural-areal reality. At the third level is the complex regional study that is developed in historical depth; it is calculated to show the functional unity of cultural, economic, and social traits of the region, as in W. P. Webb's *The Great Plains*.[14] Finally, interregional comparison furnishes an areal-cultural frame of reference for developing general theory about man, culture, or economy.

Regionalism in the United States.

In the United States, regional studies have flourished under various auspices: regional science, area studies, American studies, literary regionalism, studies of administrative and planning regions, history, and sociology. Despite the fact that New England's regional economy and culture was an early development, it was not studied as a region, nor was New York, as long as both were accepted as the expression of the national pattern. When New England lost its hegemony, Seymour Harris wrote *The Economics of New England.*[15] When the regional approach first appeared, it emanated from the West and the South, led in academic circles by Frederick Turner and Howard W. Odum.[16]

Turner, a distinguished historian of the West, developed doctrines of the frontier, the section, and sectionalism, all of which undercut the continuity of the European cultural tradition in America, particularly the European concept of "undivided nationalism." As the frontier matured, it became a distinct section, admitted to the Union but bent upon the pursuit of its own political and economic interests. Keenly aware of such developing differences, Turner viewed the United States as a sectional amalgam, something like a concert of European nations united in conflict, compromise, and adjustment. States rights, he held, functioned as the constitutional shield for sectional demands.

Odum was a sociologist whose work was devoted to the problems of the South, including its lack of development and its strong sectionalism. As an alternative to sectionalism, he proposed a regionalism that would give precedence to national values. Odum thus advocated regional-national planning that would enable all areas to participate and benefit equally from the nation's resources, its capital wealth, and its social and political organization. He believed that the development of regional-national integration was necessary to the nation's survival.

Critics have pointed out certain limitations in regionalism, and it is true that, at its most superficial level, it approaches the method of the cataloguer. For example, the early geographers sought only to determine and list the geographic relationships and influences existing in the region; the criterion of a successful report was the number of traits catalogued. Moreover, the abandonment of the doctrine of determinism appeared to rule out the search for causation, and thus the cultural region and the physical region appeared juxtaposed but unrelated. In the early 1900s, economic and social differentials gave impetus to studies of regional equilibrium and integration, but as development furthered the trend toward economic equality, the obliteration of rural-urban differences, and the diffusion of a uniform culture, the basis for both regional analysis and regional ideology, appeared to diminish. Today, however, the problems of the newly independent, underdeveloped countries accent, as never before, the basic differentials in the status of world regions. The emerging problems inherent in international stratification highlight pressing dilemmas in population policy and regional-national planning.[17] Unfortunately, however, these problems are now concealed in the ideological conflict between communism and the Western world. During the era of expanding colonial empires, European scientists made excellent cultural and regional surveys of colonial areas preliminary to planning and development. Few such surveys are being made today; instead, reliance is placed on political dogmas. Thus supersensitive ex-colonials often expend aid funds to no appreciable economic advantage. The first of the new nations to return to the pragmatism of the older regionalism may prove the first to break out of this ideological impasse.

NOTES

1. Hedwig Hintze, "Regionalism," *Encyclopaedia of the Social Sciences*, vol. 13 (New York: Macmillan, 1934), pp. 208–18.

2. Robert Ardrey, *The Territorial Imperative: A Personal Inquiry into the Animal Origins of Property and Nations* (New York: Atheneum, 1966).

3. Paul Vidal de la Blache, *Principles of Human Geography* (New York: Holt, 1926 [1922]). First published posthumously as *Principes de géographie humaine*.

4. Paul Vidal de la Blache, "Tableau de la géographie de la France," in Ernest Lavisse, *Histoire de France depuis les origines jusqu'à la Révolution*, vol. 1, part 1, (Paris: Hachette, 1903).

5. William L. Thomas et al., eds., *Man's Role in Changing the Face of the Earth* (Chicago: University of Chicago Press, 1956).

6. Derwent S. Whittlesey, "The Regional Concept and the Regional Method," in *American Geography: Inventory and Prospects*, ed. Preston E. James and Clarence F. Jones (Syracuse: Syracuse University Press), pp. 36–37.

7. Donald J. Bogue, "Nodal Versus Homogeneous Regions, and Statistical Techniques for Measuring the Influence of Each," International Statistical Institute *Bulletin* 35 (1957): 377–92.

8. Jean Gottmann, *Megalopolis: The Urbanized Northeastern Seaboard of the United States* (Cambridge: M.I.T. Press, 1964 [1961]).

9. Johann H. von Thünen, *Der isolierte Staat in Beziehung auf Landwirthschaft und Nationalökonomie*, 3 vols. (Jena: Fischer, 1930).

10. Walter Christaller, *Die zentralen Orte in Süd-deutschland: Eine ökono-*

misch-geographische Untersuchung über die Gesetzmassigkeit der Verbreitung und Entwicklung der Siedlungen mit städtischen Funktionen (Jena: Fischer, 1933); Charles J. Galpin, *The Social Anatomy of an Agricultural Community*, Research Bulletin No. 34 (Madison: University of Wisconsin, Agricultural Experiment Station, 1915).

11. Clark Wissler, *The Relation of Nature to Man in Aboriginal America* (New York and London: Oxford University Press, 1926); William R. Bascom and Melville J. Herskovits, eds., *Continuity and Change in African Cultures* (Chicago: University of Chicago Press, 1962 [1959]).

12. Isaiah Bowman, *The Pioneer Fringe* (New York: American Geographical Society, 1931).

13. Rudolf Heberle, "Regionalism: Some Critical Observations," *Social Forces* 21 (1943): 281–82.

14. Walter P. Webb, *The Great Plains* (Boston: Ginn, 1931).

15. Seymour Harris, *The Economics of New England: Case Study of an Older Area* (Cambridge: Harvard University Press, 1952).

16. Frederick Jackson Turner, "The Significance of the Section in American History," *Wisconsin Magazine of History* 8 (1925): 255–80; Howard W. Odum, *Southern Regions of the United States* (Chapel Hill: University of North Carolina Press, 1943 [1936]).

17. Gustavo Lagos Matus, *International Stratification and Underdeveloped Countries* (Chapel Hill: University of North Carolina Press, 1963).

23. Family and Work in the South (1971)

This contribution to a symposium at Mississippi State University in 1971 was not published until after Vance's death. Parts of it are taken verbatim from his 1948 article "Regional Family Patterns: The Southern Family." The context makes it clear that this represents not an understandable laziness but a judgment on Vance's part that his earlier generalizations were still valid, despite the economic changes in the interim. Here again, Vance takes two areas—work and family— for which demographic statistics are readily available and uses the statistics as the starting point for a wide-ranging, free-wheeling essay.

Man inhabits two worlds. One is the natural world of plants and animals of soil and air and waters which preceded him by billions of years and of which he is a part. The other is the world of social institutions and artifacts he builds for himself, using his tools, his engines, his science, and his dreams to fashion an environment obedient to human purpose and direction.

The search for a better managed society is as old as man himself. It is rooted in the nature of human experience. Men believe they can be happy. They experience comfort, security, joyful participation, mental vigor, intellectual discovery, poetic insights, peace of soul, bodily rest. They seek to embody them in their human environment.[1]

Life, as Darwin made us realize, is a struggle for survival. There are strong motives behind group contacts and struggles. Hunger provides for survival of the individual, sex for the survival of the race, and conflict for group cohesion. In social institutions humanity brings it all together. The family serves to socialize the powerful sex drive to put it at the service of mankind in procreation. The family in work takes part in economic production so that it can participate in consumption.

The family as a human institution is a complex of usages, customs, mores, and social values. To study the family of a particular area makes certain demands on the scholar. First, we may ask about the universals in

From Harold F. Kaufman et al., eds., *Group Identity in the South: Dialogue between the Technological and the Humanistic* (Mississippi State University, 1975), pp. 17–32. This article originally appeared as Chapter II, in *Group Identity in the South*, edited by Harold F. Kaufman et al., and published by Mississippi State University, 1975.

the structure, processes, and patterns of the family as compared to the differentials peculiar to the South. Two modes of approach to the analysis may be sought. What components in the South have impact on the family? How is the complex put together? Given the essence of the family,[2] how does this go over into the characteristic southern way of life?

FAMILY IN REGIONAL SOCIETY

It may be difficult to factorize the family to get all the nuances, but it is valuable to present the family in its society.[3] For the South this means regional society. Any student of sociological theory presented with our title will think of Frederick LePlay and his work.[4] The LePlay nomenclature developed the formula: place, work, and family. In translation, the region in which people live determines their occupation and income. In turn this determines the kind of family life. A metallurgist teaching in a French school of mines, LePlay was wont to ask: What is the most important product that comes up out of a coal mine? The answer, to the surprise of his students, was the coal miner.[5] The family budget, developed with skill and precision, became the chief method of analysis taught by LePlay to his students.

LePlay can be recorded as the first scientific student of the family, one to do justice to the region and to the economy. Charles A. Ellwood, writing on the LePlay budgetary analyses in an early issue of the *American Journal of Sociology*, contributed the first article on scientific method to be published in the AJS.[6] Patrick Geddes, the biologist, came into contact with the LePlay group in France, changed from his brand of biology to sociology. Knighted, Sir Patrick Geddes founded "Outlook Tower," the world's first sociological laboratory in London. He went from organism, function, and environment to *famille, travail, lieu*.[7] In his collaboration with J. Arthur Thompson in *Life*, a two-volume outline of general biology, he approached sociology.[8] In his later phases, Geddes was a regionalist and a city planner. He became a kind of universal genius, put more content in his lectures to students than in his published work and treated sociology "as a unifying discipline whose main components are geography, economics, and anthropology taken in their widest human context."[9]

Much of LePlay's family analysis was transferred to America by Carle

Zimmerman[10] who first encountered it in Pitirim Sorokin's seminar at Minnesota.[11] In the United States, Zimmerman's work was met with neglect. Howard Odum, seeking to change the place of his native South in the nation and the South's image in the eyes of its people, developed the idea of regionalism and thus became acquainted with the LePlay school. With Lewis Mumford he was instrumental in getting P. Boardman's *Patrick Geddes: Maker of the Future* published by the University of North Carolina Press (1944).

A region, Odum maintained, is a homogeneous physical and cultural area set off from the adjacent areas by lines determined by its common traits. Lacking political boundaries, it can, nevertheless, be used as a heuristic device.[12] The inhabitants of a region, like the inhabitants of a national domain, acquire a self-consciousness of their region and its differences from neighboring areas. Regional analysis in its technical aspects involves the means of delineating regions lacking in formal boundaries. Regionalism is the regional idea in action, as ideology and a basis for planning. Convinced that the South had made many wrong decisions,[13] Odum carried his analysis into power and power attitudes. Frederick Turner had seen the Federal Union as a concert of sections.[14] Odum visualized such areas in transition from sectionalism to regionalism. Instead of choosing either section or nation, Odum backed both region and nation and saw the nation as a concert of regions, participating in centers of power, finance, and technology.[15]

None of the symposia on the South included a chapter on the family. Doubtless the scheme of this chapter is likely to remind an unfriendly critic of the mythical student assigned a paper on Chinese metaphysics. He read the articles in the encyclopedia on China and metaphysics and tried to meld the two.

The family as a universal can best be viewed in terms of its function as an institution in society. A national society is a quasi-permanent group of groups confined within boundaries set by political frontiers and integrated within the jurisdiction of a common legal system. With its two jurisdictions, the federal system is well calculated to provide for regionalism. Its stark reality fused on power is shown by the fact that in Max Weber's phrase the state is the only institution possessed of the monopoly of the means of military violence. This propositional definition suggests a difference of the nation from the region.

The group or groups comprising national society are to be seen in the major institutions and their interrelations. Here is integrated the family which furnishes the human capital with the economy which produces and dispenses goods and services—in short, wealth. Part of this wealth is retained as capital for future maintenance of the economy, just as progeny furnish demographic capital to project society. Collective symbols in written and spoken language maintain communication, promote art, and ideology, and facilitate the society's acting on political decisions which hold it together. Education, usually under the aegis of the state, is ideally carried on by its professionals. Religion seeks a voluntary status and in the United States is kept separate from state structure.

In the great complex the family contributes greatly to the permanence of the total social group. The family harnesses the power of the sex drive to provide progeny for the future; it furnishes production and integrates consumption; it provides for children while they are helpless and socializes them while they are impressionable. It hands down the social structure and the social heritage. It also provides an intimate group as a refuge from the "slings and arrows of outrageous fortune."

WORK AND FAMILY

The family is an economic institution and a discussion of the related topics, work and family, is far from resembling the mythical treatise on Chinese metaphysics. Work sets family roles, occupational and otherwise. Agriculture once resembled a cottage industry carried on outdoors. It predominated in the South until it was restructured with the collapse of cotton culture and the take over of the region by the industrial hegemony. The transition involves regional history which we cannot take time to recount here.[16] The family at work changed from an integrated cottage industry "outdoors" to the partnership of two diverse people working in different establishments and pooling the proceeds in the consuming pattern of a modern family. This process, unfortunately, has never been studied in the South after the manner of LePlay.

We accept the fact of economic change in the South,[17] but we could understand the transition in work and the family much better if only analysts had been at hand to compile family budgets. In Mississippi, Dorothy Dickens gathered pertinent observations on farm and factory families in the beginning of the garment industry. Mean annual incomes of various groups depending on the type of employment are presented in Table 23.1.

TABLE 23.1

Comparative Incomes of Industrial and Farm Families, 1933–1936

Type of Family by Industrial Status[a]	Average Income per Capita	Size of Family	Average Annual Income per Family
Husband and wife industrially employed, open county residence	$259	3.9	$1010
Mill, mill village residence	246	4.1	1009
Husband, full-time farmer; wife in industry	265	3.1	822
Husband, part-time farmer; wife, farm assistant	157	4.6	721
Husband, full-time farmer; wife as farm assistant	119	4.4	524

a. Dickens, Dorothy, "Some Contrasts in Industrial, Farm, and Part-time Farm Families in Rural Mississippi," *Social Forces* 18 (December 1939): 242–55. Random samples were picked within a ten-mile radius of three garment factories in which wives worked. Based on 40–49 schedules for each type. Normal families—no welfare or work relief—worked 150 days or more. Income includes farm value of crops, etc.

In true "sweatshop" fashion cotton and tobacco culture long exploited the field labor of southern women and children, slave and free, black and white.

The low level of living for farm families revealed in the figures attests to the drastic circumstances that forced the transition of the region from agriculture to industry. Making use of her native environment, Dorothy Dickens sampled poverty conditions.[18] The period was deep depression (not to be compared with our inflation period). The area was on the fringes of adequate agriculture and industry. The workers were unskilled and semi-educated. The garment industry as an opening wedge of the new economy represented an operation of low-skilled, low capitalized industry in search of wage workers lacking alternative opportunities.

Spendable incomes going over into material and cultural goods gave the style of life available to families. The standard of living developed by

Friedrich Engels out of LePlay's data has furnished material for such studies. It is evident that a higher proportion of poverty existed in the South than elsewhere. The South, according to Rudolph Heberle, has not been a heartland of modern capitalism,[19] and the above statistics serve to show the drastic nature of the transition from agriculture to industry.

In all honesty to match the work of the family to the economic status of the region in that period is to demonstrate poverty.[20] Today official estimates reported by the Commission on Population Growth and the American Family indicate that 26 million Americans live under poverty conditions, 13 percent of the people. Over six million working adults simply do not make enough to meet minimum income standards; over three million of the poor, age 14 to 65, are sick or disabled, in school, or unable to find work. Over two million are female heads of families with responsibilities at home that keep them from working. More than eight million are children in disadvantaged circumstances.[21]

Regional breakdowns for these data are not at hand. From 25 to 30 percent of southern individuals and families can be classified as poor, as compared with less than 15 percent in other parts of the nation. The statistical South has 28 percent of the nation's population but draws only 22 percent of its personal income.[22]

A study sponsored by the same Commission on Population Growth and the American Family found that today it costs between $80,000 and $150,000 to raise two children and put them through college. Quality in human beings comes high. The larger figure includes the wages a mother might have earned if she had held a job instead of staying at home and caring for children until the younger reached age 14. The direct costs of raising one child to age 18 excluding college expenses but covering costs of child birth, housing, food, clothing, transportation, education, and medical expenses were placed at $34,464. Family life, it has been said, is a luxury beyond the reach of many. No regional breakdowns were made, but if southern costs were less, it would be because southern children got less.

The South's drastic economic transition from conditions of 1930 to those of 1970 has antecedents in various industrial revolutions the world over. Specifically, the transition has meant the transfer of workers from agriculture to manufacturing and from service to distributive occupations; the growth of urban places; and increase in per capita income. Since the region pays the gains in the increased wages of the transition, such wages obviously must come out of increased efficiency.[23]

Professor Howard Schaller has calculated that personal per capita income in the South as a proportion of such per capita income in the rest of the nation rose from 46 percent in 1929 to 51 percent in 1940 to 69 percent in 1963—a gain of 23 percentage points in 34 years. Projecting these trends to 1975, Professor Schaller was able to estimate personal income per capita of $2,422 in 1963 dollars with the South reaching 79 percent of the United States figure. At the rate at which the South has been changing since World War II, Schaller estimated that it would require a half century to overtake the rest of the country. This requires continued out-migration from the South at prevailing rates.[24]

Whatever its role, the South, it must be said, no longer represents an undeveloped economy. If one had to date it, the changes might well be placed in the census decade of 1920. As late as 1920, slightly over 50 percent of the region's labor force still worked in agriculture; in a textbook case for economic underdevelopment, W. W. Rostow holds that underdeveloped countries subject to the thrust of capitalization and expansion reach a takeoff stage after which economic growth becomes self-sustaining.[25] Indications are that the South has now entered this phase of the cycle.

Industrialization is related to the family by two social changes: the entrance of men and women into business, and as women become able to support themselves, their emancipation follows their entrance into business and industry. This is a nationwide phenomenon in which the South has fully participated.

In 1920 the southern states had 31.8 percent of its total work force engaged in trade, service, and related employments as compared to 46.8 percent for the remaining United States. In 1950 the South had 61.1 percent as compared to 62.7 in the rest of the United States. Fifty percent of southern women are now employed,[26] and the "easy" choice for women no longer seems to lie between being an "old maid" and a "bachelor girl" in business. Today, by far the majority of employed southern women are married. This trend has not gone over into decrease in marriage but increases in divorce. Black women have been leaving domestic service and with white women going into clerical services. With increased access to universities women are increasing their representation in the professions. The South has a tradition of more higher education for women than any other region.[27]

An analysis of sketches in the *Dictionary of American Biography* showed that ante-bellum southerners sought out careers in politics, statecraft, and the military. After the War, there was, however, a slight statistical shift to economic distinction.[28] Many northern businesses consisted of family firms. Due to lack of similar family background, the South had to create or import a whole new entrepreneurial class. A monograph will some day be written on the family background of the new business leaders in the South. "Buck" Duke of the America Tobacco Company and J. Spencer Love of Burlington Mills may be offered as types. The gifted Dorothy Shaver, recent head of Lord and Taylor, the New York fashion house, and the woman who has gone highest in United States corporate structure, was born in Mena, Arkansas (4,445 population).

TRAITS OF THE SOUTHERN FAMILY

Everything that can be said about the family in western culture can be said with equal truth about most families in the southern United States. If we concentrate on certain characteristics of the family institution that have grown out of regional tradition and social structure, it is with the understanding that the similarities are both more obvious and more significant than the differences.

Basic law in the United States is English Common Law except in Louisiana where the *Code Napoleon* prevails. The question of the wife's property has been settled by statute law. Under common law, marriage meant one "personality" and the personality was that of the husband. By 1830 North Carolina had provided that the wife should retain her property after marriage and be competent to manage business affairs, to sue and be sued.[29] She shared none of her husband's obligation to support the family, no matter how affluent. Other southern states soon followed in protecting women's property rights.

Domestic law in the United States, consisting as it does of statutes enacted by the various states, is subject to analysis for regional patterns. The only consistent southern pattern was uniform legislation against racial intermarriage, stricken down by a decree of the Supreme Court in 1968. The circumstances of the case indicate that the South was "asking for it." A white man married a black woman in the District of Columbia where such intermarriages are legal. He brought his bride back to Virginia. In the dead of the night, the couple were awakened by a deputy sheriff with a flash light and a warrant for illegal cohabitation. Offered a choice of jail or safe escort to the state line with a promise not to return to Virginia, the couple chose jail and a call to NAACP lawyers. As anyone but a deputy sheriff would have known, the couple were freed with all the dispatch the law allows. The case was treated as a class action; all state statutes prohibiting intermarriage were voided on the grounds that persons of color were deprived of equal protection of the law. Why Virginia ever let this case come to trial will never be known. Some people suffer under the illusion that all their prejudices are to be found enshrined in the United States constitution. Certain other southern states had quietly repealed similar statutes, hoping that the news would not be released abroad.[30]

An examination of differentials in other phases of family law reveals the lowest age of consent protecting aggressive males from prosecution for "statutory rape" is found in Delaware, hardly a southern state. Child brides and common law marriages, contrary to general belief, are no more favored by the law in the South than in other states.

"No fault divorce" is coming to the fore, replacing the legal contest. This appears to prevail as much in the South today as elsewhere. In these states, proof that spouses have lived apart under decree of separate maintenance is accepted in lieu of the usual divorce plea, the terms of separate maintenance usually being made permanent. In Louisiana and North Carolina, one year separation is grounds for divorce; in Virginia, 2 years; in Arkansas, South Carolina, and Texas, 3 years; in Kentucky, 5 years. No other southern state allows divorces on the basis of separation.[31] Desertion operates as "no fault" divorce for spouses without property— hence the term for desertion much used in the South—"poor man's divorce."

Brief reference should be made to the historical importance of the family in the South. By tradition and the influence of its governing classes the family was more important in the South than in any other section, unless it was New England. Fertility remained higher; divorce rates were low; and the emphasis on kinship made family status and heritage a sure avenue to social rank. Outside of Louisiana and Kentucky this emphasis on family solidarity owed little to the teaching of the Catholic Church. Among the upper classes its religious sanctions were largely those of the Episcopal Church; in other strata it was upheld by a Protestant puritanism that has remained strong in rural communities.

Against the area's agricultural background, the family tended to retain its economic unity and many of its functions. Its predominance maintained the private aspects of social life at the expense of the public sphere. A discerning social historian has written:

> In the decades after the Civil War the family was the core of southern society; within its bounds everything worthwhile took place. No one recognized to be a Southerner's social equal dined anywhere other than in his own house or in that of a friend. . . . This absorption in household affairs explained why strangers unacquainted with Southern home life found the social scene so dismal. They saw ugly main streets deserted after business hours, and noted an almost complete lack of public entertainment. The hotels were poorly equipped, the restaurants so drab and filthy that they repelled persons of good taste. Southerners who preserved the traditions of comfort and good manners seemed altogether oblivious to these conditions.[32]

As Simkins points out, the interminable visiting among brothers and sisters, the sheltering of elderly aunts and distant cousins, the seeking of favors from relatives in high places, and the innumerable tribal conferences whenever a daughter married or a son changed employment, as well as the young people's emphasis on keeping count of "kissing cousins," all testified to a family solidarity approaching clannishness.

It has been said by several critics, and with some insight, that the emphasis on the family reflected the southerner's preoccupation with questions of social stratification quite as much as it showed his devotion to family ideals. The manner of family life, with whatever differences there may exist in total pattern or subtle sentiments, is closely related to the social structure prevailing in the area. Dynamic changes are playing on family life as they interact on this social structure and the norms and values which it represented. Once visitors found "much talk about feminine honor and Southern virtue by those who tolerated a low age of legal consent for illicit relationships."[33] Now there is less talk and more attention to social agencies needed to deal with juvenile delinquency and broken homes.

The basis from which change, disorganization, and reorganization stem is the rural folk pattern of family life. There is as yet no adequate work on the rural family, although C. C. Zimmerman and M. E. Frampton have treated the Ozark family. Most studies indicate the difficulties that the common folk have in finding in the family satisfaction for a multi-

tude of desires—security, affection, sex, and improved living standards—
while at the same time they are carrying on the burden of involuntary
reproduction.

The particular emphasis on family solidarity characteristic of the South
had its origin in the traditional values of an agrarian ruling class. The
changing structure of southern society has not undermined the importance of the family, but the institution has become more limited in function, less authoritarian in character, and less romantic in sentiments. The
trend toward more democratic roles in all classes makes the institution
more like the family elsewhere. This has been accompanied by lowered
and lessened stability.

The size of the family will continue larger among rural people, no
doubt; but fertility is declining, partly through a differentiation into what
has been called "reflective" and "unreflective" family types. The area of
involuntary reproduction is continually being narrowed by the spread of
education, public health, and changes in status; but a major association
with unreflective fertility seems to be found in the patriarchal structure of
the rural family. The pattern of male dominance goes further than the
purse strings. It conceals a sexual aggressiveness not found in the family
based on companionship. Distinction between family types now appears
to depend on whether the wife has had high school education—a factor
that may have some meaning for the companionship family. The distinction is often drawn between conceptions of romantic and companionship
marriage. For the rural "common folk" the dichotomy seems to exist
between the companionship and the patriarchal family, with a certain
amount of realism pervading both in patterns of work, living standards,
and sex adjustment.

Two major preoccupations of the rural family on this level determine
the role of youth in courtship. The family sees little hope that the daughter wil improve her lot by marriage, and the father is thus prone to
disapprove of any suitor in her own stratum. The mother is more sympathetic but sees drudgery as her daughter's lot. If the father dominates,
no boy that the girl is able to attract is likely to be made welcome at her
home. Both parents are afraid the girl will "get into trouble with boys"
and thus they attempt to restrict her contacts outside the home. The
family exercises little control over the son's role in courtship; his troubles
come from the girl's family. The conflicts which the girl faces increase her
desire for independence and thus play a part in inducing early marriage.
After marriage the daughter is welcomed on a realistic basis, and both

families will give what help they can to get the couple started in life.

In E. Franklin Frazier's brilliant monograph, the Negro family has received more careful analysis than any other group in the United States. Its changing status may be measured against this same rural folk background. Its matriarchal form, its survival from slavery, its continued struggle against dissolution, poverty, and limited education are replaced by middle-class standards among those achieving professional status. The break in domestic manners, sex, and family standards between upper and lower classes is as complete among Negroes as in any group in western culture. Girls brought up in middle-class homes are shielded from contacts with boys whose behavior may be uncouth because of working class origins.

Upper classes were important in the South because they embodied the goals and values to which other groups aspired. While the South's new upper classes appear unlikely to perpetuate old patterns of family life, they are not prepared to inculcate new ones. Stability and decorum proved of less importance, but the new roles of men, women, and children were not revalued in rational terms that the society understood. Except for the novelists like Ellen Glasgow, no one has depicted these conflicts in family standards. Since change, like the news, directs attention to problems rather than to longtime trends, it was noted that family disorganization has increased and that Florida and Arkansas found it profitable to join Nevada as Meccas for quick divorce. Unconventional behavior, however, found no sanctions in an intellectual radicalism; family scandals were handled by lawyers in a manner befitting big business anywhere, but, like southern drunkenness, they were admittedly in the immoral pattern.

Less needs to be said about middle-class standards or the problems of the new industrial classes now rising in southern cities and mill towns. Patterns of the middle-class family are least divergent, for they represent largely the influence of general education and the acceptance of standards that prevail in urban culture. Among working-class families the problems of adequate standards, of working mothers, of juveniles on city streets, of member roles and family structure, differ in some respects from those in our great cities. Greater homogeneity of ethnic and cultural backgrounds reduces somewhat the incidence of family tensions as compared to problems faced by immigrant stocks. The smaller size of cities may give certain advantages in housing, etc., but they also afford fewer community and social case agencies for the adjustment of the problems of the underprivileged. The strain to improve family status through better education and the choice of marriage partners for youth and the competitive strain to improve living standards through application to the job are now characteristic of urban and industrial families everywhere. The patriarchal family is losing its character with the increased economic independence of women. With no large Catholic influence outside Louisiana and Kentucky, the resort to divorce is increasing in the South as elsewhere. And, as elsewhere, instability seems to accompany the movement toward a more democratic family life.

IN SEARCH OF GROUP IDENTITY

The burgeoning idea of group identity would owe, it seems, much of its insight to Charles H. Cooley's classic presentation of the looking-glass self. A person appears before a group, imagines their reactions to his appearance, and develops a feeling of self, either esteem or deprecation, in response. Our concept is concerned with the collectivity; is likely to be based on more objective data; for example, the news media and published documents.

Ferdinand Tönnies has provided us with sociology's valuable classification of groups: *Gemeinschaft* and *Gesellschaft*—community and society—in Loomis' translation.[37] To Tönnies, the basic dichotomy in society is that between association based on sentiments and that based in reasonable expectation of a return—somewhat different from the usual meaning attributed to community and society. Friendship and a corporation set up to make a profit represent the contrasting types. Association, according to Tönnies, was not association unless it was desired by those participating; that is, it represents an effort of the will. Informal grouping (it is difficult to avoid the term in thinking of *Gemeinschaft*) is the outcome of *Wesenvill*, liking. Marriage with its added sexual feeling belongs here. *Kurvill*—deliberate, calculating reason—gives us *Gesellschaft*. Here are many of our contractual groups requiring lawyers to scan the fine print which keeps the "association" in association.[38] Tönnies avoided time schemes and deliberately kept any tinge of evolution out of his typology.[39] If the family is of the essence, the tone of the family would give southern society its style of life.

Heretofore, we have concerned ourselves with the family in the context of society and the economy. The impact of factors gives us the family in the region. In terms that were used by the theologians of the Middle Ages, we may have concerned ourselves more with the accidents than with the essence of the family. Furthermore, neighborhoods and small communities are more given to informal association than great cities. In the metropolis, formal agreements are greatly needed to get things done. The recent South, it should be said, is in the process of this transition. As late as 1840, the United States census had not reported a single urban place in the states of Mississippi, Tennessee, North Carolina, and in Florida territory.[40] In the beginning our cities were populated by migrants from *Gemeinschaft*—this is true of the foreign immigrants in our great cities. The great model for the study of this phenomenon remains W. I. Thomas' *Polish Peasant in America*. It stands as one of the great losses to American sociology that this study has not been replicated with regard to the black migration.

We must return to the family as a small group, intimate, primary, and a refuge from the world of conflict. Our study of family in society and economy has been an essay in macrosociology, while the intimate group takes us into microsociology.

The motivation to functioning in family is personal happiness, if not public policy. Thomas Jefferson is known as the stateman who introduced in our public documents "the pursuit of happiness" as a principle of public action. The way in which small group studies have developed indicates that family analysis may not belong among them. But association has many leads. Cooley saw the family as a primary group, face to face in interaction, the nursery of human nature.[41] In a perceptive analysis, E. W. Burgess presented the family as a unity of interacting personalities. Taking account of birth control, the financial independence of women, and the new position of the family in its demands for middle-class standards of luxury, Burgess seemed to make trial marriage respectable as the "companionate."[42] Finally Jessie Bernard, a leading authority, sees women deserting marriage in droves.[43] Some leading proponents of Women's Lib, assuming the role of bald, bad buccaneers in love as well as in business, defend the right of emancipated women to untrammeled erotic adventure. A modern woman should be free, they claim, to issue propositions to men and not to be insulted, if refused. Modern women, they claim, must be able to issue a "No, no," that turneth away wrath if she wishes to retain any personable male friends.[44] Evidence of this phenomenon so upset the late, great Pitirim Sorokin that he wrote an emotional, unobjective account of the Sexual Revolution. Vance Packard, as usual, has cashed in on the topic. To use abstinence to reduce fertility in marriage is to multiply discord, since coition is a legal right. Certain clergymen have an answer: The right to divorce is hereby forbidden. Contemporary Catholics are shown to have a fertility no higher than other groups, whatever that may mean. The pursuit of happiness appears to have other antagonists than public policy.

Black fertility remains high but is hardly dignified with an ideology worth recounting. Birth control, some militants claim, is "whitey's" method of genocide. Welfare furnishes aid to dependent children; why not increase the poverty of black families and let "whitey" pay the bill? Black parties require more votes, etc. This ramshackle program evidently was constructed without the cooperation of black women. It deserves a cartoon with a cutting edge: a picture of white wives in a procession to a family planning center with black militant males, wearing Afros and picketing with banners: "No Blacks Need Apply."

Rudolph Heberle has reminded us that the categories *Gemeinschaft* and *Gesellschaft* are not clear-cut classifications, suitable for statistical tabulation, but represent ideal types.[45] In the South it is common to see society in transition from the social world of the family to that of the corporation. The family is the core of southern society, wrote Pitirim Sorokin; but before we reach the conclusion that *Gemeinschaft* is the essence of our regional society, Heberle has a word for us:

> It would defeat the very purpose of Tönnies' theory were one to define, for example, the family as a Gemeinschaft instead of inquiring to what extent a given family or, on a higher level of abstraction, a given type of family, approximates the ideal type of *Gemeinschaft* and to what extent it contains traits of *Gesellschaft*. Such a type will be found in the past in the European marriage of convenience.[46]

Rearing children, as important a function of society as it is, has been pictured as a cottage industry. If transferred to an industrial shed filled with play pits, sand piles and baths, an edifice to which women could repair at 8:30 A.M., mothers might gain the payment, the prestige, and respect that the importance of the family function deserves. One can visualize here the transfer from *Gemeinschaft* to *Gesellschaft* that may occur with the coming breakdown of the family, so often heralded. Since not profit, but happiness, one hopes, comes from the rearing of children, we might finance the care of undernourished male children by rearing them on commission for the armed forces.

The United States is one country which placed in its basic documents the pursuit of happiness as one of the "inalienable rights of man." The function of the family in society is reciprocal to the functioning of the family as an integrated primary group. More to be dreaded for the future of a society in which family life has become a luxury out of the reach of many is the loss of ability of a family to provide happiness. Since there is no profit in performing the social functions of the family, happiness in the affection for children and spouses remains its only reward. Bernard Shaw praised marriage as that delightful institution which offers the "maximum of temptation along with the maximum of opportunity." The sacrament of matrimony has been painted as iridescent magic which "can make the wrongest thing in the world into the rightest." The little four-year-old daughter who asked her mother, "Tell me all about sex," received the reply: "It leads to housework." Family life today suffers from the promise of great expectations in an otherwise very sad world. If not met, the feeling is that the premises should be vacated.

Today, the choice of marriage is a matter of personal values. For the region the inclination to *Gemeinschaft* is one of social values. If one were to test this with an opinion or attitude poll, *Gemeinschaft* would win in the South, for all the words have the right overtones. Those of us who know the area may be led to accept the "family core" of society as its *Gemeinschaft*, but there exists no acceptable empirical evidence. An appeal to attitude polls would be suspect for it would no doubt tend to elicit from respondents the right overtones.

NOTES

1. Barbara Ward and Rene DuBos, *Only One Earth: The Care and Maintenance of a Small Planet* (New York: Norton, 1972). Commissioned by the secretary general of the United Nations Conference on the Human Environment.
2. Elbert L. Cook, "Family Analysis: General Systems Strategy." This manuscript won the Howard W. Odum award as the best student paper submitted to the Southern Sociological Society in 1972. Made available by the author, Department of Sociology, North Carolina State University at Raleigh.
3. Floyd M. Martinson, *Family in Society* (New York: Dodd, Mead, 1971), accepted as model for section "Family in the Region." Other volumes that have

been helpful included Harold T. Christensen, ed., *Handbook of Marriage and the Family* (Chicago: Rand-McNally, 1964); R. Hill and R. L. Simpson, "Marriage and Family Sociology, 1945–1955," in H. L. Zetterberg, ed., *Sociology in the United States* (Paris: UNESCO, 1956), pp. 93–100; R. T. Smith, "Family: Comparative Structure," in David L. Sills, ed., *International Encyclopedia of the Social Sciences* (New York: Crowell Collier and Macmillan, 1968) (hereafter cited as IESS, no page, no volume).

4. Frederic LePlay, *Les Ouvriers européens*, 2d ed., 6 vols. (Tours: Mame, 1877–79).

5. Pitirim A. Sorokin, *Contemporary Sociological Theories* (New York: Harpers, 1928). Sorokin was responsible for disseminating information about LePlay in the United States. He introduced LePlay in his seminar at the University of Minnesota and devoted more time to the LePlay School than to LePlay's empirical work.

6. C. A. Ellwood, "Instruction in the Observation of Social Facts According to the LePlay Method of Monographs of Families," *American Journal of Sociology* 11 (1897): 662–79. The first article on method in the journal. Zimmerman became an outstanding student of LePlay's theories, methods, and actual procedures.

7. Phillip L. Boardman, *Patrick Geddes: Maker of the Future* (Chapel Hill: University of North Carolina Press, 1942).

8. Lewis Mumford, "Patrick Geddes," IESS.

9. Patrick Geddes and J. A. Thompson, *Life*, vol. 2 of *Outlines of General Biology* (London: Williams and Nogate, 1931), chaps. 11–13.

10. Carle C. Zimmerman and Merle E. Frampton, *Family and Society* (Princeton: Van Nostrand, 1935), largely disregarded by United States students of the family.

11. See Sorokin, *Contemporary Sociological Theories*, chap. 3, for his treatment of LePlay.

12. Rupert B. Vance, "Howard W. Odum," IESS; "Region," IESS; "Howard W. Odum and the Case of the South," unpublished paper read to the Southeastern Section of American Studies Association, Chapel Hill, North Carolina, April 11, 1970, in author's possession.

13. Vance, "Region"; "The Concept of the Region as a Tool for Research," chap. 1 in Merrill Jensen, ed., *Regionalism in America* (Madison: University of Wisconsin Press, 1955).

14. F. J. Turner, "The Significance of Sections in American History," in *Essays*, edited by M. Farrand and A. Craven (Gloucester, Mass.: Smith, 1932).

15. Howard W. Odum, "Region, Folk, and Society," in *Folk, Region, and Society: Selected Papers of Howard W. Odum*, edited by K. Jocher et al. (Chapel Hill: University of North Carolina Press, 1964).

16. Rupert B. Vance, "Education and the Southern Potential," in W. D. McClarken, ed., *High Schools in the South* (Nashville: Division of Surveys, Peabody College, 1966), chap. 2, pp. 7–22. A concise paper on southern development, concerned with industry in the region and the working force of the family.

17. The transition from an agricultural to an industrial region has had great impact on work and the family in the South. The subject is too large for treatment, but work in which I have engaged may help to explain the attitude with which I have treated the topic. They include: R. B. Vance, *Human Factors in Cotton Culture* (Chapel Hill: University of North Carolina Press, 1929); *Human Geography of the South* (Chapel Hill: University of North Carolina Press, 1932); "The Old Cotton Belt," in Carter Goodwin, ed., *Migration and Economic Opportunity* (Philadelphia: University of Pennsylvania Press, 1936), pp. 124–63; *All These People* (Chapel Hill: University of North Carolina Press, 1945); and *Wanted: The South's Future for the Nation* (Atlanta: Southern Regional Council, 1946).

18. Dorothy Dickens, "Some Contrasts in Industrial, Farm, and Part-Time Farm Families in Rural Mississippi," *Social Forces* 18 (December 1939): 242–55. The whole body of work by Dorothy Dickens should be examined. Some day we shall have a report on Miss Dickens. Compare her work with the amount of money and the paucity of brains expended on the Consumer Purchases Study—not a conclusion in a car load. "Added little that can be salvaged from an inchoate mass of unrelated facts," O. D. Duncan. One of the regrets of my life is that when offered a chance to review this work, I turned down the opportunity to give it the "panning" it deserved.

19. Rudolph Heberle, chap. 1 in Rupert B. Vance and N. J. Demerath, eds., *The Urban South* (Chapel Hill: University of North Carolina Press, 1954), p. 7.

20. United States Government, *Report on the Population and the American Family* (Cliffside Heights, N.J.: Signet Books, 1972), p. 29; Office of Economic Opportunity, *The Poor in 1970: A Chartbook* (Washington, D.C.: Office of Economic Opportunity, [1972]); *Hunger, U.S.A. Revisited: A Report by the Citizen's Board of Inquiry into Hunger and Malnutrition in the United States*, published in cooperation with the National Council on Hunger and Malnutrition and the Southern Regional Council, no place, no date.

21. A 1970 census return.

22. Rupert B. Vance, "Southern Labor Comes of Age," *Monthly Labor Review*, 92, no. 3 (March 1968): 1–4; "Personal Incomes by States and Regions," *Survey of Current Business* (Washington, D.C.: Government Printing Office, August 1964), pp. 15–23.

23. Vance and Demerath, *The Urban South*.

24. Howard G. Schaller, "Changes in the Southern Economy," in *Manpower Resources and Human Resources Adjustment* (Raleigh: Agricultural Policy Institute, May 1965), series 15, pp. 1–14.

25. W. W. Rostow, *The Process of Economic Growth* (New York: Norton, 1956).

26. Vance and Demerath, *The Urban South*.

27. Vance, *All These People*, pp. 441–42, figure 671, table 137.

28. Ibid., pp. 448–65. See also Rupert B. Vance and Nadia Davilesky, "The Geography of Distinction: The Nation and the Region, 1790–1927," *Social Forces* 17 (December 1939): 168–72.

29. *Reader's Digest*, "You and the Law," Henry Poor, ed. (Pleasantville, N.Y.,

1971). See section entitled "Your Family," a gem of a compilation, fully authoritative.

30. *Lovengood et Uxor v. State of Virginia,* United States Supreme Court Reports, 1969.

31. Max Rheinstein, *Marriage Stability, Divorce, and the Law* (Chicago: University of Chicago Press, 1972), "Common law marriages" are recognized in three states commonly regarded as southern, Alabama, Georgia, and South Carolina, and two western, Oklahoma and Texas. Florida repealed such a law as of January 1, 1968, and Mississippi as of April 5, 1956.

32. Francis Butler Simkins, *The South: Old and New* (New York: Knopf, 1947), p. 294.

33. Ibid.

34. Wilbert E. Moore and Robin M. Williams, "Stratification in the Antebellum South," *American Sociological Review* 7 (June 1942): 331–51; Rudolf Heberle, "Social Change in the South," *Social Forces* 25 (October 1946): 9–15.

35. Simkins, *The South.*

36. Margaret Jarman Hagood, *Mothers of the South* (Chapel Hill: University of North Carolina Press, 1939), pp. 108–69. Nora Miller, *The Girl in the Rural Family* (Chapel Hill: University of North Carolina Press, 1935), pp. 7–92, describes the role of the adolescent girl in eight types of southern rural families: dependent, mountain farm, coal mining, cotton farm, tobacco farm, potato farm, fishing community, and superior families. Gilbert W. Bebee, in *Contraception and Fertility in the Southern Appalachians* (Baltimore: Williams and Wilkins, 1942), pp. 56–85, found fertility higher because of uncontrolled conception and marriage two years earlier than among women in the poorer classes elsewhere in the nation.

37. Ferdinand Tönnies, *Community and Society (Gemeinschaft and Gesell-schaft,* 1887), translated and edited by Charles P. Loomis (East Lansing: Michigan State University Press, 1957).

38. Rudolf Heberle, "Ferdinand Tönnies," IESS.

39. Ibid.

40. T. Lynn Smith, chap. 11 in Vance and Demerath, *The Urban South,* p. 25.

41. C. H. Cooley's work comes to mind here.

42. Ernest W. Burgess, "The Family as a Unity of Interacting Personalities," *Family* 7 (1929): 309; E. W. Burgess et al., *The Family from Institution to Companionship* (New York: American Book Company, 1962 [1945]).

43. Jessie Bernard, *The Future of Marriage* (New York: World, 1972).

44. Robin Morgan, ed., *Sisterhood Is Powerful: An Anthology of Writing from the Woman's Liberation Movement* (New York: Random House, Vintage Books, 1970). See section 4, "Up from Sexism," pp. 295–421.

45. Rudolf Heberle, "Ferdinand Tönnies," IESS.

46. Ibid.

Bibliography of the Works of Rupert B. Vance

Compiled by Lynn Whitener

"Stuart-Harmon: Social Distance in Twin Towns." In Jesse F. Steiner, *American Community in Action: Case Studies of American Communities*, pp. 226–45. New York: Henry Holt and Company, 1928.

"Cotton Culture and Social Life and Institutions of the South." *Publications of the American Sociological Society* 23 (1929): 51–59.

Human Factors in Cotton Culture: A Study in Social Geography. Chapel Hill: University of North Carolina Press, 1929.

"The Concept of Region." *Social Forces* 8 (1929): 208–18.

"A Karl Marx for Hill Billies: Portrait of a Southern Leader." *Social Forces* 9 (1930): 180–90.

"The Southern Labor Supply." *University of North Carolina Extension Bulletin* 10 (1930): 16–21.

"Human Aspects of the Geography of the American South." *University of North Carolina Extension Bulletin* 11 (1931): 12–24.

"The Frontier: Cultural and Geographical Aspects." *Encyclopedia of the Social Sciences* 5 (1931): 503–5.

Human Geography of the South: A Study in Regional Resources and Human Adequacy. Chapel Hill: University of North Carolina Press, 1932.

"Aycock of North Carolina." *Southwest Review* 18 (1933): 288–306.

"The Profile of Southern Culture." In *Culture in the South*, edited by W. T. Couch, pp. 24–39. Chapel Hill: University of North Carolina Press, 1933.

"Braxton Bragg Comer: Alabama's Most Audacious." *Southwest Review* 19 (1934): 243–64.

"Folk Rationalizations in the Unwritten Law" (with Waller Wynne, Jr.). *American Journal of Sociology* 39 (1934): 483–92.

"Human Factors in the South's Agricultural Readjustment." *Law and Contemporary Problems* 1 (1934): 259–74.

"Planning the Southern Economy." *Southwest Review* 20 (1934): 111–23.

"Regional Planning and Social Trends in the South." *Proceedings, Southeastern Library Association*, pp. 3–13. Memphis: University of Tennessee Press, 1934.

"What of Submarginal Areas in Regional Planning?" *Social Forces* 12 (1934): 315–29.

"Implications of the Concepts 'Region' and 'Regional Planning.'" *Publications of the American Sociological Society* 29 (1935): 85–93.

"Is Agrarianism for Farmers?" *Southern Review* 1 (1935): 42–47.

Johnson, Charles S.; Embree, Edwin R.; and Alexander, W. W. *The Collapse of Cotton Tenancy.* Edited by Rupert B. Vance. Chapel Hill: University of North Carolina Press, 1935.

"Little Man, What Now?" *Southern Review* 1 (1935): 560–67.

336

Regional Reconstruction: Way Out for the South. New York: Foreign Policy Association, 1935.

"Report on Tenant Farmers and Rural Rehabilitation in the South." In *Minority Groups in Economic Reconstruction*, pp. 244. Nashville: University of Tennessee Press, 1935.

"Cotton and Tenancy." *Problems of the Cotton Economy*, pp. 18–39. Dallas: Arnold Foundation, 1936.

How the Other Half Is Housed: A Pictorial Record of Subminimum Farm Housing in the South. Chapel Hill: University of North Carolina Press, 1936.

"Regional Planning with Reference to the Southeast." *Southern Economic Journal* 3 (1936): 55–65.

"The Economic Future of the Old Cotton Belt." *Southern Workman* 65 (1936): 85–92.

"The Old Cotton Belt." In *Migration and Economic Opportunity*, edited by Carter Goodrich, pp. 124–63. Philadelphia: University of Pennsylvania Press, 1936.

The South's Place in the Nation. Washington: Public Affairs Committee, 1936.

"The T.V.A. and the Southern Utilities." *South Today*, Southern Newspaper Syndicate, January 12, 1936.

Farmers without Land. New York: Public Affairs Committee, 1937.

"The South—Population Seedbed of the Nation." *South Today*, Southern Newspaper Syndicate, August 15, 1937.

"Rebels and Agrarians All: Studies in One Party Politics." *Southern Review* 4 (1938): 26–44.

Research Memorandum on Population Redistribution within the United States. Bulletin 42. New York: Social Science Research Council, 1938.

"Rural Distress and Relief in the Southeast." *Hearings before a Special Committee to Investigate Unemployment and Relief.* U.S. Senate, 75th Congress, 3d Session, 2:1011–16, 1556–60. Washington: Government Printing Office, 1938.

The South's Place in the Nation. New York: Public Affairs Committee, 1938.

"Conditions among Tenants and Sharecroppers." *Disadvantaged People in Rural Life. Proceedings of the Twenty-First American Country Life Conference, Lexington, Kentucky*, pp. 108–17. Chicago: University of Chicago Press, 1939.

"Racial Competition for the Land." In *Race Relations and the Race Problem*, edited by Edgar T. Thompson, pp. 97–124. Durham: Duke University Press, 1939.

"Rural Relief and Recovery." *Works Progress Administration, Social Problems Number 3.* Washington: Government Printing Office, 1939.

"The Geography of Distinction: The Nation and the Region" (with Nadia Danilevsky). *Social Forces* 18 (1939): 168–79.

"A Desirable Policy of Human Resources for the South." *Tomorrow's Children: Proceedings of the Southern Conference*, pp. 35–48. New York: Birth Control Federation of America, 1948.

"How Can the South's Population Find Gainful Employment? *Journal of Farm*

Economics 22 (1940): 198–206.

"Population and the Pattern of Unemployment in the Southeast, 1930–1937" (with Nadia Danilevsky). *Southern Economic Journal* 7 (1940): 187–203.

"Probable Trend of Migration from the Southeast." *Hearings before the Select Committee to Investigate the Interstate Migration of Destitute Citizens.* U.S. House of Representatives, 76th Congress, 3d Session, 2:406–22. Washington: Government Printing Office, 1940.

"Tennessee's War of the Roses." *Virginia Quarterly Review* 16 (1940): 413–24.

"Interrelations of Population Trends and Land Tenure in the Southeast." In *The People, the Land, and the Church in Rural South*, pp. 85–96. Nashville: Conference of the Farm Foundation, 1941.

"Regional Approach to the Study of High Fertility" (with Nadia Danilevsky). *Milbank Quarterly* 19 (1941): 356–74.

"School Life Expectations and Marriage Expectations: An Attempt to Apply the Techniques of Life Tables Construction to Other Fields of Sociology" (with Nadia Danilevsky). "Proceedings of the Conference on Analysis and Interpretation of Social and Economic Data," pp. 72–78. Raleigh: State College, 1941 (mimeographed).

"The South's Human Resources in Total Defense." *Essays on Southern Life and Culture: A Symposium in Commemoration of the Semicentennial*, pp. 41–54. Arkadelphia, Arkansas: Henderson State Teachers College, 1941.

The South's Place in the Nation. New York: Public Affairs Committee, 1941.

Regional Planning: Part XI. The Southeast. National Resources Planning Board. Washington: Government Printing Office, 1942. Rupert Vance contributed to the introduction and part 2, pp. 8–11, 42–46.

"Human Resources and Public Policy: An Essay toward Regional-National Planning." *Social Forces* 21 (1943): 20–25.

"The Future of the South." *Predictions of Things to Come* 1 (Summer 1943): 83–86.

"Wanted: The Nation's Future for the South." *Virginia Quarterly Review* 19 (1943): 622–27.

"Economic Research in the Interests of Peace." *Approaches to World Peace: Fourth Symposium of the Conference on Science, Philosophy, and Religion*, pp. 199–202. New York: Harper and Brothers, 1944.

"Social Security and Adjustment: The Return to the Larger Community." *Social Forces* 22 (1944): 363–70.

"Tragic Dilemma: The Negro and the American Dream." *Virginia Quarterly Review* 20 (1944): 435–45.

All These People: The Nation's Human Resources in the South (with Nadia Danilevsky). Chapel Hill: University of North Carolina Press, 1945.

"Social Planning for England." *Virginia Quarterly Review* 21 (1945): 467–69.

"Sociology." In *Library Resources of the University of North Carolina*, edited by Charles E. Rush, pp. 242–47. Chapel Hill: University of North Carolina Press, 1945.

"The Place of Planning in Social Dynamics." *Social Forces* 23 (1945): 331–34.

"Toward Social Dynamics." *American Sociological Review* 10 (1945): 123–31.

"Ernest R. Groves, 1877–1946." *American Sociological Review* 11 (1946): 754–55.

New Farms for Old: Rural Public Housing in the South (with Gordon W. Blackwell). Birmingham: University of Alabama Press, 1946.

"Rural Public Housing" (with Gordon W. Blackwell). *Housing Progress* 2 (1946): 16, 32–33.

"Wanted: The South's Future for the Nation." *New South* 1 (1946): 30.

"Report to the Chairman of the Committee IV on Action to Improve the Conditions of Farms Laborers and Share Croppers." Conference on Family Farm Policy, Farm Foundation, Chicago, February 15–20, 1946. Published as chapter 18 in *Family Farm Policy*. Chicago: University of Chicago Press, 1947.

The South's Place in the Nation. New York. Public Affairs Committee, 1947.

"Design the Community for Better Living." *The School Executive* 67 (1948): 50–52.

"Malthus and the Principle of Population." *Foreign Affairs* 26 (1948): 682–92.

"Regional Family Patterns: The Southern Family." *American Journal of Sociology* 53 (1948): 426–29.

"Social Organization for the Use of Industrial Resources" (chap. 8), "Human Resources and Social Organization" (chap. 10). In *Scientists Look at Resources: Bulletin of the Bureau of Social Sciences*, vol. 20. Lexington: University of Kentucky, 1948.

Exploring the South (with John E. Ivey, Jr., and Marjorie Bond). Chapel Hill: University of North Carolina Press, 1949.

"Church Types and Social Structure: A Contribution of the Sociology of Religion to American Studies." Prepared for the Conference on Studies in Religion: Committee on American Civilization, American Council of Learned Societies, Chicago, April 23–24, 1950 (Mimeographed).

"Economic Research in the Interests of Peace." In *Perspectives on a Troubled Decade: Science, Philosophy, and Religion*, chap. 23. New York: Harper and Brothers, 1950.

"The Regional Concept as a Tool for Social Research." In *Regionalism in America*, edited by Merrill Jensen, chap. 3. Madison: University of Wisconsin Press, 1951.

"Social Structure and Social Change." *Social Forces* 30 (1952): 238.

"Is Theory for Demographers?" *Social Forces* 31 (1952): 9–13.

"Ivory Towers to Let." *Saturday Review* 35 (1952): 18.

"The Demographic Gap: Dilemma in Modernization Programs." *Approaches to Problems of High Fertility in Agrarian Societies*, pp. 9–17. New York: Milbank Memorial Fund, 1952.

"Freedom and Authority in the Social Structure: A Problem in the Interrelations of Institutions." In *Freedom and Authority in Our Time*, edited by Lyman Bryson and others, chap. 29. New York: Harper and Brothers, 1953.

"Social Change, Social Status, and the Law: A Sociological View." *Journal of Public Law* 3 (1954): 39–46.

'The Ecology of Our Aging Population." *Social Forces* 32 (1954): 330–35.

"The South's Changing Political Leadership." *Journal of Social Issues* 10 (1954): 13–18.

The Urban South (with N. J. Demerath, editors). Chapel Hill: University of North Carolina Press, 1954.

"Howard W. Odum, 1884–1954" (with Katherine W. Jocher). *Social Forces* 33 (1955): 203–17.

"The Urban Breakthrough in the South." *Virginia Quarterly Review* 31 (1955): 223–32.

"Howard Washington Odum, 1884–1954" (with Guy B. Johnson and Louis Round Wilson). In *The Kenan Professorships*, edited by A. C. Howell. Chapel Hill: University of North Carolina Press, 1956.

"Is Theory for Demographers?" Reprinted in *Population Theory and Policy*, edited by J. J. Spengler and O. D. Duncan, pp. 88–94. Glencoe, Illinois: Free Press, 1956.

"Differential Sex Mortality: A Research Design" (with Francis C. Madigan, S.J.). *Social Forces* 35 (1957): 193–99.

"Social Change, Social Status, and the Law." In *Race*, edited by E. T. Thompson and E. C. Hughes, pp. 440–46. Glencoe, Illinois: Free Press, 1958.

"Prerequisites to Immigration: Elements of National Policy." *Selected Papers of Migration since World War II*, pp. 75–88. Also discussion, pp. 166–68: 216–17. New York: Milbank Memorial Fund, 1958.

"The South's Image and the American Dream: Notes for a Fourth of July Oration out of Season." *The Lamar Lectures*. Macon: Georgia Wesleyan College, 1958.

"The Development and Status of American Demography." In *The Study of Population*, edited by Philip M. Hauser and Otis Dudley Duncan. Chicago: University of Chicago Press, 1959.

"The Southern Family Today." In *This Is the South*, edited by Robert West Howard, pp. 254–59. Chicago: Rand McNally, 1959.

"Regionalism and Ecology: A Synthesis?" (with Charles M. Grigg). *Florida State University Research Report in Social Sciences* 3 (August 1960): 1–11.

"The Sociological Implications of Southern Regionalism." *Journal of Southern History* 25 (1960): 44–56.

"The Region: A New Survey," and "The Region's Future: A National Challenge." In *Southern Appalachian Region: A Survey*, edited by Thomas R. Ford, pp. 1–8, 289–300. Lexington: University of Kentucky Press, 1962.

"Travels in the New South, 1900–1955." In *The Twentieth Century South Viewed by English Speaking People*, edited by Thomas D. Clark, pp. 1–107. Norman: University of Oklahoma Press, 1962.

"Security and Adjustment: The Return to the Larger Community." In *Sociology and History: Theory and Research*, edited by Werner Cahnman and Alvin Boskoff, pp. 376–88. Glencoe, Illinois: Free Press, 1964.

"An Introductory Note." In *Yesterday's People*, edited by Jack E. Weller, pp. v–ix. Lexington: Working Press, 1965.

"Beyond the Fleshpots: The Coming Culture Crisis in the South." *Virginia Quarterly Review* 41 (1965): 218–30.

"Social Change in the Southern Appalachians." In *The South in Continuity and Change*, edited by Edgar T. Thompson and John C. Mckinney, pp. 404–17. Durham: Duke University Press, 1965.

"The Changing Density of Virginia's Population: Urbanization and Migration." In *Exploring Virginia's Resources*, edited by Roscoe D. Hughes and Henry Leidhauser, pp. 35–53. Charlottesville: University Press of Virginia, 1965.

"The Growth of the American Population." In *Population: The Vital Revolution*, edited by Ronald Freedman, pp. 137–48. Chicago: Aldine Publishing Company, 1965.

"Education and the Southern Potential." In *High Schools in the South: A Fact Book*, pp. 7–22. Nashville: George Peabody College for Teachers, 1966.

"The Changing South, 1940–1956." In the yearbook, *Collier's Encyclopedia*, 1967.

"The South Considered as an Achieving Society." In *Perspectives on the South: Agenda for Research*, edited by Edgar T. Thompson, pp. 59–70. Durham: Duke University Press, 1967.

"Howard W. Odum." In *International Encyclopedia of the Social Sciences*, edited by David L. Sills, Vol. 11, pp. 270–72. New York: Macmillan, 1968.

"Region." In *International Encyclopedia of the Social Sciences*, edited by David L. Sills, vol. 13, pp. 377–82. New York: Macmillan, 1968.

"When Southern Labor Comes of Age." *Monthly Labor Review* 91 (March 1968): 1–4.

"North Carolina Insured Employment and Wage Payments." *University of North Carolina Newsletter*, December, 1969.

"Samuel Huntington Hobbs, Jr." *Social Forces* 48 (1970): 412.

"Howard Odum's Techniways: A Neglected Lead in American Sociology." *Social Forces* 50 (1972): 456–61.

"Family and Work in the South." In *Group Identity in the South: Dialogue between the Technological and the Humanistic*, edited by Harold F. Kaufman et al., pp. 17–32. Mississippi State University, 1975.

Index

AAA (Agricultural Adjustment Administration), 73, 126 (n. 23); and cotton cultivation, 78, 79, 82, 87, 109, 113–14, 116
Adams, James Truslow, 198
Agee, James, 285–86
Agrarianism, 60–74 passim, 252, 293, 327
Agrarians: Vance's acquaintance with, xii, 60; program of, 55–56, 60, 62, 73–74; failure of, 252; and W. H. Nicholls, 293
Agriculture: significance of in South's economy, ix, x, 56, 84, 87, 272, 290, 303–4, 320, 321, 322, 323; South's need for diversification of, xvii, 50, 52, 211, 264–65; and population increases, xviii, 64; condition of workers in, 21, 56, 146, 302, 306; commercial and precommercial character of in South, 45, 64–67, 72–73; in Appalachia, 45, 221, 222–23, 224, 225, 231; income from in South compared with U.S., 56, 84; dominated by cotton cultivation in South, 56, 253; and industrialization, 62, 144–45, 199, 276, 281, 282, 291, 304, 320, 321, 322; and Agrarians, 63; federal aid for, 71–72, 254; effect of depression on, 109–10, 176; exodus of Southern workers from, 118, 144–45, 177, 180–81, 182, 212, 246, 248, 272, 276, 278, 281, 282, 302, 306, 322; and forestry, 121; and education, 144; regional-national planning for, 147–48; and urbanization, 235, 246, 248; improved efficiency in, 264–65, 272–73, 278, 291; and economy of uniform regions, 312
Agriculture, Department of, 21, 24, 83, 110, 223
Alabama: wages and income in, 56, 84, 91–92; cotton cultivation in, 89–90, 97–98, 99–100, 102, 105; urbanization in, 94; birth rate in, 95, 143; Negroes in, 99, 258, 270; rural rehabilitation in, 122–23; educational deprivation in, 283; common law

marriage in, 335 (n. 31)
Alexandria, Va., 235, 244
Almack, R. B., 164, 187
American Dream, the, 198–207
American Legion, 10, 12, 13
American Sociological Society, x
American Tobacco Company, 32, 324
Anthropology: and regionalism, 156, 161, 163, 169–70; and sociology, 318
Appalachia: underdevelopment of, xx, 82, 213–14, 220–21, 234, 251; physical and human geography of, 44–46, 221–22; need of for population redistribution, 46, 58; birth rate in, 93, 94, 335 (n. 31); and TVA, 120; economic and social change in, 222–28; regional planning for, 228–32; educational deprivation in, 283
Ardrey, Robert, 310
Area Redevelopment Administration, 229, 230–31
Aristocracy. See Elite, Southern
Arkadelphia, Ark., xii
Arkansas: Vance's birth and youth in, ix, xi–xii; Jeff Davis and politics in, 28–42; industrialization in, 94, 235; birth rate in, 95; cotton cultivation in, 97–98, 99, 102, 104, 111; divorce in, 153, 325, 328; population migration out of, 267; educational deprivation in, 283
Arkansas, University of, 31, 41
Arlington County, Va., 236, 244
Armsby, H. P., 21
Arnold, Fred, 100
Asheville, N.C., 214, 221–22
Association of American Universities, 285
Atkinson, J. W., 292
Atlanta, Ga., 47, 53; and "New South," x, 212–13; metropolitan population of, 179, 278; as second order metropolis, 179–80, 277

Baker, O. E., xxi, 19, 117
Baltimore, Md., 180, 277

343